INTRODUCTION TO
HOMELAND
SECURITY

INTRODUCTION TO HOMELAND SECURITY

UNDERSTANDING TERRORISM PREVENTION AND EMERGENCY MANAGEMENT

Second Edition

DAVID A. MCENTIRE, PHD
Utah Valley University

WILEY

Library of Congress Cataloging-in-Publication Data

Names: McEntire, David A., author.
Title: Introduction to homeland security : understanding terrorism prevention
   and emergency management / David A. McEntire.
Description: Second edition. | Hoboken, NJ : John Wiley & Sons, Inc., 2019.|

   Includes bibliographical references and index. |
Identifiers: LCCN 2018023897 (print) | LCCN 2018028227 (ebook) | ISBN
  9781119430674 (Adobe PDF) | ISBN 9781119430636 (ePub) | ISBN
9781119430650
  | ISBN 9781119430650(pbk.)
Subjects: LCSH: Terrorism—United States—Prevention. | Terrorism—Government
   policy—United States. | Emergency management—United States. | Computer
   security—Government policy—United States. | United States—Military
   policy.
Classification: LCC HV6432 (ebook) | LCC HV6432 .M3854 2018 (print) | DDC
   363.340973—dc23
LC record available at https://lccn.loc.gov/2018023897

For Mason, Madison, Kailey, and Ashley
and the future of children everywhere

CONTENTS

ABOUT THE AUTHOR

David A. McEntire, PhD, is the dean of the College of Health and Public Service at Utah Valley University. Prior to this appointment, he was a professor in the Emergency Administration and Planning (EADP) Program in the Department of Public Administration at the University of North Texas. Dr. McEntire has taught emergency management and homeland security courses in both the undergraduate and graduate programs. His academic interests include emergency management theory, international disasters, community preparedness, response coordination, terrorism, and vulnerability reduction.

Dr. McEntire has received several Quick Response Grants (funded by the National Science Foundation through the Natural Hazards Center at the University of Colorado), which allowed him to conduct research on disasters in Peru, the Dominican Republic, Texas, New York, and California.

Dr. McEntire is the author of *Disaster Response and Recovery* (Wiley) and *Comparative Emergency Management* (Federal Emergency Management Agency (FEMA)) and the editor of *Disciplines, Disasters and Emergency Management* (C.C. Thomas). His research has also been published in *Public Administration Review*, the *Australian Journal of Emergency Management*, *Disasters*, the *International Journal of Mass Emergencies and Disasters*, *Journal of Emergency Management*, *International Journal of the Environment and Sustainable Development*, *Sustainable Communities Review*, *International Journal of Emergency Management*, *Towson University Journal of International Affairs*, *Journal of the American Society of Professional Emergency Planners*, and the *Journal of International and Public Affairs*. His articles in *Disaster Prevention and Management* received Highly Commended and Outstanding Paper awards.

Dr. McEntire completed an instructor guide for FEMA and is a contributing author to the *Handbook of Disaster Research* and the *Handbook of Disaster Management*. He also has a chapter in *Emergency Management*, a book published by the International City/County Management Association.

Dr. McEntire has received grants to conduct terrorism response training for FEMA in Arkansas and Oklahoma. He has been a contributing author for a study of Texas homeland security preparedness for the Century Foundation as well as two IQ reports for the International City/County Management Association. In addition, McEntire has presented papers in Hungary, Mexico, Norway, and at the National Science Foundation, the National Academy of Sciences, and the Higher Education Conference at FEMA's

Emergency Management Institute in Emmitsburg, Maryland. He is a former member of Congressman Michael C. Burgess's Homeland Security Advisory Council and a current member of the Fire Protection Publications Advisory Board. He has reviewed books for Delmar Learning and is on the editorial staff for the *Journal of Emergency Management*.

In a prior position at the University of North Texas, Dr. McEntire served as an undergraduate coordinator, Ph.D. coordinator, assistant chair, associate dean, and director of summer session. Prior to his first academic appointment, Dr. McEntire attended the Graduate School of International Studies at the University of Denver. While pursuing his degree, he worked for the International and Emergency Services Departments at the American Red Cross.

FOREWORD

While violence has been part of the human experience long before there was the ability to write, and thus record it, we know that, then and now, violence is particularly frequent when there is competition between various populations, ethnic groups, and cultures over access to resources and power. As the size of the human population continues to grow, so also does the probability of violence. Open warfare is often, but not always, a function of one state (or country) against another. In the twentieth century, we saw groups of countries fighting against another group of countries, such as in both World War I and World War II. In these conflicts, it was relatively easy to identify who was involved on each side of the conflicts and their declared reasons for taking up arms against another country.

Since the end of World War II, we have seen numerous smaller local and regional wars, such as wars of independence (as in Algeria, Bangladesh, Indonesia), and proxy wars between major power blocs, but fought out in smaller countries, such as Vietnam, Nicaragua, and Korea. In all these cases, it was relatively clear who the combatants were, what their stated goals were, and that established armies were the main fighters.

We are now in an era in which conflicts between groups are often fought by small cadres, seeking to instill fear and societal breakdown by way of attacks against general civilian populations. While these attacks can be directly related to access to resources, we are also seeing the use of violence designed to instill fear in established societies, often for ideological reasons. These attacks, often called *terrorism*, frequently include physical violence, but may also use cyber tools to threaten individuals or entire societies. They threaten *homeland security*, with attacks popping up where we live, work, and travel. And while the media may concentrate on attacks that are inspired from outside of our own country, increasingly, mass violence is the preferred tool of local groups or even individuals, who want to make a statement of some kind or another.

So, how do we minimize the suffering that can be delivered by terrorism? What are the tools available to us? How do we organize prevention, mitigation, preparedness, response, and recovery from terrorist events? How do we make sure that the organizations and agencies that are tasked with protection against terrorism are fully collaborative with, on the one hand, the national military with all of its tools and strategies and, on the other hand, fully interactive with and partnered with public health, law enforcement, and civilian emergency management agencies at all levels of government? Failure at any of these junctions can result in massive suffering and loss.

This second edition of Dr. David A. McEntire's well-regarded book *Introduction to Homeland Security: Understanding Terrorism Prevention and Emergency Management* is filled with information focused on the new realities regarding threats, organizational boundaries, skills, methods, strategies, and cultures, as well as the challenges of working together across organizations on behalf of the public. This volume recognizes that the details will continue to change and, therefore, provides a solid overview of the fundamental goals, strategies, and objectives of homeland security, which provide the basis upon which agencies act and interact, regardless of changing circumstances and challenges. The book strives to help each reader become a solid resource in protecting the public, regardless the kind of event or the type of organization in which the reader works or intends to work. The wide-view approach is designed to help you to be as effective and flexible as possible in a world of changing circumstances.

On a final note, I would like to thank each and every reader of this book for your commitment to using your skills, energy, and time here on Earth to improving the lives of humans everywhere. This book will help you along the way.

Rick Bissell, PhD, MS, MA
Professor of Emergency Health Services
University of Maryland–Baltimore County

United States disaster policy has witnessed an ever-present history of tension between the security and emergency management points of view. Since the late 1940s, there has been recurring disagreement about the priority given to conflict events versus other types of hazards. Two events elevated the stakes in this debate and created urgency for finding some sort of consensus about future priorities.

First, 9/11 underscored the fact that the threat of terrorism needs to be taken seriously by disaster scholars and emergency managers. No one should pretend that the world is the way it once used to be.

Second, Hurricane Katrina reminded homeland security officials that they must not disregard human vulnerability to natural hazards. The frequency of natural disasters is simply too great to ignore and their impact is getting worse over time.

With these observations in mind, it is the opinion of this author that both homeland security and emergency management priorities need to be addressed in the future. Terrorist attacks are increasing in frequency and impact. While the possibility of terrorism involving weapons of mass destruction or cyberterrorism remains fairly low, the consequences of such attacks would indeed be overwhelming. More resources will be needed to address every type of threat. However, resource distribution should also take into account the broad aspects of homeland security. Terrorism has been given the lion's share of public support in recent years, but this attention should not be allowed to overshadow the essential function and contributions of emergency management.

Unfortunately, policy makers unintentionally created a substantial divide between the homeland security and disaster communities. Politicians may have overreacted to 9/11, and their decisions initially diminished the existing emergency management system of the 1990s. This has caused some ill-feelings among emergency managers toward the military and the law enforcement communities, which is not a good situation when one considers the fact that terrorists have vowed to kill Americans everywhere (including at home).

This book, *Introduction to Homeland Security: Understanding Terrorism Prevention and Emergency Management, Second Edition*, aims to lay a foundation that could assist in spanning the chasm between the disaster and terrorism communities. Its focus on terrorism may help to educate those who do not yet understand the need to prepare for this expanding threat. Its concentration on emergency management will remind homeland security officials that reinventing of the wheel is not only unnecessary but problematic.

Of course, taking this middle ground could result in increased antagonism between the different parties. It is also possible that the author has not adequately portrayed the specific details pertinent to all of the actors involved in the broad and interdisciplinary array of homeland security and emergency management activities. Nevertheless, it is the author's hope that this work will educate those working in each area and help promote a synergy of effort.

Chapter 1, "Understanding a New Global Priority: Terrorism, Homeland Security, and Emergency Management," examines the enormous impact of the terrorist attacks on 9/11 on world history, defines homeland security, and supplements homeland security with an emergency management perspective, thereby offering a broader view of how to deal with terrorist attacks.

Chapter 2, "Identifying Terrorism: Ideologically Motivated Acts of Violence and Their Relation to Disasters," identifies the numerous definitions and perspectives of terrorism, comparing how these are both alike and dissimilar, and also looks at the connections among terrorism and other types of disasters.

Chapter 3, "Recognizing the Causes of Terrorism: Differing Perspectives and the Role of Ideology," explores what motivates people to participate in terrorism, paying special attention to how historical conflicts, mistakes in foreign policy, and extreme levels of poverty may impel some to engage in terrorist attacks.

Chapter 4, "Comprehending Terrorists and Their Behavior: Who They Are and What They Do," assesses the nature of individual terrorists and those associated with groups and states and identifies how they finance operations, communicate with secret codes, and carry out attacks.

Chapter 5, "Uncovering the Dynamic Nature of Terrorism: History of Violence and Change over Time," explores why terrorism initially emerged, how it evolved in other nations, and the ways it has manifested in the United States.

Chapter 6, "Evaluating a Major Dilemma: Terrorism, the Media, and Censorship," looks at the difficult relationship between terrorism and the media, how to predict how reporters view terrorism, and the drawbacks and limitations of censorship.

In Chapter 7, "Contemplating a Quandary: Terrorism, Security, and Liberty," you learn why, as a participant in homeland security, it is imperative that you assess the tradeoffs between security and rights, and why terrorism exploits the tension between them.

Chapter 8, "Preventing Terrorist Attacks: Root Causes, Law, Intelligence, Counterterrorism," addresses the root causes of terrorism and explores primary ways of preventing attacks, like promoting laws that prohibit terrorism and punish those who support it, protecting all points of entry into the United States, and relying on human and other sources of intelligence to apprehend terrorists before they strike.

In Chapter 9, "Securing the Nation: Border Control and Sector Safety," the permeability of the US border is mentioned along with measures to prevent the infiltration of terrorists onto American soil. It also discusses the vulnerability of various economic sectors and describe ways to secure railways, air transportation, sea ports, and chemical facilities.

Chapter 10, "Protecting Against Potential Attacks: Threat Assessment, Mitigation, and Other Measures," looks at the benefits of mitigation practices, such as working with others to assess threats posed to critical infrastructure, key assets, and soft targets, as well as differentiating between structural and nonstructural mitigation methods.

In Chapter 11, "Preparing for the Unthinkable: Efforts for Readiness," we learn that preparing for terrorism is one of the central responsibilities in homeland security. In order to help your community prepare for possible terrorist attacks, you will need to be familiar with the executive orders and legislation issued by the president and congress, and set the foundation for preparedness by creating an advisory council, passing ordinances, acquiring monetary resources, and establishing an EOC.

Chapter 12, "Responding to Attacks: Important Functions and Coordination Mechanisms," examines effective ways to react to terrorist attacks, including the numerous functions involved, such as investigation, the protection of first responders, and the treatment of the victims of terrorist attacks.

Chapter 13, "Recovering from Impacts: Short-term and Long-term Measures," addresses the variety of recovery measures that need to be performed after a terrorist attack takes place, including declaring a disaster or state of emergency, addressing mass fatality issues, disposing debris, and providing emotional support for those who have been emotionally impacted by the event.

Chapter 14, "Assessing Significant Threats: WMD and Cyberterrorism," assesses the probability that terrorists will launch more unique and devastating attacks. It identifies the threat of radiological, nuclear, biological, and chemical weapons along with numerous recommendations to counter such assaults. The chapter also describes the risk of cyberterrorism and mentions the measures being taken to increase preparedness in this area.

In Chapter 15, "Looking Toward the Future: Challenges and Opportunities," the need for accountability in homeland security is identified. A discussion about policy occurs, and recommendations are provided for both researchers and practitioners.

PRE-READING LEARNING AIDS

Each chapter of *Introduction to Homeland Security: Understanding Terrorism Prevention and Emergency Management, Second Edition* features a number of learning and study aids, described in the following sections, to activate students' prior knowledge of the topics and orient them to the material.

Do You Already Know?

This bulleted list focuses on *subject matter* that will be taught. It tells students what they will be learning in this chapter and why it is significant for their careers. It also helps students understand why the chapter is important and how it relates to other chapters in the text.

The online assessment tool in multiple-choice format not only introduces chapter material but also helps students anticipate the chapter's learning outcomes. On focusing the students' attention on what they do not know, the self-test provides students with a benchmark against which they can measure their own progress. The Pre Test is available online at www.wiley.com/go/mcentire/homelandsecurity2e.

What You Will Find Out and What You Will Be Able To Do

This bulleted list emphasizes *capabilities and skills* that students will learn as a result of reading the chapter and notes the sections in which they will be found. It prepares students to synthesize and evaluate the chapter material and relate it to the real world.

WITHIN-TEXT LEARNING AIDS

The following learning aids are designed to encourage analysis and synthesis of the material, support the learning process, and ensure success during the evaluation phase.

Introduction

This section orients the student by introducing the chapter and explaining its practical value and relevance to the book as a whole. Short summaries of chapter sections preview the topics to follow.

In the Real World

These boxes tie section content to real-world organizations, scenarios, and applications. Engage stories of professionals and institutions–challenges they faced, successes they had, and their ultimate outcome.

Summary

Each chapter concludes with a summary paragraph that reviews the major concepts in the chapter and links back to the "Do You Already Know" list.

Key Terms and Glossary

To help students develop a professional vocabulary, key terms are bolded when they first appear in the chapter and are also shown in the margin of page with their definitions. A complete list of key terms with brief definitions appears at the end of each chapter and again in a glossary at the end of the book. Knowledge of key terms is assessed by all assessment tools (see below).

EVALUATION AND ASSESSMENT TOOLS

The evaluation phase consists of a variety of within-chapter and end-of-chapter assessment tools that test how well students have learned the material and their ability to apply it in the real world. These tools also encourage students to extend their learning into different scenarios and higher levels of understanding and thinking. The following assessment tools appear in every chapter.

Self-Check

Related to the "Do You Already Know" bullets and found at the end of each section, this battery of short-answer questions emphasizes student understanding of concepts and mastery of section content. Though the questions may be either discussed in class or studied by students outside of class, students should not go on before they can answer all questions correctly.

Understand: What Have You Learned?

This online Post Test should be taken after students have completed the chapter. It includes all of the questions in the Pre Test so that students can see how their learning has progressed and improved. The Post Test is available online at www.wiley.com/go/mcentire/homelandsecurity2e

Applying This Chapter

These questions drive home key ideas by asking students to synthesize and apply chapter concepts to new, real-life situations and scenarios.

Be a Homeland Security Professional

Found at the end of each chapter, "Be a..." questions are designed to extend students' thinking and are thus ideal for discussion or writing assignments. Using an open-ended format and sometimes based on web sources, they encourage students to draw conclusions using chapter materials applied to real-world situations, which foster both mastery and independent learning.

INSTRUCTOR AND STUDENT PACKAGE

Introduction to Homeland Security: Understanding Terrorism Prevention and Emergency Management, Second Edition is available with the following teaching and learning supplements. All supplements are available online at the text's Book Companion Website, located at www.wiley.com/go/mcentire/homelandsecurity2e

Instructor's Resource Guide

The Instructor's Resource Guide provides the following aids and supplements for teaching a Homeland Security course:

- **Text summary aids:** For each chapter, these include a chapter summary, learning objectives, definitions of key terms, and answers to in-text question sets.

- **Teaching suggestions:** For each chapter, these include at least three suggestions for learning activities (such as ideas for speakers to invite, videos to show, and other projects) and suggestions for additional resources.

- **PowerPoints:** Key information is summarized in 10–15 PowerPoints per chapter. Instructors may use these in class or choose to share them with students for class presentations or to provide additional study support.

- **Test Bank:** The test bank features one test per chapter, as well as a midterm and two finals–one cumulative and one noncumulative. Each includes true/false, multiple-choice, and open-ended questions. Answers and page references are provided for the true/false and multiple-choice questions, while page references are given for the open-ended questions. Tests are available in Microsoft Word and computerized formats.

ACKNOWLEDGMENTS

I express appreciation to those individuals who have made substantial contributions to *Introduction to Homeland Security*. I am indebted first and foremost to Laura Town and Brian Baker (two editors at Wiley) for their critical assessment of the text and their useful recommendations for improvement. I am also grateful to the other members of the Wiley staff—Stefanie Volk, Katrina Maceda, and Hari Priya J—who helped format the text and find pictures for the entire document. Others including Kailey Birchall, Ashley Layton, Tres Layton, and Madison McEntire provided valuable assistance in the preparation of this manuscript.

I am likewise appreciative of several reviewers for their beneficial suggestions on earlier versions of the manuscript. This includes:

- Robin Ebemyer, Utah Valley University
- Vincent J. Doherty, Naval Postgraduate School
- Scott D. Lassa, Milwaukee Area Technical College
- David W. Lewis, University of Maryland
- Ryan Vogel, Utah Valley University

While I am solely responsible for the content of this book, I am thankful for all those who have shared valuable insights and unique perspectives. Their areas of expertise and years of experience have undoubtedly assisted me during the publication process.

Finally, I would be remiss if I did not recognize the many scholars and practitioners that I have come across during my involvement in this field. Your knowledge and professionalism have not only helped to educate me about terrorism and disasters; you have also underscored the significant need for homeland security and emergency management functions in our society. More importantly, I am cognizant that your persistent efforts will enable our nation to reduce vulnerability and increase our ability to react effectively when exigency exists. For this I am truly thankful.

David A. McEntire, PhD

ABOUT THE COMPANION WEBSITE

This book is accompanied by a companion website:

www.wiley.com/go/mcentire/homelandsecurity2e

The instructor website includes:

- Instructor's resource material
- Powerpoint slides
- Pre-test
- Post-test
- Test bank
- Image gallery

The student website includes:

- Pre-test
- Post-test
- Image gallery

CHAPTER 1

UNDERSTANDING A NEW GLOBAL PRIORITY

Terrorism, Homeland Security, and Emergency Management

Do You Already Know?

- Why we should be concerned about terrorism
- If terrorist attacks are becoming more frequent
- Why 9/11 changed the world
- How to define homeland security
- Why many professions, including emergency management, can help deal with terrorist attacks

 For additional questions to assess your current knowledge of terrorism and homeland security, go to **www.wiley.com/go/mcentire/ homelandsecurity2e**

What You Will Find Out	What You Will Be Able To Do
1.1 Examples of terrorism in the United States	• List terrorist activity in recent years
1.2 The possibility of additional attacks in the future	• Evaluate the possibility of future attacks
1.3 The far-reaching effects of 9/11	• Relate how the world changed after the 9/11 hijackings
1.4 Definitions of homeland security	• Describe homeland security
1.5 The breadth of organizations involved in homeland security	• Assess how various disciplines help practitioners deal with terrorism

Introduction to Homeland Security: Understanding Terrorism Prevention and Emergency Management,
Second Edition. David A. McEntire.
© 2019 John Wiley & Sons, Inc. Published 2019 by John Wiley & Sons, Inc.
Companion website: www.wiley.com/go/mcentire/homelandsecurity2e

INTRODUCTION

Welcome to the important field and profession of homeland security as well as the perplexing study of why violence is employed for ideological purposes! If you are interested or involved in dealing with the threat of terrorism, it is imperative that you understand the nature of this type of violence and why it occurs. The following book has the purpose of helping you achieve these goals as well as to comprehend the fundamental principles of homeland security. While reading this introductory chapter, you will gain an understanding of the growing threat of terrorism and the numerous reasons why this problem should be addressed now and in the future. You will learn how the terrorist attacks on 11 September 2001 changed the world and opened up a new era in global history. You will be able to discuss the mission and scope of homeland security along with the challenges it currently faces. The importance of approaching homeland security from a holistic perspective is then mentioned, enabling you to recognize why many professions including emergency management must form an integral part of efforts to deal with terrorism.

1.1 TERRORISM IS THE NEW NORMAL

Terrorism:
The use or threat of violence to support ideological purposes.

In simple terms, **terrorism** is the use or threat of violence to support ideological purposes. Recent events might cause you to think that terrorist attacks are more frequent and deadly than in the past. Your instinct is certainly justified according to the London Institute for Economics and Peace (Cassidy 2015). Although some visible politicians have intentionally downplayed attacks to give the impression that they are effective leaders, terrorism is ever present and cannot be denied. Attacks are not only more common than the past, they are more consequential as well. Three cases illustrate the "new normal" we are facing today.

1.1.1 Boston Marathon Bombing

On 15 April 2013, Chechen brothers Tamerlan and Dzhokhar Tsarnaev detonated two homemade pressure cooker bombs at the Boston Marathon in Massachusetts. The bombs exploded in the late afternoon about 200 yards apart near the finish line of the race on Boylston Street. Three people died from the blasts and over 260 others were injured. The Marathon was suspended while athletes and bystanders were directed to safety with the help of the Boston Police Department. A massive manhunt was soon underway to find those involved in the attack. One of the brothers was killed during a confrontation with police. The other was caught and is now facing prosecution.

1.1.2 San Bernardino Regional Center Shooting

On 2 December 2015, a mass shooting took place in San Bernardino, California, at the Inland Regional Center. The perpetrators were Syed Rizwan Farook and his wife, Tashfeen Malik. The married couple killed

14 people and injured 22 when they opened fire at a holiday party for the city's Department of Public Health. While already devastating, the incident could have been more consequential. Three pipe bombs found at the scene failed to explode. The terrorists were killed in a shootout with police a short time later.

1.1.3 Orlando Nightclub Shooting

On 12 June 2016, a security guard named Omar Mateen instigated one of the deadliest mass shootings in US history. With the use of a pistol and a semiautomatic rifle, he killed 49 people and wounded 53 others at the Pulse – a gay nightclub in Orlando, Florida. After a three-hour standoff, the terrorist was shot and killed by the Orlando Police Department. The carnage was one of the worst mass shooting in US history to date.

1.1.4 Other Notable Attacks

The above attacks are not isolated. The list of such events has increased over the past 15 years. For instance, Hesham Mohamed Hadayet opened fire at the El Al ticket counter at the Los Angeles Airport. His attack killed two people and injured four others on 4 July 2002. On 3 March 2006, Mohammed Reza Taheri-azar intentionally drove a vehicle into a crowd at the University of North Carolina at Chapel Hill. He injured nine people. In November of 2009, Nidal Malik murdered 14 people at the Fort Hood military base in Texas.

Figure 1-1

Mass shootings like the Orlando nightclub shooting reveal the significant impact a lone terrorist can have on innocent citizens.
Source: © US State of Florida.

A disgruntled man named Joseph Stack flew his private plane into an Internal Revenue Service building in Austin, Texas, on 18 February 2010. In the small town of Moore, Oklahoma, Alton Nolen beheaded a woman at a Vaughan Foods plant on 24 September 2014. Robert Lewis Dear killed three people at a Planned Parenthood clinic in Colorado Springs, CO, on 27 November 2015. In one of the worst police shootings in the United States, Micah Xavier Johnson killed five police officers on 7 July 2016. This sniper attack took place in Dallas, Texas, at a Black Lives Matter protest. It wounded nine others, including two civilians.

Unfortunately, the list of terrorism seems to be never ending. Ten other attacks illustrate the persistence of attacks along with a diversity of targets and methods:

1. Bruce Edwards Ivins mailed several letters containing anthrax spores to news outlets and two Democratic senators. Five people were killed and 17 others were injured from 18 September to 9 October 2001.
2. John Allen Williams and Lee Boyd Malvo (the "Beltway Snipers") murdered 10 people and injured 3 others in Washington, D.C., Maryland, and Virginia over a three-week period in October 2002.
3. John Patrick Bedell injured two police officers at the entrance of the Pentagon on 4 March 2010.
4. Wade Michael Page gunned down six people at a Sikh Temple in Wisconsin on 5 August 2012.
5. Ali Muhammad Brown killed three civilians in Seattle, Washington, during a period from 27 April 2014 to 1 June 2014.
6. Zale Thompson attacked two police officers with a hatchet in Queens, New York, on 23 October 2014.
7. Ismaaiyl Brinsley killed two police officers in an ambush in Brooklyn, New York, on 20 December 2014.
8. Elton Simpson and Nadir Soofi opened fire at a conference that was hosting an exhibition of a cartoon of the prophet Muhammad in Garland, Texas, on 3 May 2015.
9. Muhammad Youssef Abdulazeez shot and killed four marines and a sailor at a military base in Chattanooga, Tennessee, on 16 July 2015.
10. Finally, Faisal Mohammad attacked students with a knife at a university in Merced, California, on 4 November 2015.

The terrorist attacks mentioned above were not the first to occur in the United States or around the world. Nor will they be the last ones to take place in our country or elsewhere. There have been many unsuccessful attacks in New York as well as in Arkansas, New Jersey, Illinois, Dallas, Michigan, Washington, D.C., Florida, Missouri, etc. This is to say nothing about terrorist attacks initiated in other nations.

One of the most consequential bouts of terrorism occurred on 13 November 2015 when terrorists carried out a number of coordinated attacks in France and Belgium. Six locations were targeted in the assaults, ranging from the Stade de France stadium to popular bars in and around Paris. The

IN THE REAL WORLD

Failed Attacks

A number of attacks have been thwarted since the start of the new millennium. Four are particularly noteworthy:

Richard Colvin Reid (also known as the "shoe bomber") attempted to detonate explosives hidden in his shoes on an American Airlines flight from Paris, France, to Miami, Florida. Fortunately, Reid was subdued before he could successfully light the fuse on 22 December 2001.

A terrorist plot involving homemade liquid explosives (disguised as sports drinks) was thwarted before it could be carried out on several commercial airlines flights in 2006. Over 20 suspects were arrested after British police uncovered the scheme.

On 1 May 2010, Faisal Shahzad (also known as the "Times Square Bomber") attempted to detonate a car bomb in New York City. Fortunately, the explosives failed to detonate, and security was notified when people noticed smoke coming from a car.

Robert Lorenzo Hester, Jr., aka Mohammed Junaid Al Amreeki, was charged for his attempt to provide material support to a foreign terrorist organization on 17 February 2017. Hester believed he was helping ISIS to launch an attack, but in reality he was communicating with undercover FBI agents. This federal law enforcement agency became aware of Hester's intentions after he posted several statements regarding his desire to attack the United States.

bloodshed began when suicide bombers wearing explosives detonated them near a major soccer match being played between France and Germany. A few minutes later, gunmen began unleashing heavy gun fire at several restaurants in Paris. The most fatal of the attacks occurred in the Bataclan theater. Three gunmen entered the concert hall and fired assault rifles into the audience. Some members of the crowd were able to escape through exits, but 89 people lost their lives and many more were wounded. By the time all of the attacks concluded, 130 people were killed and 368 were injured in the coordinated massacres, which were claimed by the Islamic State of Iraq and the Levant (ISIL). Some of the gunmen were neutralized in the firefight with police, and others (including Abdelhamid Abaaoud) were arrested. Unfortunately, the same cell responsible for the attacks in November also launched additional suicide bombings in Belgium on 22 March 2016. They killed 32 innocent civilians and wounded over 300 others at the Brussels Airport and a Brussels' metro station. A few of the terrorists died in the incident, and law enforcement was able to apprehend some of the other perpetrators. This series of events was one of the worst attacks in Europe. More attacks – whether successful and unsuccessful – will certainly follow here and elsewhere.

SELF-CHECK

1. Terrorism might be considered as the "new normal." True or False?
2. Terrorist attacks have increased over the past few years. True or False?
3. Terrorist attacks have occurred at what locations?
   (a) Bars and restaurants
   (b) Military bases
   (c) Government buildings
   (d) Sports stadiums
   (e) All of the above
4. What is an example of a recent terrorist attack?

1.2 A GROWING THREAT

If you pick up a national or international newspaper on any given day or scan the Internet for news, you will probably find several articles discussing the rising menace of terrorism. Headlines frequently highlight possible threats and recent attacks:

- Terrorists Infiltrate the United States
- Man Attempts to Detonate Shoe on Plane
- Aviation Security Still Weak
- Oregon Professor Charged with Terrorism
- Sea-born Cargo a Likely Target
- Eco-terrorism Occurs in California
- Officials Detain Man after Filming Chicago Bridge
- Explosives Missing in Georgia
- Agro-terrorism a Real Possibility
- Industrial Security Still Lacking
- Pipelines Targeted in Possible Attack
- Cruise Ship Receives Threatening Letter
- Bombs Obliterate Spanish Resort
- Australia Weary about Potential Terrorists
- Plot Busted in Pakistan
- Bus Ripped Apart by Blast in London
- Children Taken Hostage in Russia
- Cartoon of Mohamed Inflames Terrorists in Europe
- Iran Seeks Nuclear Weapons
- Terrorists Set Sights on Olympics

Figure 1-2

The news is dominated with stories about terrorism and terrorist attacks. Source: © Shutterstock/Getty Images. Reproduced with permission of Getty Images.

Islamic State of Iraq and Syria (ISIS):
A group that seeks to establish an Islamic government and is now the most feared and well-known terrorist organization in the world.

In addition, the media will likely provide numerous reports about the **Islamic State of Iraq and Syria (ISIS)**. This particular group seeks to establish an Islamic government in the Middle East and is now the most feared and recognized terrorist organization in the world (Cockburn 2016; Weiss and Hassan 2016). Their actions show no mercy toward victims, and their methods involve the most brutal forms of violence imaginable. These terrorists have illustrated their willingness to kill hundreds and thousands of enemies through mass executions, with power saws, via drownings, and by dousing people with gasoline and lighting them on fire. ISIS members have thrown homosexuals off of rooftops and placed the severed heads of their victims on railings or posts. Their actions are not just atrocious, but intentional efforts to induce migration, conduct genocide, or force policy change.

Recognizing these observed threats and actual terrorist activity, many conclude that politically motivated acts of violence will be more common in the future. Several years ago Senator Richard Lugar, R-Ind, stated, "The bottom line is this: For the foreseeable future, the United States and other nations will face an existential threat from … terrorism." In 2016, FBI Director James Comey reiterated this warning by stating that terrorists will infiltrate Western Europe and the United States and that future attacks will be on "an order magnitude greater" than those of the past.

1.2.1 Reasons to Anticipate More Attacks

There are numerous reasons why we may witness additional and more impactful attacks in the future. For instance, the promise of Western forms of economic development has not materialized in many nations, and poverty may be associated with increased terrorist activities. The poor nations 50 years ago are predominantly the poor countries today, and they are breeding grounds for terrorist organizations. In addition, the end of the Cold War resulted in the resurgence of deep-seated ethnic or political rivalries. Chechnya desires autonomy and independence from Russia. Furthermore, US military power and involvement in the Middle East has angered many Arabs. Many view American presence as a new form of colonialism. Also, there is fear that countries like Iran and North Korea will develop, use, or share nuclear weapons and materials with others. Some religious and social movements have become more extreme over time. Fundamentalist Muslims and other interest groups want change now and are willing to promote it through violent behavior. Furthermore, protecting all of the vulnerable locations that the terrorists could attack is virtually impossible. Government buildings, ports, shopping malls, and schools are all likely targets. Furthermore, training and preparedness for terrorism response could be inadequate. As an example, we do not know enough about how to deal with poisonous substances used by terrorists.

Five other factors may ultimately lead terrorists to enact their deadly craft in the years to come:

a. Prior military conflicts among nation-states persist, and patience to resolve them is growing thin (e.g. the creation of the state of Israel several decades ago has resulted in ongoing tensions in the Middle East).

b. Citizens are frustrated with the harsh conditions of dictatorship or the unresponsiveness of certain democratic governments (e.g. they desire political change and think that their needs are not being met in an expeditious manner).

c. It is extremely difficult for intelligence analysts to know who the "enemy" is (e.g. how can one pinpoint a terrorist when they often blend into the crowd?).

d. Technology and education will allow terrorists to develop and use more sophisticated weapons (e.g. even typical household chemicals can be combined in such a way as to make bombs).

e. The ideology of terrorists has become so radical that their brutality knows no boundaries.

Should more and worse terrorist attacks occur as predicted, the United States can expect increased loss of life, financial hardship, social disruption, dramatic political changes, and other negative consequences. As an example, it is not out of the possibility to have casualties in the thousands, hundreds of thousands, or even higher due to modern weapons that employ today's advanced knowledge and technology. The economy will surely suffer after major attacks and financial losses can total in the millions or billions. Travel and shopping may be severely hampered as well, and impending attacks could be geared toward an alteration of people's way of life. Terrorism could likewise result in a massive transformation of government and the introduction of new laws pertaining to security, travel, and immigration. Further consequences and changes will certainly be under-taken when terrorists strike again in the United States and elsewhere. All of this is to say that terrorism is now recognized as a consistent feature of our time, and it cannot be discounted or ignored. In short, "terrorism has become the plague of the twenty first century" (Franks 2006, p. 1).

IN THE REAL WORLD

Bin Laden's War Against the United States

Terrorists like the now-dead Osama bin Laden declare war against Western nations. He and his subsequent followers disapprove of the foreign policy of the United States in the Middle East, and they declare it is the responsibility of all Muslims to attack the "infidels." Reports from intelligence analysts indicate that terrorist groups like Al-Qaeda and ISIS are working hard to launch new attacks in the United States and elsewhere around the world. Most experts believe that their efforts will be successful unless significant counterterrorism measures are undertaken in the future.

SELF-CHECK

1. There are very few reports of terrorist threats in newspapers. True or False?

2. Terrorist attacks create several negative consequences ranging from death and injuries to social and economic disruption. True or False?

3. Reasons to be concerned about terrorism include:
    (a) Resurgence of ethnic rivalries
    (b) Poverty in many nations around the world
    (c) More extreme religious attitudes
    (d) Availability of weapons
    (e) All of the above

4. Will we have more attacks in the future? If so, why?

1.3   9/11: A WAKE-UP CALL

9/11:
The terrorist attacks involving hijacked planes against the United States.

The most consequential attack up to the time of this publication occurred on 11 September 2001. **9/11**, as it is known, will forever be remembered as the terrorist attacks involving hijacked planes against the United States. It ushered in a new era in world history and illustrates why terrorism has to be taken seriously.

Al-Qaeda:
An extreme Islamic fundamentalist terrorist organization.

After years of planning, 19 hijackers affiliated with Osama bin Laden and **Al-Qaeda** (an extreme Islamic fundamentalist organization) boarded four commercial planes to initiate a massive campaign of terror against the United States. American Airlines Flight 11, departing from Boston to Los Angeles,

Figure 1-3

Terrorists used passenger jets to attack the United States on 11 September 2001. Source: © FEMA.

was overtaken by men with box cutters or other sharp instruments. It was then deliberately flown into North Tower of World Trade Center in New York City. United Airlines Flight 175, also departing from Boston to Los Angeles, was diverted and used as a missile to kill people working in the South Tower of the World Trade Center. Within minutes, American Airlines Flight 77, departing from Dulles to Los Angeles, was crashed into the Pentagon in Arlington, Virginia. Another plane, United Airlines Flight 93, departing from Newark to San Francisco, was also hijacked. By this time, passengers on board became aware of other incidents and attempted to take back the aircraft. Unfortunately, the plane was deliberately flown into the ground a short time later in an empty field southeast of Pittsburgh.

The brave efforts of passengers on Flight 93 amounted to a symbolic victory for the United States. Nevertheless, the hijackers succeeded in their goal of bringing attention to their hatred of Western culture and disapproval of American foreign policy. At least 266 passengers and crew were killed in the orchestrated attacks. Over 2500 more people died in the subsequent collapses of the World Trade Center towers in New York and in the fire at the Pentagon in Virginia. In addition to the loss of life, America experienced fear near or on par of Pearl Harbor. Economic disruption occurred on an unprecedented scale, and damages alone totaled more than $40 billion. Terrorism had certainly captured the attention of the United States.

When informed of the situation, President Bush ordered any additional hijacked planes be shot down should they be encountered. He also requested the grounding of all other flights to prevent further loss of life and damage. In the meantime, firefighters, police officers, paramedics, hospital personnel, and government officials immediately began to address the needs of the terrorists' victims. Volunteers, businesses, and numerous local, state, and federal agencies also arrived to consider how they would address long-term rebuilding activities. When flights resumed a few days later, new measures were taken at US airports to minimize the probability of similar events in the future.

After determining who was responsible for these attacks, US troops were sent into Afghanistan to topple the Taliban. The **Taliban** is the name of the government that provided a safe haven for Al-Qaeda. Intelligence efforts were also augmented, and a successful manhunt was undertaken to find Osama bin Laden, the leader of the Al-Qaeda terrorist network. In time, Congress passed numerous laws to repel terrorist activity by improving border control, increasing public security, and promoting readiness for future terrorist plots. Elected officials, public servants, law enforcement agencies, corporations, and many others are now working together to prevent further terrorist attacks or react effectively should they occur.

The above narrative describing 9/11 brings up three central questions that will be addressed in the remainder of this book:

Taliban:
The **Taliban** is the name of the government that provided a safe haven for Al-Qaeda

- What is terrorism?
- Why and how does terrorism occur?
- What can and should be done to deal with it in an effective manner?

SELF-CHECK

1. Terrorism may be described as the pursuit of ideological purposes through violent means or the threat of violence. True or False?
2. 9/11 is the name given to the terrorist attacks on the World Trade Center and the Pentagon. True or False?
3. The attacks on 11 September 2001 involved:
    (a) Explosives
    (b) Guns
    (c) Hijacked airplanes
    (d) Hand grenades
    (e) None of the above
4. Why did 9/11 change the world?

1.4   THE NATURE OF HOMELAND SECURITY

The foregoing discussion indicates the need for what is now known as "homeland security." Discussions about this field and emerging profession did not begin after 9/11. President Clinton acknowledged the threat of terrorism after a number of attacks were initiated in the 1990s. Later on, President Bush created an office to assess the growing threat of terrorism after his election. However, homeland security did not move to the forefront of the policy agenda until after 9/11. The events of this day revealed the reality of what was heretofore unthinkable as well as the need to address it in a systematic fashion. Today, homeland security is now a "primary public policy area just like education, healthcare, environment, nation defense, and others" (Jones 2008, p. 95).

1.4.1 Definitions of Homeland Security

Homeland security:
A concerted national effort to prevent terrorist attacks within the United States, reduce America's vulnerability to terrorism, and recover from and minimize the damage of attacks that do occur.

When **homeland security** was initially conceived by national leaders, it was defined as "a concerted national effort to prevent terrorist attacks within the United States, reduce America's vulnerability to terrorism, and recover from and minimize the damage of attacks that do occur" (Office of Homeland Security 2002, p. 2). While this definition captures the essence of current efforts to deal with terrorism, consensus on the term is not universal. For instance:

Department of Homeland Security (DHS):
A newly created organization that desires to prevent terrorist attacks or react effectively.

- *Citizens believe homeland security refers to the federal agency in charge of preventing terrorist attacks in the United States.* The **Department of Homeland Security (DHS)** was created, and this organization is composed of over 170 000 employees from 22 federal agencies. Its mission is to prevent terrorist attacks and react to those that may occur.
- *Elected officials view homeland security as a policy framework.* Its purpose is to organize "the activities of government and all sectors of society to detect, deter, protect against, and if necessary, respond to domestic attacks such as 9/11" (Kamien 2006, p. xli).
- *Scholars see homeland security as an area of study or emerging academic discipline.* It is considered a multi- or interdisciplinary research endeavor that involves academic fields such as international relations, criminal justice, public administration, and even medicine.
- *Practitioners regard it to be a function or functions performed in response to the terrorist threat.* In this sense, homeland security deals with intelligence gathering, border control, airport security, fire suppression, public health, and emergency medical care.
- *The military asserts that homeland security is the new priority in the post-Cold War era.* Since relations between the Cold War ended in the late 1980s, attention in national security has shifted to a significant degree toward individual terrorists, terrorist organizations, and the states that support terrorism.

1.4.2 Agreement About Homeland Security

Even though homeland security means different things to different people, there are several points of agreement. First, homeland security was created to counter the threat of terrorism in the United States and is consequently a unique blend of national security and emergency management. According to the initial National Strategy for Homeland Security, there are six essential missions of homeland security. These include:

- **Mission Area 1: Intelligence and Warning.** One goal of homeland security is to identify possible terrorist attacks before they occur. This eliminates surprises and permits the implementation of protective measures if potential targets can be identified.

- **Mission Area 2: Border and Transportation Security.** Another purpose of homeland security is to prevent the infiltration of terrorists into the United States. Protecting our land, water, and air transportation systems from attack is also a major objective of homeland security.

- **Mission Area 3: Domestic Counterterrorism.** This aim focuses on interdicting terrorist activity and prosecuting those who fund or engage in terrorism. The goal here is to thwart terrorist plans and apprehend those involved in attacks against America.

- **Mission Area 4: Protecting Critical Infrastructures and Key Assets.** This strategy desires to defend vital buildings, roadways, utilities, technology, etc. Steps must also be taken to prevent attacks against important monuments, valued industries, and national symbols (e.g. the Statue of Liberty).

- **Mission Area 5: Defending against Catastrophic Threat.** The intention of this mission is to prevent the proliferation of dangerous weapons. Homeland security also wants to quickly detect and deal with the impact of major attacks.

- **Mission Area 6: Emergency Preparedness and Response.** The final priority of homeland security is to plan, train, and equip police, fire, and paramedics to react successfully to terrorism. There is also a need to promote recovery with the assistance of disaster specialists.

In the 2010 Quadrennial Homeland Security Review, the missions were revised slightly and reflect a more specific focus on the DHS (rather than the broad functions pertinent to the goals of homeland security). The mission areas now include (i) preventing terrorism and enhancing security, (ii) securing and managing our borders, (iii) enforcing and administering our immigration laws, (iv) safeguarding and securing cyberspace, (v) ensuring resilience to disasters, and (vi) maturing and strengthening the homeland security enterprise. Regardless of this shift in mission, it is clear that homeland security is a major undertaking. It definitely requires a comprehensive approach (Martin 2017).

A second and widely held view espoused in 2016 by the DHS is that this endeavor requires integrated efforts on the part of many people. According to Richard Falkenrath, an expert on international conflict,

> Men and women from dozens of different disciplines – regional experts, terrorism analysts, law enforcement officials, intelligence officers, privacy specialists, diplomats, military officers, immigration specialists, customs inspectors, specific industry experts, regulatory lawyers,

doctors and epidemiologists, research scientists, chemists, nuclear phys-
icists, information technologists, emergency managers, firefighters,
communications specialists, and politicians, to name a few – are currently involved in homeland security (in Kamien 2006, p. xxvi).

In other words, there are a variety of participants in homeland security. Some
may represent the government at local, state, and national levels. Many cities
and states now have homeland security agencies like the DHS. Tribal governments are also involved in homeland security efforts. Others will assist in
homeland security efforts from the business and nonprofit communities. Corporations play a huge role in transportation and shipping, while organizations
like the American Red Cross help to educate the public about terrorism preparedness. Even citizens may fulfill homeland security functions by notifying
officials of potential terrorist activity (e.g. "see something, say something"
public education campaign). Although much of the activity in homeland security occurs within the domestic arena among individuals, businesses, and
cities or states, the assistance of national and international organizations is
also required. National intelligence agencies share information about terrorists operating abroad, and the United Nations has passed resolutions on how
the international community should confront terrorism.

A third area of agreement is that tensions have reemerged or resulted
at times from homeland security initiatives (Canton 2016). The most visible
examples concern the problems homeland security initially produced for
those responsible for dealing with disasters. For example, the **Federal
Emergency Management Agency (FEMA)** – the national entity in charge
of disaster management – lost much of its budget and autonomy when it
was integrated into the newly created DHS. A significant portion of the
operating funds from FEMA's small budget (at least by federal standards)
were poured into the DHS to cover start-up costs, and the ability of this
disaster organization to influence the direction of policy was severely hampered. FEMA, which had cabinet-level status in a prior administration, saw
its direct ties to the President severed when its Director was placed under
DHS. Furthermore, FEMA's interest in all types of hazards, disaster mitigation programs, and even certain preparedness functions were overlooked.
Under the DHS, terrorism seemed to take precedence over all other concerns, and efforts to address other types of disasters were neglected. The
heavy military and law enforcement approach to homeland security also
had an impact upon interagency collaboration. Information sensitivities as
well as command and control/top-down communication structures hindered
coordination across organizations horizontally and among governments
vertically. Morale at FEMA started to deteriorate under these conditions,
and many knowledgeable disaster professionals retired or switched careers
as a result. Such problems were in part responsible for the slow and disjointed response to Hurricane Katrina in fall 2005. Neither FEMA nor DHS
officials could effectively coordinate important post-disaster functions such
as mass care, sheltering, and evacuation. After several congressional investigations into these failures, efforts have been made to correct them. In
particular, there is growing recognition that homeland security cannot focus
on the threat of terrorism alone or without the help of organizations like

**Federal Emergency
Management Agency
(FEMA):**
The national entity in
charge of disaster
management.

Figure 1-4

This shield illustrates that the Federal Emergency Management Agency is an organization within the Department of Homeland Security. Source: © FEMA.

FEMA. In fact, the mission of DHS was adapted in 2007 to include a greater emphasis on all types of disasters along with a recognition of the importance of preparedness.

Finally, individuals like Representative Jeff Duncan (R-SC) have recently argued that homeland security has had mixed results during its short existence. On the one hand, the United States has been successful in preventing major terrorist attacks like 9/11 against the homeland. Efforts in this area are to be commended because several terrorist plots against Americans have been foiled. This, probably more than any other factor, is a major achievement against terrorism. On the other hand, the DHS has gone through several growing pains because of its hasty creation and the enormous challenges it faces pertaining to its mission. For instance, there have been numerous allegations that the start-up funding devoted to homeland security lacked careful controls to prevent fraud, waste, and abuse. At least some of the money designated for homeland security has not gone to legitimate purposes. Stories abound of communities using homeland security money to buy dump trucks, polo shirts, and other items that seem at first glance to be unrelated to terrorism. Other problems, like border control, are yet to be resolved due to the politics relating to illegal immigration. For these reasons, the impact of homeland security is somewhat inconclusive. Of course, it is necessary to recognize that it is not easy to assess what success means in the context of homeland security. This is because you cannot always publicize threats or evaluate responses to attacks that have been thwarted. Regardless of these concerns, homeland security remains a vital function for national interests.

IN THE REAL WORLD

The National Plans to Deal with Disasters and Terrorism

After 9/11, the government developed a new strategy for dealing with terrorist attacks. Rather than building upon or altering the prior Federal Response Plan (FRP), a new plan was created. The National Response Plan (NRP) added layers of bureaucracy to federal response operations and obfuscated responsibility for numerous disaster functions. The plan was criticized as it was being created and especially after it failed dramatically in Hurricane Katrina. Part of the problem was a result of placing too much attention on terrorism and downplaying other types of hazards. The Director of FEMA also lost direct ties to the President, which hindered communication. The challenges that have resulted indicate why the Federal Emergency Management Agency (FEMA) should be more involved in homeland security policies. This is because FEMA plays a lead role in preparing for and coordinating post-disaster responses. Fortunately, efforts are being made to clarify agency tasks in all types of disasters. The National Response Framework (NRF) is a new document that was created to correct the weaknesses of the NRP.

SELF-CHECK

1. Homeland security is defined as efforts to prevent terrorist activity, reduce vulnerability, and recover from attacks. True or False?
2. Everyone views homeland security in the same way. True or False?
3. The goals of homeland security are to:
   (a) Gather intelligence
   (b) Protect borders and infrastructure
   (c) Prepare for major catastrophes
   (d) Answers a and b only
   (e) Answers a, b, and c
4. Why is it important to take a broad view of homeland security?
5. Has homeland security been effective thus far? Why or why not?

1.5 DISCIPLINES INVOLVED IN HOMELAND SECURITY AND THE EMERGENCY MANAGEMENT PROFESSION

If you are to work in the important field of homeland security, you must be aware of its academic underpinnings and the disciplines that contribute to its knowledge base. It is true that some question if homeland security is an academic discipline (Falkow 2013). The argument is that homeland security is still emerging and does not yet have an agreed-upon set of concepts and theories. However, others assert that homeland security is a "meta" discipline. This suggests that homeland security is a combination of many areas of study including international relations, criminal justice, public administration, and public health, among others. These fields and others offer important insights into terrorism and for homeland security:

International relations:
A discipline and profession that deals with the conflicts among nation-states and nonstate actors (e.g. why terrorism occurs and what governments are doing about it).

Criminal justice:
A discipline and profession interested in intelligence gathering, terrorist investigation, prosecution, border control, and other security measures.

Public administration:
A discipline and profession that directs attention to the formation policy and the best organization to deal with difficult societal problems.

Public health:
A discipline and profession that concentrates on understanding diseases and how to treat them (e.g. identifying how to react from a medical standpoint to the use of nuclear, biological, chemical, or radiological weapons).

- **International relations** focuses on the conflicts among nation-states and nonstate actors. It identifies why terrorism occurs and what governments are doing about it.
- **Criminal justice** is interested in intelligence gathering, terrorist investigation, and prosecution. It also has relation to border control and other security measures.
- **Public administration** directs attention on the formation and implementation of policy. It also helps to identify the best form of organization to deal with difficult societal problems.
- **Public health** concentrates on understanding diseases and how to treat them. It plays an important role in preparing for terrorists' use of nuclear, biological, chemical, or radiological weapons.

Other academic disciplines are also important to the study of homeland security. National security and military studies explore intelligence gathering and lessons from counterterrorism operations. Anthropology enables an understanding of the culture of terrorism. Sociology facilitates comprehension of human behavior in crisis situations. Political science and law address policy making and human rights issues, which are vital as democratic governments fight terrorism. Journalism permits comprehension of terrorists' use of the media for increased publicity. Engineering provides valuable advice on protecting buildings and critical infrastructure from possible attacks. The physical sciences permit discussion of nuclear material, chemical reactions, and biological processes. As these and other fields are vital to homeland security, this book will approach the subject of terrorism from a holistic perspective. However, the book focuses to a great extent on the discipline and profession of emergency management. As will be seen, emergency management plays an especially important role in homeland security.

1.5.1 The Role of Emergency Management

Emergency management:
A discipline and profession that addresses how to prevent or react successfully to various types of disasters.

Emergency management is a profession that specifies how to prevent or react successfully to various types of disasters (McEntire 2014). It includes four functional phases described as the life cycle of disaster: mitigation, preparedness, response, and recovery. Each of these concepts is important for the study of terrorism and the homeland security profession.

Mitigation:
Activity that attempts to avoid disasters or minimize negative consequences.

Prevention:
Counterterrorism operations such as intelligence gathering and preventive strike activity.

Protection:
Antiterrorism operations such as border control and infrastructure protection.

Preparedness:
Readiness measures in anticipation of a disaster.

Response:
The immediate reaction to an emergency situation, like a terrorist attack.

Recovery:
Long-term activities to rebound after disasters or terrorist attacks.

Crisis management:
A law enforcement function that concentrates on identifying, anticipating, preventing, and prosecuting those involved in terrorism.

Consequence management:
An emergency management function that stresses planning, emergency medical response and public health, disaster relief, and restoration of communities.

Civil defense:
The government's initiative to prepare communities and citizens to react effectively to a nuclear exchange during the Cold War.

Mitigation is activity that attempts to avoid disasters or minimize negative consequences. Mitigation is also closely associated with two terms that are frequently discussed in homeland security:

- **Prevention** includes counterterrorism operations (such as intelligence gathering and covert military activities) or other functions like border control.
- **Protection** incorporates antiterrorism operations such as infrastructure protection and increased security surveillance at locations like airports and sporting events.

There are three other important phases in emergency management. **Preparedness** includes readiness measures in anticipation of a disaster. Planning, training, and exercises are examples of preparedness initiatives. **Response** is the immediate reaction to an emergency situation like a terrorist attack. In homeland security, response refers most often to evidence collection and emergency medical care functions. **Recovery** refers to long-term activities to rebound after disasters or terrorist attacks. It includes emotional recovery as well as rebuilding with future hazards and threats in mind.

Since its inception, homeland security has focused most of its attention on prevention, protection, and prosecution activities. These activities have been labeled as **crisis management.** However, homeland security initially downplayed the need for preparedness, response, and recovery operations. These undertakings are known as **consequence management**. While it is imperative to perform both crisis and consequence management functions, there is growing realization that they should not be treated as isolated actions. Doing so only leads to coordination difficulties. In addition, while it is crucial to stress prevention, protection, and prosecution measures, the assumption that this will be possible 100% of the time must be avoided. For these reasons, emergency management is an increasingly vital component of homeland security.

Emergency management has a long history of dealing with a plethora of natural, technological, and man-made disasters. It has generated important recommendations for dealing with conflict and collective stress situations (Drabek 1986). What is more, scholars such as Bill Waugh (2001) and McEntire et al. (2001) indicate the close relation between terrorism and emergency management. Others also see unique ties among emergency management and homeland security (Bullock et al. 2005).

In spite of this close relation, homeland security did not draw sufficiently from the research and practice of emergency management when it was created. There is definitely a need to integrate emergency management and homeland security (Kiltz 2012). The failure to adequately integrate these efforts has created many challenges pertaining to terrorism. Some of today's problems are reminiscent of those during the civil defense era (Alexander 2002). **Civil defense** is the name given to the government's initiative to prepare communities and citizens to react effectively to nuclear war against the Soviet Union. The primary focus of the Cold War was on responding to nuclear weapons with a top-down, military, command, and control approach. During this period, natural and technological hazards as well as collaboration with nonmilitary organizations were not given serious consideration.

EMERGENCY MANAGEMENT

Definition, Vision, Mission, Principles

Definition

Emergency management is the managerial function charged with creating the framework within which communities reduce vulnerability to hazards and cope with disasters.

Vision

Emergency management seeks to promote safer, less vulnerable communities with the capacity to cope with hazards and disasters.

Mission

Emergency management protects communities by coordinating and integrating all activities necessary to build, sustain, and improve the capability to mitigate against, prepare for, respond to, and recover from threatened or actual natural disasters, acts of terrorism, or other man-made disasters.

Principles

Emergency management must be:

1. **Comprehensive** – Emergency managers consider and take into account all hazards, all phases, all stakeholders, and all impacts relevant to disasters.

2. **Progressive** – Emergency managers anticipate future disasters and take preventive and preparatory measures to build disaster-resistant and disaster-resilient communities.

3. **Risk driven** – Emergency managers use sound risk management principles (hazard identification, risk analysis, and impact analysis) in assigning priorities and resources.

4. **Integrated** – Emergency managers ensure unity of effort among all levels of government and all elements of a community.

5. **Collaborative** – Emergency managers create and sustain broad and sincere relationships among individuals and organizations to encourage trust, advocate a team atmosphere, build consensus, and facilitate communication.

6. **Coordinated** – Emergency managers synchronize the activities of all relevant stakeholders to achieve a common purpose.

7. **Flexible** – Emergency managers use creative and innovative approaches in solving disaster challenges.

8. **Professional** – Emergency managers value a science and knowledge-based approach based on education, training, experience, ethical practice, public stewardship, and continuous improvement.

Homeland security officials have made similar mistakes in recent years. Those in charge of policy focused initially and almost exclusively on terrorism and favored a law enforcement or paramilitary approach. Leaders failed to recognize that the United States is prone to many different types of hazards (Mileti 1999). Homeland security also ignored to its own peril the research that suggests that coordination with others is of paramount importance if responses to disasters are to be successful (Auf der Heide 1987).

Homeland Security Advisory System (HSAS):
The nation's method for warning the population of potential and actual terrorist attacks.

The most vivid example of these mistakes was the creation of the **Homeland Security Advisory System (HSAS)**. The HSAS was the nation's method for warning the population of potential and actual terrorist attacks. It illustrated a failure to consult with the emergency management community or incorporate its lessons learned from prior disasters. For instance, research on disasters and emergency management provides solid advice for improved warning functions (McEntire 2014). Evidence from decades of research illustrates that warnings have to be clear, consistent, and credible. They must also help communities and citizens understand exactly what they are supposed to do when disasters and terrorist attacks occur.

In contrast to these recommendations, many argue that HSAS lacked clarity as well as specific and useful information for citizens (Aguirre 2004; Knight 2005). For example, what is implied when the threat level was raised from yellow to orange? Did it mean an attack has occurred? How should citizens react? Why would a change in color status help promote successful responses? Since the HSAS was not based on emergency management research, it had difficulty in successfully providing answers to these questions. The HSAS therefore became the focus of many jokes on late night television and has since been replaced with a different warning system. This situation and others reveal that emergency management is an important discipline for homeland security.

Figure 1-5

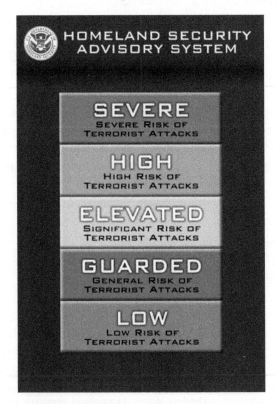

The Homeland Security Advisory System did not warn citizens about what to do if a terrorist attack should occur. Source: © US States Department of Homeland Security.

1.5.2 Important Terminology

While emergency management knowledge can help in many areas, one of the greatest potential contributions to homeland security is in reference to this profession's views about hazards, vulnerability, and risk. The term **hazard** was introduced by geographers, and it almost always refers to physical or other agents that may trigger or initiate disaster events and processes (Alexander 2002, p. 29). While hazards such as an earthquake, industrial plant explosion, or terrorist attack are real and menacing, focusing on them excessively can create many problems for those involved in homeland security and emergency management. For instance, giving priority to certain hazards often leads to dramatic and detrimental shifts in policies as we have recently seen with the almost exclusive emphasis on terrorism (Waugh 2004). Placing ultimate priority on hazards likewise downplays human role and responsibility in all types of disasters (McEntire 2004). What is more, since we cannot eliminate or control all extreme events, there is growing recognition that vulnerability is a stronger determinant of disaster than the hazards themselves (Alexander 2006, p. 2; Cutter 2005, p. 39). For these and other reasons, many recommend moving from an "agent-centered approach" to one that gives greater attention to a broad conceptualization of vulnerability (Perry 2006, p. 9; Weichselgartner 2001).

As defined in the research literature, **vulnerability** implies a high degree of disaster proneness and/or limited disaster management capabilities. One school of thought suggests that vulnerability is the likelihood of a disaster occurring and that individuals or the community as a whole will experience negative impacts from hazards (e.g. injuries, death, property damage, financial losses, social disruption, etc.). There are several scholars that accept this viewpoint (Anderson 1995, p. 41; Bolin and Stanford, 1998, p. 9; Boulle et al., 1997, p. 179; Maskrey, 1989, p. 1; Mitchell, 1999, p. 296; Salter, 1997/98, p. 28; Wisner et al., 2004, p. 11).

Another perspective on vulnerability relates to capacity or capability. This line of thought centers on the ability or inability of people and social systems to anticipate, prevent, prepare for, cope with, respond to, or recover from the impact of a hazard. It is also supported by many researchers (Schroeder 1987, p. 33; Vasta 2004, pp. 10–11; Warmington 1995, p. 1; Wisner et al. 2004, p. 11). Vulnerability is thus regarded as a multifaceted concept that the literature almost always conveys it in terms of proneness and capabilities (Chambers 1989; Comfort et al. 1999; Pelling and Uitto 2001; Watts and Bohle 1993).

Hazards and vulnerability are closely associated with the concept of risk. Some scholars assert that hazards and vulnerability are determinants of risk, or the likelihood of occurrence (Mileti 1999). Others assert that risk deals with exposure to disaster agents or possible losses (Alexander 2002). The truth of the matter is that risk is determined by both of these types of variables. **Risk** is therefore a measure of probability and consequences alike. The concept of risk permits an understanding of what can happen and how bad it could be. Although it is difficult to know how much weight to give to probability versus consequences, the notion of risk is valuable to the emergency management community.

Hazard(s):
The physical or other agent(s) that may trigger or initiate disaster events and processes.

Vulnerability:
A high degree of disaster proneness and/or limited disaster management capabilities.

Risk:
A measure of probability and consequences.

Interestingly, this same framework of risk can also be applied to terrorism and homeland security. For instance, limited intelligence, porous borders, and weak security are factors that must be corrected if the probability of attacks is to be minimized. Furthermore, inadequate prevention and preparedness abilities will likely increase the consequences of attacks during response and recovery operations. Probabilities and consequences thus seem to be extremely important concepts for both the homeland security and emergency management professions. Consequently, this book will approach terrorism by discussing many themes that relate to and determine both probability and consequences.

IN THE REAL WORLD

Risk and 9/11

The attacks on 9/11 clearly illustrated the risk facing the United States. Terrorists managed to enter the United States in virtually an unnoticed manner. They trained for their attacks in American flight schools and were able to smuggle box cutters onto planes. Once the hijackings were underway, a system was not fully in place to interdict the hijacked aircraft. After the planes were flown into the World Trade Center, firefighters and police had a difficult time communicating with each other. Many died in part because information could not be shared among agencies. After the buildings collapsed, it took some time before different pieces of intelligence could be utilized to determine who was responsible for the attacks and how they were funded. Recovery also took time and taxed many government agencies and the businesses that were impacted. 9/11 showed that a variety of efforts are needed to minimize the probability of attack and successfully deal with their consequences.

SELF-CHECK

1. International relations and criminal justice are related to homeland security. True or False?

2. Homeland security and emergency management have no relationship whatsoever. True or False?

3. Vulnerability implies:
   (a) An ability to deal with terrorism effectively
   (b) A high degree of proneness and limited capabilities
   (c) A low degree of proneness and enhanced capabilities
   (d) That terrorism will not occur
   (e) That we can respond successfully

4. What is meant by the terms "liability reduction" and "capacity building?"

SUMMARY

In this chapter, you have learned about recent terrorist attacks that have plagued the United States. You have been exposed to evidence that suggests that further attacks will take place in the future. The enormous impact of the terrorist attacks on 9/11 in relation to world history was discussed. The chapter defined homeland security – a concerted national effort to prevent terrorist attacks within the United States, reduce America's vulnerability to terrorism, and recover from and minimize the damage of attacks that do occur. It also discussed the mission of homeland security and the need for a holistic framework. Emergency management was noted as an important component of homeland security. By supplementing homeland security with an emergency management perspective, you will be better able to deal with the threat and impacts of terrorist attacks.

ASSESS YOUR UNDERSTANDING

UNDERSTAND: WHAT HAVE YOU LEARNED

 Go to **www.wiley.com/go/mcentire/homelandsecurity2e** to assess your knowledge of terrorism and homeland security.

SUMMARY QUESTIONS

1. The United States has not had a number of terrorist attacks in the past 10 years. True or False?

2. Terrorism is not an important topic in today's world. True or False?

3. Osama bin Laden and Al-Qaeda were responsible for the 9/11 terrorist attacks. True or False?

4. The 9/11 hijackers flew two of the four hijacked planes into the World Trade Center buildings. True or False?

5. Scholars, elected officials, military personnel, practitioners, and citizens have a common view of homeland security. True or False?

6. Corporations and nonprofits do not play an important role in homeland security. True or False?

7. Emergency management addresses the prevention of and reaction to different types of disasters. True or False?

8. The Homeland Security Advisory System does a good job of informing citizens on how to take action in a crisis period. True or False?

9. There is or should be an important relationship between emergency management and homeland security. True or False?

10. A community that has a low degree of disaster proneness and sufficient access to resources has a high degree of vulnerability. True or False?

11. What government organization was responsible for supporting the 9/11 attacks?

    (a) Hamas

    (b) The Taliban

    (c) Hezbollah

    (d) China

12. Included in the National Strategy for Homeland Security's six missions are:

    (a) Border and Transportation Security

    (b) Extensive Academic Research on Terrorism

    (c) Defending against Catastrophic Threat

    (d) a and c

13. Since the formation of the Department of Homeland Security:

    (a) There have been no terrorist attacks whatsoever.

    (b) There have been allegations that money devoted to homeland security lacks controls to prevent fraud, waste, and abuse.

  (c) The Department of Homeland Security has positively impacted FEMA's ability to perform effectively.

  (d) All of the above

14. Emergency management deals with:

  (a) Natural disasters

  (b) Technological disasters only

  (c) All types of disasters

  (d) Terrorist attacks only

15. Homeland security involves which of the following disciplines?

  (a) International relations

  (b) Criminal justice

  (c) Public administration

  (d) All of the above

16. Which of the following increase vulnerability to terrorism?

  (a) Secure borders

  (b) Limited intelligence

  (c) Preparedness

  (d) Both b and c

APPLYING THIS CHAPTER

1. Why were the terrorist attacks on 9/11 so significant? Explain how this event has had an impact on American way of life.

2. In this chapter, there is list of reasons why we may witness a greater number of more violent attacks in the future. Pick a terrorist attack found in recent events and explain it in terms of one or more of the reasons listed earlier.

3. Discuss what the response to a terrorist attack could look like with successful collaboration between citizens, cities, states, nonprofits, businesses, and the federal government. How would it be different if there was no collaboration?

4. State the importance of "liability reduction" and "capacity building" in homeland security. How do these ideas tie back into the concept of vulnerability?

BE A HOMELAND SECURITY PROFESSIONAL

Explaining Homeland Security

You work for the Department of Homeland Security as a public information officer. During an interview, you noticed that the press is struggling to understand what homeland security is. How would you define it for them? What is the mission of homeland security? How could you describe it as a function or agency? What else could you say to help them understand this concept?

Educating the State Legislators

As the lead member of the New York Division of Homeland Security and Emergency Management, you have been assigned to speak in front of the legislators to defend your budget. You must clearly state why it is important to have lots of resources at your disposal. Make a case as to why terrorism is a significant threat and why the state needs to take it seriously.

Tensions in Homeland Security

Homeland security illustrates some tensions between a law enforcement and emergency management perspective. Explain why both viewpoints are needed and how their goals may complement one another.

KEY TERMS

Al-Qaeda	An extreme Islamic fundamentalist terrorist organization
9/11	The terrorist attacks involving hijacked planes against the United States
Civil defense	The government's initiative to prepare communities and citizens to react effectively to a nuclear exchange during the Cold War
Consequence management	An emergency management function that stresses planning, emergency medical response and public health, disaster relief, and restoration of communities
Criminal justice	A discipline and profession interested in intelligence gathering, terrorist investigation, prosecution, border control, and other security measures
Crisis management	A law enforcement function that concentrates on identifying, anticipating, preventing, and prosecuting those involved in terrorism
Department of Homeland Security (DHS)	A newly created organization that desires to prevent terrorist attacks or react effectively

Emergency management	A discipline and profession that addresses how to prevent or react successfully to various types of disasters
Federal Emergency Management Agency (FEMA)	The national entity in charge of disaster management
Hazard(s)	The physical or other agent(s) that may trigger or initiate disaster events and processes
Homeland security	A concerted national effort to prevent terrorist attacks within the United States, reduce America's vulnerability to terrorism, and recover from and minimize the damage of attacks that do occur
Homeland Security Advisory System (HSAS)	The nation's method for warning the population of potential and actual terrorist attacks
International relations	A discipline and profession that deals with the conflicts among nation-states and nonstate actors (e.g. why terrorism occurs and what governments are doing about it)
Mitigation	Activity that attempts to avoid disasters or minimize negative consequences
Prevention	Counterterrorism operations such as intelligence gathering and preventive strike activity
Preparedness	Readiness measures in anticipation of a disaster
Protection	Antiterrorism operations such as border control and infrastructure protection
Public administration	A discipline and profession that directs attention to the formation policy and the best organization to deal with difficult societal problems
Public health	A discipline and profession that concentrates on understanding diseases and how to treat them (e.g. identifying how to react from a medical standpoint to the use of nuclear, biological, chemical, or radiological weapons)
Recovery	Long-term activities to rebound after disasters or terrorist attacks
Response	The immediate reaction to an emergency situation, like a terrorist attack
Risk	A measure of probability and consequences
Taliban	The name of the government that provided a safe haven for Al-Qaeda
Terrorism	The use or threat of violence to support ideological purposes
Vulnerability	A high degree of disaster proneness and/or limited disaster management capabilities

REFERENCES

Aguirre, B.E. (2004). Homeland security warnings: lessons learned and unlearned. *International Journal of Mass Emergencies and Disasters* 22: 103–115.

Alexander, D. (2002). *Confronting Catastrophe*. New York: Oxford University Press.

Alexander, D. (2006). Globalization of disaster: trends, problems and dilemmas. *Journal of International Affairs* 59 (2): 1–24.

Anderson, M.B. (1995). Vulnerability to disaster and sustainable development: a general framework. In: *Disaster Prevention for Sustainable Development: Economic and Policy Issues* (ed. M. Munasinghe and C. Clarke), 41–60. Washington, DC: International Decade for Natural Disaster Reduction/World Bank.

Auf der Heide, E. (1987). *Disaster Response: Principles of Preparation and Coordination*. St. Louis, MO: Mosby.

Bolin, R. and Stanford, L. (1998). *The Northridge Earthquake: Vulnerability and Disaster*. New York: Routledge.

Boulle, P., Vrolijks, L., and Palm, E. (1997). Vulnerability reduction for sustainable urban development. *Journal of Contingencies and Crisis Management* 5: 179.

Bullock, J.A., Haddow, G.D., Coppola, D. et al. (2005). *Introduction to Homeland Security*. New York: Butterworth-Heinemann.

Canton, L.G. (2016). Emergency management vs. homeland security: can we work together? *Emergency Management* (30 September).

Cassidy, J. (2015). The facts about terrorism. *The New Yorker* (24 November). http://www.newyorker.com/news/john-cassidy/the-facts-about-terrorism (accessed 10 October 2017).

Chambers, R. (1989). Editorial introduction: vulnerability, coping, and policy. *IDS Bulletin* 2 (2): 1–7.

Cockburn, P. (2016). *The Rise of the Islamic State: ISIS and the New Sunni Revolution*. New York: Verso.

Comfort, L., Wisner, B., Cutter, S. et al. (1999). Reframing disaster policy: the global evolution of vulnerability communities. *Environmental Hazards* 1: 39–44.

Cutter, S. (2005). Are we asking the right question? In: *What Is a Disaster? New Answers to Old Questions* (ed. R.W. Perry and E.L. Quarantelli), 39–48. Philadelphia, PA: Xlibris.

Drabek, T.E. (1986). *Human System Responses to Disaster: An Inventory of Sociological Findings*. New York: Springer-Verlag.

Falkow, M.D. (2013). Does homeland security constitute an emerging academic discipline? Thesis. Monterey, CA: Naval Post Graduate School.

Franks, J. (2006). *Rethinking the Roots of Terrorism*. New York: Palgrave Macmillan.

Jones, D. (2008). Homeland security: emerging discipline challenges, and research. In: *Homeland Security Handbook* (ed. J. Pinkowski), 95–127. Boca Raton, FL: CRC Press.

Kamien, D. (ed.) (2006). *The McGraw-Hill Homeland Security Handbook*. New York: McGraw Hill.

Kiltz, L. (2012). The benefits and challenges of integrating emergency management and homeland security into a new program. *Journal of Homeland Security Education* 1 (2): 6–28.

Knight, A.J. (2005). Alert status red: awareness, knowledge and reaction to the threat advisory system. *Journal of Homeland Security and Emergency Management* 2 (1): Article 9.

Martin, G. (2017). *Understanding Homeland Security*. Thousand Oaks, CA: Sage Publications, Inc.

Maskrey, A. (1989). *Disaster Mitigation: A Community Based Approach*, Development Guidelines, vol. 3. Oxford: Oxfam.

McEntire, D.A. (2004). Tenets of vulnerability: an assessment of a fundamental concept. *Journal of Emergency Management* 2 (2): 23–29.

McEntire, D.A. (2005). Revisiting the definition of "hazard" and the importance of reducing vulnerability. *Journal of Emergency Management* 3 (4): 9–11.

McEntire, D.A. (2014). *Disaster Response and Recovery: Strategies and Tactics for Resilience*. New York: Wiley.

McEntire, D.A., Robinson, R., and Weber, R.T. (2001). Managing the threat of terrorism. *IQ Report* 33: 1–19.

Mileti, D.S. (1999). *Disasters by Design: A Reassessment of Natural Hazards in the United States*. Washington, DC: Joseph Henry Press.

Mitchell, J.K. (ed.) (1999). *Crucibles of Hazard: Megacities and Disasters in Transition*. Tokyo: United Nations University Press.

Office of Homeland Security (2002). *National Strategy for Homeland Security*. Washington, DC: Office of Homeland Security.

Pelling, M. and Uitto, J.I. (2001). Small island developing states: natural disaster vulnerability and global change. *Environmental Hazards* 3: 49–62.

Perry, R.W. (2006). What is a disaster? In: *Handbook of Disaster Research* (ed. H. Rodriguez, E.L. Quarantelli and R.R. Dynes), 1–15. New York: Springer.

Salter, J. (1997/98). Risk management in the emergency management context. *Australian Journal of Emergency Management* 12 (4): 22–28.

Schroeder, R.A. (1987). *Gender Vulnerability to Drought: A Case Study of the Hausa Social Environment*. Madison, WI: University of Wisconsin.

Vasta, K.S. (2004). Risk, vulnerability, and asset-based approach to disaster risk management. *International Journal of Sociology and Social Policy* 24 (10/11): 1–48.

Warmington, V. (1995). *Disaster Reduction: A Review of Disaster Prevention, Mitigation and Preparedness*. Ottawa: Reconstruction and Rehabilitation Fund of the Canadian Council for International Cooperation.

Watts, M.J. and Bohle, H.G. (1993). The space of vulnerability: the causal structure of hunger and famine. *Progress in Human Geography* 17: 43–67.

Waugh, W.L. (2001). Managing terrorism as an environmental hazard. In: *Handbook of Crisis and Emergency Management* (ed. A. Farazmand), 659–676. New York: Marcel Dekker.

Waugh, W.L. (2004). The "all-hazards" approach must be continued. *Journal of Emergency Management* 2 (1): 11–12.

Weichselgartner, J. (2001). Disaster mitigation: the concept of vulnerability revisited. *Disaster Prevention and Management* 10 (2): 85–94.

Weiss, M. and Hassan, H. (2016). *ISIS: Inside the Army of Terror*. New York: Regan Arts.

Wisner, B., Blaikie, P., Cannon, T., and Davis, I. (2004). *At Risk: Natural Hazards, People's Vulnerability and Disasters*. New York: Routledge.

CHAPTER 2

IDENTIFYING TERRORISM
Ideologically Motivated Acts of Violence and Their Relation to Disasters

Do You Already Know?

- How to define terrorism
- The nature of terrorism
- Types of terrorism
- The relation of terrorism to other disasters

 For additional questions to assess your current knowledge of how to identify terrorism, go to **www.wiley.com/go/mcentire/ homelandsecurity2e**

What You Will Find Out	What You Will Be Able To Do
2.1 What terrorism is	• Distinguish among different perspectives of terrorism
2.2 The common characteristics of terrorism	• Predict the typical features of terrorism
2.3 Examples of terrorism	• Catalog the distinct manifestations of terrorism
2.4 The relation of terrorism to other disasters	• Compare how terrorism is similar and different than other disasters

INTRODUCTION

If you are to work effectively in homeland security, the first and most important step for you to reduce the probabilities and consequences of terrorism is to understand exactly what this phenomenon is. The following chapter provides several definitions of terrorism and compares the similarities and differences among the divergent viewpoints. You will then assess the common characteristics of terrorism, thereby helping you determine if a certain activity can be considered as such phenomena. The types of terrorism are then covered in order to help you discover its various manifestations. Finally, this chapter explores the relationship between terrorism and other types of disasters.

2.1 DEFINING TERRORISM

There are literally hundreds of definitions of terrorism, but little agreement on a single concept that captures the essence of what the term actually means. Much of the difficulty in defining terrorism is a result of the fact that the term is emotionally charged and laden with value judgments. It is a common adage that "one person's terrorist in another person's freedom fighter" (Martin 2003, p. 22). A case in point is the US patriots seeking independence from Britain in the late 1700s. Did the activities of these citizens during the revolutionary war constitute terrorism? Those in England and in the New World certainly had different perspectives on this question. The British most likely viewed the Boston Tea Party and the unconventional combat tactics similar to terrorist activities today. In contrast, the Americans regarded their behavior as a legitimate form of protest or an effective method to level the playing field against the better trained and equipped redcoats.

The problem of defining terrorism continues today among practitioners and scholars alike. For instance, the US government has developed several definitions of terrorism:

Department of State (DOS):
The government agency in charge of diplomatic relationships among nations.

- The **Department of State (DOS)** is the federal agency in charge of diplomatic relationships among nations. It asserts terrorism is "premeditated, politically motivated violence perpetrated against noncombatant targets by sub-national groups or clandestine agents, usually intended to influence an audience."

Department of Defense (DOD):
The government agency responsible for the military.

- The **Department of Defense (DOD)** is the public entity responsible for the military. It declares that terrorism is "The calculated use of violence or the threat of violence to inculcate fear; intended to coerce or to intimidate governments or societies in the pursuit of goals that are generally political, religious or ideological."

Federal Bureau of Investigation (FBI):
The government agency that concentrates on the enforcement of US law.

- The **Federal Bureau of Investigation (FBI)** is a government organization that concentrates on the enforcement of US law. It states that terrorism is "The unlawful use of force against persons or property to intimidate or coerce a government, the civilian population, or any segment thereof, in the furtherance of political or social objectives."

Department of Homeland Security (DHS):
A newly created organization which desires to prevent terrorist attacks or react effectively.

- The **Department of Homeland Security**, in one of its planning documents, describes terrorism as "Any activity that (i) involves an act that (a) is dangerous to human life or potentially destructive of critical infrastructure or key resources; and (b) is a violation of the criminal laws of the United States or of any State or other subdivision of the United States; and (ii) appears to be intended (a) to intimidate or coerce a civilian population; (b) to influence the policy of a government by intimidation or coercion; or (c) to affect the conduct of a government by mass destruction, assassination, or kidnapping" (Department of Homeland Security, 2004, p. 73).

Each of these definitions reflects the unique mission and perspective of the sponsoring agency. The DOS takes an international view and concentrates attention on nonstate actors around the world. The DOD recognizes that terrorism impacts national security and has the objective of influencing foreign policy. The FBI reveals that terrorism is illegal since their violent behavior is not permitted under the law. Finally, the DHS focuses heavily on the destruction of critical infrastructure. While each definition provides an important view of terrorism, it is important to recognize the benefit of a holistic perspective. Any single definition may limit our understanding of the phenomena and therefore hinder efforts to deal with the threat of terrorism.

Scholars have also described terrorism in divergent ways. Brian Jenkins "calls terrorism the use or threatened use of force designed to bring about a political change" (in White 2002, p. 8). Walter Laqueur says "terrorism constitutes the illegitimate use of force to achieve a political objective by targeting innocent people" (in White 2002, p. 8). And Cindy Combs believes that terrorism "is the synthesis of war and theater, a dramatization of the most proscribed kind of violence – that which is perpetrated on innocent victims – played out before an audience in the hope of creating a mood of fear, for political purposes" (Combs, 2000, p. 8).

Figure 2-1

Terrorists often launch attacks in visible locations to achieve maximum visibility and publicity. Source: © FBI.

The differences among these definitions are likewise noteworthy. As a case in point, Jenkins accepts the threat of force as terrorism, whereas Laqueur and Combs do not. The definitions by Laqueur and Combs focus on noncombatants as victims. Their inclusion of innocent people reiterates that governments are not the only ones targeted by terrorists. Furthermore, Combs implies that the media is utilized to broadcast messages to further the aims and intentions of terrorists. Fear is mentioned in some of the definitions and not in others. Only one of the definitions stresses the influence of ideology on terrorism, even though people's attitudes and values seem to have a significant role in this type of violent activity (issues that will be taken up in Chapter 3).

Although there are clearly distinct ways of looking at terrorism, the definitions provided above share remarkable similarities. All of these views acknowledge the use or threat of force and the goal of obtaining specific purposes or objectives. Terrorism is clearly related to violent activity or the threat of violence to influence the behavior of others. At the same time, none recognize the disruption of society that occurs because of terrorism. This is ironic in that terrorism may adversely impact government policies (e.g. with the creation of new laws), business activities (e.g. due to computer viruses), and citizen behavior (e.g. as a result of the reluctance to travel). Disruption is therefore another major, but unrecognized, goal of terrorists.

SELF-CHECK

1. There are many different definitions of terrorism. True or False?
2. Definitions of terrorism do not reflect the values of missions of different people and organizations. True or False?
3. In Combs definition of terrorism, the term "theater" implies:
    (a) The location of the terrorist attack
    (b) The widespread publicity of an attack
    (c) The importance of national security
    (d) The disruption caused by terrorism
4. Compare and contrast the different definitions of terrorism.

2.2 COMMON CHARACTERISTICS OF TERRORISM

Taking the above definitions and considerations into account, we may conclude that there are a number of crucial components of terrorism. Terrorism is often:

- **An act of disruption, violence, or the threat of violence.** It is not like a protest, a sit-in, or a strike with a picket line. Instead, it involves illegitimate activities that are not sanctioned by law. Terrorism creates many social, political, and economic problems for targeted populations, societies, and the international community. Some of the violent means of terrorism may include guns or bombs.

- **Performed by an individual, group, or state that espouses an ideology.** Terrorism results from unique ways of looking at the world that attempt to rationalize illegal behavior. For instance, the ideology of terrorism often neglects or subverts negotiation, diplomacy, and democratic processes.

- **Conducted against governments or citizens as targets and shown to an audience.** Certain people may be injured, killed, or otherwise affected by terrorism. But terrorism also intends to spread adverse impact far beyond those who were immediately targeted in attacks. Victims may be produced directly through terrorism or indirectly through publicity of the attacks.

- **Accompanied with fear and coercion.** Terrorism relies on shock, outrage, horror, discouragement, disruption, and intimidation to impel some sort of activity on the part of its victims. This includes both those targeted and the audience observing the attacks.

- **Directed toward the attainment of goals and objectives.** Terrorism may have the aim of promoting political independence, social justice and human rights, environmental protection, religious freedoms or dominance, and other objectives (e.g. free reign of drug cartels or the halting of abortions).

When actions and events incorporate most or all of these traits, you may have increasing confidence that the activity is terrorism. Conversely, if these features are not present, the incident in question cannot be considered in this light. Activities without these characteristics are more likely to be related to social movements or other types of violence.

SELF-CHECK

1. Terrorists have a goal that they promote through their violent activity. True or False?

2. Only groups are involved in terrorism. True or False?

3. Which of the following is not a common characteristic of terrorism?
   (a) An act of disruption or violence
   (b) Performed by someone who espouses an ideology
   (c) Accompanied with fear
   (d) A strike at the company headquarters

4. Restate why terrorists target innocent citizens.

2.3 TYPES OF TERRORISM

In spite of common features, terrorism may take on unique forms at any given time. Feliks Gross, an expert on terrorism in Russia and Eastern Europe, affirms that terrorism manifests itself in five different ways

(Gross, 1990, p. 8). These include mass terror, dynastic assassination, random terror, focused terror, and tactical terror.

Mass terror:
Terrorism by the government in power against its own citizens.

- **Mass terror** is terrorism by the government in power against its own citizens. This is a situation in which the ruling regime suppresses the opposition to maintain control. The efforts of Saddam Hussein and his Republican Guard fall into this category. The Iraqi leaders used poison gas on the Kurds in the northern part of the country and killed or imprisoned anyone who dared to speak out against the dictatorship and military in this nation.

Dynastic assassination:
The murder of the head official in government.

- **Dynastic assassination** is the murder of the head official in government. Some may assert that the shooting of President Lincoln falls into this category. After shooting this leader, Booth shouted "Sic semper tyrannis," which translated means "Thus always to tyrants."

Random terror:
An attack on large numbers of people wherever they gather.

- **Random terror** is an attack on large numbers of people wherever they gather. The coordinated attacks on Spanish trains on 11 March 2004 are an example of random terror. These blasts killed nearly 200 people and injured over 2000 others.

Focused terror:
Terrorism directed toward a specific group of people deemed as the enemy.

- **Focused terror** is terrorism directed toward a specific group of people deemed as the enemy. The Polish Underground, an organization that opposed German occupation during World War II, practiced focused terror. They detonated explosives at a café where Nazi officers dinned (Combs 2000, p. 9).

Tactical terror:
The use of attacks against the government for revolutionary or other purposes.

- **Tactical terror** is the use of attacks against the government for revolutionary or other purposes. The 1995 bombing of the Murrah Federal Building in Oklahoma City by Timothy McVeigh is an example of tactical terror.

Figure 2-2

Car bombings, such as this one in 2017 in the Ukraine, are examples of random terror. © Source: Shutterstock. Reproduced with permission of Shutterstock.

Besides the five types of terrorism described by Gross, it may be necessary to add other important categories. You are probably aware of the frequent terrorist attacks on American troops in Iraq or Afghanistan. These events frequently involve a sudden and surprise strike with small arms or bombs and a quick retreat. How would you describe this type of terrorism? Many suggest that this is guerilla warfare. **Guerilla** is a Spanish term for little war, which is an armed protest of occupying forces (Simonsen and Spindlove 2000, p. 35). Guerilla warfare is similar to **asymmetrical warfare**, which implies terrorist attacks on the part of the militarily weak against those who are powerful.

Terrorism has also been categorized in other ways. **Domestic terrorism** is terrorism that occurs within a single country. The release of nerve gas on 19 March 1995 in a subway by the Japanese religious group Aum Shinrikyo is an example of this type of terrorism. **International terrorism**, on the other hand, is terrorism that spans two or more nations. This is terrorism that is initiated by individuals, groups, or the government within one country and targets the people or the leaders of another. The bombing of the USS Cole in Yemen on 12 October 2000 can be considered international terrorism.

Although classifying terrorism as being domestic or international in origin or scope is helpful, it is not always so clear-cut. Sometimes it is difficult to determine where an attack was instigated as well as the extent of the incident. The bombings of two Russian planes on 24 August 2004 by a Chechen field commander and the 12 October 2002 Bali bombings in Indonesia by Jemaah Islamiyah are examples of this dilemma. Although the attacks took place in these countries, they included terrorists and victims from many nations around the world.

There are numerous complexities relating to each of the above categories of terrorism. For instance, the bombing of the Federal Murrah Building by Timothy McVeigh was tactical terror, but it could also be described as asymmetrical warfare and domestic terrorism. In contrast, the warfare in Iraq is focused and international in scope and not just a guerilla variant. Therefore, caution should be used when classifying terrorism into distinct alternatives.

Guerilla:
Spanish term for little war, which is an armed protest of occupying forces.

Asymmetrical warfare:
Terrorist attacks on the part of the militarily weak against those who are powerful.

Domestic terrorism:
Terrorism that occurs within a single country.

International terrorism:
Terrorism that spans two or more nations.

IN THE REAL WORLD

Classifying the 1993 WTC Bombing

Suppose you were working as a CIA analyst when the World Trade Center was bombed on 26 February 1993. Ramzi Yousef, along with nine other Arab Islamic terrorists, devised a plan to park a van full of urea nitrate fuel in the underground garage of the North Tower. Their goal was to destroy the foundation of Tower One so that this building would then collapse onto Tower Two. Although their intentions ultimately failed, the bomb did kill 6 people and injured more than 1000. If you had to write an after-action report on this attack, how would you classify it? Is there more than one way to look at this terrorist event?

SELF-CHECK

1. All terrorist attacks manifest themselves in the same fashion. True or False?

2. The shooting of the president is an example of tactical terrorism. True or False?

3. Which type of terrorism is implemented by the government to control citizens?
   (a) Focused terror
   (b) Mass terror
   (c) International terrorism
   (d) Random terror

4. Differentiate among the five types of terrorism proposed by Gross.

2.4 RELATION OF TERRORISM TO OTHER DISASTERS

Conflict disaster:
A socially disruptive and divisive event that involves a riot or some type of warfare.

Consensus disaster:
A socially disruptive event like an earthquake or tornado that brings the community together.

Terrorism can also be viewed from the perspective of emergency management. Some scholars, such as Quarantelli (1993), assert that terrorism is a "conflict disaster" and that it is qualitatively different from "consensus disasters." A **conflict disaster** is an event that involves a riot, violence, or some type of warfare. It often illustrates division within or across societies. A **consensus disaster**, on the other hand, is an event like an earthquake or tornado that brings the community together. After natural disasters, for example, people join efforts to respond and recover. Quarantelli asserts that a major difference between these two types of events is that conflict disasters include a person or group that is intentionally trying to inflict harm or distress on others. Alternatively, a consensus disaster is characterized by individuals and groups that come together to solve mutual challenges. According to Quarantelli, the first type of disaster divides society, while the other unites it.

Quarantelli's study raises an interesting question about how to classify terrorism. Is terrorism a conflict disaster or a consensus disaster? A case can be made for both arguments. Terrorism is obviously based on social conflict, but it may also lead people to work together to react to the devastation. Regardless of the answer to this question, Gary Webb (2002) provides evidence that social behavior in terrorism is very similar to consensus disasters. As an example, he declares that there is very little panic in most consensus disasters and that people also act rationally in spite of major events such as 9/11. He relays the fact that police and fire personnel are remarkably reliable in virtually all disasters and that no one abandoned their post after the World Trade Center was attacked. Webb also states that response is characterized by improvisation in most disasters, and this was certainly the case as organizations adapted to difficult circumstances in New York City. While his research recognizes the need for additional

Figure 2-3

9/11 has features of both conflict and consensus disasters. It was initiated by international terrorists, but unified American sentiment. Source: © Getty Images. Reproduced with permission of Getty Images.

studies on terrorism, Webb asserts that the defining features of 9/11 are remarkably similar to consensus disasters.

Research by Lori Peek and Jeannette Sutton (2003) likewise seems to illustrate that terrorism does not always fall easily into a single category. They discuss six hypotheses to make their argument:

- **Proposition 1:** Both pro- and antisocial behavior occurred after 9/11. In most disasters, people forget prior divisions in society, and they work jointly to reach important goals. This behavior was evident on 9/11 since people helped one another evacuate the World Trade Center towers and donated blood to help potential victims. However, there was also some intolerance and hostility toward Muslims and others of Arab descent after the attacks in 2001.

- **Proposition 2:** People experienced negative consequences owing to 9/11. In consensus disasters, most people do not suffer any lengthy psychological disturbances or health repercussions. Preliminary evidence suggests that this was not the case with the attacks on New York City. Many people experienced post-traumatic stress and depression, and emergency personnel developed respiratory problems due to the dust debris they encountered from the collapsed buildings.

- **Proposition 3:** The response to 9/11 was made more difficult due to continuing security concerns. During consensus disasters, organizations often struggle to accomplish the monumental tasks that they are required to meet. After the attacks on the World Trade Center, air, water, and road transportation systems were shut down. In addition, control over the disaster area was strictly guarded in case further attacks were to occur. These measures complicated efforts to respond to the disaster.

- **Proposition 4:** Political change was dramatic after 9/11. Most consensus disasters often do not result in massive transformations in society. This was not the case after the 2001 terrorist attacks. New legislation was quickly devised and passed, and the government underwent a massive transformation to deal with homeland security issues. These changes were impressive in terms of speed and scope.

- **Proposition 5:** Preparing for terrorism involves measures beyond consensus-type disasters. Natural and technological disasters require planning, training, and exercises. Terrorist attacks such as 9/11 introduce a new complication in that it is very difficult to anticipate and predict where the next attack will occur. In this sense, it could be more challenging to prepare for terrorism than consensus-type disasters.

- **Proposition 6:** Long-term change will be a defining feature of the 9/11 attacks. Most disasters do not impact or influence societies in any significant way. The events in New York seem to have resulted in substantial financial loss and unemployment, created disagreement about rebuilding plans, and led to the implementation of new security measures around the nation.

Based on these six propositions, Peek and Sutton therefore believe that terrorism is a complex phenomenon that exhibits features of both conflict and consensus-type disasters.

IN THE REAL WORLD

Responding to the Boston Bombing

After the 2012 Boston Marathon bombing, people from all walks of life worked together in a harmonious fashion to treat the injured and find the perpetrators. Police officers, health-care professionals, and citizens rushed to the scene and risked their own safety to assist those in need. The injured were assessed based on the severity of their injuries. Wounds were quickly dressed with anything available, including the shirts off people's backs. Hospitals were notified of the event within two minutes so they could prepare for the distribution of victims. The 264 patients were transported from the scene by 64 ambulances within 22 minutes, and they received expert care from EMTs, paramedics, nurses, and doctors. In fact, everyone who made it to a hospital survived. Within 30 minutes after the bombing, scores and scores of individuals and businesses had shared footage of suspects with the FBI. Local, state, and federal law enforcement initiated a major manhunt, and citizens in the community shared information about the whereabouts of the terrorists. The 129-page after-action report by the Massachusetts Emergency Management Agency called the coordinated response a "great success." In spite of a few minor areas for improvement, the Boston Marathon bombing is an excellent example of a consensus-type disaster.

McEntire and his colleagues accept the findings from Webb as well as Peek and Sutton. They state that "managing the threat of terrorism is both similar to and different from the management of other types of disasters" (McEntire et al. 2002, p. 1). On the one hand, those involved in planning for or reacting to terrorism must be able to perform functions that are routine to almost any disaster. This would include communicating with the population, evacuating the affected area, sheltering impacted residents, and providing emergency medical care as needed.

On other hand, terrorism poses new challenges that have not been experienced by emergency management personnel in the past. For instance:

- Intelligence gathering is a new and important task for terrorism prevention and has now filtered down to local police departments.
- Planning in homeland security must give a greater amount of emphasis to the military, the FBI, and public health.
- Response operations incorporate law functions (e.g. investigation) to a greater extent than in the past.
- Recovery may be lengthy or impossible if an area has been contaminated by deadly radiation or harmful chemicals.

Thus, the nature of terrorism complicates traditional emergency management operations and makes working harmoniously in homeland security even more imperative. Even though you might generally expect people to behave as they normally do in consensus disasters, we probably do not have sufficient evidence to predict with full certainty how they will react to terrorist events that are unfamiliar (e.g. a large-scale biological attack). More research will be required to improve understanding of terrorist disasters in the future.

SELF-CHECK

1. Terrorism is always exactly like any other type of disaster. True or False?

2. A conflict disaster is often characterized by a riot or some type of violent behavior. True or False?

3. Which of the following is true about the 9/11 terrorist attacks?
   (a) There was no indication of antisocial behavior afterward.
   (b) It resulted in new laws and significant changes in government.
   (c) Security measures did not impact response operations.
   (d) Muslims were not the target of hatred or discrimination.

4. Quarantelli asserts that terrorism is a conflict disaster. Support or critique this proposition.

SUMMARY

In this chapter you learned that one of the first steps to addressing the probability and consequences of terrorism is to comprehend the nature of this phenomenon. After reviewing numerous definitions about this complicated concept, you compared how the various perspectives are both alike and dissimilar. The prevalent features of terrorism were revealed, which will enable you to appraise if terrorism has occurred or is about to take place. Although there are recurring features of terrorism, this should not imply that every situation is similar. There are many different types of terrorist attacks. The chapter also examined the connections among terrorism and other types of disasters. Based on the evidence provided, it appears that terrorism has features of both conflict and consensus-type disasters.

ASSESS YOUR UNDERSTANDING

UNDERSTAND: WHAT HAVE YOU LEARNED

 Go to **www.wiley.com/go/mcentire/homelandsecurity2e** to assess your knowledge of how to identify terrorism.

SUMMARY QUESTIONS

1. Definitions of terrorism are all objective and free of value judgments. True or False?

2. Terrorists only want to affect those directly impacted by the attack. True or False?

3. Feliks Gross says that terrorism manifests itself in five different ways: mass terror, tactical terror, focused terror, dynastic assassination, and random terror. True or False?

4. Guerilla warfare is the opposite of asymmetrical warfare. True or False?

5. It can be difficult to determine whether a terrorist attack is categorized as domestic or international. True or False?

6. Consensus disasters involve some kind of conflict or warfare. True or False?

7. According to Peek and Sutton's Proposition 4, it is not common for extreme political and societal changes to occur after a disaster. True or False?

8. All of the following agencies have established definitions for terrorism except:

   (a) The Department of Defense
   (b) The Department of Homeland Security
   (c) The Department of Housing and Urban Development
   (d) The Department of State

9. The definition of terrorism provided by the Department of Homeland Security emphasizes:

   (a) The importance of infrastructure
   (b) The illegal nature of terrorism
   (c) Terrorisms' effects on foreign policy
   (d) The role of nonstate actors in the terrorist event

10. Which of the following best describes "random terror?"

    (a) Terrorism by a government against its citizens
    (b) Terrorism against a group of people who are considered the enemy
    (c) Terrorism used for revolutionary purposes
    (d) A terrorist attack on a large group of people in any gathering place

11. Each of the following is a crucial component of the definition of terrorism except:

    (a) An act of disruption, violence, or the threat of violence
    (b) Carried out on a large scale by many terrorists
    (c) Accompanied with fear and coercion
    (d) Directed toward the attainment of goals and objectives

12. Which of the following definitions best describes guerilla warfare?

    (a) A large military attack
    (b) A small, planned military attack on those who are less powerful
    (c) An armed protest against occupying forces
    (d) An anticipated attack from terrorists

13. Which of the following is not an aspect of a consensus disaster?

    (a) It brings the community together.
    (b) It often takes the form of a natural disaster.
    (c) It is socially disruptive.
    (d) It involves a person or group intentionally causing harm to others.

APPLYING THIS CHAPTER

1. What is meant by the adage "one person's terrorist is another person's freedom fighter?" How does this complicate the process of defining or dealing with terrorism?

2. It is suggested that terrorism is directed toward both victims and an audience. How do the victims and target audience, in the view of terrorists, impact the ability of terrorists to reach their goals and objectives?

3. There are many different classifications for terrorist activity. Why is it so difficult to put a terrorist attack into one specific category?

4. Briefly discuss terrorism in terms of conflict disasters and consensus disasters. What are some examples of how terrorist attacks take on characteristics of both kinds of disasters? Are all terrorist acts the same?

BE A HOMELAND SECURITY PROFESSIONAL

Defining Terrorism in a Public Document

You have been assigned to write the strategic plan for the police department. Your boss wants you to discuss terrorism. How would you define terrorism? Is it similar to or different than other types of illegal behavior? How so?

Writing a Report on Terrorism

As an analyst for the FBI, you have been asked to write a report stating the common characteristics of terrorism and the different manifestations it has had over time. The report will be given to members of congress who oversee national security issues. What would you include in your statement?

Assessing Terrorism and Disasters

While attending a conference on homeland security, you observe disagreement among scholars and practitioners regarding terrorism. Some suggest that it is similar to natural and technological disasters, while others state that it has the defining features of conflict events. Could you make a comment that would satisfy both sides of the argument? What would you say?

KEY TERMS

Asymmetrical warfare	Terrorist attacks on the part of the militarily weak against those who are powerful
Conflict disaster	A socially disruptive and divisive event that involves a riot or some type of warfare
Consensus disaster	A socially disruptive event like an earthquake or tornado that brings the community together
Department of Defense (DOD)	The government agency responsible for the military
Department of Homeland Security (DHS)	A newly created organization which desires to prevent terrorist attacks or react effectively
Department of State (DOS)	The government agency in charge of diplomatic relationships among nations
Domestic terrorism	Terrorism that occurs within a single country
Dynastic assassination	The murder of the head official in government
Federal Bureau of Investigation (FBI)	The government agency that concentrates on the enforcement of US law
Focused terror	Terrorism directed toward a specific group of people deemed as the enemy
Guerilla	Spanish term for little war, which is an armed protest of occupying forces
International terrorism	Terrorism that spans two or more nations
Mass terror	Terrorism by the government in power against its own citizens
Random terror	An attack on large numbers of people wherever they gather
Tactical terror	The use of attacks against the government for revolutionary or other purposes

REFERENCES

Combs, C.C. (2000). *Terrorism in the Twenty-First Century*. Upper Saddle River, NJ: Prentice Hall.

Department of Homeland Security (2004). *National Response Plan*. DHS: Washington, DC.

Gross, F. (1990). *Political Violence and Terror in Nineteenth and Twentieth Century Russia and Eastern Europe*. New York: Cambridge University Press.

Martin, G. (2003). *Understanding Terrorism: Challenges, Perspectives and Issues*. Thousand Oaks, CA: Sage Publications.

McEntire, D.A., Robinson, R.J., and Weber, R.T. (2002). Managing the threat of terrorism. *IQ Rep. 33 (12)*. Washington, DC: ICMA.

Peek, L.A. and Sutton, J.N. (2003). An exploratory comparison of disasters, riots and terrorist attacks. *Disasters* 27 (4): 319–335.

Quarantelli, E.L. (1993). Community crises: an exploratory comparison of the characteristics and consequences of disasters and riots. *Journal of Contingencies and Crisis Management* 1 (2): 67–78.

Simonsen, C.E. and Spindlove, J.R. (2000). *Terrorism Today: The Past, The Players, The Future*. Upper Saddle River, NJ: Prentice Hall.

Webb, G.R. (2002). Sociology, disasters, and terrorism: understanding threats of the new millennium. *Sociological Focus* 35 (1): 87–95.

White, J.R. (2002). *Terrorism: An Introduction*. Belmont, CA: Wadsworth.

CHAPTER 3

RECOGNIZING THE CAUSES OF TERRORISM

Differing Perspectives and the Role of Ideology

Do You Already Know?

- Why history, foreign affairs, and economic conditions lead to terrorism
- How political variables are associated with terrorism
- If religion and culture are causes of attacks
- The role of ideology in terrorism

 For additional questions to assess your current knowledge of the causes of terrorism, go to **www.wiley.com/go/mcentire/homelandsecurity2e**

What You Will Find Out	What You Will Be Able To Do
3.1 If historical grievances, foreign policy, and poverty cause terrorist attacks	• Evaluate the most frequently mentioned causes of terrorism
3.2 How numerous political variables are associated with terrorism	• Differentiate among the numerous political origins of terrorist attacks
3.3 Why terrorism results from religion and culture	• Predict how terrorism may be influenced by values and beliefs
3.4 The role of ideology in terrorism	• Appraise the impact of ideology on the phenomena of terrorism

Introduction to Homeland Security: Understanding Terrorism Prevention and Emergency Management,
Second Edition. David A. McEntire.
© 2019 John Wiley & Sons, Inc. Published 2019 by John Wiley & Sons, Inc.
Companion website: www.wiley.com/go/mcentire/homelandsecurity2e

INTRODUCTION

If you are to reduce the likelihood and impact of terrorism, it is necessary to understand its causes so you may take steps to alleviate them. Ian Lesser asserts that terrorism "has systemic origins [or root causes] that can be ameliorated" (1999, p. 127). You should therefore recognize that historical conflicts, foreign policy, and poverty may aggravate terrorism. Internal political factors, culture, and religion may also influence those who implement terrorist attacks. While there are many possible causes of terrorism, you must pay special attention to the role of ideology. People's beliefs always have significant bearing on terrorism. The following chapter will help you understand why terrorism occurs so you can do something about such causes.

3.1 FREQUENTLY MENTIONED CAUSES OF TERRORISM

You've probably wondered what drives people to engage in terrorist attacks – even to the point that they are willing to kill themselves and others. It is commonly said that there are perhaps as many causes of terrorism as there are terrorists. Some of the frequent explanations deal with historical grievances, foreign policy decisions, and poverty, among others (Sultalan 2008). Each of these will be explained in turn.

3.1.1 Historical Grievances

One perspective of why terrorism occurs focuses on the wrongs people feel they have encountered over time. The assertion here is that small initial conflicts among different groups of people have been perpetuated and aggravated over time. There is ample evidence to support this claim, and the Middle East provides a strong case in point.

There have been continual conflicts between Arabs and the Jews in this part of the world. The historical narrative in the Bible is full of such struggles, and it records several violent acts among different groups of people. Numbers 25: 1, 6–8 reveals how Phineas killed an Israelite man and a Midianite woman who were involved in illicit sexual relations. In Joshua 10: 1–14 we learn that Joshua attacked the city of Hazor, killed all of the inhabitants, burned the buildings, and took all of the remaining livestock.

Crusades:
Wars endorsed by the Pope to recapture the Holy Land of Jerusalem from the control of Muslims.

Muslims:
Those following the prophet Muhammad and adhering to the religion of Islam.

During the Middle Ages, there were wars in the Middle East as Christians tried to spread their beliefs during the Crusades. The **Crusades** were wars endorsed by the Pope to recapture the Holy Land of Jerusalem from the control of **Muslims** – those following the prophet Muhammad and adhering to the religion of Islam. These wars, which had religious and another motivations, took place between 1100 and 1300 A.D. Because of the intolerance and cruelty exhibited in the Crusades, Christians were opposed by those espousing Islam. Nevertheless, the Christians pushed back against the Muslims, who lost their empire and leadership in science, art, and trade.

Figure 3-1

Many Arabs oppose the establishment of Israel in the Middle East
Source: © Shutterstock/Getty Images. Reproduced with permission
of Getty Images.

In time, other events would add to the frustration of those residing in the Middle East. During World War II, the German leader, Adolf Hitler, denounced the Jews in Europe and desired to eradicate those professing this faith. The hatred against this religious group resulted in the **Holocaust** – the extermination of approximately six million Jews by the Nazi regime. Recognizing the plight of the Jewish people under the Nazis, the United Nations established the state of Israel in 1948. This country was created with the purpose of serving as a safe haven for Jews. Unfortunately, this move of compassion intensified a long-standing dispute over territory that is sacred to both Jews and Muslims. Conflict and terrorism have therefore been prevalent features of this part of the world for centuries. Both sides claim self-defense against the enemy aggressor. It seems as if terrorism has been omnipresent in the Middle East because of the events of the past.

Holocaust:
The extermination of approximately six million Jews by the Nazi regime during World War II.

3.1.2 US Foreign Policy

Another explanation for terrorism focuses on the foreign policy decisions of the United States. Under this view, American activities abroad are to blame for the terrorist attacks against us. Many Islamic terrorists have made this explicit in their justification for their aggression against the United States.

For instance, Osama bin Laden said he and his followers were justified for attacking Americans for at least six reasons. He asserted that the United States:

Theocracy:
A government run by clerics in the name of God.

1. *Does not understand the history and desires of Middle Eastern countries.* The United States does not recognize the preference of Muslims for **theocracy**, a government run by clerics in the name of God.

2. *Participates in colonialism in the area and is involved in exploitative policies.* The United States has military bases in Saudi Arabia, and he declared our reliance on oil has caused us to meddle in the affairs of sovereign nations.

3. *Supports puppet governments that are repressive regimes.* Saddam Hussein was initially an ally of the United States during the Iran–Iraq war, and he was a brutal leader.

4. *Founded the state of Israel and continues to fund their military capability.* This resulted in the loss of Arab land and is regarded to pose a threat to neighboring countries.

5. *Neglects human rights.* Palestinians assert they have fewer political rights than their Israeli counterparts.

6. *Sends American troops to the Middle East.* This desecrates sacred land and is associated with increased conflict and war.

Some of bin Laden's claims appear to have merit, but others might be considered debatable or even hypocritical. It is true that people in the United States do not fully comprehend the Middle East. It is a very complicated region. Also, America does rely heavily on oil from the Middle East. And the United States did support Saddam Hussein as a means to counter the military threat posed by Iran after this country experienced revolution and sanctioned the taking of hostages from the US embassy. At the same time, the intentions of America and other nations to find a safe haven (i.e. the state of Israel) for persecuted Jews after World War II were understandable. The democratic form of government in America provides more freedoms and rights to its citizens than theocratic governments (i.e. women may not have the same political status of men in some Arab nations). In addition, bin Laden was allied with the Taliban, a Sunni government that restricted the rights of women and oppressed the Hazara (Shia) minority.

In spite of the above observations, US foreign policy may certainly influence the degree terrorist activity around the world. Paul Pillar states that many "of the issues underlying … terrorism are to be found overseas" and that decisions on how to prevent or react to terrorism "must be formulated as an integral part of broader US foreign policy" (2001, p. 10).

3.1.3 Poverty

Relative poverty: Situation in which people are less wealthy than their fellow citizens.

Absolute poverty: Situation in which people lack so many resources that they cannot even meet basic necessities such as food, clothing, and shelter.

Another common causal explanation for terrorism is poverty (Krueger 2007). It is painfully evident that destitution is omnipresent around the world. But the lack of economic prosperity is not found equally in all societies. This brings up the notion of **relative poverty**, meaning that some people are less wealthy than their fellow citizens or peers in other countries. However, absolute poverty is even more concerning. **Absolute poverty** implies that people lack so many resources that they cannot even meet basic necessities such as food, clothing, and shelter. In this case, the deficiency and want are so significant that life is full of misery, illness, and even death. Unfortunately, there are millions of people around the world that fall into this latter category. For instance, over one billion people make less than $400 annually. It is possible that this number could grow in the future, particularly in Africa (Weatherby et al. 2000, p. 14).

The causal link between poverty and terrorism has been noted by many individuals including scholars and the leaders of various countries. For instance, it is reported that "the head of the World Bank even proclaimed that terrorism will not end until poverty is eliminated" (Francis 2002, p. 1). The argument here is that people become so frustrated with their impoverished conditions that they express their aggravation through violent activity including terrorism.

There is evidence that seems to support this viewpoint in certain situations. Alberto Abadie notes that "much of the modern-day transnational terrorism seems to generate from grievances against rich countries" (Lozada 2005, p. 1). A study of the Basques in Spain revealed that the lower economic classes were more likely to engage in political violence than the wealthy (Crenshaw 2010). A 2011 study in Germany revealed that unemployment was related to right-wing extremist crimes (Falk et al. 2001). Poverty can therefore be a cause of terrorism. However, it is important to remember that not all poor people engage in terrorist activity. In addition, per capita income is not always associated with terrorism. Research reveals that "protest, violence, and even terrorism can follow either a rising or declining economic tide" (Krueger and Maleckova in Francis 2002, p. 1). Regardless, poverty does need to be addressed, and it is a logical explanation for the occurrence of terrorism.

SELF-CHECK

1. Historical events may lead some people to engage in terrorism. True or False?

2. Bin Laden endorses terrorism because US foreign policy:

   (a) Disavows support of puppet governments
   (b) Places US troops in the Middle East
   (c) Does not support Israel
   (d) Benefits poor countries

3. Why would poor people be involved in terrorism?

3.2 POLITICAL CAUSES

Terrorism has an inherent relation to political disagreements. It may also result from the nature of political systems as well as their functions and structures. Conflict over priorities, the inability of political systems to adapt, the performance of government, and the structural arrangements of the ruling regime may all impact the possibility of terrorist attacks.

3.2.1 Politics

Politics:
Refers to the authoritative allocation of values in society.

Political disputes are another possible explanation for terrorism. **Politics** has been defined as the authoritative allocation of values and resources in society (Easton 1953). Politics therefore concerns the process of determining who gets what in a community or nation through the creation and enforcement of law. Since there are often conflicting views on values (such as what constitutes "good government") and because designing and running an effective government is inherently a political process, disagreements and even conflict may occur.

Any reading of early and modern political thought would likely reveal numerous suggestions on how to best govern societies. For some, the establishment of good government is based on acquiring knowledge, creating and enforcing beneficial laws, and promoting justice. While most people would agree with these recommendations, there are other points of significant disagreement.

For instance, some assert that majority rule should be promoted, while others believe the rights of minorities must be guaranteed. Political equality is espoused by many as a way to ensure that all viewpoints are taken into consideration, yet others assume that some individuals are better suited to shape public policy because of their education, leadership, and communication skills. Armed revolution against corrupt leaders is regarded as a plausible method for the foundation of good government by certain groups, but a divergent view is that order and stability are necessary to promote safety and security. Another disagreement centers on the contributions of leaders and citizens. One perspective is that wise elected officials will promote good government. Another school of thought is that it is citizen involvement that makes political decisions legitimate.

The major implication of this explanation is that values and what constitutes good government are issues of considerable debate. This being the case, it is to be expected that terrorist attacks will occur. In other words, if individuals or groups do not feel that their values and priorities are given attention, then it follows that they could engage in violent activity to increase the chance that their preferences will be sufficiently recognized and implemented. For instance, if a person feels that environmental degradation is wrong and that society is not protecting natural resources, then there is a possibility that he or she may act violently against those who profit from such activity. There have been several cases where extreme environmentalists have burned SUVs on dealers' lots as a way to protest the vehicle's gas mileage.

Political system:
A government that operates in a self-contained environment (e.g. a national territory).

3.2.2 Political Systems

Another thought about terrorism is based on the ability of political systems to adapt and change. A **political system** is a governing body that operates

Figure 3-2

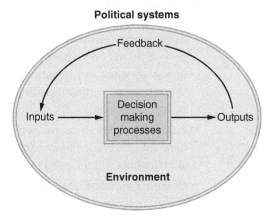

Without sufficient feedback and adaptation, a political system may be affected by terrorism.

in a self-contained environment (e.g. a national territory). David Easton (1953), one of the most recognized political scientists in the United States, suggests that political systems are composed of inputs (i.e. taxes and demands for service), decision-making processes (i.e. debates about proposed pieces of legislation), and outputs (i.e. policy choices and government programs). Easton also notes that political systems are influenced by feedback – meaning that the inputs, decision-making processes, and outputs can change over time and adjust to new needs and preferences. In Easton's view, this feedback loop is essential for the successful performance of political systems. In other words, if the political system does not adapt to unfolding situations, it will fail.

Applying this model to terrorism, it may be argued that terrorism may result when political systems do not react to the preferences of citizens. An example would be the desire of people to own a gun. If the system is viewed as not protecting citizen rights to possess weapons, then some may become disgruntled and engage in acts of terrorism as a result. The Viper Militia in Arizona is a group that attempted to engage in terrorism due to concerns over weapons rights. Its members plotted to blow up several federal offices in Arizona in 1996. Fortunately, this group was caught before the plans could be implemented (Hoffman 1998, p. 109).

3.2.3 Political Functions

A closely related view is that the performance of government functions may also be regarded as a cause of terrorism. Work in this area is similar to the research by Easton, and it has been espoused by Gabriel Almond and James S. Coleman. In their book, *The Politics of the Developing Areas*, Almond and Coleman suggest that it is imperative to examine how government works (1960). In particular, they note that the most important functions government performs include system requirements, inputs, outputs, and maintenance.

System requirements: Functions that must be performed to maintain operation of a political system.

- **System requirements** are functions that must be established to maintain the operation of a political system. They include routinization of the way things are done (e.g. elections and policy debates), integration of parts (e.g. political parties working together), and goal attainment (e.g. the satisfying of wants).

Input functions: Activities that influence priorities in the political system.

- **Input functions** are activities that influence priorities in the political system. These include interest articulation (e.g. agenda setting) and interest aggregation (e.g. formation of political parties).

Output functions: Activities emanating from the political system.

- **Output functions** are activities emanating from the political system. They incorporate rule making (e.g. policy decisions), rule application (i.e. policy enforcement), and rule adjudication (e.g. court decisions about policy).

Maintenance: The feedback function of the political system.

- **Maintenance** is the feedback function of the political system. It is composed of socialization (e.g. teaching rules of appropriate political behavior), political recruitment (e.g. the joining of interest groups), communication (e.g. calling your senator or state of the union speeches), and symbolism (e.g. a parade to increase pride and trust).

Applying this theoretical perspective to terrorism, it is presumed that political systems that do not perform these functions to a certain standard would be prone to attack. For instance, if a person does not believe law adequately protects animals in medical testing, then he or she may be more inclined to engage in violence against the government. In essence, it is maintained under this perspective that the functioning of government determines if terrorism is likely to occur.

Structure: Refers to the organizational relationships within a political system.

3.2.4 Political Structure

A final political explanation for terrorism is related to the structure of government in society. **Structure** refers to the organizational relationships within the political system. There are at least four different structures that can be identified:

Group competition: A model of politics that asserts that interest groups interact with or counteract one another in their attempt to sway government policy.

1. The **group competition model** asserts that interest groups interact with or counteract one another in their attempt to sway government policy. Some might assert that the United States is an example of this particular perspective.

Economic class model: A model that suggests a division of society based on the amount of wealth one possesses (e.g. bourgeoisie, middle class, proletariat).

2. The **economic class model** suggests a division of society based on the amount of wealth one possesses (e.g. upper, middle, and lower classes). Depending on your viewpoint, the United States or Latin American countries might also be seen in this light.

Political elite model:
A model in which the leaders are ruling over the masses.

Corporatist model:
A model that stresses the integration of various components of society into the state government (e.g. close ties to business, churches, clubs, etc.).

3. The **political elite model** is a situation where the leaders are ruling over the masses. Iraqi citizens, under the control of Saddam Hussein and his Republican Guard, would fall under this category.

4. The **corporatist model** stresses the integration of various components of society into the government (e.g. close ties to business, churches, clubs, etc.). Germany, during World War II, would be a logical example of this model.

The implication of the political structure argument is that certain forms of government will experience violence in different ways and for different reasons. For instance, if a special interest organization feels its needs are not being met in the group competition model, then it might participate in terrorism. In 2006, some Muslims in France burned McDonald's restaurants due to a law that would allow the company to fine them for violating corporate policy. In another case, if one class is being exploited economically by another, then terrorism may result. For instance, the Tupamaros, a revolutionary organization in Uruguay, engaged in terrorism to nationalize economic resources and distribute them in such a way as to reduce poverty. Other political structures, including the political elite and corporatist models, may be accompanied by state-sponsored terrorism against its own citizens. Joseph Stalin used violence as a way to maintain his power over the masses in Russia, and Francisco Franco executed many opponents of his fascist regime after the Spanish Civil War. Alternatively, terrorist activity may result in this structure as people rise up against the government. The movie "Valkyrie" depicts how some military leaders in Germany attempted to topple the Nazi regime through bombings and other activities.

IN THE REAL WORLD

State Terrorism in Russia

Although the Russian revolution of 1917 had the goal of promoting economic equality, it soon became apparent that a dictatorship had been formed. Vladimir Lenin promoted the Bolshevik take-over, and his government began to repress those who voiced opposition. Many artists, intellectuals, and clergy soon became targets of the new regime. When Lenin died, Joseph Stalin took over as the absolute ruler in what would become the Soviet Union. He was the communist leader from 1929 to 1953. During his tenure, Stalin also ruled with an iron fist. He introduced new laws to crack down on those who dissented. His secret police executed thousands and sent millions to labor camps. It is estimated that he killed 800 000 people. In addition, approximately 1.5 million people died due to the extreme conditions associated with labor camps. This experience seems to suggest that authoritarian or totalitarian political structures, where an elite group rules over the citizens, may be closely associated with mass terror.

SELF-CHECK

1. Because politics is about competing values, it is not associated with terrorism. True or False?
2. Which part of the political system is most likely to aggravate terrorism?
   (a) Inputs
   (b) Outputs
   (c) Feedback loop
   (d) Decision making
3. If the government always met the needs of individuals, would terrorism occur?
4. Is terrorism related to political structure? If so, how?

3.3 CULTURAL AND RELIGIOUS CAUSES

Culture:
The lifestyle of groups, including their shared history, language, religion, and moral system.

Religion:
The beliefs and practices espoused by those sharing a common spiritual faith.

Other potential explanations for terrorism focus on culture and religion. **Culture** is the lifestyle of groups based on their shared history, language, religion, and moral system. **Religion** specifically deals with the beliefs and practices espoused by those sharing a common spiritual faith. Both culture and religion are assumed to be related to terrorist activity, and there is ample literature on these subjects that makes this case.

3.3.1 Cultural Dimensions of Terrorism

One of the most well-known discussions about the impact of culture comes from Samuel Huntington, an American political scientist. In 1993, he wrote an article in *Foreign Affairs* describing how the world had changed when the Cold War ended. He asserted that the conflicts of the past were a result of (i) kings seeking power, safety, or wealth, (iii) nations seeking territory or sovereignty, and (iii) governments seeking to promote democracy or communism around the world. Huntington believed conflict of the future would revolve around culture.

Specifically, Huntington declared that there are numerous civilizations around the world (e.g. Western, Confucian, Japanese, Islamic, African, Hindu, Slavic, Latin American). Although there are conflicts within these civilizations, he was more concerned about the possibility that some of the world's civilizations may oppose Western culture because the United States is so powerful militarily, economically, and politically. He also suggested that others may counter American values because of its focus on individualism, constitutional government, human rights, and democracy. As a result, Huntington affirms that conflict could result from this "clash of civilizations."

Others including Benjamin Barber (1996) have followed up on this theme. In his book *Jihad vs. McWorld*, Barber asserted that the tribal values of certain cultural groups (e.g. Islamic fundamentalists) are diametrically opposed to those who espouse the Western capitalist economic system (which is symbolized by the fast-food chain McDonalds). Such differences of opinion are reasons why conflict exists today. In particular, Barber insinuated that the people who oppose globalization "argue the virtues of ancient identities, sometimes in the language of bombs" (Barber 1992, p. 5). He declares that "the aim of many of these small-scale wars is to redraw boundaries, to implode states and re-secure parochial identities … War … [is also] an emblem of identity, an expression of community, and an end in itself" (Barber 1992, p. 5).

Huntington and Barber bring up some intriguing points related to the cultural dimensions of terrorism. It is certainly clear that there are significant disagreements about culture and that acts of violence have emanated because of opposing traditions and viewpoints. As an example, the Basques created a terrorist organization known as the Euskadi ta Askatasuna (ETA). Their desire is political separatism in order to protect their language and other cultural attributes and preferences.

3.3.2 The Role of Religion in Terrorism

Religion has also been cited as a reason why conflict occurs and there appears to be a unique relationship among faith and terrorism (Juergensmeyer 1993; Hoffman 1995). Terrorism has occurred by those professing Christian, Jewish, Muslim, and other faiths.

Terrorism in the name of Christianity has taken place many times in history. In Ireland, Catholics and Protestants used "religion to identify people with politics" (White 2002, p. 57). Terrorists on both sides relied on their faith as the means to promote Irish independence or continue national association with the United Kingdom. Terrorism in the name of Christianity has also occurred

Figure 3-3

Timothy McVeigh was influenced by *The Turner Diaries* and this led him to bomb the Murrah Federal Building in Oklahoma City.

elsewhere. There have been some situations where those professing Christianity have bombed abortion clinics and killed doctors involved in such practices.

Terrorists in the United States have at times intertwined Christianity with racist or anti-government overtones. *The Turner Diaries*, written by a white supremacist named William Pierce (1978), discusses the fictitious story of a man who joins a terrorist organization. The man learns about God's alleged plan for a pure race and becomes violent toward others. Sadly, this made-up and disappointing story has had real-life implications. In fact, Timothy McVeigh was influenced by this book. Although he did not appear to have racist sentiment, McVeigh and other people relied on such teachings to reinforce their hatred toward the government. It is alleged that McVeigh got the idea of how to bomb the Murrah Federal Building in Oklahoma City while reading this work.

According to Jonathan White, groups like Aryan Nations, Posse Comitatus, and the American Institute of Theology have adopted a religious view that claims that whites are superior to other races. Jonathan White states that the fringe Christian Identity movement "is strongly anti-Semitic, claiming that humans originated from two seed lines. Whites are direct descendants from God, while Jews originated from an illicit sexual union between the devil and the first white woman. Nonwhite races evolved from animals and are categorized as sub-humans. Identity Christians believe that biblical covenants apply only to the white race and that Jesus of Nazareth was not a Jew, but the white Israelite son of God" (White 2002, p. 59). It is extremely unfortunate that people support such attitudes and that these beliefs translate into actions that are discriminatory and even violent.

IN THE REAL WORLD

Racist Attack

On 17 June 2015, a 21-year-old named Dylann Roof opened fire at the Emanuel African Methodist Episcopal Church in Charleston, South Carolina. He killed nine people and wound one other. This hate crime was racially motivated against black Americans. Roof's website, *The Last Rhodesian*, was discovered just days after the shooting and details his white supremacist views and racist beliefs. In January of 2017, Roof was sentenced to death and is currently on death row.

There are also terrorists that have associated with the Jewish faith. Rabbi Meir Kahane was an American cleric who was deeply offended by the violence against Jews in Israel. He created the Jewish Defense League as a way to ensure the survival of the Israeli state. His views claim that God made a covenant with Abraham to maintain biblical lands. Kahane's followers were involved in terrorist attacks in the United States in the 1960s. Although he was later assassinated, his son established a new organization (named Kahane Chai) to carry out similar missions. One member of his group killed 12 Muslims in a mosque in 1994.

Today, the major threat of religious terrorism comes from radical Muslim extremists. The vast majority of Muslims are peaceful. However, many

Wahhabism:
A very stringent and legalistic religious movement that attempts to ensure the purity of the Muslim faith with no deviations whatsoever.

Jihad:
Means an internal struggle to pursue righteousness or a war of self-defense, but has been used by terrorists to denote an offensive attack.

Fatwa:
A religious edict.

of the Islamic terrorists follow and support **Wahhabism**, a very stringent and legalistic religious movement that attempts to ensure the purity of the Muslim faith with no deviations whatsoever. There are many fundamentalists that engage in terrorism under the banner of this doctrine. For instance, Hezbollah means the "Party of God," while the Mujahideen are known as "holy fighters" in Afghanistan. Hamas is a name given for the Islamic Resistance Movement, and it is located in the Gaza Strip and in the West Bank. It is an offshoot of the Muslim Brotherhood and was founded in 1925 to denounce the national borders drawn up by colonial powers in Europe. Groups like Hamas and the Muslim Brotherhood oppose the creation of the Jewish state and desire to unify all Arabs under a pure Islamic government. These groups have been willing to kill anyone who supports peace.

The term Jihad is often used to describe terrorism that is influenced by Islamic fundamentalists. **Jihad** has a few different meanings. It is an internal struggle to pursue righteousness or could be construed as a war of self-defense. However, terrorists, such as Osama bin Laden, have altered this term to encourage his followers to engage in a "holy war" against nonbelievers or infidels. He stated in his **fatwa** (a religious edict) that it is the individual duty of every Muslim to fight against Israel and murder Americans everywhere. Many individuals and organizations around the world have followed this religious call to arms, and it seems as if related attacks occur on a daily basis.

IN THE REAL WORLD

The Emergence of the Irish Republican Army

During the Protestant Reformation, King Henry VIII separated himself from the Catholic Church and created the Church of England. About the same time, Elizabeth, the king's daughter, sanctioned the creation of the Ulster Plantation in Ireland, which resulted in the displacement of many of the Catholic inhabitants. Thousands of Irish Catholics who lost their land eventually perished because of malnourishment. This, coupled with a new law passed in 1801 (the Act of Union) to join Ireland under the United Kingdom, created serious tensions between Irish Catholics and Protestants from England. Witnessing the plight of their kin, many of the Irish who had migrated to the United States created the Irish Republican Brotherhood (IRB). Although the IRB had the intention of helping poor relatives in their old country, it soon became apparent that Irish independence was desired. The IRB mutated into a revolutionary organization. Its members traveled back to Ireland and later became known as the Irish Republican Army (IRA). The founder, Michael Collins, used religion as a way to recruit members to fight the British Protestants. The IRA was responsible for many bombings in Ireland and England in the 1970s and 1980s. Although various peace accords have been signed between England and the terrorists, attacks continued for some time. Luckily, terrorism does not have as close of ties to religion in Ireland today.

Terrorism is not confined to Christian, Jewish, or Islamic religions, however. Shoko Asahara, the leader of Japan's Aum Shinrikyo (Supreme Truth), stated he had been called as a messenger for God. After returning from a trip to the Himalayas, he prophesied that Armageddon would occur at the end of the 1900s and that only a divinely appointed race would survive in Japan. His religious views mixed Buddhism and Hinduism along with strong anti-American sentiment. On 20 March 1995, his followers used sarin gas to attack commuters on five subways in Tokyo. The attacks had the purpose of delaying police investigation into the groups' acquisition of deadly chemical weapons (Hoffman 1998, p. 126).

In each of these cases, terrorists use religion as a tool of violence and claim to act in God's name. Under these circumstances, "believers must identify with a deity and believe they are participating in a struggle to change history. They must also believe in cosmic consequences; that is, the outcome of the struggle will lead to a new relationship between good and evil. When they feel the struggle has reached a critical stage, violence may be endorsed and terrorism may result" (White 2002, p. 52).

SELF-CHECK

1. According to Samuel Huntington, culture will be the major source of conflict in the future. True or False?

2. According to bin Laden, Jihad refers to:
   (a) Internal struggle
   (b) Holy war
   (c) Fatwa
   (d) Wahhabism

3. Do all Muslims support terrorist attacks?

4. What are examples of religious terrorism?

3.4 IDEOLOGY

Based on the above discussion, it appears that historical grievances, poverty, foreign policy, political factors, culture, and religion are often regarded to be positively correlated with terrorism. Nevertheless, it is obvious that these variables cannot always be considered as the only motivating "cause" of terrorist phenomena. For instance, the overwhelming majority of poor people do not participate in terrorism. Ineffective political systems do not always produce citizens who engage in terrorism. Not all Muslims attack the United States, even if they disagree with Western foreign policy or culture. It consequently appears that there must be an additional reason as to why terrorism occurs. Gus Martin suggests that while "not all extremists become terrorists, some do cross the line to engage in terrorist violence. For them, terrorism is a calculated strategy. It is a specifically selected method that is used to further their cause" (2003, p. 56). Ideology is therefore a logical explanation for the occurrence of terrorism. In fact, Michael Chertoff has asserted that "Al Qaeda and like-minded organizations are inspired by a malignant ideology, one that is characterized by contempt for human dignity and freedom and a depraved disregard for human life" (2009, p. 22).

So, what is ideology? The word ideology is based on the prefix "idea." An **ideology** is consequently a set of beliefs related to values, attitudes, ways of thinking, and goals (Plamenatz 1970). In other words, ideologies are comprehensive theoretical viewpoints that often recommend certain types of political action. For this reason, ideologies are often referred to as "secular religions." The notion of ideology has roots in early political philosophy from prominent intellectuals such as Socrates, Plato, and Aristotle. But the term ideology did not appear until the late 1700s when a man named Destutt de Tracy attempted to discredit the political institutions in France. He claimed that the king was not divinely appointed and argued that the government did not represent the interests of the people. Destutt de Tracy's ideology opened up the possibility of political change in France. This was one of the first examples of how ideology is used for broad political purposes.

Ideology:
A set of beliefs related to values, attitudes, ways of thinking, and goals.

3.4.1 The Nature of Ideologies

Ideologies cover a broad range of subjects and may be related to numerous questions (MaCridis and Hulliung 1996):

- What is truth and how can it be pursued?
- What makes political authority or a political system legitimate?
- Should individual rights be promoted or should the majority rule?
- Is it important to espouse political freedoms or economic equality?
- Is the acquisition of wealth justified or is protecting the environment more vital?
- Should you follow the laws of men or God's commandments? As can be seen, ideologies therefore serve several purposes. They help promote understanding and they simplify a complex world. They facilitate communication among individuals and generate identity and emotional fulfillment in groups. They are also used as tools by leaders and provide guidelines for the behavior of followers. An ideology not only endorses certain viewpoints (while rejecting others) but also helps to mobilize people in the accomplishment of goals and priorities. Ideologies can therefore be very powerful motivators in the lives of their adherents.

Although all ideologies share many similarities, they differ in dramatic ways. Ideologies may discourage change, promote revolution, or accept incremental reform (MaCridis and Hulliung 1996). They may unite some groups and cause divisions with others. Roy MaCridis and Mark Hulliung (1996, pp. 16–17) suggest that ideologies may be assessed on five bases:

Scope:
The subjects covered by an ideology.

Coherence:
The internal logic of an ideology.

1. **Scope.** What subjects does the ideology cover? Does it focus on human rights or environmental issues?
2. **Coherence.** Does the internal logic make sense? In other words, does the ideology contradict itself?

Pervasiveness:
How long an ideology has been in existence.

Extensiveness:
How many people share a particular ideology.

Intensiveness:
The strength of attachment to an ideology.

3. **Pervasiveness.** How long has it been in existence? Is it a relatively new ideology like feminism, or has it been prevalent for centuries?

4. **Extensiveness.** How many people share that particular belief? What is the number of people that support it?

5. **Intensiveness.** What is the strength of attachment? Are people casually associated with the ideology, or are they fully committed to their particular beliefs?

3.4.2 Ideological Dimensions of Terrorism

According to Mostafa Rejai, an Indian scholar, there are five dimensions that are integral to any ideology (1991). Rejai states that all ideologies have a **cognitive dimension.** This refers to the knowledge and beliefs of the ideology. Ideologies are also related to **affect dimension** – specific feelings or emotions that are generated in conjunction with beliefs. **Valuation dimension** deals with the norms and judgments of the ideology. **Programs dimension** conjure up the plans and actions to support goals. And the **social base dimension** refers to the individuals or groups that espouse the ideology.

Cognitive dimension:
Refers to the knowledge and beliefs of the ideology.

Affect dimension:
Specific feelings or emotions that are generated in conjunction with an ideology.

Valuation dimension:
The norms and judgments of an ideology.

Programs dimension:
The plans and actions to support goals.

Social base dimension:
The individuals or groups that espouse an ideology.

These dimensions are useful to understand the ideologies associated with terrorism. Terrorists favoring radical Islam have unique attitudes about the world (e.g. they see the United States as a problem and assert that its influence needs to be countered or eliminated). Such groups have strong sentiments to a particular issue (e.g. a desire to retain a pure version of Islam). They are passionate about values and preferences (e.g. they are willing to injure others or even kill themselves if that is required). Radical Islamic terrorists also develop methods to accomplish their objectives (e.g. training and operational planning are needed to carry out attacks). Organizations are clearly identified to support this ideology (e.g. Al-Qaeda and ISIS members endorse violence, while most Muslims prefer peace).

Of course, it is important to recognize that there is no shortage of ideologies that may be related to terrorism. Some conservative ideologies have been associated with political regimes that engage in violence against the masses in order to maintain the power of the ruling elite. In contrast, a liberal ideology may endorse terrorism as the means to expand rights to individuals and citizens. Some terrorists also favor nationalistic movements, thereby attempting to promote a group with a particular culture, ethnicity, or language. Terrorism may have a relation to Marxist ideology. In this case, some people denounce capitalism and see a violent revolution as a way to promote economic equality. Other ideologies, like fascism and Nazism, sanction terrorism in order to expand a nation or promote racial superiority. At times, extreme conservationists engage in terrorism to avert global environmental degradation. Religious beliefs may be used by some people to endorse terrorism and counter the advances of secular society. Others, like anarchists and post-modernists, question all types of authority structures and accept violence as a way to protect individual freedoms. When you understand these ideological sources of conflict, you are in a better position to start dealing with the causes and consequences of terrorism.

IN THE REAL WORLD

Terrorist Ideology and Abortions

People have at times engaged in terrorist activities to halt abortions in the United States. The ideology of these individuals and groups has all of the elements identified by Mostafa Rejai. The cognitive dimension of their belief is that abortion is wrong and that this practice has increased dramatically since it was legalized. A feeling of deep sorrow for the loss of innocent life is the affect dimension of this ideology. The preference to protect unborn children is the value dimension. With this in mind, some terrorists have relied on a program of violence against doctors to halt abortions. The social base of this ideology is composed of certain fundamentalist Christians. While many of those adhering to Christianity oppose abortions, they are not willing to kill others to stop them from participating in this practice. Being able to detect which people are willing to participate in terrorism is one reason why it is necessary to have a solid understanding of the impact of ideology.

SELF-CHECK

1. Ideology is not related to beliefs, ideas, or attitudes. True or False?
2. Marxism has been used as an ideology to support terrorism. True or False?
3. Which is not one of the five dimensions of ideologies suggested by Mostafa Rejai?
   (a) Program
   (b) Cognitive
   (c) Affect
   (d) Coherence
4. Think of the terrorist attacks that have occurred in recent history. Can you identify the ideology of the responsible terrorists in each case?

SUMMARY

If you are to reduce the probability of terrorism, it is imperative that you understand what motivates people to participate in this type of behavior. In this chapter, you discovered that historical conflicts, mistakes in foreign policy, and extreme levels of poverty may impel some to engage in terrorist attacks. It was also illustrated that political systems, political functions, and political structures are often associated with terrorism.

Diverse cultures and extreme religious beliefs may likewise be used by terrorists to justify violent or disruptive activity. While all of these variables may influence terrorist behavior, it is likely that ideology is a better predictor of terrorism. People's beliefs seem to play a large role in terrorism. Once you recognize this fact, you can begin taking steps to identify terrorists and implement other measures to prevent future attacks.

ASSESS YOUR UNDERSTANDING

UNDERSTAND: WHAT HAVE YOU LEARNED

 Go to **www.wiley.com/go/mcentire/homelandsecurity2e** to assess your knowledge of the causes of terrorism.

SUMARY QUESTIONS

1. There have been continual conflicts in the Middle East. True or False?
2. Absolute poverty implies that everyone is poor or lacks desired resources. True or False?
3. There is considerable disagreement about what constitutes good government. True or False?
4. The economic class model is not related to terrorism. True or False?
5. Language is an aspect of culture, but not moral systems. True or False?
6. Terrorism has only been undertaken by those professing the Islamic faith. True or False?
7. The intensiveness of an ideology may have a direct bearing on terrorism. True or False?
8. The wars committed by Christians against the Muslims were known as:
   (a) Crusades
   (b) Wahhabism
   (c) Fatwas
   (d) Holocaust
9. An environment that has inputs, decision processes, outputs, and feedback is known as a(n):
   (a) Maintenance
   (b) Structure
   (c) Political system
   (d) Corporatist model
10. What is the religious movement that adheres to a strict interpretation of Islam?
    (a) Fatwa
    (b) Wahhabism
    (c) Marxism
    (d) *The Turner Diaries*
11. The cognitive dimension of an ideology refers to:
    (a) Feelings
    (b) Norms and judgments
    (c) Plans and actions
    (d) Knowledge and beliefs

12. According to bin Laden, Al-Qaeda is justified in attacking America because the United States:

(a) Supports Israel

(b) Distrusts Israel

(c) Distrusts puppet governments

(d) Is opposed to colonialism

APPLYING THIS CHAPTER

1. You are the public information officer for the Department of Homeland Security. The media wants to know why terrorism occurs. List at least five causes of terrorism and evaluate which explanation makes the most sense.

2. If you were in charge of US foreign policy, what causes of terrorism should you be aware of?

3. You are a scholar with expertise in terrorism. While appearing on the news show *60 Minutes*, you are questioned about the political systems and terrorism. Diagram the components of a political system and explain how the feedback loop may or may not relate to terrorism.

4. As an FBI analyst, your job is to identify potential terrorists. Predict why some people may use Christian, Jewish, and Islamic faiths to justify terrorism.

5. While discussing terrorism, a friend questions your knowledge about the characteristics of ideologies. Contrast the difference between pervasiveness and extensiveness in terrorist ideologies.

BE A HOMELAND SECURITY PROFESSIONAL

Briefing the President

You are a political advisor with expertise in homeland security. The President has asked you to brief him/her on the causes of terrorism. What would you say? What are the differing perspectives on this matter? Which one(s) is(are) most important?

Promoting Cultural Understanding

You are the Secretary of State, and it is your job to improve relations among groups and nations internationally. An important aspect of your position is to foster cultural understanding. Explain how this might ease the occurrence of terrorism around the world. Do you think it would be possible to eliminate culture as a cause of terrorism? Why or why not?

Assignment: Understanding Ideology

Write a paper about the impact of ideology on terrorism. Be sure to discuss what an ideology is, what the common characteristics of ideologies are, and the types of ideologies that may lead to violence.

KEY TERMS

Absolute poverty	Situation in which people lack so many resources that they cannot even meet basic necessities such as food, clothing, and shelter
Affect dimension	Specific feelings or emotions that are generated in conjunction with an ideology
Cognitive dimension	Refers to the knowledge and beliefs of the ideology
Coherence	The internal logic of an ideology
Corporatist model	A model that stresses the integration of various components of society into the state government (e.g. close ties to business, churches, clubs, etc.)
Crusades	Wars endorsed by the Pope to recapture the Holy Land of Jerusalem from the control of Muslims
Culture	The lifestyle of groups, including their shared history, language, religion, and moral system
Economic class model	A model that suggests a division of society based on the amount of wealth one possesses (e.g. bourgeoisie, middle class, proletariat)
Extensiveness	How many people share a particular ideology
Fatwa	A religious edict
Group competition	A model of politics that asserts that interest groups interact with or counteract one another in their attempt to sway government policy
Holocaust	The extermination of approximately six million Jews by the Nazi regime during World War II
Ideology	A set of beliefs related to values, attitudes, ways of thinking, and goals
Input functions	Activities that influence priorities in the political system
Intensiveness	The strength of attachment to an ideology
Jihad	Means an internal struggle to pursue righteousness or a war of self-defense, but has been used by terrorists to denote an offensive attack
Maintenance	The feedback function of the political system

Muslims	Those following the prophet Muhammad and adhering to the religion of Islam
Output functions	Activities emanating from the political system
Pervasiveness	How long an ideology has been in existence
Political elite model	A model in which the leaders are ruling over the masses
Political system	A government that operates in a self-contained environment (e.g. a national territory)
Politics	Refers to the authoritative allocation of values in society
Programs dimension	The plans and actions to support goals
Relative poverty	Situation in which people are less wealthy than their fellow citizens
Religion	The beliefs and practices espoused by those sharing a common spiritual faith
Scope	The subjects covered by an ideology
Social base dimension	The individuals or groups that espouse an ideology
Structure	Refers to the organizational relationships within a political system
System requirements	Functions that must be performed to maintain operation of a political system
Theocracy	A government run by clerics in the name of God
Valuation dimension	The norms and judgments of an ideology
Wahhabism	A very stringent and legalistic religious movement that attempts to ensure the purity of the Muslim faith with no deviations whatsoever

REFERENCES

Almond, G.A. and Coleman, J.S. (1960). *The Politics of the Developing Areas*. Princeton, NJ: Princeton University Press.

Barber, B. (1992). Jihad vs. McWorld. *The Atlantic* (March). http://www.theatlatntic.com/doc/print/199203/barber (accessed 21 September 2017).

Barber, B. (1996). *Jihad vs. McWorld: How Globalism and Tribalism Are Reshaping the World*. New York: Ballantine Books.

Chertoff, M. (2009). *Homeland Security*. Philadelphia, PA: University of Pennsylvania Press.

Crenshaw, M. (2010). *Terrorism in Context*. State College, PA: Penn State Press.

Easton, D. (1953). *The Political System*. New York: Alfred P. Knopf.

Falk, A., Khun, A., and Zweimuller, J. (2001). Unemployment and right-wing extremist crime. *The Scandinavian Journal of Economics*. 113 (2): 260–285.

Francis, D.R. (2002). Poverty and low education don't cause terrorism. *The NBER Digest* (September), pp. 1–2.

Hoffman, B. (1995). Holy terror: the implications of terrorism motivated by a religious imperative. *Studies in Conflict and Terrorism* 18: 271–284.

Hoffman, B. (1998). *Inside Terrorism*. New York: Columbia University Press.

Huntington, S.P. (1993). The clash of civilizations. *Foreign Affairs* 72 (3): 22–49.

Juergensmeyer, M. (1993). *The New Cold War? Religious Nationalism Confronts the Secular State*. Berkeley, CA: University of California Press.

Krueger, A.B. (2007). *What Makes a Terrorist?* Princeton, NJ: Princeton University Press.

Lesser, I.O. (1999). Countering the new terrorism: implications for strategy. In: *Countering the New Terrorism* (ed. I.O. Lesser, B. Hoffman, J. Arguilla, et al.). Santa Monica, CA: Rand.

Lozada, C. (2005). Does poverty cause terrorism? *The NBER Digest* (May), p. 1.

Martin, G. (2003). *Understanding Terrorism: Challenges, Perspectives, and Issues*. Thousand Oaks, CA: Sage Publications.

McCridis, R.C. and Hulliung, M.L. (1996). *Contemporary Political Ideologies: Movements and Regimes*. New York: HarperCollins.

Pierce, W. and (aka Andrew MacDonald) (1978). *The Turner Diaries*. Hillsboro, WV: National Vanguard Books.

Pillar, P.R. (2001). *Terrorism and US Foreign Policy*. Washington, DC: Brookings Institution Press.

Plamenatz, J. (1970). *Ideology*. New York: Praeger.

Rejai, M. (1991). *Political Ideologies: A Comparative Approach*. New York: M.E. Sharpe.

Sultalan, Z. (2008). The causes of terrorism. *Organizational and Psychological Aspects of Terrorism* 43 (1): 1–11.

Weatherby, J.N., Cuikshanks, R.L., Evans, E.B. Jr. et al. (2000). *The Other World: Issues and Politics of the Developing World*. New York: Longman.

White, J.R. (2002). *Terrorism: An Introduction*. Belmont, CA: Wadsworth.

COMPREHENDING TERRORISTS AND THEIR BEHAVIOR

Who They Are and What They Do

Do You Already Know?

- How to classify terrorists based on their intentions
- The common attitudes and personality traits of terrorists
- Similarities and differences among terrorist organizations
- The tactics used by terrorists

For additional questions to assess your current knowledge of terrorists and their behavior, go to **www.wiley.com/go/mcentire/ homelandsecurity2e**

What You Will Find Out	What You Will Be Able To Do
4.1 Examples of individuals, groups, and states involved in terrorism	• Classify terrorists based on their intentions
4.2 The cultural and personal traits of terrorists	• Critique stereotypical views about terrorists
4.3 How terrorist organizations are similar and unique	• Predict frequent terrorist behavior
4.4 The ways terrorists operate	• Anticipate how terrorists plan and carry out attacks

Introduction to Homeland Security: Understanding Terrorism Prevention and Emergency Management,
Second Edition. David A. McEntire.
© 2019 John Wiley & Sons, Inc. Published 2019 by John Wiley & Sons, Inc.
Companion website: www.wiley.com/go/mcentire/homelandsecurity2e

INTRODUCTION

If you are to increase your ability to deal with the threat and consequences of terrorism, it will be imperative that you comprehend who terrorists are and how they operate (Yayla et al. 2007). In this chapter, you will examine terrorists – whether they are acting alone or in conjunction with others. You will be able to categorize terrorists based on personality traits and evaluate their similarities and differences. By assessing the behavior of terrorists, you will be able to recognize how they recruit and train members, support their activities financially, and plan and carry out attacks. Thus, the following chapter will enable you to understand terrorists and what they do.

4.1 TERRORISTS AND TERRORIST ORGANIZATIONS

Who is a terrorist? What groups are involved in terrorism? Are nations also engaged in terrorism? These are important questions that must be addressed by those involved in homeland security. As will be seen, some terrorists are well known, while others are not. Certain terrorists are new to the scene, and others have been engaged in violence for years and decades. Specific proponents of terrorism have given up their violent activities, while different organizations remain heavily involved at the current time. Numerous examples of terrorists can be given, and the list seems to grow each day. Terrorists often have many similarities, but there are significant differences as well.

Anders Behring Breivik:
A terrorist who espoused far-right ideology and conducted one of the worst terrorist attacks in Norway.

Anders Behring Breivik is one example of a terrorist. He espoused far-right ideology and conducted one of the worst terrorist attacks in Norway. He decried Islam, criticized feminism, and rejected the cultural Marxism that was being witnessed in Europe. To spread his ideology, Breivik detonated a bomb in a van, which killed eight people on 22 July 2011. He then traveled to a summer camp on the island of Utøya and shot and murdered another 69 individuals.

Theodore "Ted" Kaczynski:
A terrorist known as the "Unabomber" who opposed technological advances.

Other examples of individual terrorists include Richard Baumhammers (a neo-Nazi who attacked people in Pennsylvania in April 2000) and Ramzi Yousef (the ringleader of the World Trade Center [WTC] bombing in 1993). **Theodore "Ted" Kaczynski** also comes to mind when discussing an individual terrorist. Known as the Unabomber (because he attacked universities and major airlines), he opposed technology and even wrote a manifesto decrying advances in this area. His attacks were aimed mainly at university professors and corporate leaders. He was responsible for at least 15 bombings around the United States that killed 3 people and injured 22 others. Individuals who act alone are sometimes described as **lone-wolf terrorists**. They are often the most difficult terrorists to uncover and capture.

Lone-wolf terrorists:
Individual terrorists that act alone

IN THE REAL WORLD

Excerpt of the Unabomber Manifesto

1. The Industrial Revolution and its consequences have been a disaster for the human race. They have greatly increased the life-expectancy of those of us who live in "advanced" countries, but they have de-stabilized society, have made life unfulfilling, have subjected human beings to indignities, have led to widespread psychological suffering (in the Third World to physical suffering as well) and have inflicted severe damage on the natural world. The continued development of technology will worsen the situation. It will certainly subject human beings to greater indignities and inflict greater damage on the natural world, it will probably lead to greater social disruption and psycho-logical suffering, and it may lead to increased physical suffering even in "advanced" countries.

2. The industrial-technological system may survive or it may break down. If it survives, it MAY eventually achieve a low level of phys-ical and psychological suffering, but only after passing through a long and very painful period of adjustment and only at the cost of permanently reducing human beings and many other living organ-isms to engineered products and mere cogs in the social machine. Furthermore, if the system survives, the consequences will be inevi-table: There is no way of reforming or modifying the system so as to prevent it from depriving people of dignity and autonomy.

3. If the system breaks down the consequences will still be very painful. But the bigger the system grows the more disastrous the results of its breakdown will be, so if it is to break down it had best break down sooner rather than later.

4. We therefore advocate a revolution against the industrial system. This revolution may or may not make use of violence: it may be sudden or it may be a relatively gradual process spanning a few decades. We can't predict any of that. But we do outline in a very general way the measures that those who hate the industrial system should take in order to prepare the way for a revolution against that form of society. This is not to be a POLITICAL revolution. Its object will be to overthrow not governments, but the economic and tech-nological basis of the present society.

Besides individual terrorists, there are literally scores and scores of terrorist groups and organizations around the world. Examples include Abu Nidal, Armed Forces of National Liberation, Democratic Front for the Liberation of Palestine, Earth Liberation Front, German Red Army

Faction, Hamas, Irish National Liberation Army, the Liberation Tigers of Tamil Eelam, and the Revolutionary Armed Forces of Colombia. There are literally too many terrorist groups to mention, and new organized appear continually.

The **Japanese Red Army** (JRA) was one such terrorist organization that emerged in the 1960s. Its members protested the presence of the US military in Japan after World War II, disapproved of the Vietnam War, and rejected capitalism. Its first operation was in 1970 when it hijacked an airplane headed to North Korea. This extreme left-wing organization has been involved in attacks in the Middle East, Italy, and in Japan, although its activities have waned in recent decades.

Abu Sayyaf is another terrorist organization. Abu Sayyaf is a jihadist separatist group in the Philippines that desires an independent Islamic state in Mindanao. As a splinter group of the Moro National Liberation Front, it opposes any type of colonialism or foreign involvement in the Philippines. Abu Sayyaf has been involved in kidnappings and has used its hostages to acquire lucrative ransoms from family members or large corporations that are associated with their captured prisoners.

In addition to the various groups involved in violent activity, there are also many states that have participated in terrorism, and individual country reports can be accessed through the US Department of State (2016). **Libya** is a country in Africa that has been sympathetic to the Palestinian cause in Israel. Under the direction of Muammar Qadhafi, this nation had involvement in the 1986 La Belle discotheque bombing in Berlin. It also was responsible for the Pan Am Flight 103 bombing over Lockerbie, Scotland, in 1988. This attack killed 270 people. Because of sanctions imposed by the United Nations and the threat of retaliation from the United States after 9/11, Libya has dramatically reduced its involvement in terrorism. It was subsequently taken off the list of nations supporting terrorism.

The Sudan and Iraq have provided arms, funding, safe haven, and diplomatic assistance to terrorists in the past. The Sudan harbored Osama bin Laden, while certain groups in Iraq have attacked US troops stationed there. Syria is another nation that supports terrorism currently. It has been involved in major episodes of ethnic cleansing within and around its borders. However, **Iran** is the state in the Middle East that has a long-standing history of participation in terrorism. After it underwent a revolution sponsored by Ayatollah Khomeini, this country increasingly denounced the United States and promoted anti-Western propaganda. Since this time, it has provided funds to terrorist organizations like Hezbollah. In addition, the Shia government in Iran had a role in attacks on US and French embassies and on the Marine barracks in Beirut during the 1980s. Most recently, evidence suggests that Iran is providing bombs to terrorists who are trying to destabilize Iraq and other parts of the Middle East. Both the United States and the United Nations are concerned that Iran is currently trying to develop nuclear weapons.

Japanese Red Army: A left-wing terrorist organization that emerged in the 1960s to protest US military presence in Japan after World War II, the war in Vietnam, and capitalism.

Abu Sayyaf: An Islamic separatist group in the Philippines that desires an independent state in Mindanao.

Libya: A country in Northern Africa that supported terrorism heavily in the 1980s.

Iran: A state in the Middle East that denounces the United States, promotes anti-Western propaganda, and has a long history of participation in terrorism.

Abu Musab al-Zarqawi:
A Sunni terrorist responsible for many atrocities in Iraq, including the beheading of an American businessman named Nicholas Berg.

Al-Qaeda:
A well-known terrorist organization whose name refers to the "base" – the location from which its supporters attacked the Soviet Union to free Afghanistan.

Cell:
A terrorist branch or unit operating in locations away from the organization's headquarters.

Terrorists – whether individuals, groups, or states – may have unique forms of organization and hierarchy. At times, terrorists may be under the direction of a single individual. For instance, many terrorists in Iraq support the ideology and vision promoted by **Abu Musab al-Zarqawi**. Al-Zarqawi was a Sunni terrorist who was responsible for many atrocities in Iraq, including the beheading of an American businessman named Nicholas Berg. Terrorists groups may also have a central headquarters. As an example, **Al-Qaeda** actually means the "base." This term refers to the location from which the Afghan war against the Soviet Union was coordinated. At other times, terrorists have **cells** (or branches with members) around the world. It is believed that Khifa had units in New York, Chicago, Pittsburgh, and Tucson at one time. In contrast, Jemaah Islamiyah has presence in Malaysia, Singapore, and Indonesia. Terrorist organizations also interact one with another. The Red Army Faction was trained by other terrorists in the Middle East. Al-Qaeda has also consulted with Jemaah Islamiyah. Terrorists are increasingly decentralized and transform themselves to avoid detection. It is hard to tell exactly who belongs to certain terrorist organizations. There are also many splinter groups with similar ideologies. Both the Irish Republican Army (IRA) and Palestinian Liberation Organization (PLO) have fragmented over time, especially when disagreements arose regarding the organization's stance (e.g. hard line or willingness to negotiate and compromise).

4.1.1 Terrorist Classification

Regardless of individual attributes or organizational structure, terrorists may be classified in one of three ways. Frederick Hacker (1976), a doctor who later became an expert in hostage negotiation, suggests that terrorists may be labeled as criminals, crusaders, or crazies. A terrorist that is a **criminal** seeks personal gain. Abu Sayyaf is an example of a criminal terrorist organization. It seems to be more interested in making money through extortion and less motivated by its initial founding goals of national independence. A **crusader** is a terrorist that promotes high moral goals. Examples of this type of terrorist include left-wing groups seeking economic or political equality, right-wing groups desiring to limit government interference in their lives, and environmental groups attempting to protect the Earth's resources. Nationalist groups advocating for separatism or religious groups trying to promote their beliefs and impose them on others are also examples of this category. A terrorist that is **crazy** is regarded to be psychologically disturbed. Ted Kaczynski might be regarded as falling into this type of terrorist since the reasoning for his attacks is not logical to others. Of course, it is important to recognize that some terrorists may exhibit elements of all three classifications. It is not always easy to distinguish among criminals, crusaders, and crazies. "The categories are not mutually exclusive; any terrorist group could contain a variety of these … types" (White 2002, p. 25).

Criminal:
A terrorist that seeks personal gain through illegal means (e.g. drugs or crime).

Crusader:
A terrorist that promotes high moral goals (e.g. Islamic fundamentalists).

Crazy:
A terrorist that is regarded to be psychologically disturbed (e.g. Ted Kaczynski).

Figure 4-1

Some individuals, like Eric Rudolph pictured above, use terrorist tactics to achieve moral objectives.

IN THE REAL WORLD

Saddam Hussein's Al-Anfal Attacks on the Kurds

While Saddam Hussein reigned with his Ba'ath Party in Iraq, he implemented state terrorism to rid his nation of the Kurdish people (Martin 2003, p. 104). He dropped chemical weapons on villages in northern Iraq to halt their desire for political separatism and autonomy. The mustard gas and nerve agents produced a yellow cloud that smelled like onions. When people inhaled the smoke, they would fall to the ground, and blood would spew from their mouths. Between 50 000 and 100 000 died, and 2.5 million Kurds were displaced as result. This series of attacks, which occurred in 1988, was named Al-Anfal. It is reported to have been in reference to revelations given by the Prophet Mohammed after his first great victory. The scripture advised the Prophet to kill unbelievers when necessary. It is an example of a crusader-type attitude that is common among many terrorists today.

SELF-CHECK

1. Terrorists always act alone. True or False?

2. Which country has been the largest supporter of terrorist attacks in Iraq?

   (a) Sudan
   (b) Syria
   (c) Iran
   (d) Sri Lanka

3. How can you classify terrorists?

4.2 PERSONAL CHARACTERISTICS

Regardless of how terrorists are classified, it is apparent that they share remarkable similarities (Holtmann 2014). In the *Language of Violence*, Edgar O'Balance (1979) states that terrorists are often dedicated, brave, and stoic. Terrorists are willing to sacrifice their time, energy, possessions, and lives for what they believe in. They are calm in light of the possibility of being subjected to prison, torture, or even death. Terrorists often lack emotions and show no pity or remorse for their attacks.

Beyond these characteristics, terrorists have other striking similarities across their belief systems (Combs 2000, p. 39). Terrorists:

1. *See the world simplistically in terms of right and wrong.* They may not accept the complexity of issues or recognize the pros and cons of certain points of view. For instance, they might have a negative perception of capitalism and fail to acknowledge any possible benefits from this type of economic system.

2. *Are disturbed by the current situation.* They are disappointed by societal problems and are able to identify what should be changed. As an example, Islamic fundamentalists assert that Western culture is responsible for the secularization of Arab societies.

3. *Have a unique image of themselves.* They feel that they are in a morally superior position to others. Terrorists are self-regarded to be the means for change and improvement. For instance, a terrorist who opposes abortions may view himself or herself as a messenger or servant from God.

4. *Identify the enemy and have strong feelings against them.* Terrorists frequently place blame and discredit those they regard to be at fault. Extreme nationalists dehumanize those of other ethnic groups as a way to mobilize action and limit guilt. They view others as enemies, collateral damage, or instruments of change. It is alleged that Michael Collins (IRA founder) stated after killing 14 men: "They were undesirables by whose destruction the very air is made sweeter" (Taylor 1958, p. 17).

5. *Believe terrorism is justified.* Recognizing their inferior position in terms of numbers or capacity as well as their inability to work through democratic processes, terrorists are willing to promote their goals through illegal means. Violence brings attention to a certain plight and speeds up the resolution to problems. To those participating in violence for religious reasons, terrorism may even bring salvation. Before being executed for killing an abortion doctor, a terrorist named Paul Hill stated that he expected a great reward in heaven once he was executed.

4.2.1 Distinct Differences

Although terrorists may have several common personality traits, there are major differences among them as well. This divergence can be seen in terms of age, gender, education, and economic status.

Most terrorists are younger adults in their twenties. This trend is seen throughout the world since young people have high ideals and possess more agile physical capabilities than older adults. However, age is not always an accurate predictor of who will engage in terrorism. During the 1970s many of the terrorists captured in Ireland were as young as 12 years old. Arab terrorist groups today also include a large number of teenagers in their ranks. There are even young children who engage in terrorism today. Nevertheless, older terrorists contradict these expectations. Osama bin Laden was in his mid-forties when the 9/11 attacks occurred. Thus, terrorists cannot be defined by a particular age. What we can state with more certainty is that the leaders tend to be older and those who implement attacks are younger.

The typical terrorist is regarded to be male. Men have traditionally been involved in the dangerous activities of planning and carrying out terrorist attacks. In fact, terrorism has frequently been a male-dominated enterprise. However, women have always played a significant support role in terrorism, and some have even participated in spying and actual operations (Griset and Mahan 2003; Ness 2008). Many females were involved in terrorism in Germany (i.e. Baader-Meinhof Gang and Red Army Faction). About half of the terrorists in Sri Lanka (i.e. Tamil Tigers) are girls or women, and they are particularly deadly in their craft. While it is true that most terrorists are men, you should not expect that this will always be the case.

The educational status of terrorists is also in question. Many terrorists are well educated, obtaining degrees in difficult subjects such as engineering, chemistry, or computer science. In fact, some of the leaders of Al-Qaeda earned college degrees in the United States and elsewhere. Not all terrorists are highly educated though. Many of the terrorists in the Middle East receive basic education in schools known as **Madrasahs**. These institutions may indoctrinate orphan students in extreme Islamic thought as occurs in some remote areas of Pakistan. Other terrorists may lack any formal type of education whatsoever.

Madrasahs: Schools in Pakistan and elsewhere that at times indoctrinate students in extreme Islamic thought.

It is sometimes difficult to predict terrorists based on economic class. Some terrorists, like Abu Nidal, were born into the lap of luxury. These

Figure 4-2

Many, but not all, terrorists are young. During a march in Pakistan on
5 October 2001, a boy holds a pistol. Thousands of demonstrators
shouted anti-American sentiment. Source: © Getty Images.
Reproduced with permission of Getty Images.

and other terrorists rejected their parents' middle-class lifestyle in the
1960s to fight for economic equality. Osama bin Laden is another excep-
tion to this rule. He was an extremely rich terrorist who acquired millions
of dollars from a number of oil and construction industries his family
owned. Today, many of the terrorists around the world are poor and lack
the basic necessities of life. Thus, "it remains true that to generalize about
the 'typical' terrorist can be very difficult with any degree of accuracy"
(Combs 2000, p. 51).

IN THE REAL WORLD

Rearing Terrorists in the Middle East

Socialization into the world of terrorism is a common practice among
many of the terrorists in the Middle East today. Children are brought up
to support terrorist organizations such as Hamas and Hezbollah. They
attend parades that celebrate militancy, and they are taught at an early
age to fire guns and use knives. Children dress in camouflage uniforms
and proudly wave the colors or flags of their terrorist organization. Car-
toons illustrate the blessings of violence and songs extol the virtue of
terrorist heroes. Under these circumstances, it is no wonder that the
ultimate goal in life for children is to die as a martyr. Others have even
executed enemies when asked to do so. This is one of the reasons why
terrorism is proving to be the enduring problem of our time.

SELF-CHECK

1. Terrorists are not willing to sacrifice for their cause. True or False?
2. Terrorists often see themselves as the means for change. True or False?
3. Terrorists:
   (a) Are always younger
   (b) Are not always male
   (c) Are never rich
   (d) Are always educated
4. How are terrorists similar?

4.3 THE BEHAVIOR AND TACTICS OF TERRORISTS

To a certain extent, terrorist activities follow certain patterns (Clutterbuck and Warnes 2011). Terrorists are involved in propaganda, recruiting, financing, and training. They also acquire false documents, travel, seek safe haven, use code words and secret communications, plan attacks, and search for weapons. Eventually, terrorists will launch attacks against their enemies. They also learn from experience to plan more deadly attacks in the future.

4.3.1 Propaganda

Al Jazeera:
A TV station based in Qatar that is popular in the Middle East and used to disseminate terrorist information.

Terrorists actively promote their ideological goals (Martin 2003). For instance, the Palestinian Islamic Jihad has a "manifesto." It rejects any peaceful solution to the Palestinian cause and lays out the goal of destroying Israel and ending Western influence in the Middle East. This document has been circulated widely among countries in the area. The media is often used to publicize the interests of terrorists. **Al Jazeera** (the most widely viewed TV station based in Qatar) often serves as the vehicle to disseminate information. Terrorists use it to call for the end of Western occupation in the Middle East and encourage viewers to "cut the head off of the snake" (i.e. destroy the United States). News material often shows video of actual or recreated attacks as well as training activities. In other cases, terrorists use the media to denounce their enemies in very visible ways. For instance, the torturing of prisoners in the Abu Ghraib prison from 2003 to 2004 horrified the Western world. However, these actions by US soldiers were also publicized widely by terrorists to spread hatred against America. In other cases, members of Al-Qaeda or ISIS swear loyalty to religious or political leaders and film a martyrdom statement. Videos of these terrorists are then mass-produced and given to people in Saudi Arabia, Yemen, and elsewhere. Young men and women are told about the benefits of terrorism. In one case, a 16-year-old terrorist apprehended in Israel said "A river of honey, a river of wine and 72 virgins. Since I have been studying the Quran, I know about the sweet life that waits there" (Daraghmeh 2004, p. 27a).

ISIS also publishes a newsletter named Rumiyah. This magazine calls for the overthrow of Western civilization and provides recommendations on ways to attack their enemies. For instance, ISIS encouraged its supporters to kill infidels with anything, including vehicles. On 22 March 2017, a terrorist in England ran over several people and then stabbed a police officer. Five people died and over 40 people were injured before the perpetrator was shot and killed.

4.3.2 Recruiting

Terrorists also attempt to recruit new members (Combs 2000). They may seek out other individuals or groups that espouse similar ideologies (e.g. anti-government groups or anti-American groups). In this situation, the terrorist may use well-developed websites to share their views with others. In different cases, terrorists may seek out students at universities who often have idealistic views of the world. Those pursuing education are aware of the world's problems, have specific technical knowledge sets, and desire change to make things better. Military personnel are often in high demand among terrorist organizations because they have understanding of how to use weapons or manufacture explosives. Crooked law enforcement officers may be another ideal terrorist, especially if they help the terrorists to operate with impunity.

Terrorists may also be recruited at prisons (Dunleavy 2011). One New York Commissioner of Prisons said that "our prisons are stuffed full of people who have a hatred to the prison administration, a hatred towards America and have nothing but time to seethe about it" (Associated Press 2016). An example is José Padilla (a.k.a. Abdullah al-Muhajir). Padilla was thrown in jail after pulling a gun on another driver in the United States. Padilla converted to Islam while in prison and traveled to Afghanistan and Pakistan in the late 1990s.

Those who are recruited into terrorist organizations often join to fill unmet emotional needs (Gerwehr and Daly 2006, p. 85). It has been illustrated that individuals who are prone to adhere to terrorist ideology are dissatisfied, are disillusioned, and lack strong family ties. Before recruitment, they often have no value system and desire clarity of purpose instead of ambiguity.

Once the terrorists are recruited, they are questioned extensively. For instance, terrorists are asked: What brought you to Afghanistan? How did you hear about us? What attracted you to the cause? How did you travel here? What is your educational or professional background? Such inquiries not only help to filter out spies but also determine the usefulness of new recruits.

4.3.3 Financing

Terrorist groups also seek to obtain financial resources to support their activities (Emerson 2006). At times, terrorist organizations may appear to resemble large corporations (Napoleoni 2005). Cindy Combs has researched these issues, and she concludes that terrorism is a "big business" (Combs 2000). Two organizations seem to illustrate her point very well.

Irish Northern Aid (NORAID) was established by Michael Flannery in 1969. This organization had headquarters in the Bronx (New York City) at 273rd East and 194th Street. Its goal was to assist the IRA through fundraising. On several occasions it sponsored dinners and gathered between $20 000 and $30 000 in cities around the United States. James Adams, one expert on terrorism, asserted: "From the onset of modern terrorism in Northern Ireland in 1969, the United States has played a key role in its support. The enormous Irish-American population has always felt a strong sentimental attachment to the 'old country,' and this has been translated into a steady stream of cash and guns to the IRA, which has, in part, enabled them to survive" (in Combs 2000, p. 95). Fortunately, this is less of a problem today.

Another example is the PLO, which was led by Yasser Arafat. Its initial office was in Damascus where it has a bank of computers as well as accountants and other employees from MIT and Harvard. Much of its funds were acquired through dairy and poultry farms as well as cattle ranches or duty-free stores in airports. The PLO also invested in stocks on Wall Street. Money acquired from these transactions is stored in bank accounts in Switzerland and Germany or passed through the Arab Bank for Economic Development. Combs asserts that this organization would be on the Fortune 500 list if it were a company (Combs 2000, p. 90). In 1985 it was worth an estimated $5 billion. The PLO was considered to be a terrorist organization up until 1991. Mahmoud Abbas took over the organization when Arafat died in 2004. The organization has experienced political turmoil recently, but it still promotes the cause of the Palestinian people today.

Terrorists may also obtain money from their involvement in the drug trade. There is often a very close connection between terrorism and narcotics. In fact, the word assassin comes from Arabic term "hashashin" – one who eats or is addicted to hashish (Combs 2000, p. 18). Centuries ago, Muslim leaders gave drugs to terrorists who acted against the crusaders. Marco Polo noted this in his travels to the Middle East. During the 1980s it was reported that "Lebanese hashish helps to pay for everything from hijacking and bombing spectaculars in Europe and the Middle East to a simmering revolt by Muslim insurgents in the Philippines" (U.S. News & World Report 1987, pp. 36–37). In December 2003, US investigators found 54 bags of hashish weighing 70 pounds each. In another case, 600 kg of heroine was traded to buy stinger missiles in a case that included suspects from Chicago and New York. The Sendero Luminoso also makes money from cocaine production. More recently, Al-Qaeda operatives were caught with drugs in Persian Gulf. Al-Qaeda also sells opium to finance their terrorist operations. For these reasons, narco-terrorism is described by *U.S. News & World Report* as "the unholiest of alliances, a malevolent marriage between two of the most feared and destructive forces on modern society – terror and drugs" (U.S. News & World Report 1987).

Money for terrorism may also come from other illegal activities. The Red Army Faction in Germany robbed banks and automobiles. Ahmed

Ressam, the LAX bomber, stole the chemicals that were used in his explosives. Al-Qaeda has relied on African clans' production of conflict diamonds to raise money. Gemstones are also used to buy weapons for terrorists in Liberia. Children trafficking supports Jemaah Islamiyah and Abu Sayyaf. Corrupt charities, such as the Haramain Islamic Foundation, are used to support terrorism. Counterfeiting perfume, software, and music CDs has also been undertaken to raise money. In the United States, cigarette smuggling (from states with low taxes/prices to states with higher taxes/prices) resulted in $8 million in profits. Nearly $100 000 of this was sent to Hezbollah to purchase stun guns, night vision equipment, and other devices (Emerson 2006, p. 217).

Terrorists may also get their financial resources from individuals or governments. Osama bin Laden received a large inheritance from his father. He also owned several construction companies. A significant proportion of Al-Qaeda's operating budget ($30 million annually) came from bin Laden, and he used some of this to pay off the Taliban for safe harbor. Shoko Asahara also played a large financing role in Japan. His terrorist organization, Aum Shinrikyo, obtained its money from the sale of books and computers. In other cases, states have sponsored terrorism. During the 1980s, Libya frequently provided terrorists with monetary resources. Iran is a major financier of terrorism today and has worked diligently to depose Western leadership in Iraq and Syria. Terrorists therefore seem to be able to raise significant amounts of funds for their operations.

4.3.4 Training

Terrorists seek to educate themselves and others about their deadly craft. For instance, in 1986, there was an international terrorist congress in Germany. 500 people attended including terrorists from France, Ireland, Portugal, Spain, and Latin America (Combs 2000, p. 89). Similar conferences have taken place in the United States. One event was held in 1990 in Dallas, Texas. It is reported to have hosted more radical Muslims under one roof in America than any other event up to that point in history (Reeve 2002, p. 224). Such events seek to reiterate the need for terrorist activities and discuss the best methods for accomplishing violent goals.

Training camps are also favored by terrorists. There have been training camps in Cuba, Bulgaria, Czechoslovakia, East Germany, Lebanon, Libya, North Korea, South Korea, and Syria. The Mes Aynak training camp was located in an abandoned copper mine in Afghanistan. In secluded areas such as this, terrorists may participate in advanced commando courses. They may be taught how to raise money, recruit others, gather tactical information, disguise themselves, travel discretely, fit into a foreign culture, read maps, and understand cryptology. At other camps they may be taught to speak English or German and be introduced to weapons manufacturing. Some training locations help terrorists use knives by butchering sheep or implement gas attacks on dogs. According to the Federal Bureau of Investigation (FBI), there are even a number of these training sites in the United States in isolated locations. It is argued that 22 jihadist camps have been identified in America and that they have been operated by Jamaat al-Fuqra. Video footage has demonstrated the use of automatic weapons and hand-to-hand combat in isolated compounds. The nature of this threat has been disputed, but the situation does produce concern among citizens and law enforcement officials.

In many situations, terrorists will be given a kit, manual, or literature to educate them further (Griset and Mahan 2003, p. 196). Ramzi Yousef's materials included bomb-making instructions, false identification documents, videos denouncing the United States, and operational guidance. Other documents found at training camps include sections on how to acquire and make chemical explosives as well as the best location to place charge on bridges and overpasses. An Al-Qaeda manual illustrates how terrorists may enter the United States through Canada. It also suggested in these documents that terrorists should avoid hanging out at radical mosques, use cash only for expenditures, and rely on public Internet access to send e-mails. Terrorists have also advised in manuals to use pay phones to communicate or throw away cell phones once they are used.

4.3.5 False Documents, Travel, and Safe Haven

According to the 9/11 Commission (2003), terrorists often seek to obtain fraudulent documents. They also travel frequently and seek safe haven among sympathizers. For instance, Al-Qaeda had an office in the Kandahar airport. Personnel in this facility helped some of its members obtain Yemeni passports. Terrorist organizations are able to substitute photos and add or erase entry stamps. They also can submit false paperwork in an attempt to acquire visas. For instance, Mohammed Atta told US officials that he lost his old passport. Because he was worried about visas from Pakistan, he ordered a new one. This allowed him to enter the United States with ease prior to 9/11.

As terrorists go about their activities, they may travel extensively. Khalid Sheikh Mohammed journeyed to India, Indonesia, and Malaysia. Others fly frequently between Afghanistan and the United States. Terrorists have traveled through Iran, which neglected to stamp passports. As they move about to conduct their business, terrorists will seek safe haven. Both Sudan and Afghanistan provided bases for Osama bin Laden. Weak countries with remote areas are attractive to terrorist organizations. When terrorists enter enemy territory, they are picked up by associates and taken to homes or apartments where food, shelter, and other necessities of life can be met.

4.3.6 Code Words and Secret Communications

In order to avoid detection, terrorists are very cautious about their communications. When discussing the timing to pick up bomb, one terrorist told his colleague that they were in the "ninth month of pregnancy." In another situation, a bin Laden supporter in Yemen said his impending "marriage" would be a "surprise." This was in reference to an attack that was being planned. However, leaders of terrorist organizations do not always tell their subordinates everything about operations. For instance, bin Laden wanted to limit the information his recruits possessed in case they were caught. Terrorists may also use the Internet to communicate. In March 2001, Al-Qaeda used hidden script on web pages. Known as steganography, this technique allows terrorists to hide maps, photos, and letters in chat rooms or pornographic sites. Louis Freeh, a former FBI director, says, "uncrackable encryption is allowing terrorists – Hamas, Hezbollah, Al-Qaeda and others – to communicate about their criminal intentions without fear of outside intrusion" (Thetford 2001, p. 252).

4.3.7 Planning

Terrorists spend a great deal of time planning attacks (9/11 Commission 2003). In researching possible targets, terrorists may rely on the Internet and open-source records (e.g. library or government documents), insider information (e.g. knowledge from employees), electronic equipment (e.g. police scanners or phone taps), or physical surveillance (e.g. casing a location) (Pluchinsky 2006).

Terrorists are meticulous planners. In 1994, Khalid Sheikh Mohammed designed the Manila air plot. He and other terrorists intended to bomb 12 US jets over the Pacific Ocean during a two-day span. They started casing flights and purchased timers and nitrocellulose to make bombs. Fortunately, the Philippine government discovered the plot and was able to thwart it. Terrorists involved in the embassy bombings in Africa used state-of-the-art video cameras for reconnaissance purposes. They obtained this equipment from dealers in China and Germany. They were interested in traffic patterns, building construction, and occupancy rates to inflict maximum casualties. The 9/11 plot was discussed seven or eight years before it actually occurred. It was initially supposed to have about 10 planes but was scaled back due to complexity. Nevertheless, the terrorists involved in the 9/11 attacks cased flights frequently to determine the best time to hijack the planes. These terrorists also went to flight school in the United States so they could maneuver the aircraft.

An important function of planning is to find a symbolic date or location so terrorist attacks can occur and have maximum impact (Martin 2003). The bombing of the Murrah Federal Building took place on the anniversary of Waco. Timothy McVeigh was frustrated with the way the ATF and FBI dealt with the Branch Davidians, and he wanted to get even. Similarly, the targets on 9/11 were not selected by chance. Their airlines – American Airlines and United Airlines – had reference to America and the United States. The WTC was chosen because it is the heart of the Western capitalist economy. The Pentagon was selected as a target because it signified the strength of the US military. Although Flight 93 never arrived at its intended location, many believe it was headed for the White House or the Capitol Building (which included the political leadership of the country). The meticulous planning and choice of targets adds to the death, damage, social disruption, and visibility of the event.

Figure 4-3

Terrorists spend a lot of time planning attacks, as was the case in the twin African Embassy bombings. Source: © FBI.

 IN THE REAL WORLD

Nice Truck Attack

On 14 July 2016, 31-year-old Mohamed Lahouaiej Bouhlel carried out a terrorist attack while people were celebrating Bastille Day in the French city of Nice. Bastille Day is the national independence holiday in France, and it commemorates the beginning of the French Revolution with the storming of the Bastille prison on 14 July 1789.

Bouhlel was born in Tunisia but lived in Nice and worked as a delivery truck driver. The attack began when he purposely drove a large rented truck (weighing about 19 tons) into crowds of people along the Promenade des Anglais. Bouhlel also fired a gun at French police officers while driving the truck. The violent assault ended when police officers shot into the vehicle, killing him. However, Bouhlel was responsible for killing 84 people and injuring over 200 others in this horrific event.

Bouhlel was identified after the attack, and his belongings and apartment were investigated by law enforcement. They discovered that Bouhlel had a previous criminal record, but was not on intelligence services' radar. He also had a history of violence toward his family, and in 2004, a psychiatrist described him as edging on psychopathy. Bouhlel was apparently depressed after his wife divorced him and likely became radicalized very quickly.

Evidence shows Bouhlel was in contact with Islamic radicals and planned the terrorist attack for over a year with several accomplices who have since been taken into custody (none of whom were previously known to have any connections to Islamic radicals). The Islamic state claimed responsibility for the incident shortly after it occurred, but Bouhlel may have acted independently with the same radicalized ideology.

4.3.8 Weapons

Sometime before, during, or after terrorists plan attacks, they will also acquire weapons (Martin 2003). These may range from simple devices to advanced military armaments. Such weapons may impact one or a few people, or even hundreds and thousands. For instance, mace, pepper spray, or box cutters were used against some of the passengers and crew on 9/11. Knives have been used by ISIS to cut off the ears of those who desert their cause. In other cases, terrorists will obtain and use pistols and light artillery. Guns and rocket-propelled grenades are also commonly used by terrorists. Incendiary devices (e.g. Molotov cocktails that start fires) are used when destruction of property is desired.

WMD:
Acronym for weapons of mass destruction.

NBC:
An acronym for nuclear, biological, and chemical weapons.

CBRNE:
An acronym for chemical, biological, radiological, nuclear, or explosive devices.

Terrorists have been increasingly interested in weapons of mass destruction (**WMDs**), which will be discussed in depth in Chapter 14. Common acronyms for WMDs are **NBC** or CBRNE. NBC stands for nuclear, biological, and chemical weapons. CBRNE is a more recognized acronym since it is more comprehensive. **CBRNE** stands for chemical, biological, radiological, nuclear, or explosive devices. Chemical weapons may include typical household cleaning agents that have been mixed into hazardous or unstable combinations. Terrorists may also try to find military weapons such as mustard gas or nerve agents. Shoko Asahara spent an estimated $30 million to make anthrax. Biological agents include pathogens, toxins, or viruses. Larry Wayne Harris was a member of the Aryan Nations. After illegally ordering the plaque from a research facility, he was arrested in Arizona and caught with the deadly agent in the glove box of his car. Radiological weapons are devices that contain and emit alpha-, beta-, or gamma-emitting material. Radiological material has been reported lost at a number of industrial or medical facilities. A nuclear weapon is far different than a radiological weapon. Nuclear weapons are large bombs created by fusion or fusion processes. They can decimate entire cities. At one point, it is reported that bin Laden was working with a Sudanese military officer to purchase weapons-grade uranium. Explosive devices are other names for bombs. Improvised explosive devices (**IEDs**) are increasingly sought by insurgents in Iraq and used in Afghanistan. Pipe bombs are examples of IEDs. They can pierce armor and kill or maim soldiers and police officers.

IED:
Improvised explosive devices.

4.3.9 Acts of Civil Disorder or Terrorisms

Once terrorists plan attacks and obtain weapons, they launch attacks (Pluchinsky 2006). There have been numerous cases where individuals have mailed letters with white powdery substances. These hoaxes and threats instill fear and intend to disrupt society. They require large numbers of responders and can shut down businesses and government facilities for hours and even days. At other times, sabotage is preferred. This includes virus attacks through computer programs. In the Northwest, the Rajneeshee group sprayed salmonella on a salad bar at a restaurant in Dalles, Oregon. 700 people became ill as the group tried to influence the outcome of local elections.

Terrorists also hijack planes or seagoing vessels. The 9/11 attacks that resulted in so much destruction in New York and Virginia began with the take-over of aircraft. Hostage taking and kidnapping are also frequent ploys of terrorists. Some hostages are used for ransom or killed if the demands of terrorists are not met. For instance, Nicholas Berg was a contractor that was beheaded in Iraq. Other people are murdered in through assassinations and ambushes. Yitzhak Rabin, a prime minister of Israel, was shot to death on 4 November 1995 by a person who opposed the Oslo Peace Accords. In another case, Al-Qaeda terrorists pretended to be reporters. They met with Ahmed Shah Massoud (a Northern Alliance leader) and killed him with a bomb on 9 September 2001.

IN THE REAL WORLD

Boko Haram

The Jama'atu Ahlis Sunna Lidda'awati wal-Jihad is an Islamist terrorist group that emerged in 2002 in Nigeria. In Arabic, this official name means "People Committed to the Propagation of the Prophet's Teachings and Jihad." However, this group is better known by the name Boko Haram, the loose translation of which sheds light on their ideology to forbid Western education. Mohammed Yusuf united his followers to form the group. Under his leadership, Boko Haram created an Islamic school and took actions to establish an Islamic state. It was categorized by a campaign of violence, and the group's headquarters were seized in 2009 by Nigeria's security forces. Many of Boko Haram's members were captured, and Yusuf was killed.

Boko Haram regrouped under Abubakar Shekau and continued their insurgency with assassinations, explosions, raids, and other attacks. Perhaps one of the most widely publicized of these incidences was the 2014 abduction of 276 schoolgirls from Chibok in Borno (northeastern Nigeria). The girls were between 16 and 18 years old. About 50 of the girls were able to escape soon after being abducted. Shekau threatened to sell the remainder of the girls into slavery, and it is likely they have been brutalized and forced to convert to Islam.

The kidnapping gained international attention and spurred a discussion on social media with the hashtag #BringBackOurGirls, which many powerful celebrities and high-ranking officials participated in, including Michelle Obama. Boko Haram continues to abduct women and children as they seek to control more of Nigeria and the surrounding regions. Some victims have since escaped or been rescued from captivity, and speculation has arisen on whether any of the Chibok girls were among those recovered. Despite the wide media coverage and government efforts in Nigeria, the United States, and other countries, over 200 Chibok girls are still missing.

Boko Haram is still a very active threat to the region with a force estimated to be around 9000 men. It is suspected that the group may have alliances with foreign groups and extremists like Al-Qaeda. As the conflict continues, Boko Haram has focused on regaining their captured prisoners and building an Islamic state, and it is clear that the poverty-stricken and chaotic state of the Nigerian government has only fueled the group's insurgency.

Arson is a frequent choice of terrorists and it has been used to intimidate members of black religious congregations. Bombings are the most prevalent type of attack, accounting for nearly 75% of violent actions committed by terrorists. They have taken place at abortion clinics, the WTC (in 1993), the Marriott hotel in Indonesia, the African embassies, and the USS Cole. In the Middle East, such attacks are frequently initiated by suicide bombers. These death squads wear or carry explosive that they detonate around others. It may be a matter of time before these occur in the United States.

While WMDs have not been used often, terrorists did use sarin in an attack on the subway in Tokyo. Terrorists have recently started using chemicals such as chlorine in their bombings in Iraq. Syria recently launched gas attacks against certain villages to "cleanse" the area of ethnic groups of which they disapprove. There is fear that this will be more commonplace in the future. If terrorists survive attacks, they will quickly flee the scene. For instance, after the first WTC bombing, Ramzi Yousef fled to Pakistan. He remained there for two years until he was caught by the special agents from the FBI.

IN THE REAL WORLD

Operations of the Tamil Tigers

The Tamil Tigers seek independence in northeastern Sri Lanka. When India gained autonomy at the end of World War II, both the Sinhala and Tamil ethnic groups shared political authority. In 1955, Sinhala-only policies were implemented, and the Tamils became disgruntled due to their loss of power. After assassinating the Sinhala leader in 1959, the Tamil Tigers emerged as a serious terrorist threat. They easily recruited members to join their cause. Funding was obtained through bank robberies. Training camps were founded in India, and members received instruction from terrorists in the Middle East. The Tamil Tigers built a navy to attack Indian fleets. In 1991 they killed the Indian prime minister. The Tamils prefer bombings and suicide attacks are common to this day.

SELF-CHECK

1. Terrorists want to recruit others, but they are also careful who they allow to join with them. True or False?

2. Training does not appear to be a major priority of terrorists. True or False?

3. Terrorists:
   (a) Often obtain false documents
   (b) Do not travel frequently
   (c) Spend little time on planning attacks
   (d) Do not prefer explosives

4. Why do terrorists select some targets over others?

SUMMARY

Understanding who terrorists are and how they operate is extremely important if you are to reduce the number and extent of potential attacks. In this chapter, you have assessed the nature of individual terrorists and those associated with organizations and nation-states. You have recognized common personality traits as well as significant differences among terrorists. Your review of terrorist behavior has enabled you to identify how they finance operations, communicate with secret codes, and carry out attacks. Such knowledge is imperative if you are to work successfully in homeland security.

ASSESS YOUR UNDERSTANDING

UNDERSTAND: WHAT HAVE YOU LEARNED

 Go to **www.wiley.com/go/mcentire/homelandsecurity2e** to assess your knowledge of terrorists and their behavior.

SUMMARY QUESTIONS

1. The Japanese Red Army is a terrorist organization that supports capitalism. True or False?

2. Leaders of Libya were responsible for the bombing of Pan Am Flight 103. True or False?

3. Individuals who commit terrorist acts are sometimes referred to as lone-wolf terrorists. True or False?

4. Abu Sayyaf is an Islamic separatist group that wants foreign involvement in the Philippines. True or False?

5. Terrorist groups may be led by a single individual, a headquarter station, or several cells throughout the world. True or False?

6. Terrorists often see the world as a complicated place with many different interpretations of what is right and wrong. True or False?

7. Terrorists groups avoid using the Internet as a means of communication. True or False?

8. Which of the following answers does not accurately describe Meir Kahane?
   (a) He was a Jewish rabbi.
   (b) He founded the Jewish Defense League.
   (c) He founded the Palestinian Jihad.
   (d) He was assassinated in 1990.

9. Theodore "Ted" Kaczynski was known for his:
   (a) Opposition to technology and studies in this field
   (b) Loyalty to professors and corporate leaders
   (c) Collaboration with terrorist organizations
   (d) Efforts to combat terrorist activity

10. All of the following nation-states have recent involvement in sponsoring terrorism except:
    (a) Iran
    (b) Syria
    (c) Sudan
    (d) France

11. Left-wing groups seeking economic or political equality through terrorist acts are an example of what kind of terrorist group?

(a) Criminals

(b) Careless

(c) Crusaders

(d) Crazies

12. Terrorist groups use all of the following techniques to raise funds except:

(a) Drug sales and other illegal activities

(b) Mass mail-outs to households

(c) Using organized "big business" techniques

(d) Funding from individuals and governments

13. CBRNE stands for:

(a) Chemical, biological, radiological, nuclear, or explosive devices

(b) Chemical, biological, radiological, nuclear, or explosive disasters

(c) Catastrophic, biological, radiological, nuclear, or explosive devices

(d) Catastrophic, biological, radiological, nuclear, or expensive devices

14. Bombings account for what percentage of terrorist attacks?

(a) 25%

(b) 50%

(c) 75%

(d) 80%

APPLYING THIS CHAPTER

1. Pick a terrorist attack not mentioned in this chapter and describe it based on the following criteria:

(a) What was the terrorist act?

(b) Was it performed by an individual or group?

(c) Would the terrorist(s) be classified as a criminal, crusader, or crazy? Why?

2. Using the same terrorist attack you picked for question one, describe what personal characteristics the person or group involved in the act has in common with other terrorists described in this chapter. Are there differences? If so, what?

3. Terrorist groups often recruit new members to grow their organization and increase their influence. What groups of people do terrorists often recruit? What are some reasons why people join terrorist groups? What happens once they are recruited?

4. Why is it important for us to understand the various behaviors and tactics of terrorist groups? Using the information in the chapter, describe how we can use information on terrorist groups to help monitor and suppress terrorist activity.

BE A HOMELAND SECURITY PROFESSIONAL

Common Terrorist Characteristics

You are an analyst with the FBI. Your boss would like you to write a report on common terrorist profiles. How could you describe terrorists? In what ways could you classify them?

Similarities and Differences Among Terrorists

Write a three-page paper about the personal characteristics of terrorists. Be sure to discuss if terrorists are similar or different from one another. Mention why it is important to understand who terrorists are.

Looking for Terrorists

You work as a member of a terrorist task force in law enforcement in local government. Your job is to identify potential terrorists before they launch attacks. What type of behavior are you looking for? Explain at least five activities that you would want to consider.

KEY TERMS

Abu Musab al-Zarqawi	A Sunni terrorist responsible for many atrocities in Iraq, including the beheading of an American businessman named Nicholas Berg
Abu Sayyaf	An Islamic separatist group in the Philippines that desires an independent state in Mindanao
Al Jazeera	A TV station based in Qatar that is popular in the Middle East and used to disseminate terrorist information
Al-Qaeda	A well-known terrorist organization whose name refers to the "base" – the location from which its supporters attacked the Soviet Union to free Afghanistan
Anders Behring Breivik	A terrorist who espoused far-right ideology and conducted one of the worst terrorist attacks in Norway
CBRNE	An acronym for chemical, biological, radiological, nuclear, or explosive devices
Cell	A terrorist branch or unit operating in locations away from the organization's headquarters
Crazy	A terrorist that is regarded to be psychologically disturbed (e.g. Ted Kaczynski)

Criminal	A terrorist that seeks personal gain through illegal means (e.g. drugs or crime)
Crusader	A terrorist that promotes high moral goals (e.g. Islamic fundamentalists)
Japanese Red Army	A left-wing terrorist organization that emerged in the 1960s to protest US military presence in Japan after World War II, the war in Vietnam, and capitalism
IED	Improvised explosive devices
Iran	A state in the Middle East that denounces the United States, promotes anti-Western propaganda, and has a long history of participation in terrorism
Lone-wolf terrorists	Individual terrorists that act alone
Libya	A country in Northern Africa that supported terrorism heavily in the 1980s
Madrasahs	Schools in Pakistan and elsewhere that at times indoctrinate students in extreme Islamic thought
Theodore "Ted" Kaczynski	A terrorist known as the "Unabomber" who opposed technological advances
WMDs	Acronym for weapons of mass destruction

REFERENCES

9/11 Commission (2003). *The 9/11 Commission Report: Final Report of the National Commission on Terrorist Attacks Upon the United States.* New York: W.W. Norton and Company.

Clutterbuck, L. and Warnes, R. (2011). *Exploring Patterns of Behavior in Violent Jihadist Terrorists: An Analysis of Six Significant Terrorist Conspiracies in the UK.* Santa Monica, CA: Rand Corporation.

Combs, C.C. (2000). *Terrorism in the Twenty-First Century.* Upper Saddle River, NJ: Prentice Hall.

Daraghmeh, A. (2004). Family: teen exploited for bomb mission Dallas Morning News (Friday, 26 March), p. 27a.

Dunleavy, P.T. (2011). *The Fertile Soil of Jihad: Terrorism's Prison Connection.* Washington, DC: Potomac Books.

Emerson, S. (2006). *Jihad Incorporated: A Guide to Militant Islam in the U.S.* New York: Prometheus Books.

Gerwehr, S. and Daly, S. (2006). Al Qaida: terrorist selection and recruitment. In: *The McGraw-Hill Homeland Security Handbook* (ed. D.G. Kamien), 73–89. New York: McGraw-Hill.

Griset, P.L. and Mahan, S. (2003). *Terrorism in Perspective.* Thousand Oaks, CA: Sage.

Hacker, F.J. (1976). *Crusaders, Criminals, Crazies: Terror and Terrorism in Our Time.* New York: Norton.

Hickey, Jennifer. 2016. Ripe for radicalization: federal prisons 'breeding ground' for terrorists, say experts. *Fox News* (5 January). http://www.foxnews.com/us/2016/01/05/ripe-for-radicalization-federal-prisons-breeding-ground-for-terrorists-say-experts.html.

Holtmann, P. (2014). Terrorism and jihad: differences and similarities. *Perspectives on Terrorism* 8 (3): 140.

Martin, G. (2003). *Understanding Terrorism: Challenges, Perspective, and Issues.* Thousand Oaks, CA: Sage.

Napoleoni, L. (2005). *Terror Incorporated: Tracing the Dollars Behind the Terror Networks.* New York: Seven Stories Press.

Ness, C.D. (2008). *Female Terrorism and Militancy: Agency, Utility and Organization.* New York: Routledge.

O'Balance, E.O. (1979). *The Language of Violence: The Blood Politics of Terrorism.* Presidio: San Rafael, CA.

Pluchinsky, D.A. (2006). A typology and anatomy of terrorist operations. In: *The McGraw-Hill Homeland Security Handbook* (ed. D.G. Kamien), 365–390. New York: McGraw-Hill.

Reeve, S. (2002). *The New Jackals: Ramzi, Yousef, Osama bin Laden, and the Future of Terrorism.* Lebanon, NH: Northeastern University Press.

Taylor, R. (1958). *Michael Collins.* London: Hutchinson.

Thetford, R.T. (2001). The challenge of cyberterrorism. In: *Terrorism: Defensive Strategies for Individuals, Companies and Governments* (ed. L.J. Hogan), 239–257. Frederick, MD: Amlex, Inc.

US Department of State (2016). Country Report on Terrorism. https://www.state.gov/j/ct/rls/crt/2016/.

U.S. News & World Report (1987). Narcotics: terror's new ally. US News & World Report (4 May), pp. 36–37.

White, J. (2002). *Terrorism: An Introduction*. Belmont, CA: Wadsworth.

Yayla, A.S., Ekici, S., Durmaz, H., and Sevinc, B. (2007). *Understanding and Responding to Terrorism*, NATO Security Through Sciences Series. Amsterdam: IOS Press.

5

UNCOVERING THE DYNAMIC NATURE OF TERRORISM

History of Violence and Change Over Time

Do You Already Know?

- The early history of terrorism
- How terrorism has evolved in other countries
- Ways terrorism impacts the United States
- The differences between traditional and modern terrorism

For additional questions to assess your current knowledge of the dynamic nature of terrorism, go to **www.wiley.com/go/mcentire/ homelandsecurity2e**

What You Will Find Out	What You Will Be Able To Do
5.1 When terrorism emerged	• Synthesize the factors influencing the appearance of terrorism
5.2 The manifestation of terrorism in other countries	• Assess the evolution of terrorism in other countries
5.3 The experience of terrorism in the United States	• Evaluate the impact of terrorism in the United States
5.4 How modern terrorism is different than terrorism of the past	• Judge how terrorism has changed over time

Introduction to Homeland Security: Understanding Terrorism Prevention and Emergency Management,
Second Edition. David A. McEntire.
© 2019 John Wiley & Sons, Inc. Published 2019 by John Wiley & Sons, Inc.
Companion website: www.wiley.com/go/mcentire/homelandsecurity2e

INTRODUCTION

One of the best ways to decrease the probabilities and consequences of terrorism is to understand how it has evolved over time. Terrorism has probably always existed in one form or another, but it has changed throughout history. In this chapter, you will learn how the use of ideology, violence, and fear has impacted the emergence of terrorism. You will then acquire an understanding of the dynamic nature of terrorism around the world and be able to describe the history of terrorism in the United States. Finally, this chapter will help you defend the assertion that terrorism is different today than it was in prior decades. Understanding the dynamic nature of terrorism is imperative for anyone working in homeland security. Recognizing how terrorism has changed over time may help you to anticipate what to expect next in the future.

5.1   THE APPEARANCE OF TERRORISM

Violence with an eye toward creating fear among an enemy has occurred repeatedly throughout history (Chalian and Blin 2007, p. 5). The examples of warriors painting their faces, brandishing weapons, and yelling loudly at their opponents are too numerous to mention. In such cases, this activity could be regarded as effort to intimidate and dissuade the violent intent of the adversary. Averting conflict by having the enemy give up was the goal of engaging in such behavior.

If hostilities did break out, ruthlessness was made painfully evident to illustrate the consequences of combating with the victor. Those from the opposing tribe were killed, and their lifeless bodies were displayed visibly for everyone to see. For instance, bodies were hung in trees and skulls were placed on poles. In addition, homes were burned, property and cattle were taken, women were raped, and children were enslaved. These types of actions were a vivid message regarding the strength of the prevailing party. In this sense, the fear associated with war is somewhat similar to that associated with terrorism. However, the two cannot be considered synonymous.

Violent activities undertaken with the goal of obtaining ideological objectives – which is an integral aspect of terrorism – can be traced back to the Roman and Greek republics (Combs 2000, p. 18). Aristotle was a famous Greek philosopher who lived from 384 to 322 BC He asserted that killing despotic rulers could be justified. If such leaders failed to serve the interests of the people, they should be eliminated. Others felt similarly. For example, when Brutus killed Roman emperor Julius Caesar, Cicero observed: "there can be no such thing as fellowship with tyrants, nothing but a bitter feud is possible ... [Such] monsters ... should be severed from the common body of humanity" (in Griset and Mahen 2003, p. 2). Thus, people have rationalized violence based on their perception of the behavior of others, suggesting that it is "just" and necessary.

In addition, assassinations of political leaders, as the previous paragraph indicates, have been a prevalent form of terrorism throughout history. For example, in 1605, Guy Fawkes was caught in an attempt to murder King James I and other leaders of the British Parliament (Griset and Mahan 2003). The cause of his **"Gunpowder Plot"** was a disagreement between King Henry VIII and Pope Clement VII. King Henry desired an annulment of his marriage to Catherine in order to wed Anne Boleyn. Because the Pope disapproved this request, King Henry denounced Catholicism and created the Church of England. Monasteries were closed and cathedrals were taken over by those loyal to the king. Catholics were suppressed in England and lost their ability to worship as they saw fit.

Fawkes and others were angry with these circumstances. They desired to reinstall the Pope as the religious head of England by blowing up the Palace of Westminster. When the king was notified of the scheme, Fawkes was immediately captured. He and the other conspirators were drawn and quartered by galloping horses in front of the public that gathered at Westminster.

While Fawkes' attempt to kill the king may be regarded as an act of terrorism, the word "terrorism" did not appear until the Enlightenment. The **Enlightenment** was a period in history when a new way of looking at the world emerged. For instance, advances in scientific knowledge offered an alternative to the religious explanations of nature during that period. Improvements in communications and travel increased the sharing of ideas within and across nations. As these and other changes took place, the divine appointment of kings was subsequently questioned. Common people started to demand political rights and freedoms. Democratic governments began to emerge as a result. The feudal economic system gave way to capitalism, and sociopolitical structures were altered. This transformation is evidenced by such events as the movement for independence in the United States (1775–1783) and the French Revolution (1789–1795).

The revolutionary war in North America resulted from the questioning of the religious authority of the King as well as taxation without representation. It was successful in that it only required a transfer of power from the King in England to the elite in America. The ambitions in France were loftier in that middle classes desired to oust reigning nobility. However, those seeking "liberty, equality, and fraternity" could not accomplish their goals. The Jacobin party acquired control of France and began to repel the revolutionary movement. During this period, an estimated 20 000 persons were killed by France's Committee of Public Safety. The state-sponsored violence against its own citizens is what Edmund Burke and others called the **"Reign of Terror."** Marie Antoinette was one of the most notable casualties in this conflict. She was beheaded on 16 October 1793.

Gunpowder Plot:
An attempted terrorist attack in 1605 against King James I and other leaders of Parliament to reinstate Catholic involvement in England.

Enlightenment:
A period in history when a new way of looking at social, political, and economic structures emerged.

Reign of Terror:
A period during the French Revolution where an estimated 20 000 persons were killed by France's Committee of Public Safety.

SELF-CHECK

1. In many ways, violence, fear, and terrorism have always existed. True or False?

2. When did the word "terrorism" appear?

    (a) During Aristotle's time
    (b) In medieval times
    (c) During the Enlightenment
    (d) Long after the American revolutionary war

3. Discuss why Guy Fawkes wanted to kill King James I.

5.2 THE EVOLUTION OF TERRORISM ABROAD

Terrorism has changed dramatically since the Enlightenment. However, the history of terrorism is not simple or linear. Instead, the evolution of terrorism is complex, and numerous manifestations of violent activity have coexisted at times (Chalian and Blin 2007). This history is best understood when considered as an unfolding transformation.

Terrorism took on distinct forms as the nineteenth century got underway. In the late 1700s, Napoleon Bonaparte gained control of France and then began to spread his empire to the rest of Europe. His armies were meticulously trained, sufficiently staffed, and well equipped. Nevertheless, the Spanish attempted to repel Napoleon's invasions in 1808. Hit-and-run tactics were common in this war for liberation. Spanish resistance was aided by the support of the British military.

Nationalist Movements:
Efforts on the part of a group or nation to obtain political independence and autonomy.

Nationalist movements like this have been common in many parts of the world. The associated attacks have had significant and far-reaching impacts. For instance, World War I was triggered on 28 June 1914. A nineteen-year-old member of the Black Hand (a Serbian terrorist organization) opposed the Austro-Hungarian Empire. He was therefore recruited to assassinate the Archduke Franz Ferdinand. Terrorism with nationalistic overtones has been evident in many countries ever since. Numerous terrorist acts have occurred in the Middle East, Ireland, and India. Countless and cruel acts have also been witnessed in the Balkan region (i.e. Yugoslavia) and in African nations (e.g. Rwanda) during the 1990s.

Anarchists:
Those opposing specific governments or all governments.

Anarchists – those opposing specific governments or all governments – also launched numerous terrorist attacks in the 1800s. In Russia, men like Michail Bakunin sought to dismantle the czarist state. He and others disapproved of the government and desired a major transformation of society. As a means to accomplish his goal, Bakunin advocated the selective killing of Russian officials. Sergei Nechaev, another Russian, also recommended that terrorism be used in his publication, *Revolutionary Catechism*. He stated that the anarchist must "have one single thought, one single purpose: merciless destruction. With this aim in view, tirelessly and in cold blood, he must always be prepared to kill with his own hands anyone who stands in the way of achieving his goals" (Venturi 1966, p. 366). In 1879, Zemlya i Volya (a terrorist organization knows as the Will of the People) was created in Russia. This group used terrorism often as a form of political protest against the ruling elite (Combs 2000, p. 25).

In the early and mid-1900s, fascist governments were involved in terrorist attacks against their own citizens. **Fascism** is an ideology that promotes the uniting of citizens in support of the state. It is an extreme right-wing movement aimed at protecting government interests. Fascist regimes existed in Spain under Francisco Franco and Italy under Benito Mussolini. Of course, the most egregious use of force against the populous occurred in Germany. Adolf Hitler killed an estimated six million Jews during the Holocaust. Others, including the Aryan Nations today, have been influenced by Hitler's hatred toward those of Jewish descendants.

In the mid-to-late 1900s, **communism** was a driving force of terrorism. Communism is an ideology that sympathizes with the poor and downtrodden. It attempts to do away with private property and exploitative class relations. Communists have commonly been involved in terrorism in Latin America. During the Cold War, the United States supported many military dictators in an attempt to halt Russian political influence in the area. As a result, many peasants and intellectuals began to attack the governments they saw as illegitimate in the 1960s, 1970s, and 1980s.

One vivid example is from El Salvador. Máximo Hernández ruled with an iron fist and persecuted anyone suspected of having ties with Russia. In some cases, he forced alleged communists to dig ditches that were then filled after their executions. Some historians assert that the US Marines were stationed offshore in case their assistance in the effort was needed. One of the prominent leftists of the time, Farabundo Marti, was put to death during the purge known as the Matanza (the killing). This resulted in the creation of the Farabundo Marti Liberation Front (FMLF). The FMLF was involved in guerilla-type activities in El Salvador until a peace accord was signed with the government in 1992.

Fascism:
An ideology that promotes the uniting of citizens in support of the state.

Communism:
An ideology that sympathizes with the poor and downtrodden and attempts to do away with private property.

Figure 5-1

Many leaders in Latin America have employed terrorist tactics in the name of communism. Source: © US Department of Justice.

There have been many other terrorist organizations that have fought for economic justice including the Zapatista National Liberation Army in Mexico and the Rebel Armed Forces in Guatemala. The Morazanist Patriotic Front, Sandinistas, and Revolutionary Armed Forces were other left-wing terrorist organizations in Honduras, Nicaragua, and Colombia, respectively. Bolivia, Chile, Uruguay, Argentina, and Brazil also witnessed many terrorist attacks in the name of communism. The Shining Path and Tupac Amaru Revolutionary Movement (TARM) have similar ideologies in Peru. They desire to rid their country of outside imperial influence. TARM was responsible for the assassination of General Enrique López Albújar.

In the 1970s and 1980s, state-sponsored terrorism was common in the Middle East (Combs 2000). For instance, Syria provided help for the Marine barracks bombing in 1983. It supported terrorists who delivered a truck bomb against US forces in Lebanon, killing 241 soldiers. This nation was also involved in bombings in France and plane hijackings. It has frequently provided training and safe haven for terrorists operating in the area. In addition to Syria, Sudan has supported many terrorist groups. In the 1990s, it was the home of Osama bin Laden and his followers. Because of international pressure, however, Al-Qaeda was asked to leave this country, and this terrorist organization took up presence in Afghanistan. The Taliban (the ruling government in Afghanistan) then allowed bin Laden to use the country as a terrorist headquarters. In return, bin Laden paid these leaders to permit the organization's presence and operation in this country. Terrorists have often benefited from states that support their ideological objectives. Both terrorists and states in the Middle East oppose Israel and the United States for political and religious reasons.

Islamic Fundamentalists: Individuals or groups of Muslims that violently oppose Israel and the United States.

Today, it is widely held that the major threat of international terrorism comes from radical **Islamic fundamentalists**. Israel has been dealing with such violence for decades, but the groups opposing the Jewish people and the United States have been growing in number, political strength, and operational sophistication. Russia has likewise been dealing with attacks from similar groups who desire independence in Chechnya. There are many other Islamic fundamentalist organizations throughout Africa, the Middle East, and Europe and in nations such as the Philippines and Indonesia. Arab and Muslim extremists are now viewed as the most dangerous terrorists because of events like 9/11, the bombing of trains in Spain in 2004, and the attacks on buses and subways in England in 2005. Such extremists appear to have no reservations dying as martyrs for their cause.

This brief history of terrorism abroad generates at least two lessons for those involved in homeland security. First, terrorism has been manifested in different ways over time. On some occasions, citizens rose up against governments. There have been countless cases where political leaders have been assassinated by those who felt mistreated. Later on, states engaged in terrorism against their own people. Russia, under Joseph Stalin, had a deplorable history of state-sponsored terrorism. The government killed millions of people. So did Cambodia. From 1975 to 1978, it is believed that Pol Pot (the leader of the Khmer Rouge in Cambodia) executed as many as two million people. He accomplished this through executions, starvation, and the grueling conditions of forced labor (Simonsen and Spindlove 2000, p. 227). Terrorism has also been related to nationalistic and communistic movements. States have sponsored terrorist groups over time, and a major threat today emanates from radical Islamic fundamentalists around the world.

A second point to be recognized is that terrorism often breeds violent counterterrorism activity. Terrorism in France, Spain, Russia, Latin America, and other parts of the world often generated long-standing conflicts among those promoting and opposing this violent behavior. For instance, the civil war in El Salvador lasted from 1980 to 1992. It resulted in the death of 75 000 citizens and displaced millions of people. The perception that violence is an effective solution to ideological disagreements cannot always be supported with evidence. In most cases, violence has only brought more problems to those seeking a better way of life. Terrorism creates a cruel cycle of viciousness (Combs 2000, p. 24).

IN THE REAL WORLD

Chechen Terrorism in Russia

When the Soviet Union disintegrated at the end of the Cold War, pent-up ethnic tensions and rivalries began to emerge. Many Chechens disliked Russian involvement in the political decisions that affected them and desired increased independence. In addition, Chechens share greater affinity for Islamic tradition than their Russian counterparts, and this has been a notable source of conflict among the two areas. Because of the continued presence and influence of Russia over the affairs of this nation, Chechens have launched numerous terrorist attacks against them. On 24 August 2004, two passenger aircraft departing from Moscow were blown up in coordinated terrorist attacks. The explosive hexogen was used to bring down the planes. The bombing resulted in the death of over 85 passengers and crew members. It is believed that two females from the Islambouli Brigades and a Chechen field commander were responsible for the attack.

SELF-CHECK

1. World War I was initiated in part due to a terrorist attack. True or False?
2. Which ideology was not involved in the early development of terrorism?
   (a) National liberation
   (b) Anarchism
   (c) Environmentalism
   (d) Communism
3. What are some of the major lessons we learn from terrorism in other nations?

5.3 TERRORISM AND THE UNITED STATES

It is imperative that those involved in homeland security realize that terrorism is not just a foreign problem. In fact, certain historians believe that US citizens and its government have participated in terrorism. For instance, and as mentioned earlier in this book, it is asserted that the tactics used against the British during the American Revolution bear close relation to those of terrorists. Others suggest that the US government sponsored terrorism abroad while it fought communism during the Cold War. As an example, it is alleged that the United States spent $7 million dollars to finance opposition groups to destabilize the leftist government in Chile. The CIA is even reported to have been involved – directly or indirectly – in an attack on Rene Schneider, a commander of the Chilean Army. Evidence also suggests that the United States tried to assassinate Fidel Castro from 1961 to 1962.

Operation Mongoose:
An attempt by the United States to kill Cuban leader Fidel Castro with a poison cigar.

Operation Mongoose, as it was known, involved an attempt to poison the Cuban leader with a cigar. It is believed that the United States tried to hire Castro's former girlfriend to kill him later on. This plot was also unsuccessful. Politicians at the time claimed that Castro was threatening the security of the United States. Cuba had close ties to the Soviet Union, and Castro accepted the placement of Russian nuclear missiles in this Caribbean nation. For these reasons, other scholars argue that the United States was not engaged in terrorism, but was instead involved in violence for geopolitical purposes. This case reiterates that it is not always easy to define terrorism.

The United States may or may not have been involved in terrorism as a participant (depending on your political view). However, this country has definitely been the target of terrorism throughout its history. For instance,

Molly Maguires:
A group of Irish citizens that joined together to dispute the treatment of coal mine workers in the United States.

the **Molly Maguires** was one of the many organizations involved in terrorism in this nation after it was founded. The Mollies, as the organization was commonly known, were a group of citizens that joined together in Ireland to dispute the treatment of tenants by landlords. At times, their protests were violent in nature. In the early 1800s, many members of this group migrated to the United States and settled in Pennsylvania. Feeling that they were being treated unfairly in the coal mines of this area, they began to engage in acts of violence. The Mollies killed many of the mine superintendents in protest. The situation became so bad in the 1870s that Franklin Gowen, president of the Philadelphia and Reading Railroad, told detectives that they were "to remain in the field until every cut-throat has paid with his life for the lives so cruelly taken" (Lejeune 2001, p. 208). Nineteen members of the Molly Maguires were subsequently killed in the late 1800s.

Disputes over workers' rights and compensation also led to additional terrorist acts in large cities across the United States (Lejeune 2001, p. 208). In 1886, labor unions requested an eight-hour work day. They felt the existing and strenuous work hours were unreasonable. As strikes and picketing took place in Chicago, skirmishes broke out among police and rioters. One person was shot and killed in the riot. A few days later, a protest was held to denounce the death. When police tried to disperse the crowd, a bomb was detonated. Eight police officers died in the blast. Explosives were also set off elsewhere to protest political and economic issues. In New York City, a horse-drawn carriage was taken near J.P. Morgan's house. Its deadly cargo killed 35 people and injured hundreds more. The perpetrators, who were believed to have Bolshevist or anarchist leanings, were never apprehended.

Ku Klux Klan (KKK):
A white supremacist group that has been involved in terrorism in the United States since the Civil War.

The **Ku Klux Klan (KKK)**, a white supremacist group, has also been involved in terrorism in the United States. The KKK emerged after the Civil War era (Simonsen and Spindlove 2000, p. 40). It is alleged that six Confederate veterans were talking around a fireplace one night in Tennessee in the late 1800s and decided to create a secret society. After coming to agreement on a name to represent the group, they disguised themselves in sheets and rode through the town on horseback. The regalia they wore gained so much attention that the KKK adopted white hooded clothing as a symbol of the organization. In time, more people joined, and the KKK began to threaten blacks. This behavior was evident during the civil rights movement and again in the early and mid-1990s. Hate speech soon turned to terrorism, and the KKK was involved in "hanging, acid branding, tar-and-feathering, torture, shooting, stabbing, clubbing, firebranding, castration and other forms of mutilation" (Simonsen and Spindlove 2003, pp. 41–42). Thousands of African Americans were killed or attacked by members of the KKK. Fortunately, such activities have waned dramatically in recent years. But this type of activity has yet to be completely eliminated. Small neo-Nazi groups also share much of the ideology of the KKK. They desire to establish a white-controlled government in the United States.

Figure 5-2

The United States has had to deal with terrorist organizations, like the Ku Klux Klan in Madison County, Mississippi. Source: © FBI.

During the 1950s, 1960s, and 1970s, terrorists in the United States also came from the political left. Individuals and groups like Bill Ayers and the Weather Underground Organization identified with Marxist class struggles and desired equal rights. The terrorists planted bombs in public areas, police stations, and military bases (Griset and Mahan 2003, p. 87). They also protested the Vietnam War. Others, like the Symbionese Liberation Army (SLA), had utopian visions for society. This organization desired a unified populous based on cooperative economic institutions. The SLA was responsible for several bank robberies, kidnappings, and assassinations. The **Black Panthers**, in contrast, sought revenge for the mistreatment of African Americans by the KKK. Their activities have become less notable over time, although there was a resurgence of violence at the end of the twentieth century. They remain active today due to recent police shootings in the United States. It was asserted that Black Panthers may have also intimidated voters at one polling place in the 2012 elections.

Black Panthers:
An organization composed of African Americans to revenge the actions of the KKK and other white supremacists.

In the 1970s and early 1980s, much of the terrorist activity in the United States came from Puerto Rican terrorists. The **Armed Forces of National Liberation (FALN)** emerged in 1974. The goal of this insurgency was to obtain liberation of Puerto Rico, and its supporters were willing to utilize violent means if necessary. The FALN was responsible for at least 100 bombings in the United States in the mid-to-late 1970s. Since that time, many other Puerto Rican groups formed and launched attacks against the United States. "Between 1982 and 1994, approximately 44 percent of terrorist incident committed in the United States and its territories are attributed to Puerto Rican terrorist groups" (Lejeune 2001, p. 211).

Armed Forces of National Liberation (FALN):
A Puerto Rican terrorist organization seeking liberation of Puerto Rico from the United States.

In the 1980s and 1990s, terrorism was associated with many different advocacy issues. Some right-wing terrorist organizations opposed the government. They disliked taxes as well as US involvement in the United Nations. Other conservative groups wanted to protect individual rights to own firearms, or they opposed Jews and homosexuals. People like Eric Rudolph have been involved in terrorism for these reasons and to stop abortions. For instance, Rudolph bombed abortion clinics and the Olympic Park in Atlanta during the 1996 summer games. Numerous people were killed or injured as a result.

There are also terrorists who used violence in the 1990s to promote animal rights or environmental conservation. Examples include the **Animal Liberation Front** and the **Earth Liberation Front**. For instance, terrorists attacked research facilities that conduct tests on animals. The perpetrators are concerned about cruel procedures in meat packing facilities as well. Auto dealers have also been targets of arson and bombings because of the low gas mileage of their trucks and SUVs. New neighborhood developments have likewise been vandalized or set ablaze to discourage the destruction of forests (for wood) or the expansion of urban sprawl. Sadly, "Earth Now, one militant environmental group in the United States rationalized that, if it was necessary to kill people to save the trees, then they would be justified in killing people" (Combs 2000, p. 43).

Animal Liberation Front:
A terrorist organization that opposes cruelty to animals.

Earth Liberation Front:
A terrorist organization that opposes environmental degradation.

All of these cases illustrate that the United States has been affected by terrorism long before the first World Trade Center attack in 1993, the bombing of the Murrah Federal Building in 1995, or the 9/11 attacks in 2001. It is also evident that terrorists in the United States come from diverse ideological interests as well. These facts illustrate the complicated nature of terrorism in our modern era.

SELF-CHECK

1. The United States is not believed to have been involved in terrorism. True or False?
2. The Black Panthers may have emerged due to the activities of the KKK. True or False?
3. Which terrorist organization emerged due to concerns over workers' rights?
    (a) Molly Maguires
    (b) The KKK
    (c) The Armed Forces of National Liberation
    (d) Animal Liberation Front
4. Explain how terrorism has manifested itself in different ways over time in the United States.

5.4 TERRORISM TODAY

Another important requisite to effectively deal with terrorism is to be aware of how different current terrorist activity is as compared with that of the past (Rubin and Rubin 2008). In recent years, notable alterations in the manifestation of terrorism have become evident. Scholars such as Veness (2001), Hoffman (2001), Kegley (2003), and Jenkins (2008) have explored how terrorism has changed over time. They cite numerous examples of significant alteration, including the following:

- In the past, terrorists were organized hierarchically. Organizations such as the PLO often had a clear leader and an identified chain of command. *More recently, terrorists around the world (like Al-Qaeda) organize in a diffuse manner and are cell oriented.* A cell is a semiautonomous terrorist organization that may be loosely affiliated with other terrorist groups. Current terrorism therefore resembles a network of many groups that operate in a loosely coordinated fashion. In other words, direction among terrorists may or may not always emanate from a central headquarters.
- Terrorists were frequently supported by states in prior years. Governments like Libya or Syria provided sanctuary and financial assistance

to those engaging in terrorism. Many terrorists, such as Hamas and Hezbollah, continue to work closely with Iran now. However, *several terrorist organizations have become more independent in terms of raising funds*. For instance, Aum Shinrikyo, a Japanese terrorist group, acquired money through religious and corporate donations. They launch attacks with or without approval from governments even if they sanction such behavior.

- In former years, it was also easier to distinguish between crime and terrorism. The differences between theft and assassinations were more readily apparent. *Currently, it is more challenging to make a distinction between criminal and terrorist activities*. Many terrorist groups rely on crime to raise money, and some organizations that were founded on terrorist aspirations now promote extortion for financial gain (e.g. left-wing groups in Latin America or the Philippines).

- In the past, citizens of the United States typically regarded terrorism to be a problem in a very limited geographic area. Terrorism has traditionally been viewed as a feature of the Middle East or, to a lesser extent, Europe. Nonetheless, terrorism has been prevalent in the United States throughout its history, and 9/11 and recent attacks brought the reality of international terrorism home. Terrorism is also making significant headway in South Asia and even Australia. No place appears to be immune.

- Historically, terrorists desired goals such as liberty, national independence, or political stability. They used violence as a way to promote freedom or strengthen government control over the masses. *At the moment, the mission of terrorists is more messianic in orientation*. There is a desire to "save" the world from abortions, environmental degradation, or the evils of Western civilization. Extreme Christian groups and the Environmental Liberation Front come to mind as examples of these types of terrorist organizations. Of course, each of these groups has their own strategies and tactics to obtain their messianic objectives. As an example, the approach of ISIS today is based firmly on providing inspiration to those who may join their cause.

- Terrorists were somewhat cautious about their statements in the past and did not always want to take responsibility for their harsh words or activities. They may have tried to avoid being ridiculed or held accountable for their actions. *Terrorists have more vocal and defiant attitudes today*. While all terrorists are not alike, many publicly denounce their enemies and are eager to take credit for their violent and disruptive behavior. ISIS is one of many organizations that publicly denounce the United States as the "great Satan." This group did not hesitate to acknowledge its role in violent behavior.

- Twenty years ago, terrorists desired to share their ideological goals and messages with the public at large. *More recently, terrorists such as Hamas or Hezbollah give greater attention to sharing their message in detail to their sympathizers*. Their goal is to improve recruitment for sustained operations. Terrorists recognize that they need continual backing if they are to be successful in the future.

- Since its birth, terrorism has largely been related to the assassination of specific leaders for clearly defined purposes. By "taking out" individual politicians (e.g. Yitzhak Rabin), the hope was to advance a particular political or ideological agenda. *Today, terrorists are increasingly willing to target citizens.* The belief is that citizens will cave into terrorist's demands due to fear, which will allow terrorist's to pursue their desires and ambitions.

IN THE REAL WORLD

The Brutality of ISIS

The Islamic State of Iraq and Syria (ISIS) is a radical militant group well known for its strict opposition to the Western world and its ruthless efforts to establish a caliphate based on fundamental Sunni Islamic principles. ISIS is also referred to as the Islamic State of Iraq and the Levant (ISIL) or simply the Islamic State. The group originally emanated from Al-Qaeda in 1999, and Abu Musab al-Zarqawi was its first leader. He professed his allegiance to Osama bin Laden in 2004 and was later killed by US forces. Abu Bakr al-Baghdadi is the current leader of ISIS, and he has continued the legacy of carnage.

ISIS is notorious for its brutality toward others who do not share their same beliefs and ideologies. Mass bombings, shootings, beheadings, and additional types of executions are common and are frequently recorded to be shared publicly. For example, in June of 2014, the group shared a series of tweets and photos on social media claiming to have mass executed 1700 Iraqi soldiers. In January of 2015, the terror cell imprisoned a pilot from Jordan, trapped him in a cage, doused him with gasoline, and burned him alive while the entire incident was captured on video. In June of that same year, ISIS released a video showing a cage full of spies slowly being lowered into a swimming pool to drown the victims. In August of 2016, ISIS publicly executed nine youth by tying them to a pole and then sliced them in half with an electric chainsaw.

On many occasions, members of ISIS have thrown men off of tall buildings because of their sexual orientation. ISIS has also been known to stone homosexuals and adulterers to death. Other forms of torture include everything from starving prisoners or boiling them alive. When taking over new territory, ISIS often takes females and uses them as sex slaves. In other situations, children are kidnapped, forced to learn Islamic beliefs, and used as informants or soldiers. The regime has also used sulfur mustard, sarin nerve, and chlorine gases as chemical weapons. In another instance, ISIS put "infidels" in a car and then launched a rocket-propelled grenade at it. The video was uploaded to the Internet for all to see. These horrendous tactics are utilized with the intent to incite terror and cause as many casualties as possible.

Figure 5-3

Coalition forces attacking ISIS – one of the most brutal terrorist organizations in the world. Source: © Shutterstock. Reproduced with permission of Shutterstock.

- Terrorists have always been willing to kill others when it advances their cause. Violence was seen as a "logical" means for goal attainment. While terrorists have periodically engaged in suicide attacks, the practice has been given more legitimacy in the late 1900s and early 2000s. *Terrorists from the Middle East and elsewhere are increasingly willing to kill themselves in the process of taking the lives of others.*

- Terrorist activities in the past were relatively small and isolated. Attacks killing more than a handful of individuals were, for the most part, rare. *Terrorism, especially international terrorism, is more deadly today.* Many attacks kill dozens of people, and there are others that have extinguished the life of hundreds and even thousands. Terrorism in Africa, the 9/11 attacks, and events in Spain, Russia, England, and France all suggest more deaths as compared with the past.

- Terrorist attacks a few decades ago were relatively simple and limited in terms of impact. A conventional explosive was used to kill the occupants of a single building. In contrast, *terrorists today employ novel techniques in attacks, and their objectives are more grandiose.* Planes are used as missiles (e.g. 9/11), and vehicles are employed to run over innocent bystanders (e.g. England and the United States). Terrorists also intentionally disrupt urban infrastructure and love to produce adverse effect on the economy.

- Terrorists in earlier decades were relatively easy to track down and capture. They were not always careful about their communications and were less than meticulous in leaving evidence that could be used for prosecution. *Terrorists are now more elusive.* They utilize technology (e.g. calling cards or the Internet) to minimize detection. They blend into the community or hide in countries with weak governments and in isolated areas that cannot be reached effortlessly. As an example, Osama bin Laden operated from remote locations in Afghanistan and Pakistan. Terrorists' obscure activities create serious challenges for those trying to thwart terrorism.

As a participant in homeland security, you should be aware of these changes and their potential impact on your profession. It is imperative that you recognize that terrorism is not static, but is instead ever changing and likely to morph in unique ways in the future. You must anticipate unprecedented and more consequential attacks from diverse terrorist organizations. Uncertainty and complexity are the characteristics of terrorism today.

IN THE REAL WORLD

Terrorism and Technology

Terrorists now increasingly exploit technology to carry out their attacks (Thetford 2001). In 1998, the Tamil Tigers sent repeated e-mails to the Sri Lankan embassies to disrupt the activities of this government. During the Gulf War in 1990, "High Tech for Peace," a group of Dutch hackers, asked Iraqi agents if they would pay $1 million to disrupt communications among bases in the United States and military units in Saudi Arabia. There have been other instances of foreigners or high school students accessing sensitive computers (e.g. 911 systems, NASA, and Pentagon). Many terrorist groups also use encryption techniques on the Internet to hide their secret communications. James Kallstrom, a chief of engineering at the FBI laboratory in Virginia, states that "In the old days . . . Fort Knox was the symbol of how we protected things of great value: we put them in buildings with thick walls and concrete. We put armed guards at the doors, with sophisticated multiple locks and locking bars. We could even build a moat and fill it with alligators ... [Today] we are not equipped to deal with ... [cyber-terrorism], both in the government and [in] private industry" (in Thetford 2001, pp. 243–244).

SELF-CHECK

1. Terrorists today are always organized hierarchically. True or False?
2. Terrorism is a problem in the Middle East only. True or False?
3. Which is not a feature of modern terrorism?
    (a) Terrorists are individually sponsored.
    (b) Terrorists attack key individuals only (e.g. politicians).
    (c) Terrorists work harder to recruit members.
    (d) Terrorism is more complex today than in the past.
4. List three ways that terrorism has changed in recent years.

SUMMARY

In this chapter, you have been exposed to the dynamic history of terrorism. You have gained a better comprehension of why terrorism emerged initially. The chapter illustrates how terrorism evolved in other nations and how it has been manifest in the United States as well. In addition, you have increased your knowledge about the differences between terrorism in the current century and that of the past. If you are to be successful in minimizing the possibility and effects of future attacks, it is imperative that you acknowledge that terrorism changes over time.

ASSESS YOUR UNDERSTANDING

UNDERSTAND: WHAT HAVE YOU LEARNED

Go to **www.wiley.com/go/mcentire/homelandsecurity2e** to assess your knowledge of the dynamic nature of terrorism.

SUMMARY QUESTIONS

1. The fear created by warriors painting their faces, brandishing weapons, and yelling loudly at their opponents is similar to the creation of fear associated with terrorism. True or False?

2. The word "terrorism" appeared during the Enlightenment. True or False?

3. Communism is an ideology that sympathizes with the poor and downtrodden. True or False?

4. Some elements of the Black Panthers have become increasingly threatening if not violent. True or False?

5. Operation Mongoose was an attempt to assassinate Saddam Hussein. True or False?

6. The Ku Klux Klan was formed in Tennessee. True or False?

7. A cell is a completely autonomous terrorist group with no affiliation to other terrorist groups. True or False?

8. Anarchists are those people who:

   (a) Want a communist nation

   (b) Oppose specific governments or all governments

   (c) Fight for a democratic state

   (d) Think that government is not doing enough

9. Syria is known for all of the following except:

   (a) Being sympathetic to US Marines

   (b) Bombing barracks in Lebanon

   (c) Bombings in France

   (d) Plane hijackings

10. Which of the following individuals was not in some way associated with of the "Gunpowder Plot?"

    (a) Pope Clement VII

    (b) King Henry VIII

    (c) Sarah Elizabeth

    (d) Anne Boleyn

11. The following groups or individuals were a part of the "Reign of Terror" except:

(a) The Jacobin party

(b) Marie Antoinette

(c) France's Committee of Public Safety

(d) The Spaniards

12. The Molly Maguires were:

(a) A Scottish group opposed to the religious state

(b) An American group opposed to immigration

(c) An Irish group supporting the elite of Ireland

(d) An Irish group that disputed the treatment of tenants by landlords

13. Which of the following groups set fire to ski resorts in Colorado?

(a) Earth Liberation Front

(b) Black Panthers

(c) Molly Maguires

(d) The Armed Forces of National Liberation

14. All of the following are characteristics of today's terrorist groups except:

(a) Some rely on crime for money.

(b) Terrorism is only considered a feature of the Middle East.

(c) The practice of suicide attacks is seen as more legitimate by many terrorists.

(d) Terrorist activity is carried out on a larger scale.

APPLYING THIS CHAPTER

1. How did the Enlightenment change the way people saw their role in society? How did it change the way they viewed their leaders? What is one reason for the increased violence and the creation of the term "terrorism" during the Enlightenment?

2. Describe the difference between the violence mentioned in the first section of the chapter and the terrorist attacks we see today.

3. The chapter makes clear the fact that terrorism is employed by groups acting against established organizations and by groups connected with government organizations. Why is it important that we understand both kinds of terrorism? Provide one example of a terrorist group rising against an established organization or government and one example of a terrorist group supported by a government organization.

4. There are several examples of different terrorist groups that have acted within the United States. What common threads run throughout these groups? Why is it important to understand these commonalities?

5. This chapter lists twelve ways in which terrorism has changed and evolved. Why is it important for those working in homeland security to understand these changes? What does the evolution of terrorism tell us about terrorism in the future?

BE A HOMELAND SECURITY PROFESSIONAL

The Emergence of Terrorism

You are an historian who has been hired as a consultant by the CIA. Your job is to write a two-page brief about the birth of terrorism. What could you say about the emergence of terrorism and its manifestations in the 1700s and 1800s?

History of Terrorism Abroad or in the United States

Write a three-page paper describing the evolution of terrorism abroad or in the United States. Be sure to describe how it has changed over time.

Differences Between Modern and Traditional Terrorism

As a local emergency manager or employee in homeland security, your job is to anticipate terrorist attacks in your community. Could the knowledge about the differences between modern and traditional terrorism help you in your job? How so?

KEY TERMS

Anarchists	Those opposing specific governments or all governments
Animal Liberation Front	A terrorist organization that opposes cruelty to animals
Armed Forces of National Liberation (FALN)	A Puerto Rican terrorist organization seeking liberation of Puerto Rico from the United States
Black Panthers	An organization composed of African Americans to revenge the actions of the KKK and other white supremacists
Communism	An ideology that sympathizes with the poor and downtrodden and attempts to do away with private property
Earth Liberation Front	A terrorist organization that opposes environmental degradation
Enlightenment	A period in history when a new way of looking at social, political, and economic structures emerged
Fascism	An ideology that promotes the uniting of citizens in support of the state
Gunpowder Plot	An attempted terrorist attack in 1605 against King James I and other leaders of Parliament to reinstate Catholic involvement in England

Islamic fundamentalists	Individuals or groups of Muslims that violently oppose Israel and the United States
Ku Klux Klan (KKK)	A white supremacist group that has been involved in terrorism in the United States since the Civil War
Molly Maguires	A group of Irish citizens that joined together to dispute the treatment of coal mine workers in the United States
Nationalist movements	Efforts on the part of a group or nation to obtain political independence and autonomy
Operation Mongoose	An attempt by the United States to kill Cuban leader Fidel Castro with a poison cigar
Reign of Terror	A period during the French Revolution where an estimated 20 000 persons were killed by France's Committee of Public Safety

REFERENCES

Chalian, G. and Blin, A. (2007). *The History of Terrorism: From Antiquity to Al Qaeda*. Berkeley, CA: University of California Press.

Combs, C.C. (2000). *Terrorism in the Twenty-First Century*. Upper Saddle River, NJ: Prentice Hall.

Griset, P.L. and Mahan, S. (2003). *Terrorism in Perspective*. Thousand Oaks, CA: Sage Publications.

Hoffman, B. (2001). Change and continuity in terrorism. Studies in Conflict and Terrorism 24: 417–428.

Jenkins, B.M. (2008). The new age of terrorism. In: *Weapons of Mass Destruction and Terrorism* (ed. R.D. Howard and J.J.F. Forest), 23–31. New York: McGraw Hill.

Kegley, C.W. Jr. (2003). *The New Global Terrorism: Characteristics, Causes, Control*. Upper Saddle River, NJ: Prentice Hall.

Lejeune, P.H.B. (2001). History and anatomy of terrorism. In: *Terrorism: Defensive Strategies for Individuals, Companies, and Governments* (ed. L.J. Hogan), 203–238. Frederick, MD: Amlex, Inc.

Rubin, B.M. and Rubin, J.C. (2008). *Chronologies of Modern Terrorism*. Armonk, NY: Routledge.

Simonsen, C.E. and Spindlove, J.R. (2000). *Terrorism Today: The Past, The Players, the Future*. Upper Saddle River, NJ: Prentice Hall.

Simonsen, C.E. and Spindlove, J.R. (2003). *Terrorism Today: The Past, The Players, The Future*. Upper Saddle River, NJ: Prentice Hall.

Thetford, R.T. (2001). The challenge of cyberterrorism. In: *Terrorism: Defensive Strategies for Individuals, Companies, and Governments* (ed. L.J. Hogan), 239–257. Frederick, MD: Amlex Inc.

Veness, D. (2001). Terrorism and counterterrorism: an international perspective. Studies in Conflict and Terrorism 24: 407–416.

Venuri, F. (1966). *Roots of Revolution: A History of the Populist and Socialist Movement in the Nineteenth Century*. New York: Norton.

6

EVALUATING A MAJOR DILEMMA
Terrorism, the Media, and Censorship

Do You Already Know?

- How the media has changed over time
- Why terrorists use the media
- If the media benefits from terrorism
- Why the portrayal of terrorism is important to government officials
- The drawbacks of media censorship

 For additional questions to assess your current knowledge of the dilemmas associated with terrorism, the media, and censorship, go to **www.wiley.com/go/mcentire/homelandsecurity2e**

What You Will Find Out	What You Will Be Able To Do
6.1 How reporting is different today than in the past	• Comprehend the features of modern news coverage
6.2 Why the media is utilized by terrorists	• Predict advantages terrorists receive from media publicity
6.3 What the media gains from terrorist activity	• Evaluate reasons for media coverage of terrorist attacks
6.4 If the government is concerned about the reporting of terrorist attacks	• Assess why reporting is of concern to government officials
6.5 Why censorship is to be avoided	• Critique the possibility of media self-censorship in the United States

Introduction to Homeland Security: Understanding Terrorism Prevention and Emergency Management,
Second Edition. David A. McEntire.
© 2019 John Wiley & Sons, Inc. Published 2019 by John Wiley & Sons, Inc.
Companion website: www.wiley.com/go/mcentire/homelandsecurity2e

INTRODUCTION

An important way for you to reduce the impact of terrorism is to comprehend the role of the media in publicizing and perhaps even facilitating this type of violent activity. You must evaluate how the media has changed over time, as well as understand the complicated relationships among terrorists and the media. It is also imperative that you recognize what the government desires from the media in addition to the drawbacks of censorship or self-censorship. Finding an appropriate way to deal with the media is one of the greatest challenges facing you and others in homeland security.

6.1 CHANGES IN THE MEDIA OVER TIME

To adequately grasp the nature of terrorism today, it is imperative that you recognize how the media has changed over time. Up until the mid- or late 1700s, there were no unofficial outlets for news. Information was distributed (and sometimes even created) by the king or political party in power. This resulted in a great deal of control over people's perspectives. News also traveled slowly as it was transmitted by horse, rail, or telegraph. The dissemination of news was thereby severely limited due to geographical distance. The lack of education also constrained the demand for information. People could not always read or understand what was being distributed.

Although authoritarian governments still control information in certain countries around the world today, things have changed dramatically for the media over the past few centuries and even in recent decades

Figure 6-1

News can be quickly broadcast around the world with modern technology. Source: © Getty Images. Reprinted with permission of Getty Images.

(Hoffman 1998, p. 136). The establishment of democratic governments and the rise of capitalism have resulted in the appearance of additional news sources. Media organizations now determine what the news is and convey it to an increasingly educated public citizenry. Furthermore, technological innovations have reduced the time it takes to share information around the world. Television, cable TV, satellite dishes, Internet, e-mail access, and cell phones with cameras have revolutionized the media. Getting news to the public once took months, weeks, or days. Now, the sharing of information is measured in hours, minutes, or seconds. News that was only given to people in large urban areas and developed communities is now accessible to anyone around the world. With the advent of the Internet, even citizens are able to become an online journalist (Mahan and Griset 2013). Social media applications like Instagram, Twitter, and Facebook are allowing people to relay news events around the world in minutes. Such changes have had dramatic consequences. On the positive side, we are more aware of what is going on, and we can share information quickly with one another. On the negative side, new technologies and the media can be fully exploited by terrorists.

 SELF-CHECK

1. Prior to the 1800s, most news came from the king or ruling elite. True or False?

2. Information traditionally traveled slowly around the world because of limitations in travel or communications. True or False?

3. What type of technology has not transformed the media in recent years?

   (a) Television
   (b) The typewriter
   (c) Satellite dishes
   (d) The Internet

4. What are the pros and cons of the modern media?

6.2 TERRORISTS AND THE MEDIA

It is increasingly accepted as fact that terrorism and the media have an extremely close relationship (Mahan and Griset 2013; Nacos 2016). Indeed, terrorists are heavily dependent on the media in our modern era. To realize their ideological goals, terrorists want to increase legitimacy for their cause, shock as many people as possible, and instill widespread fear. Terrorists also want to augment visibility (for monetary support and recruiting purposes) and destabilize the enemy (by illustrating that the government cannot cope effectively with attacks). In the mind of terrorists, the best way for them to reach their desired objectives is to rely on the assistance of reporters.

Black September:
An operational unit of the Al-Fatah terrorism organization that initiated the terrorist attacks on Israeli athletes at the Munich Olympic Games in 1972.

One of the most well-known examples of this occurred during the 1972 Munich Olympics. In an attempt to reverse real or perceived injustices against Palestinians, **Black September** – an operational unit of the Al-Fatah terrorism organization – launched an attack against Israeli athletes participating in the international games (Simonsen and Spindlove 2000, p. 140). Decrying the eviction of the PLO from Jordanian training camps in September 1970, Abu Iyad (the head of the Palestinian intelligence network) and his followers entered the Olympic Village and immediately killed two members of the Israeli team. Using the threat of AK-47 assault rifles to keep remaining the hostages at bay, the terrorists then demanded the release of 234 Palestinians held in Israeli jails. The large global audience tuned into the Olympics became very interested in the unfolding drama. Terrorists thought this would be the best method to put intense pressure on the Israeli government and cause them acquiesce their demands. The Jewish people gained sympathy from those watching the event, and the state of Israel decided not to release the prisoners. Nevertheless, government leaders in this country did allow the terrorists to fly by helicopter to Furstenfeldbruck Airport. Even though these and other terrorists were hunted down and killed, this event illustrated the potential impact of the media in negotiations.

Since this time, the media has increasingly been seen as an important tool at the disposal of terrorists. For instance, after taking hostages at

Figure 6-2

The media was used extensively by terrorists in the 1972 Olympics.
Source: © Popperfoto/Getty Images. Reproduced with permission of Getty Images.

OPEC headquarters in Vienna in 1975, Carlos "the Jackal" waited for the media to arrive before exiting the building with the oil ministers he kidnapped (Hickey 1976, p. 6). Another case is also illustrative. While 52 American hostages were being held at the American Embassy in Tehran in 1979, the mob outside only began to shake their fists, burn flags, and denounce President Carter when a Canadian broadcasting company showed up at the scene (Hoffman 1998, p. 142). In order to increase public relations, the Irish Republican Army "historically included close relationships with the print and broadcast media" (Martin 2003, p. 281). Ted Kaczynski likewise sent his 35 000-word manifesto against technology to the *Washington Post* and *New York Times*. This document denouncing economic development and the US government was published in 1995 (Griset and Mahan 2003, p. 132).

Osama bin Laden also used the media to promote Al-Qaeda's wishes. In the late 1990s, bin Laden was interviewed by Western reporters. He told them that America would be attacked if it did not withdraw its troops from the Middle East and stop supporting puppet governments in the area. On 9/11, Al-Qaeda relied on the morning news broadcasts and large international media organizations in New York to publicize the lengths it was willing to go to force the United States to cave in to its demands. In recent years, bin Laden and ISIS leaders have encouraged sympathizers to acquire weapons of mass destruction and use them against Americans or their interests, regardless of their location around the world. Thus, it is evident that the media is viewed as significant means for reaching terrorist aims.

Brian Jenkins, a well-known RAND Corporation researcher, states, "terrorists want a lot of people watching and a lot of people listening …. Terrorists choreograph dramatic incidents to achieve maximum publicity, and in that sense, terrorism is theater" (1985, p. A4). He also asserts,

IN THE REAL WORLD

Terrorism on TV

On 14 June 1985, three Lebanese terrorists hijacked TWA Flight 847 from Athens to Rome. The plane was initially then flown to Beirut, and it then made several trips between Lebanon and Algeria. During the 16-day ordeal, nearly 500 reports on nightly news programs (CBS, ABC, NBC) were devoted to the event. The terrorists skillfully used the media to publicize their cause, and they even attempted to charge networks for a tour of the plane and interviews with them. The broadcasts ended up, creating enough pressure on the US government that it negotiated with the terrorists. Everyone on board the plane was released when 756 Shi'a terrorists were freed from prison in Israel. Gus Martin believes "the hijackers masterfully manipulated the world's media" (2003, p. 294).

"terrorism is violence for effect – not primarily, and sometimes not at all for the physical effect on the actual target, but rather for its dramatic impact on an audience" (Jenkins 1985, p. 101). Others agree with Jenkins. For instance, Walter Laqueur believes the "media are a terrorist's best friend." Frederick Hacker declares emphatically that if the mass media organizations did not exist, "terrorists would have to invent them!" (see Combs 2000, p. 128).

SELF-CHECK

1. The media helps give terrorists visibility. True or False?
2. Osama bin Laden did not speak with Western media because he regarded them to be infidels. True or False?
3. Which terrorist attack was among the first to exploit international media?
    (a) Tehran hostage crisis
    (b) The OPEC hostage crisis
    (c) The Munich Olympic massacre
    (d) 9/11
4. Why is the media regarded to be the terrorist's "best friend?"

6.3 THE MEDIA AND TERRORISM

The media has a very complicated relationship to terrorism (Eid 2013). On the one hand, the media may not report terrorist attacks to shape the political narrative regarding this phenomenon. At a 2017 speech to the military at MacDill Air Force Base, President Donald Trump decried "fake news" and asserted that the dishonest press does not want to relay to the public what is actually happening. The argument is that the media is typically liberal and wants to avoid social discrimination, harsh interrogation practices, and covert military operations. After Trump's speech, the White House released a list of 78 attacks carried out by ISIS that were underreported by the media. While the media has probably downplayed terrorist attacks to protect Muslims and promote interests of the Democratic Party (e.g. lax immigration security), this has not always been the case.

The media can also be obsessed with terrorism at times, and this could have an impact on such behavior. According to former British Prime Minister Margaret Thatcher, the media provides "the oxygen of publicity on which [terrorists] depend" (in Hoffman 1998, p. 142). The media also stands to gain much from terrorists and their ideologically motivated attacks. In particular, the media desires to make "the news entertaining enough to 'sell' " (White 2002, p. 257).

Fortunately for the media, terrorist attacks offer a dramatic presentation that keeps viewers riveted. Terrorism is associated with violence, heroic responses, and unusual consequences. These are only a few of the features that keep people glued to their television, encourage them to stay tuned to the radio, or impel them to return over and over to the Internet or newspaper. Ratings are also important to the media, and, therefore, reporters exploit terrorism to its advantage. In other words, the media broadcasts terrorist attacks to maintain or increase their standings in the competitive news world.

Of course, the media does present timely portrayal of the news to keep society informed of important events (Perl 1997, p. 7). The media may also play a positive role in the resolution of some terrorist conflicts. For instance, in one case, hostages felt that reporters kept politicians interested in their plight until their situation could be peacefully resolved (Hoffman 1998, p. 147). Media involvement in terrorism is not without drawbacks, however.

One of the major problems created by the media concerns their interference in counterterrorism operations. For instance, as the ATF was making final preparations to raid the Branch Davidian compound in Waco, Texas, because of illegal weapons violations, the media told David Koresh of the impending plans. This intensified the Branch Davidian's fear of the government and may have augmented the violence that broke out on 28 February 1993. Ten people (both ATF agents and Branch Davidians) died during the exchange of gunfire, and this outbreak of violence resulted in a 51-day standoff between the two opposing parties. Another 79 Branch Davidians died when federal law enforcement agencies launched tear gas into the building and Davidian leaders ordered fires to be lit in the compound.

Figure 6-3

Aerial view of Branch Davidian compound near Waco, Texas, in flames on 19 April 1993 following a 51-day siege by the FBI and law enforcement. Source: © FBI.

Another excellent case in point concerns the Hanafi siege that occurred in Washington, D.C., from 9 March to 11 March in 1977 (Combs 2000, pp. 135–136). Twelve gunmen took over three buildings in an attempt to force the release of convicted murderers and protect the name of the Prophet Mohammad. In the process, 2 people were killed and another 149 were taken hostage. During the ordeal, the media complicated negotiations with the terrorists. One reporter who communicated with the terrorists said the police were preparing to attack. Another called the terrorist leader and stated that the police were trying to trick him. This terrorist then selected 10 hostages for execution. The assailant did not carry through with the threat, however, because the police agreed to defuse the situation by removing sharpshooters from nearby buildings. Nevertheless, the participation of the media slowed down and even reversed negotiations. One of the hostages (who also happened to be a reporter) said this about the media's mistakes during the take-over:

> As hostages, many of us felt that the Hanafi takeover was a … high impact propaganda exercise programmed for the TV screen, and for the front pages of newspapers around the world. Beneath the resentment and the anger of my fellow hostages toward the press is a conviction gained that the news media and terrorism feed on each other, that the news media and particularly TV, create a thirst for fame and recognition. Reporters do not simply report the news. They help create it. They are not objective observers, but subjective participants (Schmid and de Graff 1982, p. 172).

Besides complicating negotiations and rescues, the media may also exacerbate terrorism or attacks in other ways. For instance, by giving terrorists airtime, reporters may help the terrorists appear more powerful they actually are. In addition, continued coverage of terrorist attacks could create emotional problems for viewers. As an example, numerous children suffered from nightmares after repeatedly witnessing the World Trade Center towers collapse in media reports after 9/11. TV stations stopped airing this footage as a result. Furthermore, the media may use terrorist attacks to advance a political agenda. Reporters frequently criticized George W. Bush for his aggressive foreign policy in the Middle East. Whether justified or not, the media seemed to very critical of the decisions made under President Bush and insinuated that his actions were aggravating the ongoing conflict.

Alex Schmid offers other perspectives about the negative impact of the media on the occurrence of terrorist attacks:

Social Learning Theory:
Observing terrorist attacks in the news may generate similar type of behavior among others.

Disinhibition Hypothesis:
Violence portrayed by the media may weaken the inhibition of others to participate in terrorism.

Arousal Hypothesis:
Media reports on terrorism can increase people's interest in acting aggressively.

- **Social learning theory.** Observing terrorist attacks in the news may be the first step in generating similar type of behavior among others (e.g. people learn from what they see).

- **Disinhibition hypothesis.** Violence portrayed by the media may weaken the reticence of others to participate in terrorism (e.g. people become immune to the violence of terrorism).

- **Arousal hypothesis.** Media reports on terrorism can increase people's interest in acting aggressively (e.g. terrorism may be seen as a legitimate way to accomplish goals).

Built-in Escalation Hypothesis:
More deadly and visible attacks are required to get equal media coverage in the future.

• **Built-in escalation hypothesis.** More deadly and visible attacks in the future are required to get the same amount of media coverage as in the past (in Combs 2000).

The point to remember is that the media has a complicated relationship with terrorism and that attacks can be magnified if reporting occurs in a careless way.

IN THE REAL WORLD

The *Achille Lauro* Incident

In 1985, the Palestine Liberation Front hijacked an Italian cruise ship, the *Achille Lauro*. Their goal was to exchange passengers for 50 Palestinian terrorists imprisoned in Israel. During the incident, terrorists killed a man who was confined to a wheelchair and dumped his body into the Mediterranean Sea. The United States announced a $250 000 reward for anyone who could provide information that would lead to the arrest of the leader Abul Abbas. The government struggled in its attempt to bring Abbas to justice. However, the media was able to contact him for an exclusive interview on NBC's news program. Although some viewed the interview as tasteless, others claimed it was indeed of interest to the American people. This was an excellent case of the symbiotic relationship among terrorists and the media (Hoffman 1998, p. 144).

SELF-CHECK

1. The Hanafi hostage crisis illustrates how the media worked to effectively deal with terrorism. True or False?

2. Social learning theory implies that people will mimic the behavior they see on TV. True or False?

3. Which of the following concepts describes why people become complacent about terrorism in the media?

   (a) Social learning theory
   (b) Disinhibition hypothesis
   (c) Arousal hypothesis
   (d) Built-in escalation hypothesis

4. Explain why terrorism is appealing to the media and those interested in the news.

6.4 GOVERNMENT AND THE MEDIA

According to an editorial in the journal *Terrorism and Political Violence*, "the relationship between publicity and terror is indeed paradoxical and complicated. Publicity focuses attention on a group, strengthening its morale and helping to attract recruits and sympathizers. But publicity is pernicious to the terrorist groups as well. It helps an outraged public to mobilize its vast resources, and produces information that the public needs to pierce the veil of secrecy all terrorist groups require" (Rapoport 1996, p. viii). This complex relationship is convoluted further because the government also has an interest in using the media to counterterrorism and its impacts.

The government may take special interest in the media so it can portray itself in the best possible light with the public. This was probably the case with President Barack Obama and some of his senior leadership. Three situations revealed that his foreign policy and the war on terrorism were not as successful as he seemed to imply. First, the **Arab Spring** – a series of uprisings and armed rebellions that spread across the Middle East in 2010 and 2011 – revealed that radicalization was becoming more commonplace in that part of the world. This radicalization seemed to be downplayed in the media. Second, after four Americans were killed in Benghazi, Libya, Susan Rice (a National Security Advisor) went on five Sunday morning news programs to claim that the deaths were a spontaneous demonstration against a hateful video posted on YouTube. However, Libya President Mohamed Magariaf claimed the event was preplanned and the fact that the perpetrators had rocket launchers calls into question this assumption at least to some degree.

Third, the rising number of terrorist attacks abroad and at home indicated that not enough was being done to counter such violent extremism. Instead of acknowledging and addressing this problem, President Obama implied that the situation was improving, and he ironically called ISIS the "JV Team." This caused many to question the Administration's policies. After a string of attacks occurred in the United States, Michelle Malkin wrote a scathing article entitled "Where Was President Obama?" This political commentator asserted that instead of tackling the problem, the President was "Sabotaging our borders, restricting our gun rights, working to free Gitmo Jihadists, decrying Islamophobia, demonizing conservatives, welcoming jihad sympathizers to the White House and putting politics over national security" (Malkin 2014). This issue indicates that the government may try to spin what is happening and that reporters may question these types of assumptions and assertions.

Arab Spring:
A series of uprisings and armed rebellions that spread across the Middle East in 2010 and 2011.

IN THE REAL WORLD

Fort Hood Shooting

Nidal Hasan carried out a mass shooting against military personnel at Fort Hood, Texas, on 5 November 2009. Hasan shouted "Allahu Akbar!" (meaning "Allah is great!" in Arabic) as he opened fire at the Soldier Readiness Center. The shooting killed 13 people and injured 32 others. Hasan was shot in the incident and ended up becoming paralyzed from the waist down. Evidence later revealed that Hassan corresponded with an Al-Qaeda supporter and became radicalized. Hasan was later convicted in the trial and sentenced to death.

President Barack Obama originally claimed the shooting was workplace violence, which caused public outrage. People believed the President cast the event this way to maintain a perception that he was effective in his efforts to deal with terrorism. Because of this stance, victims were not awarded Purple Heart medals (military decoration given to those wounded or killed while serving in the military). In November of 2011, survivors and other family members of the Fort Hood shooting filed a lawsuit against the US government. The victims and relatives reprimanded the government for not taking sufficient actions to prevent the attack and demanded that it be classified as terrorism.

In December of 2014, Congress issued new legislation in the National Defense Authorization Act. The new provision now treats military personnel who are killed or wounded in domestic terrorist attacks in the same manner as those who are targeted during foreign military campaigns. The Fort Hood tragedy was also reclassified as domestic terrorism, and victims were subsequently awarded either Purple Hearts or the civilian equivalent (i.e. Defense of Freedom medals). President Obama did not begin to publicly regard the shooting as an act of terrorism until some five years later. However, when President Obama gave his farewell address in January 2017, he again reiterated that no attacks by terrorist organizations occurred in the United States during his time in office. This clear exaggeration is a striking example of how government leaders may use the media to advance their political agenda or attempt to protect their legacy.

Raphael Perl, a specialist in foreign affairs, believes that the government has several requests of the media before, during, and after terrorist attacks (1997, pp. 5–6). Government leaders generally desire to do the following:

1. Gain information about possible terrorist attacks (if those plans exist).
2. Separate the terrorists from the media in order to deny them a public platform.
3. Obtain information about terrorists if the media is aware of the location where hostages are being kept.
4. Have the media present terrorists as criminals who devalue life and ignore international or national law.
5. Diffuse the crisis through the accurate dissemination of public information, rather than contribute to an already tense situation.
6. Avoid emotional stories as media reports may place extreme pressure on officials to negotiate with terrorists.
7. Withhold information that may notify terrorists of pending counterterrorism or rescue operations.
8. Avert the sharing of details about intelligence gathering or successful operations.

9. Seek media cooperation in holding back evidence that could be used for future prosecution.

10. Boost the image of their agencies by controlling leaks to the press and avoiding undue criticism.

As can be seen, the government is at times concerned about the media's involvement in terrorism. This is because "terrorists learn their tactics and copy methods from the mass media. Media coverage also serves as a motivation for terrorism. The most serious outcome is that violence seems to increase during media coverage. The mass media have become the perfect instrument of violent communication" (White 2002, p. 262). How can this major problem be addressed? Two choices are available, but neither is totally desirable nor achievable. The first is to have the government censor the media. The second is to have the media control the content of its own broadcasts.

SELF-CHECK

1. The relationship between terrorism and the media is straightforward. True or False?

2. Which is not a reason why the government is concerned about the media's reporting of terrorism?

    (a) The government does not want the media to make money.
    (b) The media could share evidence that might hurt the prosecution of terrorists.
    (c) The media may have information about forthcoming terrorist attacks.
    (d) Emotional stories could cause officials to react to terrorism prematurely.

3. Why would the government worry if the media discusses intelligence operations?

6.5 CENSORSHIP AND SELF-CENSORSHIPS

Censorship:
The withholding, banning, or altering of information the media shares with the public.

One of the ways to limit the negative aspects of media coverage is to implement some form of government censorship. **Censorship** is the withholding, banning, or altering of information the media shares with the public. Censorship is forbidden by law in the United States. In fact, the First Amendment to the Constitution states that "Congress shall make no law … abridging the freedom of speech, or of the press." Nevertheless, there have been cases where censorship has occurred in our nation's history and elsewhere around the world. During World War II, the amount and type of information about the conflict was controlled by the government. This had the purpose of maintaining unity at home and obfuscating Germans' understanding about US war plans. Also, in the first Gulf War, the US government denied immediate access of reporters in war zones (presumably for their own safety). Britain has been particularly adept at restraining media coverage of terrorism. On various occasions, the media in the United Kingdom was forbidden to broadcast interviews or statements by members of the Irish Republican Army.

While this type of censorship is extremely controversial, some scholars suggest that restrictions on news coverage may be necessary in emergency conditions. "Lives hang in the balance during hostage crises …. Reporting and the freedom to report are not the only critical concerns in such crises: The impact of the media on the event, and media interference with police operations, have also become central issues" (White 2002, p. 263).

The proposal for censorship is far from being accepted, however. Besides being in conflict with our democratic ideals for government, censorship probably does nothing to stop terrorist activity. In fact, prohibiting the freedom of speech or of the press may actually augment terrorism. This is because people will not have a voice to express concerns about government policies or highly contentious debates. Citizens have shown a tendency over time to engage in violence if they feel their political values are not being heard or heeded by elected officials. Chechen rebels feel, for example, that Russia has limited their freedom over the press. Although censorship is possible to some degree and at different times, it will probably never occur completely in the West because of our interest in a free society.

The other option for dealing with terrorism is to have the media take more stringent measures to control their reporting of news to the public. In some ways, **self-censorship** is in the interest of news organizations. Terrorists often see reporters as pawns of their enemies and therefore seek to silence their opposition to terrorist ideology and violent behavior. Also, killing reporters is an additional way that terrorists spread fear among the population.

Self-censorship:
Media control over their reporting of news to the public.

Reporters participate in a very dangerous profession. The Committee to Protect Journalists says 110 reporters were killed around the world in 1994 (Marks 1995). While a portion of these deaths were due to accidents, most resulted from assassinations. Hot spots for attacks against journalists include countries such as Algeria, Nigeria, Russia, Turkey, Syria, and Zaire. Drug cartels in Mexico and Colombia are also quick to kill journalists who point out corruption in the government. Reporters and media organizations are also targeted in the United States. A week after the 9/11 attacks, a deranged individual sent letters laced with anthrax spores to Tom Brokaw as well as ABC News, CBS News, the *New York Post*, and the *National Enquirer*. Although Brokaw was not harmed, 5 people died and 17 others were infected by the disease.

Daniel Pearl:
A reporter with the *Wall Street Journal* who was killed by terrorists in Karachi, Pakistan.

One of the most notable cases of such attacks involved **Daniel Pearl**. Pearl was a reporter with the *Wall Street Journal*. He was investigating Richard Reid (the shoe bomber) and possible ties with Al-Qaeda and Pakistan's intelligence service. On 23 January 2002, Pearl went to interview a suspected terrorist. In the process, a group calling itself the National Movement for the Restoration of Pakistani Sovereignty kidnapped Pearl. They demanded, among other things, the release of terror detainees in Guantanamo Bay, Cuba. The terrorists also stated that they would kill Pearl if the United States did not meet their request. On 1 February 2002, Khalid Sheikh Mohammed decapitated Pearl in Karachi, Pakistan. Pearl's death

Figure 6-4

Journalists are often killed or held hostage by terrorist organizations.
Source: © Shutterstock. Reproduced with permission of
Shutterstock.

was captured on video and released with the comment that such actions would occur repeatedly if the United States did not give in to the terrorists' request. The media refused to air this brutal murder and the demands of the terrorists. In time, Ahmed Omar Saeed Sheikh and three other suspects were captured. They were charged with murder in March 2002.

Unfortunately, most of the slayings of reporters remain unsolved crimes. In Latin America, it is estimated that "95 percent of the 155 killings, 1109 known beatings, 49 kidnappings, and 205 terrorist acts against media installations ... tallied ... have gone unpunished" (Marks 1995, p. 9). Other media personnel are frequently threatened verbally or jailed for long periods of time. As an example, China has more journalists in prison than any other Asian country. Attacks against journalists continue in the Middle East to this day.

With the above in mind, one would assume that reporters and media organizations would want to limit their involvement in controversial subjects like terrorism. This is surprisingly not the case. The media wants desperately to protect citizens' right to public information. In addition, a failure to report the news results in lower ratings in a very competitive media market. Although committees among media organizations have been and can be formed to monitor news reporting, disagreement about what should or should not be reported is also frequent.

Reporters therefore do their job in spite of potential threats or disagreement about content. Horria Saihi, an Algerian TV producer, stated, "I know what awaits me in the end is a bullet in the head, but what kills me more is censorship. That would be symbolic death" (Marks 1995, p. 9). Others agree that any form of censorship is an attack on liberty. Cindy Combs states, "[w]hen a democratic society, in panic and anger, abandons one of the cherished principles of law that make it democratic, the society has inflicted on itself a greater wound than the terrorists could achieve, were they to bomb a hundred buildings" (2000, p. 131). Knowing what to do in regard to the media's involvement in terrorism remains problematic at best.

IN THE REAL WORLD

The Case of Terry Anderson

Terry Anderson was a reporter stationed in Beirut in 1985. He was snatched from his car and held for seven years by Islamic fundamentalists. When freed, he later stated, "[i]f there ever was a sense that journalists should be given some sort of immunity, it is long gone" (Marks 1995, p. 1). As Anderson's comments indicate, reporters recognize that they may be kidnapped, beaten, or killed for their comments about terrorism. Unfortunately, terrorists intentionally target the media to maximize publicity of their cause or change the way they are presented in the news.

SELF-CHECK

1. Amendments to the constitution protect freedom of the press. True or False?

2. Censorship has never occurred in democratic countries. True or False?

3. Which reporter was kidnapped and killed in Pakistan?
   (a) Richard Reid
   (b) Daniel Pearl
   (c) Tom Brokaw
   (d) Dan Rather

4. Why would the media want to censor its reporting of terrorist activity?

SUMMARY

One of the greatest dilemmas you will face in homeland security is in regard to the relationship between terrorism and the media. Because the media can relay information around the world in a matter of minutes, you should be aware of the reasons why terrorists desire to publicize their activities through reporters. However, the media also benefits from terrorist attacks because of the nature of such stories and high viewer ratings. Meanwhile, the government desires to alter how terrorism is reported to discredit terrorists or maintain their popularity. For this reason, you may need to monitor the information you give the media during a terrorist attack. You should also be aware of the drawbacks and limitations of censorship so you do not aggravate incentives for violent behavior.

ASSESS YOUR UNDERSTANDING

UNDERSTAND: WHAT HAVE YOU LEARNED

 Go to **www.wiley.com/go/mcentire/homelandsecurity2e** to assess your knowledge of the dilemmas associated with terrorism, the media, and censorship.

SUMMARY QUESTIONS

1. News that once traveled slowly can now be transmitted around the world in minutes or seconds. True or False?

2. One of the reasons why terrorists want to have media coverage is to show the inability of government to deal with their attacks. True or False?

3. Red October is the name of the terrorist group that killed Israeli athletes in the 1972 Olympic Games in Germany. True or False?

4. Terrorism is regarded to be "theater" because it is directed toward an audience and not just actual victims. True or False?

5. The media has no interest in terrorist attacks. True or False?

6. People are interested in terrorist attacks because of their drama and suspense. True or False?

7. The government wants the media to portray terrorists as criminals. True or False?

8. Censorship is the withholding, banning, or altering of information the media shares with the public. True or False?

9. We are likely to see full censorship of the media in the future in the United States. True or False?

10. Which terrorist sent a manifesto to the media to complain about modern technology?

    (a) Osama bin Laden

    (b) Timothy McVeigh

    (c) Ted Kaczynski

    (d) Khalid Sheikh Mohammed

11. Which of the following was not one of Osama bin Laden's demands issued through the media?

    (a) Withdraw US troops from the Middle East

    (b) Limit pollutants into the environment

    (c) Stop supporting corrupt puppet governments

    (d) Have Muslims acquire and use nuclear weapons against the United States

12. If a terrorist is successful in reaching his or her goals with the help of the media, others may be likely to engage in similar behavior. This is known as:

    (a) The arousal hypothesis

    (b) The disincentive hypothesis

    (c) The built-in escalation hypothesis

    (d) The inflammatory hypothesis

13. Why is the government interested in how the media conveys news about terrorism?

    (a) Because terrorists do not care about media reports about attacks

    (b) Because the government can never provide any details about what is happening

    (c) Because censorship is the best way to protect the security of the United States

    (d) Because the media can contribute to an already tense situation

APPLYING THIS CHAPTER

1. Explain why terrorists are able to have an impact on countries far away from the actual attack. Be sure to list at least three reasons.

2. Many scholars, including Brian Jenkins, state that "terrorism is theater." What is meant by this comment? How do terrorists use "theater" to get their message across?

3. What were some of the problems created by the media during the Hanafi siege? How was this resolved?

4. Raphael Perl states that the government is interested in media reporting of terrorism for at least 10 reasons. List three of them.

5. Censorship of the media is a controversial strategy for dealing with terrorism. Explain why this is the case, and be sure to discuss advantages and disadvantages of the curtailing of news information to the public.

BE A HOMELAND SECURITY PROFESSIONAL

Covering a Terrorist Attack

You are a reporter for CNN. You have just been notified that a terrorist is holding hostages in a shopping mall in Phoenix, Arizona. The terrorist group called you to ask someone to relay their grievances. They decry US involvement in the United Nations and are threatening to kill people if international policies are not reconsidered. Would your boss want you to conduct the interview? Are there any drawbacks of doing so? If so, what are they?

Public Information Officer

As the public information officer for the Department of Homeland Security, your job is to ensure that the government's perspective of terrorism is shared with the media. A bomb has just been detonated in California, and an environmental group is claiming responsibility for the destruction at a petrochemical plant. What are some of the issues or comments you would like the media to address as they cover this attack?

Your Views About Censorship

Write a two-page paper about censorship of the media in relation to terrorist activity. Be sure to discuss why some form of censorship might be considered, as well as its advantages and disadvantages.

KEY TERMS

Arab Spring	A series of uprisings and armed rebellions that spread across the Middle East in 2010 and 2011
Arousal Hypothesis	Media reports on terrorism can increase people's interest in acting aggressively
Black September	An operational unit of the Al-Fatah terrorism organization that initiated the terrorist attacks on Israeli athletes at the Munich Olympic Games in 1972
Built-in Escalation Hypothesis	More deadly and visible attacks are required to get equal media coverage in the future
Censorship	The withholding, banning, or altering of information the media shares with the public
Daniel Pearl	A reporter with the *Wall Street Journal* who was killed by terrorists in Karachi, Pakistan
Disinhibition Hypothesis	Violence portrayed by the media may weaken the inhibition of others to participate in terrorism
Self-censorship	Media control over their reporting of news to the public
Social Learning Theory	Observing terrorist attacks in the news may generate similar type of behavior among others

REFERENCES

Combs, C.C. (2000). *Terrorism in the Twenty-First Century*. Prentice Hall: Upper Saddle River, NJ.

Eid, M. (2013). The new era of media and terrorism. *Studies in Conflict and Terrorism* 36 (7): 609–615.

Griset, P.L. and Mahan, S. (2003). *Terrorism in Perspective*. Thousand Oaks, CA: Sage.

Hickey, N. (1976). Terrorism and television. *TV Guide* (31 July). Radnor, PA.

Hoffman, B. (1998). *Inside Terrorism*. New York: Columbia University Press.

Jenkins, Brian. (1985). Terrorism found rising, now almost accepted. *Washington Post* (3 December), p. A4.

Mahan, S. and Griset, P.L. (2013). *Terrorism in Perspective*. Thousand Oaks, CA: Sage.

Malkin, M. (2014). Where was President Obama. *Real Clear Politics* (24 October). http://www.realclearpolitics.com/articles/2014/10/24/where_was_president_obama_124411.html (accessed 22 June 2016).

Marks, A. (1995). Reporters at risk: war and lawlessness increasingly turn foreign correspondents into targets." *Christian Science Monitor* (10 November), pp. 1, 10–11.

Martin, G. (2003). *Understanding Terrorism: Challenges, Perspectives and Issues*. Thousand Oaks, CA: Sage.

Nacos, B.L. (2016). *Mass-Mediated Terrorism: Mainstream and Digital Media in Terrorism and Counterterrorism*. Lanham, MD: Rowman & Littlefield Publishers, Inc.

Perl, R.F. (1997). Terrorism, the media, and the government: perspectives, trends, and options for policy makers. Volume 97, Issue 960 of CRS Report for Congress. Library of Congress. Congressional Research Service, Library of Congress. Foreign Affairs and National Defense Division

Rapoport, D. (1996). Editorial: the media and terrorism: implications of the unabomber case. *Terrorism and Political Violence* 8 (1): viii.

Schmid, A.P. and de Graff, J. (1982). *Violence as Communication: Insurgent Terrorism and the Western New Media*. Beverly Hills, CA: Sage.

Simonsen, C.E. and Spindlove, J.R. (2000). *Terrorism Today: The Past, The Players, The Future*. Prentice Hall: Upper Saddle River, NJ.

White, J.R. (2002). *Terrorism: An Introduction*. Thomson/Wadsworth: Belmont, CA.

CHAPTER 7

CONTEMPLATING A QUANDARY
Terrorism, Security, and Liberty

Do You Already Know?

- The difference between terrorism and war
- Why security and freedom are important
- How terrorist attack prevention can impact liberty
- If rights can be protected in spite of terrorism

 For additional questions to assess your current knowledge of the relationship of terrorism to security and liberty, go to **www.wiley.com/go/mcentire/homelandsecurity2e**

What You Will Find Out	What You Will Be Able To Do
7.1 How terrorism is unlike traditional combat operations	• Appraise how security and liberty may be at odds with one another
7.2 Why security and freedom are vital but competing priorities	• Argue why security is necessary
7.3 Ways that liberty is adversely impacted by efforts to prevent terrorist attacks	• Evaluate reasons why more people are concerned about liberty today
7.4 How to ensure rights while promoting homeland security	• Predict ways to secure the nation against terrorism while also maintaining rights

Introduction to Homeland Security: Understanding Terrorism Prevention and Emergency Management,
Second Edition. David A. McEntire.
© 2019 John Wiley & Sons, Inc. Published 2019 by John Wiley & Sons, Inc.
Companion website: www.wiley.com/go/mcentire/homelandsecurity2e

INTRODUCTION

One of the major difficulties you will have in homeland security concerns the proper relationship between security and liberty. You must be able to make and implement decisions that will minimize terrorist attacks while also protecting values that are desired in democracies such as the United States. It is vital that you understand international law relating to conflict. You must also be able to critically evaluate the probability of terrorism and estimate the negative impact that counterterrorism and antiterrorism policies may have on rights and freedoms. Above all, you must select policies that limit the threat of terrorism but protect liberty as a cherished principle. These issues are addressed in the chapter that follows.

7.1 WAR, TERRORISM, AND LAW

All countries want to ensure their security from external or internal threats. Such dangers may come from enemy nations or from those within the country who would subvert or overthrow political leaders. If the government is unable to successfully defend itself or its citizens from these aggressors, it could logically cease to exist. All other goals – such as education, health care, and economic prosperity – would be jeopardized. For this reason, government leaders declare the need to recognize potential enemies and, if required, take measures to protect their people and way of life. Not all threats are alike however. War and terrorism both involve violent behavior, but these types of conflict are distinct in fundamental ways.

Fighting in traditional conflicts (e.g. nation against nation) poses a difficult challenge, but the enemy is typically identified and known. In most cases, the government of the opposing forces issues a formal statement of war, the enemy engages in visible conflict, and soldiers are clearly marked with their own matching uniforms. The location of the battle is also distinguishable, and efforts usually follow Geneva Convention rules. The

Geneva Conventions:
A set of internationally accepted laws pertaining to the conduct of war.

Geneva Conventions are a set of internationally accepted laws pertaining to the conduct of war. They were initiated in Europe by Henry Dunant in 1863 after he witnessed the depressing lack of medical treatment for wounded soldiers at the Battle of Solferino in 1859. He believed both sides of any conflict have a responsibility to care for the injured. Dunant was responsible for the initial development of international law pertaining to the humane treatment of soldiers.

Since this time, the conventions have undergone numerous changes. One of the most notable revisions of the Geneva Convention occurred after World War II. The United Nations felt that citizens should not be targeted in war because they have no way of protecting themselves (e.g. weapons, training, armor, etc.). Signatory nations therefore established moral guidelines to limit the most disturbing aspects of war. Nearly 200 countries have declared their support of the Geneva Convention that prohibits attacks on civilians.

Terrorism is unlike the national conflicts mentioned above. First, the perpetrator of a terrorist attack is not always distinguishable from others.

Terrorists may be foreigners or citizens of the targeted country. Second, terrorists do not typically wear uniforms that identify themselves and denote their intent to engage in conflict. Instead, they may be dressed as an ordinary person in order to carry out their attacks in a covert manner. Third, terrorists may or may not provide advanced notice of their intent to attack. They are far more likely to engage in violence and then claim responsibility afterward. Terrorists also disregard other aspects of the Geneva Conventions. Although terrorists may kill soldiers in attacks, they also prefer to target civilians in order to increase fear and publicity. It is this aspect that makes terrorism so deplorable.

The unique attributes of terrorism present other major challenges to democratic governments and the law under which they operate. One of the greatest struggles facing those involved in homeland security is to protect the United States from terrorism while also maintaining the rights we enjoy (Demmer 2004). It is argued that "the Constitution weighs heavily in both sides of the debate over national security and civil liberties" (Rosenzweig 2006, p. 1020). The President and Congress must take steps to protect the

Figure 7-1

The US Constitution promotes both liberty and security concerns.
Source: © National Archives.

nation against terrorist attacks. In addition, these leaders are also obligated to implement policies that do not infringe upon citizens' freedoms.

Some scholars and practitioners see little or no conflict between these important priorities. For instance, K. A. Taipale states:

> Within the public discourse, concerns about domestic security and civil liberties are often asserted as competing and potentially incompatible policy interests requiring the achievement of some tolerable state of balance. Implicit in this notion of balance is the smuggled assumption of a dichotomous rivalry in which security and liberty are traded one for another in a zero-sum political game. But the notion is misleading, for there is no fulcrum – as is implicitly in the metaphor of a balance – at which the correct amount of security and liberty can be achieved. Rather, security and liberty are dual obligations of civil society, and each must be maximized (2006, p. 1009).

Others, however, are quick to point out that security and liberty are conflicting goals rather than values that can be achieved in harmonious fashion. Justin Hood observes that "our history has shown us that insecurity threatens liberty. Yet if our liberties are curtailed, we lose the values that we are struggling to defend" (Murphy 2006, p. 1047). Jonathan White asks a question that may be difficult to answer: "is there a point where civil liberties can be curtailed in the name of public safety?" (White 2002, p. 275). These issues and inquiries illustrate there is an uneasy relationship among security and liberty (Gaughan 2015). Unfortunately, "terrorism exploits this tension" (Badey 2008, p. 123).

SELF-CHECK

1. War and terrorism are alike in almost every way. True or False?
2. The Geneva Convention is a law that prohibits terrorism specifically. True or False?
3. The Constitution:
   (a) Ignores security
   (b) Supports liberty only
   (c) Sees security and liberty as important priorities
   (d) Denounces liberty
4. As a type of conflict, what are the unique attributes of terrorism?

7.2 SECURITY AND LIBERTY

One school of thought asserts that security is an extremely important goal (or perhaps the most important objective) for any government. People holding this view acknowledge that national protection has become even more vital after the attacks against the United States in 2001. For instance, a spokeswoman for the Department of Justice stated that "Sept. 11th has forced the entire government to change the way we do business …. Our No. 1 priority right now is to prevent any further terrorist attacks" (in Griset and Mahan 2003, p. 285).

Others provide evidence of the current scope of the threat and indicate that terrorism is becoming more severe over time. Rosenzweig's research reveals:

- 70 000 terrorists were trained in Afghanistan before the United States deposed the Taliban.
- The State Department has compiled a list of at least 100 000 known terrorists around the world.
- Jemaah Islamiyah, a terrorist organization in Indonesia, has 3000 members and it is still growing.
- As many as 5000 Al-Qaeda operatives could be present in the United States.
- "Virtually every terrorism expert in and out of government believes that there is a significant risk of another attack" (2006, p. 1022).

Furthermore, views favoring security recognize the negative impact of terrorism. It seems as if more and more people are willing to engage in terrorism and groups like ISIS are increasingly passionate about their violent goals. Because of the possibility of acquiring weapons of mass destruction, terrorists today may develop the ability to kill hundreds, thousands, or even millions of people. Attacks will adversely affect the economy and disrupt our way of life in the process as well.

IN THE REAL WORLD

Ibrahim al-Qosi

Ibrahim al-Qosi was a jihadist leader who served as a cook, accountant, and chauffeur to Osama bin Laden. He was captured by US troops in Afghanistan in December 2001. Shortly thereafter, al-Qosi was detained at the Guantanamo Bay prison for more than 10 years – most of this time without any formal charges. The United States returned al-Qosi to Sudan in 2012 following his guilty plea to war crimes in 2010.

The hope was that al-Qosi would mend his ways and avoid a return to terrorist activity. Unfortunately, al-Qosi reemerged in a video released by the Guardians of Sharia group in December of 2015. The propaganda included his biography and showed al-Qosi and other commanders of Al-Qaeda in the Arabian Peninsula (AQAP) encouraging jihadist attacks against the United States and other Western countries. As a high-profile leader, al-Qosi's recidivism sparked a lot of controversy, and some US leaders questioned whether he should have been released in the first place. This case illustrates the potential danger in releasing terrorists since the rate of recidivism is disappointing. For example, at least 235 prisoners engaged in terrorism after being released from Guantanamo Bay. The actual rate of recidivism is difficult to calculate with certainty, but is probably between 15 and 30%. The al-Qosi case illustrates the tension between security and legal rights.

Along these lines, another assertion is that taking drastic measures to counterterrorism may be unavoidable. One intelligence chief for the Department of Homeland Security believes "things are changing, and this change is happening because [attacks] can be brought to us that we cannot afford to absorb. We can't deal with them, so we're going to . . . do something ahead of time to preclude them. Is that going to change your lives? It already has" (Murphy 2006, p. 1047). In this light, combating terrorism is seen as a crucial moral responsibility – perhaps a goal that is even more important than other government goals or the protection of civil liberties. It is better to forego a few rights, the argument goes, instead of suffering the negative consequences of terrorism. This is especially the case if the reduction of liberties occurs internationally and if the associated actions are effective (Garcia 2016).

Others disagree vehemently with this point of view. It is reported that Ben Franklin once stated that those who give up liberty for security deserve neither. His assertion is that the loss of rights would inevitably lead to insecurity and only stable governments can be established and maintained when citizens' liberty is guaranteed. Under this perspective, our rights are as valuable – or even more important – than security itself.

People who adopt this viewpoint feel that the government has gone too far in its attempt to ensure security against terrorism (Demmer 2004, p. 149). Some even assert that fewer rights in the name of security will produce more terrorist attacks (Dragu 2016). For instance,

Figure 7-2

Ben Franklin declared that those who give up liberty for security deserve neither. Source: Oil on canvas painting by Joseph Siffred Duplessis (1725–1802).

- "Critics of the government's ... policy have long argued that lawmakers overrate terrorist threats to achieve their political goals, with the result that civil liberties are sacrificed" (Griset and Mahan 2003, p. 282).

- Profiling is commonly described as one action that is inherently discriminatory. "**Profiling** is defined as the practice of law enforcement officials (including security personnel) using race, ethnicity, religion, or national origin as the decisive factors in targeting an individual for suspicion of a wrongdoing" (Starks 2008, p. 241). However, profiling was very effective in helping to find out who the Unabomber was.

Profiling
Profiling is defined as the practice of law enforcement officials (including security personnel) using race, ethnicity, religion, or national origin as the decisive factors in targeting an individual for suspicion of a wrongdoing.

- Many people today are concerned about the collection of **metadata**. Metadata includes information gathered from communication through electronic devices. Besides the content of such messages, it includes phone numbers, e-mail addresses, the device used, and electronic service provider. Other examples of metadata are automated license plate recognition systems and digital photography in public places. People worry that this private information is being collected about them and given to others without permission.

- A movement has emerged that might be called anti-antiterrorism. Its argument is that certain steps being taken domestically to prevent potential terrorist attacks are too intrusive and threaten civil liberties (Rosenzweig 2006, p. 1013).

- The American Civil Liberties Union (ACLU) states, "If we give up our freedoms, the terrorists win" (Murphy 2006, p. 1047).

As can be seen, many people assert that the government has gone too far in the war against terrorism. The argument in favor of rights has therefore gained a great deal of attention since the attacks on 9/11. However, Paul Rosenzweig, an adjunct professor at George Mason University, lists several reasons why it cannot be blamed solely on the aftermath of 9/11. He states that the liberty view has become more popular for six reasons:

1. **A more activist court.** The judicial system in the last 40 years has tended to overturn executive branch actions and congressional decisions.

2. **A more partisan Congress.** Congressional investigative authority has expanded oversight of the President's power.

3. **Investigative journalism.** Reporters have increasingly focused on activities that some might want to keep out of the public light.

4. **Public interest groups.** Organizations like the ACLU are heavily involved in public information and litigation actions.

5. **Technology.** Computers and the Internet have augmented people's ability to monitor the government.

6. **Greater awareness of civil liberties.** Citizens are more educated about rights than ever before.

Thus, the perspective favoring liberty downplays the focus on security and remains a popular paradigm to this day.

IN THE REAL WORLD

Physical Security vs. Civil Liberties

Paul Rosenzweig, an adjunct professor in the George Mason University School of Law, states that some people believe physical security is becoming more important than civil liberties (2006, p. 1023). He uses a hypothetical case of placing 10 alleged terrorists in prison. In the past, people in the United States generally accepted the rule that it is "better 10 terrorists go free than one innocent be mistakenly punished." Today, because of the high costs of terrorism, more people believe it is better to punish 10 alleged terrorists even if only one of them is actually guilty. This is because the potential for a terrorist attack increases if the guilty are released back into the general population. Such cases show the difficulty of balancing security and liberty in the United States.

SELF-CHECK

1. There are less than 10 000 terrorists around the world. True or False?
2. Some people believe that security is more important than liberty, but others believe the reverse is also true. True or False?
3. Ben Franklin stated:
   (a) Lawmakers exaggerate the threat of terrorism.
   (b) If we give up our liberties, the terrorists win.
   (c) Combating terrorism is a crucial moral responsibility.
   (d) Those who give up liberty for security deserve neither.
4. Explain why the anti-antiterrorism movement has gained momentum in recent years.

7.3 CASES AND CONSIDERATIONS

As can be seen, people feel strongly about both security and liberty. At times, these political values have been in direct conflict with one another. By trying to ensure security, policy makers have implemented decisions that have had dramatic repercussions on liberty. Rosenzweig (2006) and Griset and Mahan (2003) provide several examples from history:

- When the Civil War broke out in the United States, President Abraham Lincoln declared that anyone guilty of disloyal practices would be imprisoned. Those convicted could not seek redress through the **writ of habeas corpus** (i.e. there was no way to protect citizens from unlawful imprisonment).

Writ of Habeas Corpus:
A law protecting citizens from unlawful imprisonment.

- During World War I, over 2000 people were locked up because of their opposition to the global conflict. This eliminated virtually all antiwar sentiment in the United States, but it also jeopardized free speech.

Figure 7-3

During World War II, over 100 000 people of Japanese descent were
relocated to detention centers due to security concerns.
Source: © Library of Congress.

- After Pearl Harbor was attacked at the commencement of World War II,
  President Franklin D. Roosevelt signed Executive Order 9066. This allowed
  him to gather more than 110 000 people of Japanese descent and "relocate"
  them in detention centers in the Western Pacific region of the United States.
  This occurred even those individuals were American citizens.

- In 1953, Senator Joseph McCarthy raised fear of Russian infiltration into
  the United States. Under the banner of the "**Red Scare**," his permanent
  investigations subcommittee sent numerous Hollywood directors and actors to prison for alleged involvement in communism.

Red Scare:
Senator McCarthy's fear
of communist infiltration
into the United States.

Freedom of speech:
People are allowed to
express their opinions,
even when they criticize
the government.

Freedom of religion:
People cannot be denied
their right to worship
according to the dictates
of their own conscience.

Right to assemble:
People are permitted to
join in politically
motivated gatherings.

Right to bear arms:
Guns can be purchased
and owned without
government interference.

Such incidents have led Geoffrey Stone to suggest that "in time of war …
we respond too harshly in our restriction of civil liberties, and then, later,
regret our behavior" (in Rosenzweig 2006, p. 1017).

Liberty may also be limited or curtailed in other ways when terrorism is
taken into account. For example, citizens of the United States are guaranteed:

- **Freedom of speech.** They are allowed to express their opinions, even
  when they criticize the government or others.
- **Freedom of religion.** They cannot be denied their right to worship according to the dictates of their own conscience.
- **Right to assemble.** People are permitted to join in politically motivated
  gatherings.
- **Right to bear arms.** Guns can be purchased and owned without government interference.

While these are all liberties that Americans enjoy and desire to protect, they
do present thorny questions for those engaged in creating homeland security

policies. For instance, what if people are inciting terrorist attacks as they talk to others? What should be done with a religious group that advocates violent behavior? What if meetings have the purpose of planning attacks? What if weapons will be used by terrorists to kill others?

The rights upheld by American political values could therefore run counter to efforts to stop terrorism. Again, these issues bring up difficult questions. Should liberties be curtailed to promote security? Or, must liberty be treasured more than security? These are not just historical, hypothetical, or philosophical predicaments. We are facing very difficult choices today regarding security and liberty. A variety of recent examples can be given:

- After 9/11, the federal government immediately began to investigate the status of immigrants and visitors in the United States. Over 1000 foreigners (mostly from Arab and Muslim nations) were detained, and some of them were charged for involvement in the attacks on America, for their expired visas, or for miscellaneous violations (e.g. traffic tickets). Although this action may have prevented other attacks, some people suggest that the racial profiling and subsequent detentions were illegal (Griset and Mahan 2003, p. 285).

- As US forces captured Taliban soldiers and Al-Qaeda members in Afghanistan, they sent many of them to prisons at Guantanamo Bay, Cuba (Mahan and Griset 2013). Many of these individuals were held for indefinite periods without being charged of formal crimes. If evidence warranted further investigation, prisoners were tried in military tribunals that lacked juries and civilian oversight. These efforts have limited the number of "enemy combatants" around the world, but seem to reject our own laws pertaining to illegal seizures and fair trials.

- The State of Florida declined to issue a driver's license to a woman who did not want to remove the veil over her face when pictures were being taken (Long 2003). The woman sued and claimed religious discrimination. Howard Marks, the woman's attorney, states, "There is no public safety issue here with Sultaana Freeman, none whatsoever. Sometimes when there are fears and prejudices in our country, we react and … go overboard. We go too far. We infringe on the liberties we are fighting for; the liberties that make us the American Society." Judge Janet C. Thorpe disagrees with the lawsuit. She stated, "If you rule for the plaintiff, someday a man will present himself to a driver license office and demand a license, without a photo, based upon his religious convictions. You may have to give it to him, but we will not know if his objectives are sincere or peaceful, or if they are terrible until it is too late." Both comments are justified – but difficult to reconcile in light of the other.

- A professional emergency management organization in one state wrote Congress about its fear that sensitive public information would get into the hands of terrorists. The letter declares: "Over the past several years, government agencies across the state have been assessing our vulnerability to natural disasters and, more recently, terrorist attacks. Unfortunately,

these assessments, if publicly disclosed, can provide a road map for a person or groups intent on destroying government facilities, disrupting government services and, in some cases, causing injury and death. Such assessments are now available upon request under provisions of the Open Government Act. In addition to the assessments, other critical information is available which has the same potential to be used against the interests of governments and their constituents. This includes items such as: detailed engineering drawings of facilities such as dams, power plants and government buildings; detailed response plans and procedures; and network diagrams for information management and telecommunications systems … We propose that the Open Government Act be amended to allow officials to deny access to certain, carefully defined classes of information such as those described previously. Our goal is to restrict public access to sensitive emergency plans and information that might be valuable to persons attempting to mount an attack." Such limitations seem perfectly logical in light of the terrorist threat. However, are there potential dangers in amending the Open Government Act?

- In 2011, the US military used a drone to kill Anwar al-Awlaki. al-Awlaki was a terrorist propagandist, but he was also an American citizen engaged in Jihad abroad. Lawyers for the Obama administration argued that the Authorization to Use Military Force allowed them to carry out this mission to protect US interests abroad. However, others assert that al-Awlaki's rights were violated. He was not tried in a court and had no recourse to legal representation. Some may argue that al-Awlaki was punished in a drone strike before even being found guilty of terrorism.

- After killing five Dallas police officers and two civilians on 7 July 2015, during a Black Lives Matter rally, Micah Xavier ran into a parking lot and found himself surrounded. Because Xavier posed a risk to law enforcement officials and others, the police department sent in a remote-controlled robot. After negotiations failed, the police detonated a bomb on the robot and killed Xavier. This was the first time a suspect was killed by a remote-controlled police bomb. The threat was neutralized, but some wonder if Xavier's right to a public trial was neglected.

There are perhaps no simple resolutions to the difficult situations discussed above. For such reasons, success is not to be achieved by giving security preference over liberty or by elevating rights concerns over the goal of preventing attacks and protecting communities. Instead, both values should be carefully weighed against the other, and decisions should be somewhat fluid and never set in stone. Paul Rosenzweig affirms: "one possible lesson from history is that we should not be utterly unwilling to adjust our response to liberty and security for the sake of counterterrorism, since we have the capacity to manage that adjustment, and to readjust it as necessary" (Rosenzweig 2006, p. 1020).

Others have also provided recommendations for ensuring liberty even while we address threats associated with terrorism. David Lowe (2016) illustrates that reactions to terrorism should be based on proportionality and always be approved by judges. In a statement before Congress, Richard

IN THE REAL WORLD

FBI vs. Apple

In a technological world, privacy and security are often two seemingly divergent roads. The privacy versus security argument has been a great source of debate, with the question of whether or not governments have the right to access private, protected information that relates to a criminal case. This once again became a national topic following the mass shooting in San Bernardino by Syed Rizwan Farook and his wife, Tashfeen Malik, on 2 December 2015.

In the early months of 2016, the Federal Bureau of Investigation (FBI) asked Apple Inc. to assist in unlocking Farook's work iPhone so they could recover valuable information from it. Farook had a four-digit passcode on his iPhone that had to be inputted to access the contents. In order to unlock it, the FBI wanted Apple to create new software to override the current system that destroys all iPhone data after 10 failed password attempts.

Apple declined to help in this regard, stating that the action would set a lenient privacy precedent and lead to a slippery slope favoring security over confidentiality. Apple and other technology moguls frequently attribute encryption (like the iPhone passcode system) as a way to help secure customers' valuable information and prevent access by uninvited hackers. The FBI, on the other hand, requested cooperation to aid in their investigation in this important national security measure. As a result, a hearing was scheduled for the end of March 2016. However, prior to the hearing, the FBI found a third-party entity to unlock the phone, so the request to Apple was rescinded.

The case was legally closed, but the ensuing wave it created in the privacy debate is far from over. Many questions remain. Should there be a balance between privacy and security in the land of the free? Does the average citizen have the right to keep their information private regardless of the impact on society? Should companies like Apple (that build trust with customers by creating products that are meant to ensure personal privacy and security) be forced to violate their own standards for the sake of national security? Should the government have access to private information when it determines the safety of others? If so, how should this be facilitated? This case was one of the most high-profile examples of the security–privacy predicament, which is likely to remain complicated as time goes on.

Ben-Veniste and Slade Gorton of the National Commission on Terrorist Attacks Upon the United States stated that "The test is a simple but important one. The burden of proof should be on the proponents of the measure to establish the power or authority being sought would in fact materially enhance national security, and that there will be adequate supervision of the exercise of that power or authority to ensure the protection of civil liberties.

If additional powers are granted, there must be adequate guidelines and oversight to properly confine their use" (Murphy 2006, p. 1048).

Laura Murphy, director of the Washington Legislative Office of the ACLU, also suggests we need to apply additional tests (Murphy 2006, pp. 1049–1051):

- Do the costs of liberty outweigh the potential benefits to public safety?
- Will the measure call for, or result in, discrimination based on religion, ethnicity, race, or other group characteristics?
- Is the measure properly tailored to the desired mission, or could it result in unintended and possibly abusive consequences?
- Will the public react negatively to the measure?

If any of these questions are answered in the affirmative, Murphy recommends that the considered action be rejected in favor of less severe alternatives.

Thus, logic and evidence demands that security may require some limitations on liberty. The threat of terrorism is significant and should be taken seriously. Nonetheless, liberty should not be fully sacrificed on the security altar. One of the reasons why we should be extremely careful is because there is circumstantial evidence that terrorists are likely to emanate from politically repressed societies. The United States does not want to create more terrorists in the future as it responds to existing terrorists. If we deny rights to others, we run the risk of creating more external enemies in the future. This is nicely summarized in a statement by Lhaj Thami Breze,

IN THE REAL WORLD

Treatment of Detainees at Guantanamo Bay

After an investigation of the prison facility at Guantanamo Bay, Cuba, the FBI described the treatment of enemy combatants captured in Afghanistan or elsewhere (Ackerman 2008, p. 124). At times, detainees claimed that they had insufficient water or food. Others asserted that they had been chained to the wall and had urinated or defecated on themselves. It was also asserted that the temperature of interrogation rooms was set either too cold or too hot. Detainees were exposed to loud music by Lil' Kim and Eminem along with repeated videos of a Meow Mix commercial. Each of these incidents was authorized by Pentagon guidelines. Such cases raise challenging questions for those involved in homeland security. If such techniques could prevent a terrorist attack, would they be justified? Is it ever correct to limit people's rights and liberties? Can a proper balance between security and liberty be found? If so, how? This is a very contentious issue. Some assert that the loss of rights does nothing to prevent terrorism and it may actually promote it. Others declare that many lives have been saved by making security the top priority. It is likely that this debate will continue into the future.

president of the Union of Islamic Organizations in France. He states, "The majority of Muslims want to practice their religion in peace and in total respect of the laws. But, when you persecute, when you make fun of, when you refuse, when you don't respect beliefs, what is the consequence? The consequence is radicalization" (Associated Press 2004). Along these lines, if domestic rights are severely eroded in the name of homeland security, there is the chance that citizens in the United States may also rise up violently against their own government. Both possibilities should be avoided to the best degree possible.

SELF-CHECK

1. There have been no wars that have resulted in the loss of liberties. True or False?

2. Law in the United States protects the right to assemble, and terrorists could use this right to meet to plan attacks. True or False?

3. The search for communists in the United States after World War II was known as:

    (a) The writ of habeas corpus

    (b) The Red Scare

    (c) The Japanese internment

    (d) Executive Order 9066

4. What are some tests that could help to protect rights while we fight the war on terrorism?

SUMMARY

As a participant in homeland security, it is imperative that you assess the trade-offs between security and rights. As illustrated in this chapter, you must know why terrorism exploits the tension between these two important priorities. You should be aware of the threats terrorists pose as well as the reasons why freedoms should not be eliminated. Because there are historic and current events that illustrate the delicate balance between security and freedoms, you must educate yourself about the consequences of homeland security policies. Most importantly, you should find ways to protect security while minimizing the loss of liberty. Striving for both objectives is most likely to reduce the possibility of future terrorist attacks. It is key to successful homeland security policies and actions.

ASSESS YOUR UNDERSTANDING

UNDERSTAND: WHAT HAVE YOU LEARNED?

 WWW Go to **www.wiley.com/go/mcentire/homelandsecurity2e** to assess your knowledge of the relationship of terrorism to security and liberty.

SUMMARY QUESTIONS

1. Governments take measures to protect themselves from outside aggressors. Otherwise they may cease to exist. True or False?

2. The President and Congress have no responsibility to protect citizen freedoms and rights. True or False?

3. Security has become a much greater priority since 9/11. True or False?

4. There are no known terrorists in the United States. True or False?

5. Some government leaders feel their most important responsibility is to protect the nation from further attacks. True or False?

6. During the Civil War, President Lincoln sent people to prison if they were involved in disloyal practices. True or False?

7. The right to bear arms implies that people can purchase and own guns without government interference. True or False?

8. US citizens are guaranteed freedom of religion. This will never create a problem for homeland security since people will not use their beliefs to incite terrorist attacks. True or False?

9. What is the name of the international laws that were created to protect soldiers?

   (a) The Stafford Agreement

   (b) The Hague Convention

   (c) The Geneva Convention

   (d) The Paris Accords

10. According to the American Civil Liberties Union, if we give up our freedoms:

    (a) We are most likely to win the war on terrorism.

    (b) The terrorists win.

    (c) We will not be able to prevail against terrorism.

    (d) The terrorists will not be able to prevail against terrorism.

11. A more activist court implies:

    (a) Congressional investigative authority has expanded.

    (b) Reporters increasingly focus on rights.

    (c) Citizens are more aware of their liberties.

    (d) The judicial system has overturned executive decisions.

12. During World War II, President Roosevelt:

    (a) Sent 110 000 Japanese Americans to relocation centers.

    (b) Sent many Hollywood actors and directors to prison.

    (c) Stopped all antiwar sentiment.

    (d) Rescinded the writ of habeas corpus.

13. The State of Florida:

    (a) Does not want to give sensitive information to the public.

    (b) Did not give a license to a woman who would not remove her veil.

    (c) Held Arab and Muslims who were here illegally.

    (d) Took the US government to court because it violated the writ of habeas corpus.

APPLYING THIS CHAPTER

1. Why is terrorism different than war?

2. What are some of the reasons why security has become important after 9/11?

3. List three reasons why an appreciation for liberty and rights has increased in recent years.

4. Has there ever been a time when liberty has been curtailed in the name of security? If so, discuss this case.

5. Discuss how the right to assemble can be abused by terrorists. Does this create a dilemma for policy makers?

6. One professional emergency management organization proposed to limit public access to sensitive government information. Why was this recommendation made?

7. What are five tests that can help us to protect rights as we attempt to augment security?

BE A HOMELAND SECURITY PROFESSIONAL

The Threat of Terrorism

You have been asked to testify before Congress about the need for new laws to protect our nation. What evidence could you use to describe the threat we are facing?

The Importance of Rights

As a member of a Congressional committee on terrorism, you are concerned about rights and liberties. What questions could you ask those who are proposing more stringent security measures?

The Geneva Conventions and Terrorism

Read a book or search the Internet for information about the Geneva Convention. Write a two-page essay describing the relation between the Geneva Convention and terrorism.

KEY TERMS

Freedom of religion	People cannot be denied their right to worship according to the dictates of their own conscience
Freedom of speech	People are allowed to express their opinions, even when they criticize the government
Geneva Conventions	A set of internationally accepted laws pertaining to the conduct of war
Profiling	Profiling is defined as the practice of law enforcement officials (including security personnel) using race, ethnicity, religion, or national origin as the decisive factors in targeting an individual for suspicion of a wrongdoing
Red Scare	Senator McCarthy's fear of communist infiltration into the United States
Right to assemble	People are permitted to join in politically motivated gatherings
Right to bear arms	Guns can be purchased and owned without government interference
Writ of habeas corpus	A law protecting citizens from unlawful imprisonment

REFERENCES

Ackerman, S. (2008). Island mentality. In: *Homeland Security* (ed. T.J. Badey), 124–128. Dubuque, IA: McGraw-Hill.

Associated Press (2004). Head Scarf Ban Backlash Warning. CNN.Com, 10 February. http://www.cnn.com/2004/WORLD/europe/02/10/france.headscarves.ap (accessed 17 August 2017).

Badey, T.J. (2008). *Homeland Security*. Dubuque, IA: McGraw-Hill.

Demmer, V.L. (2004). Civil liberties and homeland security. In: *Homeland Security* (ed. T.J. Badey), 149–152. Guilford, CT: McGraw-Hill/Dushkin.

Dragu, T. (2016). The moral hazard of terrorism prevention. *Terrorism and Political Violence* 79 (1): 223–236.

Garcia, B.E. (2016). Security versus liberty in the context of counterterrorism: an experimental approach. *Terrorism and Political Violence* 28 (1): 30–38.

Gaughan, A.J. (2015). A delicate balance: liberty and security in the age of terrorism. *Drake Law Review* 63: 1015–1029.

Griset, P.L. and Mahan, S. (2003). *Terrorism in Perspective*. Thousand Oaks, CA: Sage.

Long, P. (2003). State: ID photo is security issue. *The Miami Herald* (30 May). http://www.miami.com.mld.miamiherald/news/state/5972523.htm (accessed 28 December 2005).

Lowe, D. (2016). Surveillance and international terrorism intelligence exchange: balancing the interests of national security and individual liberty. *Terrorism and Political Violence* 28 (4): 653–673.

Mahan, S. and Griset, P.L. (2013). *Terrorism in Perspective*. Thousand Oaks, CA: Sage.

Murphy, L.W. (2006). Principled prudence: civil liberties and the homeland security practitioner. In: *The McGraw-Hill Homeland Security Handbook* (ed. D.G. Kamien), 1045–1062. New York: McGraw-Hill.

Rosenzweig, P. (2006). Thinking about civil liberty and terrorism. In: *The McGraw-Hill Homeland Security Handbook* (ed. D.G. Kamien), 1013–1030. New York: McGraw-Hill.

Starks, G.L. (2008). Profiling. In: *Homeland Security Handbook* (ed. J. Pinkowski), 239–250. Boca Raton, FL: CRC Press.

Taipale, K.A. (2006). Introduction to section 12. In: *The McGraw-Hill Homeland Security Handbook* (ed. D.G. Kamien), 1009–1012. New York: McGraw-Hill.

White, J.R. (2002). *Terrorism: An Introduction*. Belmont, CA: Wadsworth.

PREVENTING TERRORIST ATTACKS

Root Causes, Law, Intelligence, and Counterterrorism

Do You Already Know?

- Why addressing the root causes of terrorism is important
- The laws that aim to stop terrorist attacks
- How information is acquired about potential terrorists
- Benefits and drawbacks of counterterrorism
- Methods to enhance border control

For additional questions to assess your current knowledge of measures to prevent terrorist attacks, go to **www.wiley.com/go/mcentire/ homelandsecurity2e**

What You Will Find Out	What You Will Be Able To Do
8.1 The difficulty of reducing the underlying causes of terrorism	• Argue ways to minimize people's desire to attack the United States
8.2 Legislation that is passed to prevent terrorist attacks	• Evaluate the nature of policies designed to prevent terrorism
8.3 The cycle used to acquire information about potential terrorists	• Plan ways to acquire intelligence about potential terrorists
8.4 The advantages and disadvantages of counterterrorism activities	• Critique the need for and impact of preemptive strikes against terrorist enemies

Introduction to Homeland Security: Understanding Terrorism Prevention and Emergency Management,
Second Edition. David A. McEntire.
© 2019 John Wiley & Sons, Inc. Published 2019 by John Wiley & Sons, Inc.
Companion website: www.wiley.com/go/mcentire/homelandsecurity2e

INTRODUCTION

As a participant in homeland security, one of your principal objectives is to prevent terrorist attacks against the United States. For this reason, it will be imperative that you take several steps to minimize the probability of terrorism. One such measure is to eliminate – if possible – grievances that encourage terrorist activity. You should also be aware of and advocate for laws that proscribe terrorist actions. Another requirement is to anticipate terrorist intentions through intelligence gathering methods. At other times, the military may need to be deployed in counterterrorism operations abroad. Each of these measures may help you to minimize terrorist attacks now and in the future.

8.1 ADDRESSING ROOT CAUSES

According to some people, the predominant approach in homeland security (i.e. the deployment of soldiers against terrorism in the Middle East) has been ineffective and even counterproductive (Lustick 2007). Instead of advocating an aggressive military response to terrorism, some scholars, war protestors, journalists, and politicians around the world assert that the United States should do its best to reverse the root causes of terrorism through other means (Shakil-ur-Rahman 2007). According to this view, one of the most important but currently underutilized activities to prevent terrorism is to eliminate terrorists' motivations to commit attacks. As noted in Chapter 3, it is believed that terrorism will rise when abject poverty prevails, when political freedoms are limited, when human rights are ignored, and when alternate viewpoints or groups of people are not respected.

For instance, the head of the World Bank stated that "terrorism will not end until poverty is eliminated" (as cited by Francis 2002). Poverty can create serious feelings on the part of the poor against the rich. It is also suggested that people have an innate desire to participate in and influence political decisions. If individuals and groups cannot shape political decisions, terrorism will result. Others assert that the United States must do more to protect the human rights of everyone around the world – and not just American citizens. Without taking a more universal approach to rights, the argument goes that violence will continue to occur abroad. In addition, a common opinion in the Middle East is that terrorism would be minimized if the West shows increased consideration of and respect toward Muslim values. There is also a belief that terrorism could be reduced if the United States and Israel avoid unfair treatment of Arabs (i.e. it is asserted that the Palestinians are denied freedoms and a political voice in that country) (Abu-Amara 2002). Furthermore, US foreign policy decisions, in the opinion of President

Mohammad Khatami of Iran, may also lead to opposition against America and generate further terrorist attacks around the world (CNN 2001). Summarizing these perspectives, Jonathan Lash, a reporter for *Science Magazine*, states, "the compound of poverty, powerlessness, lack of opportunity, and injustice is volatile" (2001, p. 1789). It is assumed that many things must be changed if the number of terrorist attacks is to be diminished in the future.

The idea of addressing such root causes is both controversial and difficult (Franks 2006). For instance, one difficulty is that countries in the Middle East may misunderstand America's intentions to increase political freedoms around the world. Israel has held elections for Arab-Israelis, and the United States has attempted to establish a state to protect Palestinian people. What is more, the expanding of democracy and human rights to other nations may actually augment the attacks we are trying to prevent because it is viewed as a threat to the theocratic governments that are preferred among certain groups of people. However, violence has continued unabated, and terrorism against Israel and the United States has required additional security measures to be taken against Palestinians and fundamentalist Muslims (thereby compounding the problem).

Furthermore, American corporations may oppose many economic practices that reduce poverty, but also limit free trade or curtail profits. And it is also true that certain dictators in the world are likewise to blame for the extreme poverty their citizens experience due to their corruption and exploitative policies. There are likewise some root causes that the United States may not be able to control. As an example, children in some countries are often taught to hate Americans and are brought up in a culture of violent behavior (Leiter 2002). It may be virtually impossible to reverse such attitudes when they are ingrained at such a young age. Consequently, there are no easy answers to the challenges terrorism poses.

Regardless of the severity of these dilemmas, it would be advisable that the US government recognize that it must do more to address root causes if homeland security is to be enhanced. Failing to do so will only lead to a more protracted conflict with individual terrorists as well as the groups and nations that support them. Reaching out to moderate Muslims in a partnership may prove useful for the generation of ideas that will help to resolve such problems. Diplomatic activity and peaceful actions are therefore the first preference.

Nonetheless, such efforts may not be enough. Terrorists may attack the United States no matter what this country does. Taking a less aggressive and more peaceful approach could also jeopardize the rights of the potential victims of terrorist attacks in the United States or elsewhere. For instance, if nothing is done to prevent immanent terrorist attacks, people will be killed and injured. This is not acceptable either. Other preventive measures may inevitably be required.

IN THE REAL WORLD

Diplomacy or Not?

During the summer 2016 Presidential debates, diplomacy became a heated subject among Democratic and Republican candidates. Most of those from the left asserted the need to engage enemy nations in dialogue and find ways to resolve conflict through diplomacy and peaceful foreign policy. Those on the right declared that negotiations with terrorists and states that support such violence are pointless since they have already stated their desire to attack the United States and kill Americans. One side saw value in diplomatic endeavors, while the other affirmed no logical reason to negotiate with well-known enemies. One camp attempts to address root causes through diplomacy while this practice is discredited by another. Diplomacy with enemy states is a politically contentious issue for sure.

SELF-CHECK

1. Addressing the root causes of terrorism is currently the most used approach to preventing terrorist attacks. True or False?
2. Some people believe that poverty and injustice will augment terrorist attacks against the United States. True or False?
3. Which is not seen as a way to address the root causes of terrorism?
    (a) Eliminating the indoctrination of children to hate the United States
    (b) Improving US foreign policy
    (c) Disregard the rights of Palestinians
    (d) Respecting different cultures around the world
4. Will poverty reduction, human rights, and the expansion of democracy prevent all terrorist attacks? Why or why not?

8.2 POLICY AND LEGISLATION

Another measure that has and should be taken to deal with the threat of terrorism is to create policies and enact laws that make terrorism illegal or criminal. The policies and regulations that outlaw terrorism may emanate from executive orders (e.g. presidential directives), congressional decisions, or state and local legislative bodies. Although law can be initiated by different branches and at all levels of government, homeland security has been driven mostly by the President and federal agencies. Some of these laws were implemented before 9/11. Others were created to promote homeland security after this fateful date.

8.2.1 Laws Prior to 9/11

Many of the laws associated with international conflict evolved from the National Security Act of 1947 and the Goldwater–Nichols Act of 1987. And, even though the United States has always been threatened by terrorism, it has only recently begun to address terrorism through policy and legislation. To be sure, the government did prosecute those engaging in terrorism. But it usually did so through other laws that dealt with murder, arson, and property destruction. In the mid-1990s, however, things began to change.

One of the first significant policies to address terrorism directly was Presidential Decision Directive 39 (e.g. the US Policy on Counterterrorism). This policy was issued after major terrorist attacks in Japan and the United States. These two events are particularly noteworthy since they had dramatic impact on policy.

On 25 March 1995, the apocalyptic cult, Aum Shinrikyo, punctured plastic bags containing liquid sarin on various subways in Tokyo and elsewhere. The attack killed 12 people and sent 5500 people to hospitals (although only 1000 had actually sustained injuries). Only a month later, on 19 April 1995, Timothy McVeigh detonated a bomb in Oklahoma City at the Alfred P. Murrah Federal Building. The blast killed 168 people and injured another 800.

Recognizing the seriousness of these events, President Clinton reiterated in Presidential Decision Directive 39 (PDD-39) that it is the policy of the United States to use all means necessary to defeat terrorism. He vowed that the government would work with friendly nations to pursue terrorists through counterterrorism operations. He also declared that the government would seek the return of any terrorist to the United States who commits acts against our national interests. President Clinton also assigned terrorism-related roles and responsibilities to many federal organizations including the Department of State, the Department of Defense, the Department of the Treasury, the Department of Energy, the Department of Transportation, the Attorney General, and the Director of the Central Intelligence Agency (CIA). PDD-39 also separated functions dealing with terrorism into two categories. As noted in Chapter 1, crisis management was a law enforcement responsibility focusing on prevention efforts as well as the apprehension and prosecution of terrorists. Crisis management was to be led by the Federal Bureau of Investigations (FBI). Consequence management dealt more with preparedness, response, and recovery activities. The Federal Emergency Management Agency was put in charge of these functions.

In the late 1990s and early part of the new millennium, Congress also began to recognize the growing threat of terrorism against the United States. It passed a few laws that instituted homeland security as a national and foreign policy goal. From this point on, America would be less concerned with enemy states in relative comparison with individual terrorists and terrorist organizations. Understanding this emerging threat, House Resolution 1158 permitted the establishment of the National Homeland Security Agency. It was passed on 21 March 2001. House Resolution 1292 allowed the President to create a strategy for homeland security. The approach was enacted on 29 March 2001. While all of these laws signified substantial change, it was not until 9/11 that most of the legislation dealing with homeland security was initiated.

8.2.2 Legislation After 9/11

Shortly after the terrorist attacks on the East Coast, President Bush issued Executive Order 13228 on 8 October 2001. This law established an Office of Homeland Security in the White House. Tom Ridge was sworn in as the first director of this office. Within a few short weeks, additional homeland security legislation would be passed. These laws would have profound impact upon the United States.

For instance, on 25 October 2001, Congress passed and the President ratified the USA PATRIOT Act. The **USA PATRIOT Act** stands for "Uniting and Strengthening America by Providing Appropriate Tools Required to Intercept and Obstruct Terrorism." Its goal was to prevent terrorist attacks and enhance law enforcement ability to investigate and punish offenders. This law relaxed restrictions on sharing information among the CIA and FBI, permitted roving wiretaps and increased surveillance over computer communications, and allowed for the detention of terrorists. The Act also mandated new measures to prevent the funding of terrorists, prohibited the harboring of terrorists, and augmented the number of border agents. The Act also eliminated the statute of limitations for terrorist acts, meaning that a person could be tried for attacks regardless how long ago they occurred. Another aspect of the PATRIOT Act deals with material support. People can be convicted for providing aid and support to terrorists. Although highly controversial because of the perceived infringement of rights and liberties, the PATRIOT Act did enhance the ability of law enforcement to find, apprehend, and prosecute terrorists. This law has since been amended, but it remains in effect today.

A short time later, the **Transportation Security Act** was passed. On 19 November 2001, Congress created this law to protect transportation systems in the United States. From this point on, only passengers could enter airport terminals. The federal government also took over airport screening operations and purchased new equipment to detect explosives in carry-on and checked baggage. These activities intended to make it more difficult for terrorists to use airplanes in future attacks.

A number of other important policies and laws were implemented in 2002 and 2003. The first of which was Executive Order 13224. On 9 August 2002, President Bush acknowledged that the government would freeze any assets belonging to terrorists to limit resources that could be used in attacks against the United States. Courts have since supported this decision, and funds supporting terrorism have been seized in the United States and elsewhere. The Justice Department released a statement noting that "freezing the assets of organizations that bankroll terror is a legitimate and important role in the government's arsenal for fighting the war against terrorism." In the most notable case, the Holy Land Foundation for Relief and Development was indicted for supporting terrorism. It is believed that this organization sent over $12 million to Hamas. This court case began in July 2007 and resulted in a hung jury in October. However, at a retrial in 2008, the jury found defendants guilty of each of the charges against them.

Another very significant law was passed on 25 November 2002. President Bush signed the **Homeland Security Act**, which would become active on 24 January 2003. This law resulted in the most dramatic reformulation

USA PATRIOT Act: A homeland security law which that stands for "Uniting and Strengthening America by Providing Appropriate Tools Required to Intercept and Obstruct Terrorism." This law aims to prevent terrorist attacks and enhance law enforcement's ability to investigate and punish offenders.

Transportation Security Act: A law designed to protect transportation systems in the United States.

Homeland Security Act: A law passed in 2002 that mandated the creation of the Department of Homeland Security.

Figure 8-1

The Seal of the Department of Homeland Security reflects its mission. The eagle's claws represent activities during peace and war. The circles surrounding the eagle symbolize DHS' aims to coordinate with other levels of government. Source: © FEMA.

of government in 50 years and led to the creation of the Department of Homeland Security (DHS). The Homeland Security Act outlined the mission of DHS and listed its responsibilities dealing with border security, infrastructure protection, and the like. This law also focused on weapon of mass destruction (WMD) countermeasures and explained how the transition to homeland security would take place. The Homeland Security Act resulted in major challenges for the federal government due to massive organizational realignments, but virtually everyone agreed that this was a first step to deal with the threat of terrorism.

An added and important piece of legislation to be mentioned here, the **Comprehensive Homeland Security Act**, was passed on 7 January 2003. This legislation resulted in many new regulations to implement the actions of the DHS. For instance, the law related to the security of critical infrastructure and railroads. It also implemented more stringent measures pertaining to border control and identified ways to halt the proliferation of WMD. Other portions of the law deal with improving intelligence gathering. Funds were likewise released to aid local law enforcement efforts to support homeland security goals.

Additional policies and pieces of legislation have been issued or passed over the past several years. In fact, new laws are being implemented virtually every day. If you are working in homeland security, it will be imperative that you stay on top of new developments. Some laws have been changed or repealed, while others are being created at a frantic pace. This can be overwhelming. Nevertheless, resources are available to help you understand your role. For instance, the National Governors Association created a Governor's Guide to Homeland Security, which can be accessed at https://www.nga.org/files/live/sites/NGA/files/pdf/1011GOVGUIDEHS.PDF.

Comprehensive Homeland Security Act:
A law passed in 2003 containing new regulations for critical infrastructure security, railroad security, and more stringent measures related to border control and weapons of mass destruction.

As can be seen, the government is desperately working to prevent terrorist attacks. Unfortunately, some of these laws have been hastily put together or are controversial for other reasons. For instance, there is a debate about the authorities given in U.S.C. Title 10 and U.S.C. Title 50. Title 10 governs the organization and function of the armed forces (e.g. Army, Navy, Air Force, Marine Corps, Coast Guard, and Reserve). Title 50 determines how the United States declares and conducts war and focuses more on intelligence issues. Some argue that the two laws overlap substantially. However, others like Wall (2011) argue that there is a clear difference between military and intelligence operations. In addition, legislation has not always provided the funds that are necessary to make homeland security effective, and allocated resources have at times been misdirected (as will be seen in Chapter 14). It is likely that the challenges confronting legislators will continue into the foreseeable future.

IN THE REAL WORLD

The Comprehensive Homeland Security Act

The Comprehensive Homeland Security Act of 2003 is one of the most important pieces of legislation guiding homeland security activities. This bill, put forward by Senator Thomas Daschle (D-SD), focuses heavily on a variety of measures to prevent terrorism. It established a task force to protect nuclear power plants from terrorist attacks. The goal of this group is to assess the vulnerability of these structures and outline actions to secure them against terrorist threats. Besides being concerned about terrorist attacks involving radioactive material, the act also mandated a national smallpox vaccination program, promoted ways to foster intelligence dissemination, increased regulations pertaining to the use of hazardous materials, and augmented financial and technical assistance to law enforcement agencies in the United States. This law will have lasting impact upon homeland security for the foreseeable future.

SELF-CHECK

1. Terrorism has always been an important subject of legislation in the United States. True or False?
2. Homeland security was discussed as a policy function before 9/11. True or False?
3. Which terrorist attacks resulted in Presidential Decision Directive 39?
   (a) 9/11 and the Oklahoma City bombing
   (b) The Tokyo subway attack and Oklahoma City bombing
   (c) The Tokyo subway attack and 9/11
   (d) The sarin gas attack and 9/11
4. What are some of the features of the Homeland Security Act and Comprehensive Homeland Security Act?

8.3 INTELLIGENCE

Intelligence:
The function of collecting, assessing, and distributing information about an enemy, criminal, or terrorist.

One of the best ways to prevent terrorist attacks is to have a sound understanding of the plans of potential terrorists. This brings up the important function of intelligence. **Intelligence** is a word that describes the function of collecting, assessing, and distributing information about an enemy, criminal, or terrorist. Governments have long been concerned about the activities of unfriendly countries. Their desire is to become aware of the threats posed by rival nations so they may take necessary defensive or offensive measures. Law enforcement officials also seek information about citizens or nonresidents who plan to break the laws that bring order to society. In this case, detectives attempt to avert theft, murder, and other crimes or to arrest those who are intent on violating the law. In the context of homeland security, intelligence about terrorist intentions is the most important priority. It is imperative to acquire knowledge about potential terrorist attacks in order to prevent their negative consequences of death, damage, and disruption.

8.3.1 The Need for Intelligence

Intelligence has been a major feature of America's national security interests since our birth as a nation. Efforts have always been undertaken to understand the activities of enemy nations and the threat they pose to the United States. This was especially the case after World War II. During this period, intelligence efforts were bound to a "Cold War" mentality. Although animosity with the former Soviet Union dissipated in the late 1980s, American political and military leaders remained fearful of potential enemy nations. In particular, the United States was spending time and energy on understanding rising powers (i.e. China, North Korea, and Iran) during the 1990s. On the domestic front, law enforcement agencies were giving attention to the war on drugs, the sale or use of illegal weapons, and civil rights violations (e.g. hate crimes). It was under this context that terrorists took America by surprise.

For instance, during President Clinton's tenure in office, the United States witnessed several terrorist attacks against American interests. On 26 February 1993, Middle Eastern terrorists bombed one of the towers at the World Trade Center. The car bomb killed 6 people and injured 1042. Fortunately, it did not bring the building down. High-profile attacks also occurred toward the end of the 1990s. Two US embassies were bombed in the African nations of Tanzania and Kenya on 7 August 1998. The near-simultaneous attacks killed over 200 people. Another attack with explosives took place against the USS Cole (a military vessel) in Yemen port on 12 October 2000. This event killed 17 and injured 39 others. Sadly, none of these were detected and denied in advance. The intelligence community was only able to deter one major attack during this period. The **Bojinka plot** – a planned attack on airliners over the Pacific Ocean – was thwarted in 1995. However, in spite of this success, it appeared that not enough was being done to anticipate the growing threat of terrorism.

Bojinka plot:
A planned attack on airliners over the Pacific Ocean.

Intelligence cycle:
A four-step process of gathering, understanding and synthesizing data, and then sharing it with those who will use it.

Intelligence collection:
Activities to gather information about terrorist organizations and their operations and potential attacks.

OPINT:
Open-source intelligence acquired through publicly available materials including academic research, newspaper articles, library books, etc.

SIGINT:
Interception and interpretation of electronic communications such as phone conversations and e-mails.

IMINT:
Geospatial imagery collected by satellites and aircraft.

MASINT:
Measurement and signature intelligence that looks for the characteristics of certain types of actions (e.g. the presence of nuclear material when one is trying to develop a nuclear weapon).

HUMINT:
Intelligence collected by people from people (and can be done overtly or covertly).

Intelligence analysis:
Efforts to make sense of the voluminous data that is gathered from the field.

Intelligence production:
The creation of written reports, briefings, images, or maps to influence operational decisions.

This trend of downplaying the threat of terrorism continued for a time when George W. Bush was elected as President. The CIA and FBI began to collect evidence specifying that Al-Qaeda was intent on attacking the United States. One analyst in Phoenix, Arizona, noted in July 2001 that potential terrorist operatives were taking flight training lessons at US schools. On 6 August 2001, President Bush was given a brief entitled "Bin Laden Determined to Strike in US" It stated that Al-Qaeda was intent on bringing the fight to America and that it was recruiting and operating in places like New York City. In spite of these clues, US officials appeared to be oblivious to the impending attacks on 9/11. After a careful study of what led up to this fateful day, the 9/11 Commission (2004) listed several reasons why the attacks were not fully anticipated: increased intelligence reports with insufficient details, an inability to share intelligence across government agencies, and a failure to appreciate the tenacity and creativity of terrorists. Terrorist attacks and government panels revealed that intelligence must be a key feature if homeland security is to be successful (Githens and Hughbank 2010).

8.3.2 The Intelligence Cycle

In an attempt to overcome prior weaknesses, Patrick Deucy (2006) recommended that those involved in counterterrorism rely on the **intelligence cycle**. This includes a four-step process of gathering, understanding and synthesizing data, and then sharing it with those who will use it:

1. **Intelligence collection** – Activities to gather information about terrorist organizations and their operations and potential attacks. Intelligence collection may be obtained through a variety of means including:
   - **OPINT** – Open-source intelligence is acquired through publicly available materials including academic research, newspaper articles, library books, etc.
   - **SIGINT** – Interception and interpretation of electronic signal communications such as phone conversations and e-mails.
   - **IMINT** – Geospatial imagery collected by satellites and aircraft.
   - **MASINT** – Measurement and signature intelligence looks for the characteristics of certain types of actions and evidence (e.g. the presence of nuclear material when one is trying to develop, smuggle, or use a nuclear weapon or dirty bomb).
   - **HUMINT** – Intelligence collected by people from people (and can be done overtly or covertly).

2. **Intelligence analysis** – Efforts to make sense of the voluminous data that is gathered from the field. This is often performed at the headquarters level where individuals and groups process information to determine what is really going on at the field level.

3. **Intelligence production** – The creation of publications, briefings, images, or maps to influence policy or operational decisions. Written reports, oral presentations, and supporting documents are examples of this stage of the intelligence cycle.

Figure 8-2

Thousands of employees help to collect, interpret, and disseminate intelligence to the President, Congress, and others who need to know. Source: © FBI.

Intelligence dissemination:
Sharing information with end users (e.g. policy makers, FBI Special Agents, homeland security personnel, etc.).

4. **Intelligence dissemination** – Sharing information with end users to increase agency awareness, warn the public, and take steps to "pre-empt, disrupt or defeat terrorism" (Kauppi 2006, p. 423). This may include policy makers, FBI Special Agents, homeland security personnel, the military, etc.

Of course, additional intelligence will be required when data collection is incomplete. In addition, the analysis phase seeks to "connect the dots," the production phase generates new questions, and the dissemination of results phase will open up new questions about future attacks. We may therefore want to add another step to this cycle and label it as **intelligence adjustment**. The intelligence cycle must adapt repeatedly based on intelligence shortfalls, insufficient information, changing priorities, new leads, and unfolding needs. The intelligence cycle therefore requires a great deal of planning, direction, and follow-up (Kauppi 2006, p. 415).

Intelligence adjustment:
Adaptation of the intelligence cycle is required when collection is incomplete, analysis seeks to "connect the dots," production generates new questions, and dissemination results in the anticipation of future concerns.

8.3.3 Challenges Facing the Intelligence Community

As can been seen, the intelligence cycle is not a simple linear process. Nor is it exempt from significant challenges. At least four major difficulties have to be overcome. The first problem relates to the types of intelligence products that are useful for homeland security purposes. During the Cold War, the United States relied heavily upon IMINT and MASINT to detect troop movements and the building of missile sites or bomb bunkers. HUMINT was also utilized during this time by spies and secret agents who understood the language, history, and culture of Russia. The problem with these sources of intelligence is that they are less useful in homeland security. IMINT and MASINT can still be utilized to detect terrorism activities, but they are of reduced value because terrorists are especially adept at operating in stealth.

The HUMINT system built up during the Cold War is also not suited to address today's homeland security needs. Besides needing a substantially larger number of agents, the United States must have operatives who understand Arabic languages, Islamic religion, and Middle Eastern cultural practices. This is no small feat when one considers the complexity of these subjects. Even as the American intelligence community retools for today's homeland security objectives, it is extremely difficult to penetrate terrorist groups and cells. Terrorists have close knit relations, and they are not likely to allow significant infiltration into their organizations. The United States will therefore have to work through Arab partners and others around the world who already understand and can assimilate into terrorist goals and activities.

A second problem with the function of intelligence is that it is heavily dependent on technology. Terrorists communicate, plan, and conduct attacks with the use of technology. Cell phones, fax machines, pagers, teleconferencing, e-mails, and the Internet are all used frequently by terrorists. This technology allows terrorists to operate with a degree of impunity. As noted in a prior chapter, FBI Director Louis Freeh stated before a US Senate Commission in March 2000 that "uncrackable encryption is allowing terrorists to communicate without fear of outside intrusion." He further stated that because of this technology "they're thwarting the efforts of law enforcement" (in Thetford 2001, p. 252). Consequently, the intelligence community must have adequate equipment and training to allow them to operate in the modern world of technology.

A third problem is that there are many organizations that provide intelligence services. Most people have heard of the well-known **Central Intelligence Agency (CIA)** and **Federal Bureau of Investigations (FBI)**. These organizations generally operate in the international and domestic spheres, respectively. However, people may not have heard about the National Security Agency (NSA), the Defense Intelligence Agency (DIA), the National Geospatial-Intelligence Agency (NGA), and the National Reconnaissance Office (NRO), to name a few. The sheer number of federal agencies (which are not mentioned in their totality here) is only eclipsed when we consider other intelligence units around state and local jurisdictions in the United States. States are developing their own terrorism intelligence units, and even the City of New York has its own dedicated agency to assess threats against this large metropolitan area in the United States.

This diversity of organizations obscures intelligence ownership and could at times discourage collaboration. As an example, before 9/11, the FBI and CIA did not have open lines of communication. The federal government did not want the CIA to spy on its own citizens, and the FBI and CIA were prohibited by law from sharing information with each other. Fortunately, new laws (such as the Intelligence Reform and Terrorism Prevention Act of 2004) have been passed to enhance the distribution of intelligence. **The Terrorist Threat Integration Center (TTIC)**, which joins the efforts of the FBI and CIA, was created to improve cooperation in the federal government. The DHS also aims to collect information on attacks planned against the United States. Efforts have similarly been undertaken to augment the sharing of intelligence internationally and to lower levels of government in the United

Central Intelligence Agency (CIA): The federal agency in charge of international intelligence operations.

Federal Bureau of Investigation (FBI): The federal agency in charge of domestic intelligence operations.

The Terrorist Threat Integration Center (TTIC): A government organization which attempts to improve coordination among the FBI and CIA.

INTERPOL:
An international police organization that is involved in intelligence.

States. For instance, **INTERPOL** is an international police organization that is involved in intelligence gathering and sharing. It has 186 member nations that collect and distribute information about terrorists and various forms of criminal behavior. The United States also works with the North Atlantic Treaty Organization (NATO) and other friendly nations. There are also many daily briefs that are distributed to state and local governments from the FBI. There are other guidelines to assist state, local, and tribal law enforcement agencies gather and act on intelligence (Carter 2009).

IN THE REAL WORLD

Fusion and Intelligence Integration Centers

In light of the information sharing weaknesses made evident on 9/11, the federal government has implemented additional measures to increase collaboration across intelligence agencies. This includes fusion centers and intelligence integration centers.

The concept of fusion centers started in the 1990s when Los Angeles County created a Terrorism Early Warning Center. However, after the terrorist attacks on 9/11, both the DHS and the Department of Justice recognized the need to improve the collection and sharing of information about terrorism and crime. For this reason, federal funding was provided to create fusion centers around the nation. These centers are typically located within local and state law enforcement agencies. However, fusion centers vary dramatically in terms of organization, reporting chains, etc. Sizes range from 4 to over 200 personnel. Some centers stress drugs and organized crime, while others focus more on disasters and emergency management. Nevertheless, fusion centers play an important role in collecting information within their jurisdictions and relaying intelligence products up to the federal government or down to local communities. Guidelines for fusion centers can be accessed at https://it.ojp.gov/documents/fusion_center_guidelines_law_enforcement.pdf.

What is more, on 1 May 2003, the TTIC was formed in the FBI. According to the government, the TTIC is an interagency body intended "to provide a comprehensive, all-source-based picture of potential terrorist threats to US. interests." It is composed of personnel from many organizations, including the CIA, the FBI, and the DHS. Each organization will continue to gather data from their respective areas of specialization: the CIA focusing on terrorists at the international level, the FBI focusing on terrorists at the domestic level, and DHS focusing on other ways to reduce vulnerabilities to known threats. The overall objective of the TTIC is to increase information sharing and avert any disconnects relating to intelligence collection and processing. In other words, the FBI, CIA, and DHS can help one another "fill in the blanks" where intelligence is lacking and find ways to "connect the dots" where it is present. A similar organization helps to inform the President regarding intelligence and counterterrorism planning. The National Counterterrorism Center (NCTC) was established by Presidential Executive Order 13354 in August 2004. It produces the President's Daily Brief (PDB) and the National Terrorism Bulletin (NTB).

Classified intelligence:
Information given only to a very specific and limited number of people to protect sources of acquisition and deny adversaries information that would lead them to alter their communications or operations.

This brings up a fourth challenge: determining with whom to share intelligence. For instance, while some information is sensitive but unclassified, much of it is classified. **Classified intelligence** is highly sensitive information given only to a very specific and limited number of people to protect sources of acquisition and deny adversaries information that would lead them to alter their communications or operations (Deucy 2006, p. 401). Classified intelligence is thus only given on a need to know basis and is strictly guarded. Unfortunately, failing to share information with others could prove dangerous as we found out on 9/11. The CIA and FBI were preventing from sharing information because of their unique missions internationally and domestically. The 9/11 Commission reiterated that it is imperative to find an appropriate balance between safeguarding intelligence and sharing it with those who "need to know."

A final problem concerns gathering intelligence about the funding of terrorism. Since 9/11, the government has been very interested in disrupting terrorist finances. Numerous laws have been passed to make it illegal to support terrorism through monetary means. A challenge arises due to the fact that terrorists are very careful about how they channel money to each other. **Money laundering** is the process of hiding where money is coming from and what it is being used for. Terrorists are adept at collecting and transferring money through legal and illegal means.

Money laundering:
The process of hiding where money is coming from and what it is being used for.

As an example, terrorists may gather funds from legitimate charities and businesses as well as fraudulent companies and organizations. These finances may then be sent through a variety of accounts in banks around the world. This covert movement of money creates significant obstacles for intelligence officers who are trying to cut off the financial lifeblood of terrorist organizations. For this reason, financial institutions are now required to report to the government wire transfers and other bank transactions that involve a significant amount of money (usually anything over $10 000).

8.3.4 Successes

In spite of notable difficulties, the intelligence community has been successful on occasion at uncovering terrorist conspiracies in the United States and around the world. For instance, on 10 August 2006, 24 suspects were arrested in the United Kingdom. These individuals intended to board 10 jets from Britain to California, New York, and Washington, D.C. They wanted to smuggle on board gel explosives in sports drink bottles and detonate them with the use of an electronic signal from an iPod or cell phone. Fortunately, officials in the United States and United Kingdom worked closely to investigate and thwart the plot.

On 8 May 2007, six men were arrested for planning to purchase automatic weapons and attack the Fort Dix Army base in New Jersey. The men talked to an employee at a store and wanted him to transfer video footage of them firing weapons to a DVD. The thoughtful citizen promptly notified the FBI, and the attack was foiled. In another case, four men were intent on blowing up terminal buildings, fuel pipelines, and fuel tanks at JFK airport in New York. This plot was prevented on 2 June 2007 and may have been only days away from implementation.

Such cases indicate the importance of working with other nations, the need for citizen involvement, and the benefit of anticipatory action. While these and other accomplishments are praiseworthy, the intelligence community must not be complacent. Terrorist leaders have said they are sending suicide bombers to the United States, and many fear it is only a matter of time before these and other attacks occur in the future. It is a common adage that terrorists only have to be successful once, while intelligence officials have to be right 100% of the time.

IN THE REAL WORLD

Gathering Intelligence

Information is vital for those involved in gathering intelligence. In order to keep track of potential terrorists, the government is turning to corporations for assistance. Companies such as ChoicePoint and LexisNexis are working closely with homeland security and intelligence officials. These businesses obtain and retain personal data about people including information about homes, relative, and criminal records. Software has also been developed to find links in the data that would be indicative of terrorist activity. While some people like former Attorney General John Ashcroft argued that these new tools are vital for homeland security. Others in the FBI fear that there is not sufficient oversight or restrictions pertaining to corporations collecting information and then sharing it with the government (O'Harrow 2008).

SELF-CHECK

1. There were no clues that the attacks would take place on 9/11. True or False?

2. IMINT is intelligence collected by electronic communication. True or False?

3. Which part of the intelligence cycle is concerned with the creation of briefings and maps?
   (a) Intelligence collection
   (b) Intelligence analysis
   (c) Intelligence production
   (d) Intelligence feedback loop

4. What are some of the challenges facing the intelligence community?

8.4 COUNTERTERRORISM

Counterterrorism:
The active pursuit of known terrorists that includes preemptive military strikes.

One of the ways the United States deals with potential threats to our nation is to engage in counterterrorism (Jones 2014). **Counterterrorism** is the active pursuit of known terrorists that includes preemptive military strikes or the involvement of law enforcement officials. It is different than detention and interrogation of terrorists by law enforcement, military custody, and CIA control. Counterterrorism relies heavily on intelligence but is used before attacks or even while they are taking place. The goal of such activities is to neutralize terrorist threats before they materialize or rescue hostages and minimize the loss of life afterward. There are numerous counterterrorism organizations in the United States and in other nations. Some of their operations illustrate the importance of adequate training. Others provide unique of failed or successful operations.

The United States has several entities that are involved in counterterrorism operations. This may include covert operatives from the CIA or law enforcement officials from the FBI. The CIA infiltrates enemy organizations and operates on foreign soil. Its main purpose today is to gather intelligence about terrorist activities internationally. However, the CIA may also actively pursue individuals in the United States if it is believed they pose a threat to the country. The FBI is also interested in intelligence issues, and it does collaborate with other law enforcement agencies abroad. In fact, the FBI has offices in at least 40 nations around the world. However, and in contrast to the CIA, the FBI is generally interested in preventing terrorist attacks at home (or against US interests abroad such as an embassy). FBI Special Agents seek to arrest individuals who threaten or plan attacks in the United States. At times, efforts for apprehension may turn violent if the alleged criminals or terrorists resist.

The military is also heavily involved in counterterrorism operations, and they have operated under mandates such as the 2001 Authorization for Use of Military Force, which helped the United States find the perpetrators of 9/11 and combat groups like the Taliban who harbored these terrorists. When authorized, the Special Operations Command (SOCOM) plays an important role in coordinating counterterrorism organizations. It oversees special reconnaissance, direct action, unconventional warfare, and counterterrorism activities. It coordinates closely with special forces of the US military.

Delta Force, or First Special Forces Operational Detachment-Delta, is one of the well-known special forces unit of the US Army. It was formed in 1977 under Colonel Charles Beckwith and is modeled after the British SAS. Although the Pentagon does not report on its activities, Delta Force is believed to be involved with reconnaissance, the rescuing hostage, and fighting against enemy forces. Delta Force is made up of about 1000 soldiers who have come from the Green Berets and the 75th Ranger Regiment. Candidates seeking to qualify for Delta Force membership are considered on an invitation-only policy. They must have been in the military for at least 4½ years and then must undergo extensive physical and psychological tests. Delta Force members look like ordinary citizens (they can let their hair grow) and often have no markings on uniforms. If accepted, they will be given a M1191.45 caliber pistol. They are expert marksmen with M14, M21, and M25 rifles. Delta Force personnel train with many other special forces around the world, and they have been deployed in numerous counterterrorism operations.

Counterterrorism is also carried out by other military forces. Some of the more well-known teams include Delta Force (US Army), Special Warfare Units (US Navy), Special Operations Wing (US Air Force), and the Anti-Terrorism Battalion (US Marine Corps). These teams are sent around the world to eliminate terrorist organizations and prevent attacks. Counterterrorism forces may work with soldiers in foreign nations, as is the case in the

Figure 8-3

The role of counterterrorism center is to thwart attacks before they happen. Source: © FBI.

Philippines. Others have been deployed to Afghanistan and Iraq to capture Al-Qaeda members or other terrorist insurgents. In several cases, US Special Forces have been highly effective at disrupting terrorists and keeping them on the run. States and local governments are now developing counterterrorism squads. They work closely with the FBI on Joint Terrorism Task Forces.

IN THE REAL WORLD

Finding bin Laden Through Operation Neptune Spear

The most notable counterterrorism operation in US history was the assassination of Osama bin Laden on 2 May 2011. Because the United States was increasingly interested in finding the whereabouts of bin Laden, the CIA established the Bin Laden Issue (Alec) Station from 1996 to 2005. Although initially unsuccessful, the CIA started to track a courier who was connected to bin Laden. Intelligence agencies began to closely monitor a compound in Pakistan. Their leads indicated that bin Laden was living in the residence with his wives and children. In the middle of the night, SEAL Team Six flew secretly into Pakistan in helicopters, landed in the compound, and sealed off the streets in the area. Team members then proceeded to clear rooms in the building. They took out bin Laden's security forces and gathered women and children in rooms until the conflict was over. When the Navy Seals found bin Laden, they shot and killed him. Before they left, the Navy Seals gathered bin Laden's documents and computers to acquire additional intelligence about his operations and key partnerships. Although one of the helicopters was damaged during landing, the event was regarded to be a huge success.

8.4.1 Risky Operations

Counterterrorism operations can be very risky and may involve a significant loss of life. Two of the most problematic counterterrorism operations in history are Operation Eagle Claw and the Moscow theater crisis. Operation Eagle Claw occurred on 24 April 1980 after 53 hostages were taken hostage in the US Embassy in Tehran, Iran. In an attempt to resolve the situation, two activities were required. First, a staging base would have to be established in Iran. Second, military units would need to approach the embassy, rescue the hostages, and extract them out of Iran. Unfortunately, things went horribly wrong from the start. Two helicopters got lost in a sandstorm and another experienced a mechanical problem. A bus of civilian Iranians also came too close to the staging area and had to be captured to limit detection and notification of the operations. In light of these challenges, President Carter called off the rescue attempt. After the mission was aborted, a helicopter crashed into a C-130 transport plane and eight airmen and marines were killed. The fiasco underscored the need for increased counterterrorism funding, better equipment, and improved training and communications.

Another counterterrorism operation also had deadly results. On 23 October 2002, approximately 40 terrorists entered a Broadway-style theater in Russia with explosives and took about 850 hostages. The terrorists demanded the withdrawal of Russian military forces from Chechnya. The Kremlin would not give into such demands, and the situation deteriorated when a girl was shot by the terrorists. After a two-and-a-half-day siege, Russian leaders decided to spray fentanyl (an anesthetic) into the building through the ventilation system, which caused everyone to fall asleep. OSNAZ (Russian Special Forces) then entered the building and killed about 30 of the terrorists with gunfire. The hostages were then taken out of the building and laid on the sidewalk. Unfortunately, many of the citizens

Figure 8-4

Russian Special Forces were able to kill terrorists at a Russian theater. Unfortunately, many citizens died in the process. Source: © Getty Images. Reproduced with permission of Getty Images.

suffered adverse reactions to the chemicals. Complicating the matter, there were insufficient ambulances on scene, and military leaders did not want to release information about the chemical agent to doctors. It is estimated that about 128 hostages died as a result.

8.4.2 Learning from Other Nations

The United States has worked diligently to develop one of the most sophisticated counterterrorism forces in the world. It has no doubt gleaned additional knowledge from countries that have a long history of responding to violent terrorist organizations. According to Cindy Combs (2000, pp. 169–176), Germany, Britain, and Israel are notable examples. A successful counterterrorism operation can also be witnessed from activities in Peru in 1996.

GSG9:
A German counterterrorism organization, whose name means "Border Guards, Group 9."

The **GSG9** is a German counterterrorism organization, whose name means "Border Guards, Group 9." The GSG9, which is now part of the Federal Police, was created after the terrorist attacks during the Olympics in Munich in 1972. As noted in a prior chapter, terrorists entered the Olympic Village where Israeli personnel were staying. The extremists killed some athletes and took other citizens as hostages. The response by the German government was less than desirable because it resulted in the death of both law enforcement officials and civilians. Wishing to minimize such problems in the future, this organization developed specialized training in counterterrorism operations. Members of GSG9 are extremely proficient in weapons use and are equipped with BMWs and BO 105 helicopters. In 1977, the GSG9 was able to enter a hijacked plane (Lufthansa Boeing 737) in Somalia and rescue 82 passengers. Four terrorists were killed in the altercation. The GSG9 has been involved in several operations against the Red Army Faction, a left-wing terrorist organization in Germany. Today they are engaged with radical Islamic terrorists.

Special Air Service (SAS):
A British counterterrorism organization.

Because Britain has experienced many terrorist attacks from the Irish Republican Army, it also has an acclaimed counterterrorism organization – the **Special Air Service (SAS)**. The SAS has developed a great deal of expertise as it has been in existence for over three quarters of a century. Those wishing to become members of this group must serve in the military for a minimum of three years. They must then pass rigorous tests of strength and endurance. According to Combs,

> Out of every 100 men who apply, only about 19 will meet the physical and mental requirements. The initial tests include a series of treks across the Welsh hills, carrying weighted packs. The final trek covers 37 miles, carrying a 55-pound pack, over some of the toughest country in the Brecon Beacons. It must be covered in 20 hours, and it is literally a killer course. Men have died trying to complete it (Combs, 2000, p. 173).

If accepted, SAS recruits will subsequently be trained in hand-to-hand combat, water warfare, and emergency medicine. They are also experienced with the use of pistols, machine guns, and enemy weapons.

The British SAS carried out a successful counterterrorism operation in 1980. During the first few days in May, members of the Democratic Revolutionary Movement for the Liberation of Arabistan took over the Iranian Embassy in downtown London. They demanded freedom of their associates who were imprisoned and also wanted to gain possession of oil field in Iran.

After a hostage was killed, officials in the United Kingdom decided to implement Operation Nimrod. In order to move SAS forces into place without detection, they ordered that all airplanes flying into London approach the airport much lower than normal. They also had a British utility company work in the area to create as much noise as possible. When the timing was right, the SAS set off a charge in the building and cut the power to the facility. SAS members then swung down from ropes and burst into the windows (after placing explosives on them first). As they entered the building, they set of stun grenades. Within a short period of time, they killed five terrorists and captured that last one remaining. Only one hostage was killed in the incident, and the rest were safely escorted from the building.

Sayeret Matkal:
A strike team devoted to finding terrorists before they attack Israeli interests.

Of all of the counterterrorism organizations, few are as well known as the **Sayeret Matkal** in Israel. Sayeret Matkal is a strike team devoted to finding terrorists before they attack Israeli interests. They were also established after the Munich massacre and shortly thereafter killed the mastermind of this attack (Ali Hassan Salameh) with a car bomb in Beirut. Because of the long-standing threat of terrorism against this country, this group of Special Forces in Israel is carefully selected. On a biannual basis, Camp Gibush is held to determine who can join the organization as new recruits. If applicants pass the constant monitoring of military officials, doctors, and psychologists, they then must train for an additional 20 months. This training is rigorous and includes, among other things, basic and advanced infantry training, parachuting, counterterrorism classes, reconnaissance, and martial arts.

The Sayeret Matkal illustrated its capabilities when a Belgian aircraft was hijacked from Vienna to Tel Aviv on 8 May 1972. While the airplane on the tarmac in Israel, 16 commandos (who were dressed as airplane technicians) told the terrorists the plane needed servicing. The terrorists let the technicians in disguise approach the plane, and the rescue operation then began. Within 10 min, two terrorists were killed and others were taken captive. Three civilians were injured and one died as a result. Benjamin Netanyahu (an Israeli prime minister) was a participant of Sayeret Matkal at the time.

Figure 8-5

Counterterrorism organizations like Grenzschutzgruppe 9, the tactical unit of the German Federal Police, participate in training exercises.

Peru also has special military forces to deal with the Shining Path and other left-wing and drug-related terrorist organizations. While Peru's special units are not as well known as those in Germany, Britain, or Israel, they did participate in a successful counterterrorism operation. On 17 December 1996, 14 members of the Tupac Amaru terrorist organization stormed a Japanese embassy. They took at least 72 people hostage, including the President Alberto Fujimori's brother. The Tupac Amaru wanted 400 people released from prison, but the government would not acquiesce to these demands. Instead, counterterrorism forces smuggled listening devices into the embassy through humanitarian workers and closely monitored the activities of the terrorists. They noticed that the terrorists would play soccer every day at 3:00 p.m. and decided this would be the best time to conduct the raid. For the next several days, the Special Forces implemented Operation Chavin de Huantar (a name referring to pre-Inca site with secret passages). While loud music was playing nearby, six tunnels were dug into the compound from nearby buildings. On the designated day (22 April 1997), several explosive charges were detonated. Special Forces then emerged from the ground, entered the embassy, and began to exchange gunfire with the terrorists. During the conflict, hostages took cover (since they were previously notified to do so through an intelligence agent who posed as a doctor). When all was said and done, each of the 14 members of the Tupac Amaru were killed. Sadly, one hostage and one soldier were killed. Nine others were also injured. Nevertheless, the operation was hailed as a national success, even though international human rights monitors believe some of the terrorists were summarily executed.

8.4.3 Controversy Regarding Counterterrorism

In spite of the successes and perhaps as a result of notable failures, counterterrorism is highly controversial. Those supporting counterterrorism argue that there are many in and outside of the United States that wish to do us harm. They assert that the government has a moral responsibility to protect its citizens and prevent attacks. Others decry counterterrorism and suggest that it is an immoral undertaking. They fear intelligence operations and oppose the preemptive and deadly use force.

This debate is especially evident in discussions about the use of unmanned aerial vehicles (UAVs) – also known as drones (Mahan and Griset 2013). Drones are popular among politicians and military leaders because they reduce the cost of conflict and they minimize risk to personnel. They can also be effective weapons. From 2004 to 2011, US drones killed between 1300 and 2100 people. For these reasons, it is asserted that drones are "cheap, safe and precise." However, others assert that drones violate the airspace of other nations as well as the privacy of individuals. Opponents also declare that drone strikes may have unintended consequences (e.g. the death of innocent civilians). These individuals consequently see them as immoral weapons.

While these opponents to counterterrorism and drones seem to overlook the enemies that wish to do us harm, they could be right when they note that counterterrorism may aggravate hostilities and breed additional violence. For these reasons, counterterrorism will likely remain a contentious and divisive policy option in the future.

IN THE REAL WORLD

Counterterrorism in Afghanistan

Shortly after 9/11, it was discovered that Osama bin Laden and Al-Qaeda were responsible for the attacks against the United States. It was also a well-known fact that the Taliban were providing these terrorists with sanctuary in Afghanistan. On 22 January 2002, special US forces flew into mountains of Kandahar to stop the instruction of terrorists at a training camp (Zaroya 2003). Before arriving at the compound, they launched a grenade to catch the terrorists off guard. They then entered the facility and began shooting at those offering resistance. While searching through the premise, one US soldier was hit over the shoulder with a large stick. He then began to fight the terrorists by hand. The soldier broke his collarbone but prevailed in the altercation. The training, tactics, night vision goggles, and other equipment were believed to have been some of the reasons for the success of this counterterrorism operation. Allies who opposed the Taliban in Afghanistan were also very helpful in this surprise attack.

SELF-CHECK

1. Preemptive military strikes are known as counterterrorism operations. True or False?
2. The FBI does not have offices in foreign countries. True or False?
3. Which nation has special forces that rescued hostages in the Iranian embassy?
   (a) The United States
   (b) Britain
   (c) Peru
   (d) Germany
4. Are there any drawbacks to counterterrorism operations?

SUMMARY

Preventing terrorist attacks is one of the main pillars of the national homeland security strategy. If you are to succeed in this area, it is vital that you realize the importance and limitations of addressing the root causes of terrorism. You should promote laws that prohibit terrorism and punish those who support such violent behavior. Relying on human and other sources of intelligence may help you to apprehend terrorists before they strike. Of course, this requires that the collected information is accurate and shared with those who need to know. At times, confronting terrorists may also require the involvement of the military in counterterrorism operations. There are countless measures you can take to prevent acts of terrorism against American citizens and others around the world.

ASSESS YOUR UNDERSTANDING

UNDERSTAND: WHAT HAVE YOU LEARNED?

 Go to **www.wiley.com/go/mcentire/homelandsecurity2e** to assess your knowledge of measures to prevent terrorist attacks.

SUMMARY QUESTIONS

1. Not everyone agrees with the military response to the threat of terrorism. True or False?

2. The United States cannot be held responsible for all of the causes of terrorism around the world. True or False?

3. Policy and legislation may emanate from presidential directives, but not congressional decisions. True or False?

4. The USA PATRIOT Act attempts to prevent terrorist attacks by strengthening law enforcement abilities. True or False?

5. The 9/11 terrorist attacks took the United States by surprise because it was operating under a Cold War mentality. True or False?

6. HUMINT includes intelligence gathered from academic research and books. True or False?

7. Counterterrorism can be defined as preemptive military strikes against terrorists. True or False?

8. The SAS is a counterterrorism force in Israel. True or False?

9. Which may be considered as a root cause of terrorism that cannot be controlled by the United States?
   (a) The treatment of Muslims around the world
   (b) The upbringing of children in the Middle East in a culture of hate and violence
   (c) American foreign policy
   (d) Respect for culture and religion

10. Which is not a feature of the Comprehensive Homeland Security Act?
   (a) Creation of the Department of Homeland Security
   (b) Protection of nuclear power plants
   (c) Increased border control
   (d) Regulations pertaining to rail security

11. PDD-39 reaffirmed:
   (a) The importance of border control
   (b) The need for improved intelligence
   (c) The value of rights and liberties
   (d) The policy of the United States to defeat terrorism

12. Which component of the intelligence cycle deals with sharing information with policy makers?

   (a) Intelligence collection

   (b) Intelligence analysis

   (c) Intelligence production

   (d) Intelligence dissemination

13. Intelligence given to specific and limited individuals is known as:

   (a) HUMINT

   (b) Classified intelligence

   (c) Categorized intelligence

   (d) IMINT

14. Which counterterrorism force is the most well known around the world?

   (a) SAS

   (b) GSG9

   (c) Sayeret Matkal

   (d) Shining Path

APPLYING THIS CHAPTER

1. While watching the news on TV one night, you hear a scholar suggest that America must address the root causes of terrorism. What does this mean and will "addressing root causes" eliminate all terrorist attacks?

2. If you were working in homeland security and someone suggested that laws will not help to reduce terrorism, what would you say?

3. A co-worker who just started working with the FBI asserts that the United States should spend more money on SIGINT? Will this type of intelligence provide the most accurate view of terrorist operations? Is there another type that is preferable?

4. As a concerned citizen, you frequently watch the presidential debates broadcasted on national television. On one occasion, there was a heated discussion about the merits of counterterrorism operations. What are the pros and cons of these types of military actions?

BE A HOMELAND SECURITY PROFESSIONAL

Homeland Security Laws

Discuss laws relating to homeland security with another student. Discuss why they are necessary and provide some examples.

Assignment: Understanding the Intelligence Cycle

Write a paper about the intelligence cycle. Be sure to mention the steps that must be taken to gather intelligence about potential terrorists.

A New Recruit

You have just joined the military and you desire to participate in counterterrorism operations. What kind of training might you undertake in the future?

KEY TERMS

Bojinka plot	A planned attack on airliners over the Pacific Ocean
Central Intelligence Agency (CIA)	The federal agency in charge of international intelligence operations
Classified intelligence	Information given only to a very specific and limited number of people to protect sources of acquisition and deny adversaries information that would lead them to alter their communications or operations
Comprehensive Homeland Security Act	A law passed in 2003 containing new regulations for critical infrastructure security, railroad security, and more stringent measures related to border control and weapons of mass destruction
Counterterrorism	The active pursuit of known terrorists that includes preemptive military strikes
Federal Bureau of Investigation (FBI)	The federal agency in charge of domestic intelligence operations
GSG9	A German counterterrorism organization, whose name means "Border Guards, Group 9"
Homeland Security Act	A law passed in 2002 that mandated the creation of the Department of Homeland Security
HUMINT	Intelligence collected by people from people (and can be done overtly or covertly)
IMINT	Geospatial imagery collected by satellites and aircraft
Intelligence	The function of collecting, assessing, and distributing information about an enemy, criminal, or terrorist
Intelligence analysis	Efforts to make sense of the voluminous data that is gathered from the field

Intelligence collection	Activities to gather information about terrorist organizations and their operations and potential attacks
Intelligence cycle	A four-step process of gathering, understanding and synthesizing data, and then sharing it with those who will use it
Intelligence dissemination	Sharing information with end users (e.g. policy makers, FBI Special Agents, homeland security personnel, etc.)
Intelligence adjustment	Adaptation of the intelligence cycle is required when collection is incomplete, analysis seeks to "connect the dots," production generates new questions, and dissemination results in the anticipation of future concerns
Intelligence production	The creation of written reports, briefings, images, or maps to influence operational decisions
INTERPOL	An international police organization that is involved in intelligence
MASINT	Measurement and signature intelligence that looks for the characteristics of certain types of actions (e.g. the presence of nuclear material when one is trying to develop a nuclear weapon)
Money laundering	The process of hiding where money is coming from and what it is being used for
OPINT	Open-source intelligence acquired through publicly available materials including academic research, newspaper articles, library books, etc.
SIGINT	Interception and interpretation of electronic communications such as phone conversations and e-mails
Special Air Service (SAS)	A British counterterrorism organization
The Terrorist Threat Integration Center (TTIC)	A government organization which attempts to improve coordination among the FBI and CIA
Transportation Security Act	A law designed to protect transportation systems in the United States
USA PATRIOT Act	A homeland security law that stands for "Uniting and Strengthening America by Providing Appropriate Tools Required to Intercept and Obstruct Terrorism." This law aims to prevent terrorist attacks and enhance law enforcement's ability to investigate and punish offenders

REFERENCES

9/11 Commission (2004). *The 9/11 Commission Report: Final Report of the National Commission on Terrorist Attacks Upon the United States*. New York: *W.W. Norton and Company, Inc.*

Abu-Amara, S. (2002). Terrorism is a result of Israel's denying a people its rights. *Dallas Morning News*. Viewpoints (Monday, 22 July), p. 9A.

Carter, D.L. (2009). *Law Enforcement Intelligence: A Guide for State, Local, and Tribal Law Enforcement Agencies*. Washington, DC: US Department of Justice.

CNN (2001). Iranian president: "root of terrorism" must be addressed. *CNN* (12 November). http://archives.cnn.com/2001/WORLD/meast/11/12/khatami.interview/index.html (accessed 19 April 2017).

Combs, C.C. (2000). *Terrorism in the Twenty-First Century*. Upper Saddle River, NJ: Prentice Hall.

Deucy, C.P. (2006). Intelligence and information sharing in counterterrorism. In: *The McGraw-Hill Homeland Security Handbook* (ed. D.G. Kamien), 391–412. New York: McGraw-Hill.

Francis, D.R. (2002). Poverty and low education don't cause terrorism. *The NBER Digest* (September).

Franks, J. (2006). *Rethinking the Roots of Terrorism*. New York: Palgrave Macmillan.

Githens, D. and Hughbank, R. (2010). Intelligence and its role in protecting against terrorism. *Journal of Strategic Security* 3 (1): 31–38.

Russell, H., Forest, J., and Moore, J. (2006). *Homeland Security and Terrorism: Readings and Interpretations*, McGraw-Hill Homeland Security Series, 1e. New York: McGraw-Hill.

Jones, K. (2014). *U.S. Counterterrorism Programs in East and Northwest Africa*. New York: Nova Science Publishers, Inc.

Kauppi, M.V. (2006). Counterterrorism analysis and homeland security. In: *The McGraw-Hill Homeland Security Handbook* (ed. D.G. Kamien), 413–430. New York: McGraw-Hill.

Lash, J. (2001). Dealing with the Tinder as well as the Flint. *Science* 294 (5548): 1789.

Leiter, K. (2002). Palestinians must remake their society before peace can come. *Dallas Morning News*. Viewpoints (22 July), p. 9A.

Lustick, Ian. (2007). The war on terror: when the response is the catastrophe. Paper presented at FEMA Higher Education Conference, Emmitsburg, MD (5 June).

Mahan, S. and Griset, P.L. (2013). *Terrorism in Perspective*. Thousand Oaks, CA: Sage.

O'Harrow, R. (2008). Mining personal data: one company keeps tabs on the public in the name of post-9/11 security. In: *Annual Editions Homeland Security* (ed. T.J. Badey), 141–143. Dubuque, IA: McGraw Hill.

Shakil-ur-Rahman, M. (2007). Root causes of terrorism must be addressed: PM. *The International News* (Monday, 13 August). http://www.thenews.com.pk/top_story_detail.asp?Id=5452 (accessed 30 January 2008).

Thetford, R.T. (2001). The challenge of cyberterrorism. In: *Terrorism: Defensive Strategies for Individuals, Companies and Governments* (ed. L.J. Hogan), 238–257. Frederick, MD: Amlex, Inc.

Wall, A. (2011). Demystifying the title 10 – title 50 debate: distinguishing military operations, intelligence activities & covert action. *Harvard National Security Journal* 3: http://harvardnsj.org/wp-content/uploads/2012/01/Vol-3-Wall.pdf.

Zaroya, G. (2003). Inches divide life, death in the Afghan darkness. *USA Today* (19 October), p. 4A.

CHAPTER

9

SECURING THE NATION
Border Control and Sector Safety

Do You Already Know?

- Methods to enhance border control
- Measures to limit attacks against air transportation
- Steps to secure rail transportation
- Efforts to avert terrorism against sea transportation
- Actions to reduce threats facing chemical facilities

 For additional questions to assess your current knowledge of measures to prevent terrorist attacks, go to **www.wiley.com/go/mcentire/homelandsecurity2e**

What You Will Find Out	What You Will Be Able To Do
9.1 Agencies related to border control	• Synthesize the variety of steps that can be taken to protect the integrity of the border.
9.2 The mandate of the Transportation Security Administration	• Project ways to secure air transportation from terrorism
9.3 Why VIPR teams patrol rail transportation systems	• Anticipate alternative measures to reduce attacks on railroad systems
9.4 The role of the private sector in port security	• Implement procedures to secure seaports and maritime trade
9.5 How chemical facilities can safeguard themselves against attacks	• Assess the effectiveness of the chemical facility safety standards

---

Introduction to Homeland Security: Understanding Terrorism Prevention and Emergency Management,
Second Edition. David A. McEntire.
© 2019 John Wiley & Sons, Inc. Published 2019 by John Wiley & Sons, Inc.
Companion website: www.wiley.com/go/mcentire/homelandsecurity2e

INTRODUCTION

A major priority to minimize the probability and consequences of terrorism is to secure the nation against possible attacks. If you are working in this profession, you must do all you can to stop the infiltration of terrorists into the United States. This suggests that the border needs to be strengthened and that immigration processes need to be changed. Policies must also be implemented to limit the risk associated with air, rail, and sea transportation. In addition, it will be imperative that you enhance chemical facilities through the enforcement of widely accepted security standards. Each of the measures discussed in this chapter may help to halt terrorist attacks now and in the future.

9.1 BORDER CONTROL

The United States is established on the principle of immigration, and the arrival of foreigners into this country has provided significant benefits over time. However, some studies suggest that legal migration diffuses terrorism around the world (Bove and Bomelt 2016). That is to say, the movement of people to other countries allows the ideological forces of terrorism to spread elsewhere too. In addition, illegal immigration may be a conduit by which terrorists enter other nations to launch attacks. It is true that "most of those entering the United States illegally are only seeking a better way of life. The fact that they can enter illegally is, however, a national security vulnerability that must be addressed" (Chertoff 2009, p. 41). If the government can control the flow of people and goods into this nation, then there will obviously be less likelihood that enemies from abroad will be able to implement terrorist acts against us. Therefore, reducing or eliminating the infiltration of terrorists and weapon of mass destruction (WMD) into the United States is a very important way to prevent possible terrorist attacks. This brings up the important subject of borders and border control.

9.1.1 What Is the Border?

Border:
The territorial boundary of any nation along with its various points of entry.

The **border** is the territorial boundary of any nation along with its various points of entry. Jack Riley, an associate director of RAND Infrastructure, Safety, and Environment, states that people and goods can enter the United States from one of four locations (Riley 2006, p. 587). This includes airports, seaports, guarded land points, and unguarded land borders and shoreline.

Airports are the transportation hubs where foreigners fly into the United States and are allowed or denied entry based on valid passports and visas for business, education, or vacation purposes. Seaports are also transportation networks that make up portions of the border. They facilitate the movement of people and likewise play a role in commerce due to the trade they facilitate. Guarded land points include border stations where people, vehicles, and trucks are processed for entry. Unguarded land borders are those locations between the United States and its neighboring countries (i.e. Canada to the north and Mexico to the south). These may be protected at times by fences and walls, but are not always secured in most cases. There are also coastlines to the northeast, east, west, and south of the United States, which are considered a part of national borders. The waterways near the Great Lakes, the Atlantic Ocean, Pacific Ocean, and Gulf of Mexico are often open to human movement and maritime shipping with limited or at least minimal oversight. Unfortunately, the sheer size and openness of our nation is an invitation to those who wish to do us harm.

9.1.2 Our Porous Border

Statistics regarding the size and fluid nature of the border are impressive or overwhelming, depending on your point of view. For instance, there are more than 100 international airports in the United States (Riley 2006, p. 587). America also has 90 000 miles of coastline (Hoffman 2006, p. 143) and "more than 1000 harbor channels and 25 000 miles of inland, intra-coastal, and coastal waterways, serving over 300 ports, with more than 3700 passenger terminals" (Benztzel 2006, p. 631). These numbers do not include, of course, the hundreds of other foreign airports and seaports around the world that are connected to counterparts in this country. What is more, there are also 9000 miles of land borders (Hoffman 2006, p. 143). The scope of the border is therefore awe-inspiring.

The extent of the border is only dwarfed by the dizzying pace of activity that takes place around it. In a single year, a "half a billion people, 125 million cars, 12 million trucks, and 33 million overseas shipments – including nearly 6 million shipping containers, 800 million planes, 2 million railcars, and over 200 000 ships – went through U.S. borders" (Hoffman 2006, p. 143). There are also thousands or even hundreds of thousands of employees that enter the country on a daily basis to work in the agricultural sector or in factories called maquiladoras along the US–Mexican border. These numbers do not include those people or goods entering the country illegally. As an example, estimates suggest that between 500 000 and 4 million people cross the border without permission each year (Knickerbocker 2006). There are numerous reasons why the border appears to be open to trade and why the United States attracts so many visitors.

Besides the millions of people who travel here for leisure or business opportunities, there are also millions who come here to seek a better way of life (e.g. economic and educational opportunities). The former group comes from all around the world, while the latter is comprised mainly of Mexican nationals and others from Latin America. Politicians on the left and right frequently prefer an open border, even if they will not admit it publicly. Some want to extend America's freedoms and prosperity to any-one wishing to obtain them. Others desire a constant supply of cheap labor to keep corporate profits high.

International commerce has likewise increased substantially in the past few decades due to improvements in transportation and the high demand for foreign goods and services. Corporations also prefer the ability to send things quickly to the United States. In fact, "many manufacturers and retailers now use the 'just-in-time strategy' to reduce the costs of carrying and storing inventory" (Riley 2006, p. 588). This has boosted global trade over the past decade.

Finally, the scope and expense of securing our borders is monumental. In 2006, "Airport officials estimate that less than 10 percent of all this cargo is physically inspected, and most airports lack the equipment to conduct inspections, especially of large containers" (Riley 2006, p. 593). Today, about 1/5 of all air cargo is inspected. One of the challenges is that there is a shortage of personnel to prevent illegal immigration or quickly process the vast numbers of people and goods that come to the United States on a daily basis. Protecting the border would require a serious investment of resources on an ongoing basis.

Regardless of the cause for the movement in and around our borders and the expense to protect them, citizens and experts alike recognize the potential danger for homeland security. If the border cannot be adequately controlled or regulated, terrorists may be able to enter the United States along with WMD. This situation has already been used to the advantage of those who wish to do us harm on 9/11. Frank Hoffman states that bin Laden "struck at America's Achilles' heel – its porous borders, transportation networks, and vulnerable economic portals" (Hoffman 2006, p. 142). He also states that "our most daunting domestic challenge is posed by the open nature of America's society: borders" (Hoffman 2006, p. 143).

IN THE REAL WORLD

Immigration Debate

During the 2016 Presidential Election, Donald John Trump, the Republican candidate, repeatedly announced his closed-door policy toward certain groups of Muslims who wished to enter the United States. He also advocated for deporting all illegal immigrants from the United States, but eased up on this mandate to some extent by clarifying his immigration policies would focus on those who pose a danger.

Following the San Bernardino, California, shooting attack in December of 2015, Trump suggested the nation should enforce a ban on Muslim immigrants. He subsequently altered his stance slightly, choosing to focus on preventing immigrants from entering the United States if they were from countries that had any ties to terrorists. This sparked an intense debate on Trump's policies, even for an already highly controversial candidate.

Notably, there are pros and cons to having such a restricted approach to immigration as Trump proposes. He and his supporters believe that the thorough monitoring and screening of immigrants would help identify those who have links to terrorists or those who condone jihadist ideals. This would allow actions to be taken to prevent them from infiltrating the United States. Trump has also spoken on the need to build a wall along the entire US–Mexico border as part of his plan. Ideally, stricter enforcement through improved immigration standards and a wall could make our nation safer and decrease our vulnerability to terrorist attacks on US soil. In addition, a more regimented border could mean increased attention on citizens' needs, rather than illegal immigrants' welfare or education. Jobs and taxpayer dollars could be focused more on helping legal citizens provide for themselves and their families.

However, stronger immigration policies would be a costly financial endeavor. Tightening immigration regulations and increasing border security as Trump advocates would require the allocation of financial and human resources. Furthermore, a closed-door immigration policy might result in economic losses since millions of jobs are filled by immigrants. Also, those who favor open immigration standards believe the United States should be a safe haven for all people who wish to take advantage of the opportunities available in this nation. Others assert the country should remain a melting pot of varying cultures, ideals, ethnicities, religions, and races. Lastly, it is stated that having more stringent regulations could potentially cause discrimination against immigrants who are already legally and lawfully residing in the United States.

It is evident that there are a multitude of advantages and disadvantages to Trump's immigration propositions, depending on your political viewpoints. Clearly, the topic of immigration will continue to be a highly discussed and disputed as time goes on.

9.1.3 Participants Involved in Border Control

There is no single entity involved in border control. Instead, there are a variety of government agencies interested in the securing of our border. This includes Immigration and Customs Enforcement as well as the Coast Guard. Corporations and international organizations also play an important role in securing our border.

Immigration and Customs Enforcement (ICE):
The largest investigative organization within the Department of Homeland Security that attempts to deter illegal immigration and the smuggling of money and materials that support terrorism.

Immigration and Customs Enforcement (ICE) is the largest investigative organization within the Department of Homeland Security. It was created in March 2003 by combining the Immigration and Naturalization Service and the US Customs Service. The goal of ICE is to enforce immigration and customs laws. The agents working for ICE specifically attempt to deter illegal immigration and the smuggling of money, drugs, and other materials that support terrorism. In an attempt to protect the homeland, ICE looks for fraudulent passports, investigates employers that hire illegal aliens, and stops the transport of weapons and sensitive military technologies.

United States Coast Guard (USCG):
A military branch within the Department of Homeland Security that is in charge of maritime law, environmental protection of waterways, search and rescue operations at sea, and interdiction of illegal aliens and contraband.

The **United States Coast Guard (USCG)** is an organization of Department of Homeland Security. It employs over 40 000 people. In terms of the border, the USCG interdicts illegal aliens and seizes illegal contraband. One of its goals is to prevent terrorists from entering US waters or gaining access to the shores of US lands. Because the Coast Guard is a military branch, its employees receive the same pay and benefits as other active and reserve personnel in the other branches of the armed forces.

Besides these agencies in the Department of Homeland Security, others also play a role in border control. For instance, "private companies such as

Figure 9-1

There are many government employees who work to secure US borders. Source: © US Department of Homeland Security.

airlines, truckers, container shippers, and manufacturers – as well as companies whose employees travel over these borders – are stakeholders" (Riley 2006, p. 588). Observant employees can do much to enhance security at the border. Corporate involvement is also vital since any attack along the border could have drastic economic consequences for their bottom line.

9.1.4 Measures to Secure Borders

Those charged with border control are implementing a number of programs to prevent terrorist attacks against the United States. The most well-known program is US-VISIT. The government and citizens are also undertaking other measures to protect the integrity of the border.

United States Visitor and Immigrant Status Indicator Technology (US-VISIT):
A computer database used to screen passengers who wish to travel to the United States.

The **United States Visitor and Immigrant Status Indicator Technology (US-VISIT)** is a computer database created and maintained by the Department of Homeland Security. It contains information about passengers who wish to travel to the United States. Those seeking visas will have their biometric data recorded (e.g. digital finger scans and photographs). When the traveler arrives in the United States, his or her biometric data will then be compared with the information stored on the system and checked against known criminals and terrorists around the world. According to Riley, "the system was first tested in Atlanta in late 2003 and became operational at all 115 international airports on 5 January 2004. Simultaneously, it was introduced at 14 major seaports served by cruise liners" (Riley 2006, p. 592). At least 90 million people have had their biometric information recorded by US-VISIT since its inception. However, citizens of 27 allied countries are excused from this system. This is a major weakness today in that some of the terrorists on 9/11 came from these exempted nations.

The government is also looking into or taking other measures to secure our borders and prevent further terrorist attacks. Some officials in the government assert that passports need to be changed continually to prevent tampering and falsification. Smart lanes and electronic passes (much like toll tags) are being developed to speed up the processing of trucks carrying goods into the United States. Unmanned aerial drones and stationary cameras are being used along the borders to detect locations where people are entering the United States illegally. In order to increase the effectiveness of border agents, the government has opened up a border patrol academy in Artesia, New Mexico. At this school, recruits are taught Spanish, learn about immigration law, practice using weapons, and develop or enhance other law enforcement techniques and skills. Patrol of the border has also increased, which has led to the discovery of tunnels and capture of illegal aliens. President Trump and Congress laws that would fund the building of a fence along the entire US–Mexican border. The goal is to make it more difficult to illegal aliens and terrorists to enter the United States.

IN THE REAL WORLD

Preventing Terrorist Entry into the United States

On 29 January 2017, an executive order was signed to allow for the proper review of standards to prevent the entry of foreign terrorists and criminals into the United States. The President argued that the most generous immigration system has been "repeatedly exploited by terrorists and other malicious actors who seek to do us harm." In order to reduce national security risks that were identified under the Obama Administration, the President wanted to halt those traveling on passports from Iraq, Syria, Sudan, Iran, Somalia, Libya, and Yemen. He asserted that Congress provided the President under section 212(f) of the Immigration and Nationality Act (INA) the ability to prevent entry of individuals who are deemed to pose a threat to national interest. The order also provided the government with the "additional resources, tools and personnel to carry out the critical work of securing our borders, enforcing the immigration laws of our nation, and ensuring that individuals who pose a threat to national security or public safety cannot enter or remain in our country." Although prior presidents have implemented similar measures, the order was met with fierce opposition from many in the public and others in the media. US District Judge Ann Donnelly issued a verdict to bar the travel ban after the American Civil Liberties Union filed a petition in court. This action was later sustained when the Ninth Circuit of Appeals ruled 3-0 to maintain the freeze on the immigration order. In response, Trump later tweeted "SEE YOU IN COURT, THE SECURITY OF OUR NATION IS AT STAKE!" The Trump Administration also rewrote the order to facilitate implementation as soon as possible. This, again, was challenged in court. However, in June of 2017, portions of the travel ban were approved by the Supreme Court. But immigration is likely to be a contentious issue into the future.

Finally, citizens are becoming more involved in measures to enhance border security. After feeling that the government was not doing enough to protect the United States against the entry of illegal aliens and potential terrorists, a group of concerned individuals in Arizona joined together to form the **Minutemen Project**. People who join the Minuteman Civil Defense Corps lobby local, state, and federal officials to do more about border security. They also organize shifts when volunteers can patrol the border and notify the government when people attempt to cross the border illegally. While the group is having an impact upon politicians' views and deterring those wishing to enter the United States illegally, some fear that this group may aggravate tensions along the border and be unprepared if conflict erupts. Regardless, hundreds of illegal immigrants have been detained as a result of the efforts of the Minutemen.

Minutemen Project: Activities to promote border security carried out by a group of volunteers that founded the Minuteman Civil Defense Corps in Arizona.

IN THE REAL WORLD

Ahmed Ressam

On 14 December, 1999, Ahmed Ressam attempted to enter the United States to conduct a terrorist attack known as the Millennial Plot. Ressam hid explosives in his car and was attempting to travel from Canada to California in order to blow up the Los Angeles International Airport on New Year's Eve. When questioned by a border agent near Seattle, Washington, Ressam became anxious and was evasive. He tried to flee the area and was shortly arrested for his activity along with a colleague from Brooklyn, New York. This case illustrated the importance of observant border patrol agents.

SELF-CHECK

1. Airports are not considered as part of the territorial boundary of the United States. True or False?

2. It is relatively easy for the United States to oversee the people and goods that enter our country. True or False?

3. Which agency is responsible for investigating companies that hire illegal aliens?
   (a) The Transportation Security Administration
   (b) Immigration and Customs Enforcement
   (c) The United States Coast Guard
   (d) The United Nations International Maritime Organization

4. What are a few of the measures taken by the Department of Homeland Security to prevent illegal immigration?

9.2 PROTECTING AIR TRANSPORTATION

As noted in earlier chapters, terrorists have repeatedly targeted ground transportation systems like buses and subways. Airplanes and airports are also favorite targets of terrorists as illustrated throughout history. In addition, terrorists may launch attacks on railroads and seaports. Chemical facilities are also likely to be targeted in the future. Each of these will be discussed in turn.

The aviation industry comprises a significant portion of the transportation sector across the globe and is consequently a major focus for terrorists. In 2015, the US Department of Transportation calculated that 685 million people flew on domestic airliners, which is an average of 1.87 million people per day. The vast number of people who use air transportation coupled with airliners' high speed capabilities and endless destination possibilities makes the aviation industry an extremely vulnerable and enticing form of transportation to exploit.

As mentioned in Chapter 1, terrorists infamously turned airplanes into WMD in the 11 September 2001 (9/11) hijacking attacks. But there have been many terrorist attacks before and after this fateful date. Terrorists have hijacked many flights throughout the history of aviation, and they bombed PAN AM 103 on 21 December 1988. Terrorists also tried to use improvised explosive devices (IEDs) to cause harm more recently, such as the Underwear Bomber in 2009. On 17 July 2014, Malaysia Airlines Flight 17 was brought down over Ukraine using surface-to-air missiles. During that same year, the threat of laser illumination (when a laser is shined into the cockpit of an aircraft) was reported 3894 times. In addition, ISIS is suspected of bombing a Russian Metrojet Flight 9268 on 31 October 2015. This event – probably resulted from a bomb placed in a soda can – that killed 224 people was the deadliest air disaster in Russian history.

These examples represent just a handful of the attacks involving or targeting the aviation industry. More will certainly follow. During a one-week period in July 2017, the TSA confiscated 96 handguns during passenger screening in the United States alone. Recent intelligence reports indicate that "terrorists continue to target commercial aviation and are aggressively pursuing innovative methods to undertake their attacks, to include smuggling devices in various consumer items" (Jansen 2017, p. 1A). In consequence, this threat prompted an international ban of personal electronics (excluding cell phones) on nine airlines from 10 countries from the Middle East and Northwest Africa. If the affected airlines do not comply, they will not be allowed to fly to the United Kingdom or the United States.

With all the potential threats to aviation, the government has instituted agencies and programs to help identify and prevent such tragedies from occurring. These include the TSA, the Federal Air Marshal Service, the Computer Assisted Passenger Prescreening System II, and Secure Flight. Airports Council International has also been established to increase security of airports and the world.

Transportation Security Administration (TSA):
A federal agency under the Department of Homeland Security created to protect our transportation systems from terrorist attacks.

Federal Air Marshal Service:
Another important organization of a few thousand marshals who act under the TSA.

Computer Assisted Passenger Prescreening System II (CAPPS II):
A former computer program utilized by the TSA to screen passengers against lists of known terrorists and others with criminal records.

The **Transportation Security Administration (TSA)** is a federal agency under the Department of Homeland Security. It was created after the 9/11 attacks to protect our transportations systems from acts of terrorism. It includes over 43 000 security officers and inspectors who share a unified goal of preventing terrorist attacks on airplanes, subways, and rail systems. The TSA screens passengers, checks luggage and cargo for bombs, deters hijackings and other attacks on transportation systems, and works with local law enforcement agencies to protect transportation systems. The TSA is most visible in airport terminals, but the employees of this organization perform many other activities behind the scenes (e.g. audits of security systems on the airfield or related hangars).

The **Federal Air Marshal Service** is another important organization of a few thousand marshals who act under the TSA. This Air Marshal Service was initially created in 1961 to maintain confidence in the civil aviation system. Today, the Federal Air Marshal Service is most interesting in identifying and halting attacks against US aircraft. Air marshals are armed security officers trained in aircraft-specific engagement tactics. They often blend in with general passengers aboard the aircraft, concealing their status as law enforcement officials. After the 9/11 attacks, the Federal Air Marshal Service grew substantially. Certain "gateway airports" require that an armed security officer is on board at least 48 flights per day. The Air Marshal is a vital program to protect our aircraft, crew, and passengers.

Another important program for the safety of aviation was the **Computer Assisted Passenger Prescreening System II (CAPPS II). CAPS II** was a database that ensured that passengers are screened by every airliner and airport that operates within the United States. This system was

Figure 9-2

TSA agents have the goal of preventing terrorist attacks against aircraft. Source: © US Department of Homeland Security.

implemented after 9/11 and was maintained by the TSA. The system collects information about passengers (including date of birth, street address, and telephone numbers). Once obtained, this data was then compared with terrorist or most wanted lists as well as federal and state warrants for arrest. A risk score would then be calculated and printed on the boarding pass so airport screeners could be notified. Because of potential rights violations, watchdog groups and the General Accounting Offices became very critical of CAPPS II. In the summer of 2004, this program was suspended. However, a new program known as Secure Flight was implemented in its place.

Secure Flight:
The proposed program to replace the Computer Assisted Passenger Prescreening System II.

Secure Flight is also an advanced passenger screening program that is administered by the TSA. Secure Flight checks passenger information with watch lists maintained by the federal government, such as the No Fly List. Therefore, Secure Flight functions similar to the CAPPS II passenger screening. However, a notable difference in Secure Flight compared with programs like CAPPS II is that the TSA is now solely responsible for passenger watch list matching. Prior to Secure Flight, airlines held the responsibility for this type of passenger screening.

In addition to US initiatives mentioned earlier, the Airports Council International helps to set global standards regarding the safety and security of airports. It has taken a more active role since 9/11. This organization shares information and best practices for training with partner nations from around the globe. The efforts of the Airports Council International are extremely important since the safety of any given aircraft is determined by the security of airports in other parts of the world. Any weak link in the international transportation system could impact the safety of others in faraway nations.

In summary, it is apparent that the aviation industry will likely remain a major target for terrorist activity. Government agencies and international partners must therefore take further precautions and continually evolve and improve their safety programs to meet the escalating threat of violence.

IN THE REAL WORLD

Airport Security

US airports are among the safest in the world. Each year, airport screeners stop the smuggling of hundreds of knives and guns on planes. However, there is concern about the 900 000 people who work at airports and have access to most locations in terminals and on the tarmac. While the vast majority of these employees are honest and hardworking, some may have ulterior motives. The bombing of a Russian airliner was the result of an insider who planted explosives on the plane. A similar activity against US aircraft is not out of the realm of possibility. The good news is that employees are vetted by TSA contractors. The private sector also has a responsibility to screen those who are working at airports and in the aviation industry.

SELF-CHECK

1. Terrorists desire to bomb aircraft to disrupt the transportation system. True or False?
2. The TSA was created before 9/11. True or False?
3. What program puts armed security personnel on aircraft?
   (a) Air Marshals
   (b) TSA Secure Flight
   (c) AIR SWAT
   (d) VIPR Teams
4. Explain why Secure Flight replaced CAPPS II.

9.3 RAIL TRANSPORTATION SECURITY

Railroads are another important part of the US transportation network and have a major impact on the economy. As an example, in 2006, the major class 1 railroads employed over 167 000 people and created $52 billion in revenue. In addition, these railroad companies moved over 1.7 trillion ton-miles of freight, which represents 41% of all the freight ton-miles carried in the United States (Goel et al. 2008).

With this information in mind, it is apparent why terrorists would potentially target rail transportation networks. Terrorists could cause significant economic harm by damaging railway infrastructure, which would prevent the flow of people and goods. Trains can be derailed by removing the spikes that hold the rail and crossties together or by throwing a switch that causes the train to travel too quickly on a curved track. Tunnels, railways, or bridges can be destroyed with explosives, and train engines also can be incapacitated through other nefarious means. All of these tactics and many more could halt rail transportation (Goel et al. 2008).

Railways are also vulnerable because they transport millions of people for both short and long distances. These passenger railroads are generally classified into two different types of rail transportation based on the distance the train travels. A commuter railroad travels short distances within metropolitan areas. In contrast, an intercity passenger railroad travels long distances. In the United States, most passenger rail transportation is carried out by commuter railroads, with over one million riders per day (American Public Transportation Association). However, Amtrak, the only domestic intercity railroad, reported a 51% increase in their passenger travel from 2001 to 2013. In 2013, 31.6 million passengers rode Amtrak, which is about 87 000 passengers per day (Imam 2014).

Terrorists are therefore likely to target passenger cars or train stations. Such an attack would be extremely deadly because these cars and locations have large numbers of people in confined spaces. For instance, approximately 1.4 million people ride commuter trains each day (Goel et al. 2008).

In fact, the MTA Long Island Rail Road in New York alone has an average ridership of 337 800 passengers per day (American Public Transportation Association 2014). For this reason, security at train stations is generally less stringent than at airports. These lower standards and the lack of sufficient monitoring make it easier for terrorists to launch an attack and then blend in with the ensuing rush of passengers to escape.

Attacks on trains and subways have occurred around the world, including in countries like India, England, and Spain. Russia experienced several train and subway attacks from 2003 to 2004. More recently, in March of 2010, two suicide bombers detonated explosives on two trains in near-simultaneous attacks. These terrorists killed 40 people and injured another 100. On 3 April 2017, a blast in a subway station in St. Petersburg killed at least 10 people and injured 50 more. These events have definitely underscored the vulnerability of the rail transportation system.

Unfortunately, railroads could be targeted by terrorists due to the cargo they carry. As an example, the **Strategic Rail Corridor Network (STRACNET)** is a network of railroads that transport Department of Defense munitions and other materials, including hazardous items. 21.6 million ton-miles of especially dangerous items, known as toxic-by-inhalation materials, are transported along this network per year. These "gasses or liquids that are known or presumed on the basis of tests to be so toxic to humans as to pose a health hazard in the event of release during transportation" (Goel et al. 2008).

Tank cars containing toxic-by-inhalation materials can be compromised as well. This could occur through gun fire, explosives, or derailments. The consequences of a tank car rupturing near a major city would be catastrophic to those in the vicinity. For instance, in 2005, a train with a tank car containing chlorine gas was derailed and damaged near Graniteville, South Carolina. This accident released 60 tons of gas, which killed nine people, injured 554 people, and required 5400 people to be evacuated from nearby homes. Indirect damages of this accident were more than $40 million (Goel et al. 2008). If terrorists were able to damage a tank car containing hazardous materials in a major city, the impact could be even more disastrous.

Because of these obvious threats to security, the US government and the railroad industry have implemented their own security measures to keep rail transportation as safe as possible. The railroad industry created the **Surface Transportation and Public Transportation Information Sharing and Analysis Center (ST-PT ISAC)** at the request of the US Department of Transportation. This organization interfaces with government leaders, intelligence agencies, law enforcement personnel, and computer emergency response teams to spread top-secret threat information among railroad operators. The railroad industry also coordinates and regulates when and where certain things are transported, such as hazardous materials and munitions.

In addition, the government employs 100 rail security officers from the TSA and 450 rail safety inspectors from the Federal Railroad Administration. These individuals monitor rail activities for potential threats and

Strategic Rail Corridor Network (STRACNET): A network of railroads that transport Department of Defense munitions and other materials, including hazardous items

Surface Transportation and Public Transportation Information Sharing and Analysis Center (ST-PT ISAC): Interfaces with government leaders, intelligence agencies, law enforcement personnel, and computer emergency response teams to spread top-secret threat information among railroad operators.

inspect the rail infrastructure, engines, and tank cars against safety standards. Companies such as the Volpe National Transportation Center, Dow Chemical, Union Pacific, and the Union Tank Car Company also collaborate with the federal government to ensure the safety and integrity of tank cars (Goel et al. 2008).

Many other government organizations and policies are related to railroad security. The Department of Homeland Security obviously has some oversight of rail security. It is concerned about the possibility of attacks against the railroad industry. However, it is the National Transportation Safety Board that has the specific task of investigating the safety of tank cars to determine which are suitable for transporting hazardous materials (Goel et al. 2008). The Association of American Railroads likewise works to track and inspect rail shipments to increase safety.

There are number of laws and regulations to enhance rail security and safety at rail stations/yards. The Department of Homeland Security issues directives that require protective security measures to be taken by passenger rail operators. The Material Transportation Act provides the legal basis for assessing the costs and benefits associated with transporting hazardous materials. New laws are being created each year to address the threat of terrorism against the rail system. This is important because the threat of terrorism is dynamic and not static.

As can be seen, railroads are a significant part of US transportation network, moving either large loads of materials (potentially toxic substances) or a high volume of passengers to destinations all over the nation on a daily basis. This makes rail transportation a prime target for terrorist attacks. As such, the national government has created agencies and instituted policies to better monitor and track railway activity. The nation and its partners in the railroad industry will continue to find new ways to better secure this form of transportation for the future.

Figure 9-3

Trains may be the target of terrorism due to the confinement of a large number of people in a small area. Source: © US Department of Homeland Security.

IN THE REAL WORLD

VIPR Teams

The Visible Intermodal Prevention and Response Team (VIPR) is a program in the Transportation Security Administration. It falls under the TSA's Office of Law Enforcement/Federal Air Marshal Service. VIPR teams search and detain risky travelers at railroad and bus stations, on ferries, in tunnels, and at weigh stations and rest areas. They also have special detection devices to identify the presence of chemical, biological, and radioactive materials present on aircraft or railcars. The goal of these teams is to increase security in all modes of transportation. They also develop plans to improve interagency responses to terrorist attacks and other emergencies.

SELF-CHECK

1. Railroads to do not ship hazardous materials. True or False?
2. A train could be derailed by removing spikes. True or False?
3. Evacuation of a city due to a chemical release occurred in what state?
   (a) South Carolina
   (b) Florida
   (c) Oregon
   (d) Kansas
4. Why is security more problematic at a train station in comparison with the airport?

9.4 PROTECTION OF SEA PORTS AND MARITIME TRANSPORTATION

Like air and rail transportation, seaports and shipping have an incredible economic impact on the United States. According to the American Association of Port Authorities, commercial seaport activities in 2014 created employment opportunities for an estimated 23.1 million Americans. $4.6 trillion of the US economy can also be attributed to waterborne commerce, and businesses paid $321.1 billion in federal, state, and local taxes on these waterborne commercial transactions. In 2014 alone, seaport activities accounted for $41 billion in federal, state, and local tax revenues (American Association of Port Authorities 2015).

As can be seen, seaports are important for the economy. They act as important hubs for mass transportation of people and goods. Seaports also help to distribute raw materials and finished products around the world. However, the very same assets that make them so valuable also contribute to their inherent vulnerabilities. It is only logical to presume that terrorists will strike US seaports because they are so important. Sadly, terrorist organizations have made it clear that they wish to harm the United States by spreading fear, causing economic damage, and inflicting mass casualties in order to accomplish their agendas. Blowing up a seaport and launching other types of attacks against these facilities could, in the mind of terrorists, help them reach their goals.

Terrorists may also attack maritime transportation. For example, terrorists may attack cruise ships to create mass fatalities, subsequently impacting the tourism industry. Such an attack would also generate mass amounts of publicity to propagate terrorists' political messages and instill fear in others. Not only are ships potential targets for terrorist activity, but such vessels can also be used to facilitate attacks that are intended for other targets. Shipping containers can be used to smuggle WMD, explosives, or other arms to inflict damage on inland targets. Ships can be turned into WMD that impact docks, and terrorists may illegally cross the border through ships in order to mount attacks elsewhere in the United States.

Additionally, terrorists are beginning to finance their violent operations through piracy. Most piracy cases occur in international waters where there is minimal law enforcement, such as the Gulf of Aden, the Red Sea, or near Indonesia, the Malacca Straits, Malaysia, Singapore Straits, and the South China Sea. The payoff from taking over a ship and its cargo ranges from $8 to $200 million per vessel. After taking over a ship, pirates can easily change their identity by getting a new registry. They may also paint their ship in a remote dock and change flags. Modern-day piracy is extremely dangerous, as was depicted in the 2013 film *Captain Phillips*. Because of this threat, the United States Navy is working hard to counter such activities around the world. The Navy has even commissioned special ships to find pirates and prevent their activity in oceans and waterways around the world.

Because of the various threats posed to seaports and sea transportation, measures must be taken to ensure the security of people and goods on the water and in ports. The USCG, the Container Security Initiative, and the Customs-Trade Partnership Against Terrorism are some of the main organizations and programs that protection sea transportation. The United Nations International Maritime Organization (UNIMO) also works to prevent piracy and improve safety and security of maritime shipping.

As mentioned earlier, the USCG is an organization of the Department of Homeland Security. It enforces maritime law, manages vessel traffic, responds to maritime pollution, and participates in search and rescue operations (due to severe weather and sinking or incapacitated boats). The USCG is a vital asset in homeland security efforts to protect the safety of maritime activities.

Container Security Initiative (CSI):
One of the first measures taken by the government to protect maritime trade and ports against terrorism.

The **Container Security Initiative (CSI)** was one of the first measures taken by the government to protect maritime trade and ports against terrorism. Launched in 2004, this program has four components (Hoffman 2006, p. 145). First, shipments are to be placed in tamper-proof containers to limit the possibility that something can be smuggled into the United States. Second, computers are used to identify potential high-risk containers – those thought to be containing questionable goods, such

Figure 9-4

The Coast Guard has specially trained teams to deter attacks that could create significant financial losses and disrupt the economy.
Source: © US Coast Guard.

as WMD. Third, high-risk containers are prescreened to limit the chances that they arrive at the intended location. Finally, high-tech detection equipment is used to identify WMD before or during shipment or after arrival. In order to accomplish this goal, US Customs officials are being deployed abroad to push the borders out and speed up the process. Cargo manifests also have to be given to US officials 24 hours before containers are loaded onto ships. Hoffman notes that 18 of the top 20 seaports have agreed to the CSI. These ports represent about 70% of all containers shipped to the United States (Hoffman 2006, p. 145). Others need to be incorporated as time goes by.

Customs-Trade Partnership Against Terrorism (C-TPAT):
An agreement between the public and private sectors to protect international commerce from terrorist attacks.

The **Customs-Trade Partnership Against Terrorism (C-TPAT)** is an agreement between the public and private sectors to protect international commerce from terrorist attacks. As of 2006, it included at least 1600 importers, manufacturers, carriers (air, rail, and sea), brokers, port authorities, and others involved in international trade. These organizations voluntarily adhere to high standards pertaining to physical security, access controls, personnel security, training and education, manifest procedures, and other requirements relating to trade. Once certified by the government, these businesses are promised fewer and quicker inspections as long as they do not let their support of the agreement lapse. C-TPAT is a novel way to support efforts to prevent terrorist attacks through international trade.

United Nations International Maritime Organization:
A UN organization that establishes security rules regarding access and security at ports.

Finally, the **United Nations International Maritime Organization (UNIMO)** is another organization that is involved in the protection of sea transportation. It has created rules on piracy as well as standard security procedures to prevent the shipment of dangerous goods such as WMD. The UNIMO also establishes rules regarding access issues and security at seaports. It is a vital partner in preventing maritime terrorism.

As can be seen, the need to protect seaports and ships from attacks and to prevent terrorists from utilizing sea transportation to further their violent agendas remains vital concerns for homeland security. The hope is that government organizations and programs will continually innovate and improve the safety of people and goods on or near the water.

IN THE REAL WORLD

Terrorism at Sea

On 27 February 2004, an eight-pound TNT bomb exploded after being placed in a television set, which was brought onto the SuperFerry 14 vessel. The bomb was detonated about an hour after the ship departed. It caused serious damage to the ship and also ignited a fire on board. The captain issued an abandon ship order at 1:30 a.m. Those who were not killed in the blast jumped over board or boarded rescue boats. While most of the 744 passengers and 155 crew were spared, the attack killed 116 people. Not only was this the Philippine's deadliest attack, but it was the world's worst terrorist event at sea. After the investigation, it was determined that Redondo Cain Dellos placed the explosive on his bunk, but got off the ship before it disembarked. The bombing occurred because the company that owned the ship refused to give protection money to Abu Sayyaf.

SELF-CHECK

1. Ports will never be attacked because they are heavily guarded. True or False?

2. The United States Coast Guard is a military organization. True or False?

3. Piracy is most likely to occur where?

   (a) In international waters
   (b) In the United States
   (c) In Russian waters
   (d) Away from the Middle East

4. Explain the benefits of the Container Security Initiative.

9.5 PROTECTION OF PETROCHEMICAL FACILITIES

As noted through this book, terrorists have made it clear that they wish to cause harm to the United States and its citizens. They can do that by damaging the transportation systems described above. But they can also attack vulnerable points in the United States that will result in mass casualties. Petrochemical facilities are one of these high value targets. These facilities contain chemicals that are known to be extremely hazardous to human health. And these materials are ever present in the United States. In fact, the Environmental Protection Agency identified 1500 facilities that contain dangerous levels of these chemicals, and many of these facilities are located in highly populated areas (Kaplan 2006). The states of California, Florida, Illinois, Michigan, New Jersey, New York, North Carolina, Ohio, Pennsylvania, and Texas are particularly susceptible due to the number of plants in their jurisdictions.

Terrorists may attempt to enter these locations to steal hazardous materials to create WMD for future terrorist attacks. This is very troublesome because of the vulnerable nature of these facilities. Investigations reveal that some chemical facility sites lack gates, guards, and other protections to prevent or minimize theft and illegal acquisition. As an example, in 2014, ISIS easily took over the chemistry lab at the University of Mosul to test and build deadlier bombs. Therefore, chemical facilities may be overtaken to allow terrorists to manufacture explosive devices. Alternatively, chemical facilities may also be the target of the attack themselves. The threat against chemical facilities and refineries is not hypothetical. On 26 June 2015, Yassin Salhi drove a van with gas canisters into chemical plant in France owned by Air Products & Chemicals. Although the van exploded, it fortunately did not impact the rest of the targeted facility.

Figure 9-5

Numerous efforts are being undertaken to prevent terrorist attacks against chemical facilities. Source: https: © US Department of Homeland Security (www.dhs.gov/sites/default/files/publications/2014-08-25-fi nal-chemical-eo-status-report-508.pdf).

Chemical Facility Anti-Terrorism Standards (CFATS): A program that identifies risk at chemical facilities and regulates standards to ensure sufficient security measures are in place.

In order to deal with these threats and vulnerabilities, Congress initiated the **Chemical Facility Anti-Terrorism Standards** (CFATS) in 2007. CFATS is a program that identifies risk at chemical facilities (as well as at power plants, refineries, and universities) and regulates standards to ensure sufficient security measures are in place. The law was reauthorized in 2014 under the Protecting and Securing Chemical Facilities from Terrorist Attacks Act. It is a broad regulation that relates to perimeter restrictions, personnel background checks, key or electronic access to sensitive locations, activities related to operations (e.g. shipping and storage), and various threats including theft, sabotage, and cyber-attacks. While this law and program has received some criticism in the past (Sadiq 2014), it is one of many important measures to protect society from terrorist attacks against chemical facilities and refineries. If you are to work in homeland security, you should be aware of this important regulation. It is one of many measures to protect people from possible terrorist attacks.

IN THE REAL WORLD

Chemical Plots and Facility Security

In 2014, Tom Coburn (a Republican senator from Oklahoma) released a report from the Senate Committee on Homeland Security and Governmental Affairs. In the report, it was revealed that right-wing terrorists have planned attacks against facilities in Texas and California in 1997 and 2000, respectively. Law enforcement officials became aware of the plans and were able to arrest the perpetrators involved. Unfortunately, Islamic terrorists have also indicated their desire to attack these facilities. Due to this threat, the government is doing what it can to fortify chemical facilities. But the efforts may be insufficient. After spending $595 million dollars, only 39 of the 4011 facilities were actually inspected. The partnership between the government and industry will be important if the vulnerability of chemical facilities is to be reduced going forward. It is one of many efforts to protect the nation from future terrorist attacks.

SELF-CHECK

1. The states of California, Texas, and Ohio may be particularly prone to terrorist attacks due to the chemical plants. True or False?
2. Facilities that contain chemicals may provide terrorists material to launch attacks or they may be the target of the attack. True or False?
3. CFATS is a federal program that:
    (a) Protects seaports
    (b) Establishes safety and security standards at chemical facilities
    (c) Prevents attacks on airplanes
    (d) Corrects unsafe practices on US railways
4. What are some measures to protect chemical facilities?

SUMMARY

As the word homeland security implies, efforts must be taken to enhance the safety of the nation. If you are working in this field, one of your priorities will be to limit all illegal points of entry into the United States by terrorists. Improved immigration standards, border walls, and other measures may prevent this from happening. You will also need to understand various forms of transportation security and the methods to halt attacks in the air, on the rails and at sea.

These modes of transportation are clearly vulnerable and require numerous measures for their protection. Another important activity is to find ways to inhibit terrorist events that could impact chemical facilities. The dangers of failing to protect these locations could be consequential. For these reasons, border security, transportation security, and chemical facility security are vital to for your efforts to minimize the probability of terrorism.

ASSESS YOUR UNDERSTANDING

UNDERSTAND: WHAT HAVE YOU LEARNED?

 Go to **www.wiley.com/go/mcentire/homelandsecurity2e** to assess your knowledge of measures to prevent terrorist attacks.

SUMMARY QUESTIONS

1. Immigration and Customs Enforcement is in charge of air transportation security. True or False?
2. The Transportation Security Administration is an agency under the Department of Homeland Security. True or False?
3. VIPR teams have the intent of protecting trains and train stations. True or False?
4. The Customs-Trade Partnership Against Terrorism (C-TPAT) is a program to limit terrorist attacks against aircraft. True or False?
5. The Coast Guard is not a military organization. True or False?
6. Terrorists target transportation locations because they are heavily populated. True or False?
7. CAPPS II replaced the Secure Flight program. True or False?
8. Which program protects ports and maritime trade?
   (a) United Nations Port and Maritime Organization
   (b) Container Safety System
   (c) Customs and Container Partnership
   (d) Customs-Trade Partnership Against Terrorism
9. What is the name of the computer database that is used to screen passengers?
   (a) US ASSIST
   (b) US PREVENT
   (c) US CARGO
   (d) US-VISIT
10. The rail network used to transport DOD munitions is known as:
    (a) Rail Secure
    (b) STRACNET
    (c) HazRail
    (d) Rail Prevent
11. Which program is meant to protect cargo at sea?
    (a) The Cargo Protection Program
    (b) The Container Safety Program
    (c) The Container Security Initiative
    (d) The Drum and Car Security Program

12. What is the government effort to protect plants that use hazardous materials in their manufacturing process?

   (a) Hazardous Materials Protection Process
   (b) Chemical Facility Anti-Terrorism Standards
   (c) Chemical Facility Prevention Program
   (d) Manufacturing Counter-Terrorism Association

APPLYING THIS CHAPTER

1. You have been hired to advise the President about the threat of terrorists infiltrating the United States through the border. What are the various ways terrorists could enter the United States illegally?

2. What is the US Air Marshal program? How does it relate to terrorism and transportation security?

3. You are a member of the VIPR team? What are you looking for and how can you help secure the US rail system?

4. Your boss has asked you to explain the Container Security Initiative (CSI) to his peers from worldwide regional trade offices. What would you say? Is this initiative important? Why?

5. As an inspector for the Chemical Facility Anti-Terrorism Standards, you need to convince the manager of ACME Manufacturing that he or she needs to enforce additional safety measures in his/her company. What would you say?

BE A HOMELAND SECURITY PROFESSIONAL

Enhancing Border Control

You have been assigned to represent DHS at a press conference on the border. Why should you be aware of the political issues surrounding border control?

Protecting Transportation Modes

You have been given the assignment to brief the Secretary of the Department of Homeland Security on threats to transportation systems. What information would you relay about terrorist preferences for these targets and the potential impact of these types of attacks?

Security Maritime Trade and Seaports

Your boss of International Maritime Trade, Inc., has hired you to protect their facilities and operations. What threats exist against sea transportation? Who could help you to enhance the security of your company?

Hired as a Security Specialist

You have just been hired as a security specialist for a major industrial firm. You have been tasked with the responsibility of ensuring the safety and security of employees. What measures can you take to reduce the possibility of an attack against your facility?

KEY TERMS

Border	The territorial boundary of any nation along with its various points of entry
Chemical Facility Anti-Terrorism	A program that identifies risk at chemical facilities and regulates standards to ensure sufficient security measures are in place
Computer Assisted Passenger Prescreening System II (CAPPS II)	A former computer program utilized by the TSA to screen passengers against lists of known terrorists and others with criminal records.
Container Security Initiative (CSI)	One of the first measures taken by the government to protect maritime trade and ports against terrorism
Customs-Trade Partnership Against Terrorism (C-TPAT)	An agreement between the public and private sectors to protect international commerce from terrorist attacks
Federal Air Marshal Service	Another important organization of a few thousand marshals who act under the TSA
Immigration and Customs Enforcement (ICE)	The largest investigative organization within the Department of Homeland Security that attempts to deter illegal immigration and the smuggling of money and materials that support terrorism
Minutemen Project	Activities to promote border security carried out by a group of volunteers that founded the Minuteman Civil Defense Corps in Arizona
Secure Flight	The proposed program to replace the Computer Assisted Passenger Pre-screening System II
Strategic Rail Corridor Network (STRACNET)	A network of railroads that transport Department of Defense munitions and other materials, including hazardous items

Surface Transportation and Public Transportation Information Sharing and Analysis Center (ST-PT ISAC)	Interfaces with government leaders, intelligence agencies, law enforcement personnel, and computer emergency response teams to spread top-secret threat information among railroad operators
Transportation Security Act	A law designed to protect transportation systems in the United States
Transportation Security Administration (TSA)	A federal agency under the Department of Homeland Security created to protect our transportation systems from terrorist attacks
United Nations International Maritime Organization	A UN organization that establishes security rules regarding access and security at ports
United States Coast Guard (USCG)	A military branch within the Department of Homeland Security that is in charge of maritime law, environmental protection of waterways, search and rescue operations at sea, and interdiction of illegal aliens and contraband
United States Visitor and Immigrant Status Indicator Technology (US-VISIT)	A computer database used to screen passengers who wish to travel to the United States

REFERENCES

American Association of Port Authorities (2015). *The National Economic Impact of the U.S. Port System 2014*. Lancaster, PA: Martin Associates.

American Public Transportation Association. (2014). Public Transportation Ridership Report Fourth Quarter & End-of-Year 2014. https://www.apta.com/resources/statistics/Documents/Ridership/2014-q4-ridership-APTA.pdf.

Benztzel, C. (2006). Port and maritime security. In: *The McGraw-Hill Homeland Security Handbook* (ed. D.G. Kamien), 631–648. New York: McGraw-Hill.

Bove, V. and Bomelt, T. (2016). Does immigration induce terrorism? *Journal of Politics* 78 (2): 572–588.

Chertoff, M. (2009). *Homeland Security*. Philadelphia, PA: University of Pennsylvania Press.

Goel, R., Hartong, M., and Wijesekera, D. (2008). Security and the US rail infrastructure. *International Journal of Critical Infrastructure Protection* 1: 15–28.

Hoffman, F. (2006). Border security: closing the ingenuity gap. In: *Homeland Security and Terrorism: Readings and Interpretations* (ed. R. Howard, J. Forest and J. Moore), 142–166. New York: McGraw-Hill.

Imam, J. (18 October 2014). The surprising comeback of train travel. CNN.com. http://www.cnn.com/2014/10/15/travel/irpt-train (accessed 7 July 2017).

Jansen, B. (2017). U.K. joins U.S. in electronics ban on flights. *USA Today* (22 March), pp. 1A, 5A.

Kaplan, E. (2006). "Targets for terrorists: chemical facilities." Council on Foreign Relations. www.cfr.org/united-states/targets-terrorists-chemical-facilties/p12207.

Knickerbocker, B. (2006). Illegal immigrants in the US: how many are there?, *Christian Science Monitor* (16 May). https://www.csmonitor.com/2006/0516/p01s02-ussc.html.

Riley, K.J. (2006). Border control. In: *The McGraw-Hill Homeland Security Handbook* (ed. D.G. Kamien), 587–612. New York: McGraw-Hill.

Sadiq, A.-A. (2014). Chemical sector security: risk, vulnerabilities and chemical industry representatives' perspectives on CFATS. *Risk, Hazards and Crisis in Public Policy* 4 (3): 164–178.

10

PROTECTING AGAINST POTENTIAL ATTACKS

Threat Assessment, Mitigation, and Other Measures

Do You Already Know?

- How to assess the threat of terrorism
- The definition of structural and nonstructural mitigation
- Ways to increase physical security

For additional questions to assess your current knowledge of protecting against potential attacks, go to **www.wiley.com/go/mcentire/homelandsecurity2e**

What You Will Find Out	What You Will Be Able To Do
10.1 Components of threat assessments	• Evaluate the threat of terrorism against key assets and soft targets.
10.2 The importance of mitigating terrorist attacks by protecting critical infrastructure	• Predict the benefits of structural and nonstructural mitigation
10.3 The need to build structures with terrorism in mind	• Implement activities that will enhance physical security

INTRODUCTION

To minimize the impact of terrorist attacks, it is imperative that you take steps to protect the nation. If you are to work in homeland security, one of your primary responsibilities is to assess the threat of terrorism. This entails an evaluation of potential targets as well as the intents of terrorist organizations. Threat assessments also require that you work closely with homeland security partners at the federal, state, and local level as well as businesses in the private sector. Once your analysis is complete, you must then take measures to secure critical infrastructure and key assets. In addition, it is imperative that you enhance structural and nonstructural mitigation through architectural design, improved construction practices, zoning and set-back requirements, and other security measures. The overarching goal of this process as noted in this chapter is to make targets less attractive to terrorists and to diminish consequences should deterrence fail.

10.1 THREAT ASSESSMENT

Protection:
An attempt to deny attacks and defend oneself from terrorism.

Because of the nature of terrorism, it will be impossible to prevent every single terrorist attack. For this reason, it is necessary that you consider the benefit of strategies to enhance protection. In homeland security, **protection** is proactive activity designed to deny the possibility of attacks and defend oneself if they occur anyway. If terrorists are able to enter the United States or plan attacks that we are not aware of, we must find ways to minimize the appeal of anticipated targets and reduce the severity of attacks that do occur.

Threat assessment:
A careful study of the targets that might be appealing to terrorists.

In order to accomplish these goals, a threat assessment of the possible attacks that could be launched against our nation, states, and communities will be required. A **threat assessment** is a careful study of the targets that might be appealing to terrorists. It is, in some ways, similar to a hazard and vulnerability analysis in emergency management. A hazard and vulnerability analysis is an assessment of risk – an evaluation of what may occur along with possible consequences. However, instead of determining the potential impact of natural or technological disasters, a threat assessment focuses specifically on potential terrorist attacks and their probable impacts. It is an educated guess about what terrorists might do along with a determination of the outcome of such actions. In this sense, the analysis is equivalent to FEMA's threat and hazard identification and risk assessment (THIRA) process.

10.1.1 Critical Infrastructure, Key Assets, and Soft Targets

Critical infrastructure:
Interdependent networks composed of industrial, utility, transportation, and other distribution systems.

When conducting a threat assessment (or hazard and vulnerability analysis), it is important that you consider both critical infrastructure and key assets. **Critical infrastructure** is defined as interdependent networks composed of industrial, utility, transportation, and other distribution systems

(Edwards 2014; Pupura 2007, p. 359). According to Nancy Wong, the deputy director of the US Critical Infrastructure Assurance Office, examples of this infrastructure include:

- Information and communication systems (computer networks, line-based phone systems, and cell towers)
- Electrical systems (power plants, step-up and step-down stations, transformers)
- Transportation systems (airports, highways, bridges, seaports)
- Petrochemical systems (oil wells, refineries, storage facilities)
- Water systems (dams, sewage treatment plants, distribution lines) (as cited by McEntire et al. 2001, p. 5).

In addition to this list of vulnerable locations, we may also want to add farms, food processing plants, and food distribution networks. They, too, may be deemed as critical infrastructure.

All of these infrastructure systems are regarded to be "critical" because "their incapacity or destruction would have debilitating impact on the defense or economic security of the United States" (Clinton 1996). For instance, the loss of the Internet or phone systems would limit our ability to conduct business and communicate with others. ATMs and credit card swiping devices would be rendered useless, and business activity would be severely hampered. Disruption of energy systems would prohibit the heating and cooling of homes in the winter or summer and limit visibility at

IN THE REAL WORLD

The Attractiveness of Certain Targets

On 2 June 2007, Russell Defreitas, a resident of Brooklyn, New York, devised a plot to blow up fuel pipelines leading into JFK International Airport. According to the US Justice Department, Defreitas stated that the attack would provide "more bang for the buck" because of the anticipated fire as well as resulting economic and psychological consequences. Pipelines such as this one may be attractive targets because it is impossible to protect them completely due to their length. The loss of pipelines could lead to a fuel shortage and rising prices. For this reason, the security of pipelines is an important priority in the National Infrastructure Protection Plan. The Department of Homeland Security, under the direction of Homeland Security Presidential Directive 7, is working with oil and petroleum companies to plan responses to future threats in this area. Many corporations are now taking steps to protect the most vulnerable locations. Improved monitoring and shutdown strategies are making pipelines less appealing targets to terrorists (Kimery 2007).

night. As noted in Chapter 9, the destruction of transportation systems would also have an enormous impact on the movement of goods and services. Likewise, if petrochemical plants are taken out of service, many aspects of our lives, including manufacturing and travel, would be in jeopardy. An attack on water systems could result in mass sickness or even the death of thousands of people. An attack on food production and food transportation systems could likewise result in severe hunger and the loss of life. Critical infrastructure must therefore be evaluated as part of a comprehensive threat assessment. This is especially important since "The United States has not invested enough in the long-term maintenance of its levees, dams and power grids" (Chertoff 2009, p. 89).

Key assets:
Facilities, sites, and structures that are believed to require additional protection from terrorist attacks.

During your threat assessment, it is also imperative that you examine possible attacks against key assets. **Key assets** include "a variety of unique facilities, sites, and structures that require protection" (White House 2003, p. 71). Examples include banks, financial institutions, major corporations, fire and police stations, hospitals, national monuments, and government property (e.g. the White House, Capitol Hill, the Supreme Court Building, the Governor's Office, City Hall, etc.). These buildings are vital for the well-being, safety, and operation of government and our way of life. Key assets also have unique symbolic importance for the United States.

Besides considering critical infrastructure and key assets in your threat assessment, you must also recognize that any location of public assembly could be attacked by terrorists. For instance, sporting venues, fairgrounds, shopping malls, grocery stores, restaurants, bus stations, subways, and train cars are all likely to be attacked. Schools are also possible targets as was witnessed in Beslan, Russia, on 1 September 2004. Chechen separatists took over 1200 adults and children hostage at a local school. A few days later, a gun battle broke out and the fighting resulted in the death of 334 people (including 186 children). Such locations are likely to be attacked

Soft targets:
Potential sites of terrorist attacks because they are open and accessible to the public.

because they are regarded to be **soft targets**, meaning they are open and accessible to the public. Soft targets are also extremely vulnerable to attacks due to the high concentration of people in a single location. The 7 July 2005 attacks on the London subway and bus systems are additional examples of soft targets. Four terrorists detonated bombs, which killed 52 people and injured over 700 more. The events illustrated that soft targets such as these are extremely difficult to protect and defend because of the freedom of movement in and around them.

Subways are vulnerable to attacks because they are accessible to terrorists and contain a large number of potential victims.

10.1.2 Collaboration with Others to Identify Threats

In order to accurately assess the threat of attacks against critical infrastructure, key assets, and soft targets, it will be imperative that you work closely with others. Government agencies, department leaders, and members of the business community have special knowledge and expertise to help you determine the likelihood of an attack along with possible consequences.

At the local and state level, there are also many departments and individuals that can help you assess terrorist threats and risks. For instance, the Department of Transportation will have vital information about traffic patterns, key interchanges, and vulnerable bridges. Transportation officials will also possess vital information about subway systems and bus terminals. River authorities can provide you with data about the age and capacity of dams, while utility departments can help you assess the criticality of wastewater systems. Engineering departments will have statistics on building age and occupancy rates and should be consulted as part of comprehensive threat assessments. Planning and development agencies can help you acquire information about zoning requirements, demographic data, and census numbers. Parks and recreation departments can be contacted to gain knowledge about athletic venues, water parks, and large community gatherings. The Chamber of Commerce can likewise help you identify commercial districts and industrial areas that could be targeted. Public health agencies can determine the dangers associated with the use of biological agents. The private sector can also be a great partner when you conduct your threat assessment. Businesses are heavily involved with critical infrastructure. In fact, it is estimated that approximately 85% of all infrastructure is owned or operated by the private sector (Ewing 2004). Therefore, contacting companies associated with communications, energy production, and other economic activity can help you to understand the threats posed to phone lines, gas systems, and electrical grids. Manufacturers and the safety managers at petrochemical plants will also be able to assist you in the threat assessment. They will have knowledge about hazardous materials that could be used in or targeted by a terrorist attack. You can also plan with hospitals to identify the consequences of major public health emergencies associated with terrorist attacks. Insurance companies are also a great resource that can help you to identify the economic losses associated with potential attack scenarios.

There are many other possible partners to help you complete your threat assessment. Farmers will have vital information about cattle and agricultural production. Biotechnology research firms may have data about the diseases and medical advances they are studying in your community. Rail companies and trucking firms are good assets to contact if you want to know what is being shipped through your county.

Emergency managers are another wonderful resource for those working in homeland security. They are increasingly adept at conducting such these types of analyses because they have undertaken such assessments for decades to determine the risks associated with hazards and vulnerabilities. The key point is to recognize that you can and should tap into the expertise of others by networking and collaborating. Without involving specialists in your threat assessment, you will fail to accurately estimate the probability of an attack in your community and the associated negative potential.

Obviously, the FBI is the most important agency involved in threat assessments. It gathers intelligence about the plans of terrorists, which is then filtered down to state and local law enforcement officials. It also works to prevent attacks on computer systems and the Internet. In addition, FBI Special Agents can help you identify the threats associated with National Special Security Events (e.g. NCAA Final Four or the Super Bowl) through

SEAR:
Special Events Assessment Rating is used by the FBI to identify the risk of terrorist attacks against major public gatherings.

what is known as a Special Event Assessment Rating (SEAR). A **SEAR** assessment is an evaluation of the public importance of an event along with the potential risk of an attack.

Philip Purpura, the director of the Security Training Institute and Resource Center, has identified several additional partners at the federal level that could help you assess risks (Purpura 2007, p. 361). Such stakeholders, along with their area of expertise, include:

- **Department of Defense.** Responsible for the physical security of military installations and the defense industrial base.
- **Department of Energy.** Oversees the safeguarding of power plants, energy infrastructure, and nuclear weapons production facilities.
- **Department of Health and Human Services.** Concentrates on health-care assets.
- **Environmental Protection Agency.** Deals with water and wastewater systems.
- **Department of Agriculture.** Focuses on the need to protect agriculture and food infrastructure.
- **Department of Treasury.** Accountable for banking and financial institutions.
- **Department of the Interior.** Conscientious about the security of national monuments, such as the Statue of Liberty, Mount Rushmore, etc.

Finally, the Department of Homeland Security (DHS) is charged with the protection of numerous sites that could be the target of terrorist attacks. These locations include telecommunication systems, postal and shipping sectors, emergency services, and transportation systems (in conjunction with the Department of Transportation). DHS also works closely with the Nuclear Regulatory Commission to oversee the security of nuclear reactors and nuclear waste sites. It likewise collaborates with the Secret Service to oversee special events and the National Cyber Response Coordination Group to monitor cyber security. Another responsibility of DHS is the protection of government facilities. The Federal Protective Service helps DHS to reach this vital goal. For this reason, no threat assessment would be complete without some type of consultation with the DHS. There are also published guidelines to help you assess the risks to and vulnerability of critical infrastructure (DHS 2011, 2013).

10.1.3 Points of Consideration

As you assess threats and associated vulnerabilities, you should take into consideration many important questions, for instance:

- Are there known groups in your jurisdiction that may desire to carry out a terrorist attack?
- What are the possible targets that they may wish to destroy?
- How easy would it be to carry out an attack against critical infrastructure through sabotage?

- What is the likelihood of key assets being attacked with traditional explosives?
- Which soft targets would result in more fatalities due to the concentration of people in the area?
- Which of the above locations are more likely to be targeted than others?
- Are any measures in place to defend these locations from an attack?
- What are the probable consequences of a terrorist attack at that specific location?
- What types of attacks would have the greatest impact on life, property, the environment, government and corporate operations, and general social disruption?

Answering these questions can lead to very formal and complex threat assessments, which could take months and even years to complete. Of course, there is always a difficulty of knowing what you should focus on: probability, consequences, or both likelihood and impact. Some attacks may be highly probable, but result in limited consequences. As an example, a conventional explosive might fall into this category. Other attacks may be improbable, but produce significant impacts. A biological attack is one type of event because it could kill hundreds of thousands of people. It is thus a challenge to know how to weigh each scenario and its resulting severity.

IN THE REAL WORLD

Risk-based Funding Prioritization

In June 2006, the Intelligence and Analysis Office in the Department of Homeland Security released the findings of a study about the risk facing states around the nation. The study examined a number of factors including population size and density, the importance of critical infrastructure, proximity to the border and ports, the presence of hazardous materials, and iconic value, among other variables. The results provided one view on how to prioritize homeland security funding around the nation. Below is a list of states and territories in rank order:

1. California	11. Georgia
2. Texas	12. Louisiana
3. New York	13. Arizona
4. Florida	14. Massachusetts
5. Illinois	15. Washington
6. District of Columbia	16. North Carolina
7. Michigan	17. Indiana
8. Ohio	18. Virginia
9. New Jersey	19. Kentucky
10. Pennsylvania	20. Minnesota

(Continued)

(Continued)

21. Maryland		37. Utah	
22. Missouri		38. West Virginia	
23. Tennessee		39. Nebraska	
24. Kansas		40. Maine	
25. Alabama		41. Rhode Island	
26. Wisconsin		42. Wyoming	
27. Mississippi		43. North Dakota	
28. Colorado		44. Hawaii	
29. Connecticut		45. Vermont	
30. Oregon		46. Idaho	
31. South Carolina		47. Delaware	
32. Oklahoma		48. Montana	
33. Iowa		49. New Hampshire	
34. Nevada		50. South Dakota	
35. Arkansas		51. Alaska	
36. New Mexico			

Nevertheless, the process of conducting a threat assessment can be simplified if you put yourself in the position of a terrorist. People playing this role are known in war games as the "red team" (while the "blue team" would include those responding to the actions of the red team). If you were a terrorist, what critical infrastructure, key assets, and soft targets would give you maximum publicity for your cause? Which of these targets would be easiest to infiltrate and operate in? How would you implement the attack to have the greatest potential impact? These thoughts are morbid, but are necessary if you are to be successful in assessing threats.

Another method to help you determine threats and vulnerabilities is a risk assessment matrix. David Alexander, a well-known scholar of emergency management, has developed a table to determine the risk of natural and technological disasters. It is based on an examination of probability and severity (Alexander 2002, p. 57). Adapting this table to the threat of terrorism, different types of events (e.g. assassination, bombings, mass shootings, attacks involving weapons of mass destruction) can be categorized in Table 10-1.

Table 10-1: Risk assessment matrix

	Probability of occurrence				
Severity	Impossible	Improbable	Occasional	Probable	Frequent
Negligible	Acceptable	Acceptable	Acceptable	Acceptable	Acceptable
Marginal	Acceptable	Acceptable	Acceptable	Acceptable	Significant
Moderate	Acceptable	Acceptable	Acceptable	Significant	Critical
Serious	Acceptable	Acceptable	Significant	Critical	Critical
Catastrophic	Acceptable	Significant	Critical	Critical	Critical

Figure 10-1

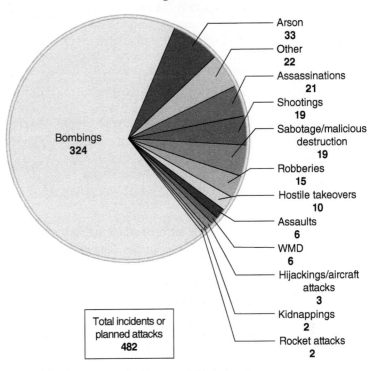

Arson
33

Other
22

Assassinations
21

Shootings
19

Sabotage/malicious
destruction
19

Robberies
15

Hostile takeovers
10

Assaults
6

WMD
6

Hijackings/aircraft
attacks
3

Kidnappings
2

Rocket attacks
2

Bombings
324

Total incidents or
planned attacks
482

Bombings are the most common threats from terrorists, but other attacks are possible and may have even greater consequences.

Terrorist attacks placed in low probability and low severity cells are described as having an acceptable level of risk. Attacks listed with a moderate degree of probability and severity is defined as having significant risk. Events described as being frequent and catastrophic are regarded to be of critical risk.

IN THE REAL WORLD

Catastrophic Scenarios

In 2004, US homeland security officials identified 15 possible catastrophic scenarios. It is interesting to note that only two of them are natural disasters, even though they are historically more prevalent than terrorist attacks.

Scenario 1: Nuclear detonation – 10-kiloton improvised nuclear weapon

Scenario 2: Biological attack – Aerosol anthrax

Scenario 3: Biological disease outbreak – Pandemic influenza

Scenario 4: Biological attack – Plague

Scenario 5: Chemical attack – Blister agent

Scenario 6: Chemical attack – Toxic industrial chemicals

(Continued)

(Continued)

Scenario 7: Chemical attack – Nerve agent

Scenario 8: Chemical attack – Chlorine tank explosion

Scenario 9: Natural disaster – Major earthquake

Scenario 10: Natural disaster – Major hurricane

Scenario 11: Radiological attack – Radiological dispersal devices

Scenario 12: Explosives attack – Bombing using improvised explosive device

Scenario 13: Biological attack – Food contamination

Scenario 14: Biological attack – Foreign animal disease (foot and mouth disease)

Scenario 15: Cyber attack

As possible terrorist attack scenarios are being described, you should determine your top priorities. The Federal Emergency Management Agency has a publication, *Building Design for Homeland Security*, that discusses how to accurately assess risks. This manual can be accessed at http://www.fema.gov/library/viewRecord.do?id=1939. It will help you be most concerned about attacks that are deemed to be significant or critical. However, the process of determining risks is subjective and cannot be determined with 100% certainty. While risk estimation may include complex mathematical models that incorporate an evaluation of costs and benefits of specific mitigation measures, the unpredictability and adaptability of terrorists make threat assessments problematic at best. Regardless, doing your best to evaluate risk, even when not perfect, is preferable to doing nothing at all.

Figure 10-2

Subways are vulnerable to attacks because they are accessible to terrorists and contain a large number of potential victims.
Source: © Shutterstock. Reprinted with permission of Shutterstock.

IN THE REAL WORLD

Homeland Security Resources

As an employee in homeland security, you may not initially understand the methods to assess the threat of terrorism. Fortunately, there are many resources available to help you fulfill this vital responsibility. Besides working with government officials in emergency management and the Department of Homeland Security, you can also acquire assistance from the private sector. Emergency & Disaster Management, Inc. is one company that can help you assess hazards and vulnerability. It employs unique methodologies to measure risk including blast analysis, entry control point studies, and impact assessments. With this information, Emergency & Disaster Management, Inc. can then help to create and implement effective mitigation strategies based on current antiterrorism standards. For further information, see www.emergency-management.net.

SELF-CHECK

1. A threat assessment is a study about what types of attacks could occur and how bad they might be. True or False?

2. Farms and food processing plants are not considered critical infrastructure. True or False?

3. Which of the following is considered a soft target?
   (a) A computer network
   (b) A petrochemical plant
   (c) A school
   (d) A sewage treatment plant

4. Why is it important to work with others to assess the threat of terrorism?

10.2 STRUCTURAL AND NONSTRUCTURAL MITIGATION

Structural mitigation
Special construction practices and materials to limit the impact of terrorist attacks.

Nonstructural mitigation
Methods beyond construction that may limit the possibility or consequences of terrorist attacks.

Besides assessing threats against critical infrastructure, key assets, and soft targets, protecting against terrorist attacks may require two types of mitigation, which are commonly discussed in emergency management. This includes structural and nonstructural mitigation. **Structural mitigation** involves special construction practices and materials to limit the consequences of terrorist attacks. For instance, installing blast-resistant glass on government buildings is an example of structural mitigation. **Nonstructural mitigation** includes other methods (beyond construction) that may limit the possibility or impact of terrorist attacks. Regulations on building location or the use of security guards are examples of nonstructural mitigation.

Both structural and nonstructural approaches are vital to homeland security. They can help to reduce injuries and deaths, limit economic losses, and minimize the disruption associated with terrorism.

IN THE REAL WORLD

Four Layers of Defense

The Federal Emergency Management Agency has described four layers of defense against terrorist attacks. These layers include the following:

Deter: Limiting access to a target or countering the weapon or tactic being used. This usually includes perimeter control, fencing, locks, and lighting.

Deny: Designing buildings and infrastructure to withstand blasts or minimize the effects of chemical, biological, or radiological weapons.

Devalue: Finding ways to minimize the consequence of an attack, thereby discouraging the desire of terrorists to attack.

Detect: Gathering intelligence to monitor threats and using security to prevent access to buildings.

10.2.1 Architectural Design and Construction

In the *Reference Manual to Mitigate Potential Terrorist Attacks Against Buildings*, the US DHS notes that building design and fabrication plays a large role in the potential impact of terrorist attacks (US Department of Homeland Security 2003). For instance, "U"- or "L"-shaped buildings should be avoided since they channel and exacerbate the force of shock waves. The use of steel reinforcement in concrete buildings, as well as the number and redundancy of support columns, may minimize also the damage or collapses created by explosive devices. Windows glazed with laminate security film may inhibit or slow down flying shrapnel and other debris. Sprinklers and fire-resistant materials can be installed to prevent arson-induced fires from spreading. Ventilation systems can also be protected in certain ways to discourage or stop hazardous materials releases. For instance, intake vents can be isolated and inaccessible to those without authorization. The great benefit of implementing these structural mitigation measures in light of the threat of terrorism is that they will often be applicable to other types of hazards (e.g. earthquakes, hurricanes, tornadoes, electrical fires, etc.). In fact, it is well known in the emergency management community that these hazards are often more likely to occur than terrorist attacks. Terrorism provides yet another reason why architects and construction companies should take structural mitigation seriously.

Figure 10-3

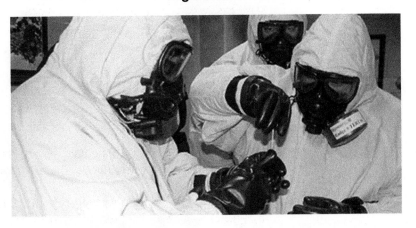

Chemical attacks are 1 of 15 anticipated attacks against
the United States. Source: © FEMA

10.2.2 Zoning and Set-back Regulations

Other ways to protect against terrorist attacks at the local level include
zoning and set-back requirements as well as unique devices to prevent the
movement of people and vehicles. **Zoning** involves regulations that delineate where buildings can be located. Just as you would not want an elemen-
tary school located near an industrial plant, you do not want a shopping
mall located near a rail yard that transports chemical tankers. In either case,
the accidental or intentional release of hazardous materials could injure or
kill scores of people, or even hundreds or thousands of individuals.
Prescribing the best location for businesses, homes, sporting venues, and
critical infrastructure could do much to limit the impact of terrorist attacks.
Planning with spatial relationships in mind can be extremely beneficial. For
instance, if no homes are located in flood plains downstream, terrorists will
be less likely to blow up dams and levees. There is minimal incentive to
carry out such an attack because the consequences will be less severe. The
added benefit of such planning is that repetitive flood losses from excessive
precipitation will also be minimized as a result. This could also save many
lives and countless dollars on the part of taxpayers.

In contrast to zoning, **set-back requirements** describe the proximity
of buildings to roads and parking lots. Many, if not most, terrorist attacks
involve vehicle-delivered bombs. Creating fewer vehicle access points near
a building, avoiding parking lots beneath structures, and moving parking
sites away from edifices will dampen the effects of explosive detonations.
For instance, if the driveway leading next to the Murrah Federal Building
in Oklahoma City were eliminated, the impact of Timothy McVeigh's 1995
bomb would have logically been minimized. A bomb a half a block away
will produce far less damage to a building and its occupants than an explosive device placed within several yards of the structure. Standoff zones can
be a great defense against acts of terrorism.

Zoning:
Regulations that delineate
where buildings can be
located.

**Set-back
requirements:**
Laws that describe the
proximity of buildings to
roads and parking lots.

Figure 10-4

1. Locate assets stored on site, but outside the building within view of occupied rooms in the facility.	8. Minimize vehicle access points.
2. Eliminate parking beneath buildings.	9. Eliminate potential hiding places near the building; provide an unobstructed view around building.
3. Minimize exterior signage or other indications of asset locations.	10. Site building within view of other occupied buildings on the site.
4. Locate trash receptacles as far from the building as possible.	11. Maximize distance from the building to the site boundary.
5. Eliminate lines of approach perpendicular to the building.	12. Locate building away from natural or manmade vantage points.
6. Locate parking to obtain stand-off distance from the building.	13. Secure access to power/heat plants, gas mains, water supplies, and electrical service.
7. Illuminate building exteriors or sites where exposed assets are located.	

There are many things that can be done to buildings to minimize the probability of an attack. Source: © US Department of Defense.

10.2.3 Other Protective Measures

There are countless other mitigation measures that can be taken to reduce the probability and consequences of terrorist attacks. Purpura (2007) and Kelly (2006) have identified several of them:

Bollards:
Metal or concrete posts installed into the earth or cement to keep vehicles from entering restricted areas.

- **Bollards,** which are metal or concrete posts installed into the ground or cement, can be used to keep vehicles from entering restricted areas. They make it difficult for cars or trucks to come closer to buildings.
- Trees and vegetation may be planted around buildings to limit the blast from explosives. They serve as a natural barrier during terrorist attacks.
- Walls, fences, and barbed wire can be employed around critical infrastructure and key assets to maintain a secure perimeter. While these devices can be broken or cut, they are a vital layer in security.

- Proper lighting can create a psychological deterrent for terrorists and enable detection if they attempt to carry out attacks at night. Terrorists might seek a location that has no lighting or it will be easier for them to be apprehended.

- Guards and guard dogs can help patrol facilities and control employee and visitor traffic. They can sense when behavior is suspicious and take appropriate measures.

- Gates and doors should have locks (whether mechanical or electromagnetic). This will prevent unauthorized access into the building or its rooms.

- Metal detectors and X-ray scanners may be used to detect weapons and explosives. Such devices are essential at courthouses and other key assets.

- Background checks can be conducted on prospective employees to determine who should be hired. This will prevent terrorism from internal sources.

- ID badges and access cards allow or restricted from movement into sensitive areas. This will help to ensure that authorized employees are only permitted to roam freely in certain locations. Note: The United States implemented the REAL ID program in 2005 to improve the security, authentication, and issuance procedures standards for state driver's licenses. All states are to be compliant by the year 2020.

- Pin numbers and biometric identifiers (e.g. fingerprint or retinal scans) are other means to permit or confine movement of employees. They are useful to gain or restrict access to mission-critical areas.

- Special attention should be given to security in lobbies, loading docks, and mail rooms. These are logical locations where terrorists might attack.

- Cameras, alarms, and intrusion systems (e.g. motion detectors) are valuable tools to monitor physical security. They can help to warn of unusual activity or solve questions of who was responsible for terrorist attacks.

Figure 10-5

Bollards like these can prevent vehicle-delivered bombs from reaching their intended targets. Source: © FEMA.

In addition, special efforts need to be undertaken for events and festivals. Advanced planning – perhaps with the use of the eSAFE system (Hu and Racherla 2008) – could help to protect such vulnerable events. The goal is to consider what could happen and take steps to enhance safety and security. In addition, when key leaders and dignitaries (e.g. CEOs and the president) are to be present at a specific location, physical security becomes even more vital. Areas may need to be "sniffed" or "swept" in advance for bombs, and access to the building or area carefully controlled. Additional security guards, bodyguards, snipers, and special force teams may need to be used to protect such officials. In addition, it is imperative to plan for emergency response needs should something unexpected occur. Escape routes and medical care for dignitaries are just of few of the things that need to be considered when national or state leaders are involved in public events and gatherings.

Where possible and when required, it would also be wise to hire someone to be in charge of security measures at any given location. According to the US Government Accountability Office, "having a chief security officer position for physical assets is recognized in the security industry as essential in organization with large numbers of mission-critical facilities" (US Government Accountability Office 2005, pp. 43–44). This person should be familiar with the American Society for Industrial Security, which has additional information about physical security. He or she might also want to "visit a local airport, jail or courthouse to see the levels of complexity in equipment, operations and management of security systems" (Evans 2001, p. 96). However, the security specialist should not be viewed as the only one in charge of security. Everyone must take more interest in security if terrorist attacks are to be minimized. This includes anyone working in the public and private sectors as well as the public at large. Attacks have been prevented by citizens who saw something out of the ordinary and reported suspicious behavior. The adage "see something, say something" is a good motto for everyone to remember and follow.

IN THE REAL WORLD

Virginia Protects Itself

After 9/11, the state of Virginia felt a need to increase security at water treatment plants, power facilities, and tunnels – all potential targets for terrorist attacks. State officials determined that these locations are extremely vulnerable and that employees could take advantage of this risk-laden situation if they had ill-intent. For this reason, it was decided that background checks would be performed on employees applying for sensitive jobs. The Cooperative Extension Service will also verify that employees in the agricultural sector are legal residents of the United States. These are only a few of the vital measures that can be taken to mitigate terrorist attacks.

SELF-CHECK

1. ID cards and pin numbers are examples of structural mitigation. True or False?
2. The shape of buildings can reduce or exacerbate the blast waves from explosions. True or False?
3. The proximity of buildings to roads and parking lots pertains to:
   (a) Zoning
   (b) Set-back requirements
   (c) Structural mitigation
   (d) Bollards
4. What special measures need to be taken to protect dignitaries?

SUMMARY

Because it may be impossible to prevent terrorism, it will also be necessary to protect locations against possible terrorist attacks. You will need to work with others to assess the threats posed to critical infrastructure, key assets, and soft targets. In addition, it is important that you understand the benefits of mitigation practices as well as the difference between structural and nonstructural mitigation. In particular, you should promote the design and construction of buildings that take terrorism into account. You will likewise need to consider zoning and set-back requirements as well as a variety of other measures to augment physical security. While no single measure will be foolproof, a strong system of self-defense will diminish the possibility and effects of terrorism.

ASSESS YOUR UNDERSTANDING

UNDERSTAND: WHAT HAVE YOU LEARNED?

 Go to **www.wiley.com/go/mcentire/homelandsecurity2e** to assess your knowledge of mitigation.

SUMMARY QUESTIONS

1. It is possible to prevent all terrorist attacks from occurring. True or False?

2. A threat assessment is an evaluation of anticipated targets of terrorist attacks. True or False?

3. Infrastructure is regarded to be "critical" if its destruction would have a severe impact upon the well-being of the United States. True or False?

4. The Department of the Interior can help you assess the threat of terrorism posed to power plants and nuclear facilities. True or False?

5. An important question to consider when assessing threat is: Are there any measures in place to deter terrorism from occurring at that location? True or False?

6. Structural and nonstructural mitigation will never reduce death, economic losses, and disruption caused by terrorist attacks. True or False?

7. Walls and fences may inhibit the ability of terrorists to launch attacks at businesses and manufacturing plants. True or False?

8. It might be wise for any organization deemed to be a likely target for attack to hire a security specialist. True or False?

9. A threat assessment is similar to:
   (a) A structural mitigation technique
   (b) A hazard and vulnerability analysis
   (c) A key asset target
   (d) A set-back requirement

10. Which is not considered to be included in critical infrastructure?
   (a) Transportation systems
   (b) Electrical systems
   (c) The White House
   (d) Information and communication systems

11. Which of the following is believed to be a soft target?
   (a) Restaurants
   (b) Police stations
   (c) An oil refinery
   (d) The Supreme Court Building

12. What organization could help you assess threats posed against dams?

   (a) The FBI
   (b) The Department of the Interior
   (c) Parks and recreation
   (d) River authorities

13. A metal posed placed in the ground to prevent movement of vehicles is best known as:

   (a) Structural mitigation
   (b) Blast reduction capacitor
   (c) Nonstructural mitigation
   (d) A bollard

14. Which measure would help to prevent someone from bringing a weapon into a building?

   (a) Fences
   (b) Background checks
   (c) Metal detectors
   (d) Cameras

APPLYING THIS CHAPTER

1. After mentioning to your neighbor that you are studying homeland security, he says that there is no point in trying to figure out where terrorists will attack next. He believes they are too unpredictable. What would you say to him about the benefit of threat assessments?

2. As an employee working in homeland security, you have been asked to conduct a threat assessment looking specifically at the private sector. How could companies help you with your responsibility?

3. As seasoned emergency manager in your community, you have just received word that the city council has approved your request to relocate the emergency operations center. What structural, zoning, and set-back measures could help protect it against terrorist attacks?

4. As the public information officer in your homeland security department, you have been asked to be interviewed about effective security procedures in buildings. What would you say in your remarks?

BE A HOMELAND SECURITY PROFESSIONAL

Meeting with the FBI

You are an official in the Department of Homeland Security. It is your responsibility to assess potential targets around the nation. The FBI has requested that you meet with them to discuss the consequences of an attack against transportation systems. They fear that a domestic terrorist organization is intent on carrying out such an attack. What would you say about the vulnerability and criticality of transportation systems?

Assignment: Things to Consider When Assessing Threats

Write a two-page paper discussing the concerns you might need to address if you were to complete a threat assessment. Be as thorough as possible.

Hired as a Security Specialist

You have just been hired as a security specialist for a major industrial firm. You have been tasked with the responsibility of ensuring the safety and security of employees. What measures can you take to reduce the possibility of an attack against your facility?

KEY TERMS

Bollards	Metal or concrete posts installed into the earth or cement to keep vehicles from entering restricted areas
Critical infrastructure	Interdependent networks composed of industrial, utility, transportation, and other distribution systems
Key assets	Facilities, sites, and structures that are believed to require additional protection from terrorist attacks
Nonstructural mitigation	Methods beyond construction that may limit the possibility or consequences of terrorist attacks
Protection	An attempt to deny attacks and defend oneself from terrorism
SEAR	Special Events Assessment Rating is used by the FBI to identify the risk of terrorist attacks against major public gatherings
Set-back requirements	Laws that describe the proximity of buildings to roads and parking lots
Soft targets	Potential sites of terrorist attacks because they are open and accessible to the public
Structural mitigation	Special construction practices and materials to limit the impact of terrorist attacks
Threat assessment	A careful study of the targets that might be appealing to terrorists
Zoning	Regulations that delineate where buildings can be located

REFERENCES

Alexander, D. (2002). *Principles of Emergency Planning and Management*. New York: Oxford University Press.

Chertoff, M. (2009). *Homeland Security*. Philadelphia, PA: University of Pennsylvania Press.

Clinton, W.J. (1996). Critical infrastructure protection: executive order 13010. *Federal Register* 61: 37347–37350.

DHS (2011). The strategic National risk assessment in support of PPD 8: a comprehensive risk-based approach toward a security and resilient nation. http://dhs.gov/xlibrary/asssets/rma-strategic-national-risk-assessment-ppd8.pdf (accessed 2 August 2017).

DHS (2013). Supplemental tool: executing a critical infrastructure risk management approach. https://www.dhs.gov/sites/default/files/publications/NIPP-2013-Suppment-Executing-A-CI-Risk_Mgmt-Approach-508.pdf (accessed 2 August 2017).

Edwards, M. (2014). *Critical Infrastructure Protection*, NATO Science for Peace and Security Series. Amsterdam: IOS Press.

Evans, R.J. (2001). Public works and terrorism. In: *Terrorism: Defensive Strategies for Individuals, Companies and Governments* (ed. L.J. Hogan), 95–100. Washington, DC: Amlex, Inc.

Ewing, L. (2004). The missing link in the partnership. *Homeland Security* 1.

Hu, C. and Racherla, P. (2008). eSAFE: the knowledge management system for safe festivals and events. In: *Homeland Security Handbook* (ed. J. Pinkowski), 267–279. Boca Raton, FL: CRC Press.

Kelly, R.J. (2006). Role of corporate security. In: *The McGraw-Hill Homeland Security Handbook* (ed. D.G. Kamien), 745–765. New York: McGraw-Hill.

Kimery, A. (2007). Petrojihad: the next front? *HS Today: Insight and Analysis for Homeland Security Decision Makers* 4 (9): 36–42.

McEntire, D.A., Robinson, R. J., and Weber, R.T. (2001). Managing the threat of terrorism. *IQ Rep. 33 (12)*. Washington, DC: International City/County Management Association.

Purpura, P.P. (2007). *Terrorism and Homeland Security: An Introduction with Applications*. Burlington, MA: Butterworth-Heinemann.

US Department of Homeland Security (2003). *Reference Manual to Mitigate Potential Terrorist Attacks against Buildings*. FEMA: Washington, DC.

US Government Accountability Office (2005). Homeland security: actions needed to better protect national icons and federal office buildings from terrorism. www.gao.gov/cgi-bin/getrpt?GAO-050681 (accessed 8 May 2017).

White House (2003). The national strategy for the physical protection of critical infrastructure and key assets. www.whitehouse.gov (accessed 23 October 2017).

CHAPTER 11

PREPARING FOR THE UNTHINKABLE
Efforts for Readiness

Do You Already Know?

- The importance and nature of preparedness
- The role of an advisory council
- How to write an emergency operations plan
- The benefit of training and community education

 For additional questions to assess your current knowledge of preparedness, go to **www.wiley.com/go/mcentire/homelandsecurity2e**

What You Will Find Out	What You Will Be Able To Do
11.1 How to define preparedness	• Evaluate the different roles of federal and state governments
11.2 Why an advisory council is vital	• Compose a city emergency management ordinance
11.3 The need for budgets and grants	• Develop an emergency operations plan
11.4 How to train and educate the community	• Design and conduct terrorism exercises

INTRODUCTION

One of your important roles in homeland security is to anticipate and prepare for possible acts of terrorism. In order to accomplish this objective, you must understand the concept and nature of preparedness. It is also vital that you are aware of federal and state activities that increase readiness levels as well as steps that must be taken for preparation at the local level. In particular, you must establish a preparedness council, designate and equip an emergency operations center, and plan for the impacts of possible terrorist attacks. Training of first responders and education of citizens will also improve your ability to react if terrorism occurs. By undertaking the measures identified in this chapter, you will enhance your community's capability to deal with the negative effects of terrorist attacks.

11.1 THE IMPORTANCE AND NATURE OF PREPAREDNESS

No matter what steps are taken to prevent terrorist attacks or mitigate their adverse impacts, it is always possible that terrorism will occur anyway. A common saying is that homeland security is similar to the game of soccer. Goalies and homeland security officials have to be effective 100% of the time to reach their objectives. In contrast, forwards and terrorists only have to be successful once to accomplish theirs. This reality poses an enormous challenge for those working in the field and profession. There is simply too much vulnerability in comparison to the resources and capacity we have at hand at any given period of time. Richardson (2007, p. 176) puts it this way: "If victory means making the United States invulnerable to terrorist attack, we are never, ever going to be victorious."

For instance, if our intelligence officers are able to intercept one communication stream, terrorists will switch to another. If counterterrorism forces close down a training camp in a specific location, it is likely that a new one will emerge elsewhere. If the United States is able to control legal entry through passports and visas, terrorists will work to find ways to cross the border illegally. If we spend time and energy protecting dams, national monuments, and government buildings, terrorists will simply attack schools, churches, and shopping malls. Prudence therefore dictates that our nation takes adequate measures to prepare for potential terrorist attacks (Donahue 2014). This brings up the concept of preparedness.

Preparedness is not simple or straightforward. Even though it has been the subject of attention in emergency management for years, there is no agreement on a single definition (Kirschenbaum 2002). Godschalk views preparedness as "actions taken in advance of an emergency to develop operational capabilities to facilitate an effective response" (1991, p. 136). Gillespie and Streeter (1987) suggest that preparedness includes numerous actions taken to improve the safety and effectiveness of a community's response during a disaster. While these views seem to downplay the relation of preparedness to recovery, the Department of Homeland Security (DHS) believes preparedness is related to all aspects of dealing with terrorism.

According to the DHS, preparedness is "the range of deliberate, critical tasks and activities necessary to build, sustain, and improve the operational capability to prevent, protect against, respond to and recover from domestic incidents" (Department of Homeland Security 2004, p. 134). For the purposes of this chapter, prevention and protection are more concerned about avoidance, deterrence, denial, and mitigation. Therefore, **preparedness** assumes terrorist attacks will occur and therefore promotes concerted efforts to improve response and recovery capabilities. Preparedness is thus necessary for more effective post-terrorism operations. It is often driven by policy and activity at the federal and state levels.

Preparedness:
Concerted efforts to improve response and recovery capabilities.

11.1.1 Federal and State Initiatives

Responsibility for national preparedness falls to the federal government in general and the DHS and Federal Emergency Management Agency (FEMA) in particular. However, in an attempt to improve the readiness of the nation for terrorist attacks, the President often issues policies to encourage improved preparedness programs. As an example, on 4 May 2007, President Bush issued Homeland Security Presidential Directive (HSPD) 20. This order establishes continuity of operation requirements for all executive departments and agencies. **Continuity of operation** deals with the maintenance of government functions after terrorist attacks through the identification of leader succession, alternate work sites, and resumption of operational activities. The idea is the government must continue to serve the American people if its leaders, departments, and missions fall victim to terrorism. While continuity of operations plans existed among some federal entities before HSPD 20, this directive clarified their purpose and mandated further compliance.

Continuity of operation:
The maintenance of government functions after terrorist attacks through the identification of leader succession, alternate work sites, and resumption of operational practices.

Congress also passes many laws to enhance our nation's preparedness for terrorist attacks. Such pieces of legislation started in the 1990s and have become more frequent over time. Examples of such laws are numerous and include:

- The National Defense Authorization Law, which was passed after the World Trade Center bombing in 1993. It specified that FEMA and other federal agencies should devote more attention to planning for future terrorist attacks.

- The Antiterrorism and Effective Death Penalty Act of 1996, which required additional training for first responders and provided funds to accomplish this goal.

- The Defense Against Weapons of Mass Destruction Act (also known as the Nunn, Lugar, and Domenici Act) was also approved in 1996, and it mandated improved preparedness measures in 120 cities around the United States regarded to be vulnerable to terrorist attacks.

- The Public Health Security and Bioterrorism Preparedness and Response Act of 2002 provided local and state governments $4.6 billion to improve public health readiness around the nation.

- The Comprehensive Homeland Security Act of 2003 recommends improvement in the area of interoperable communications for first responders.

Figure 11-1

Congressional officials pass laws to help the nation prepare for terrorist attacks. Source: © FEMA.

There are additional laws that deal more specifically with preparedness for all types of disaster scenarios. One important example is the Robert T. Stafford Disaster Relief and Emergency Assistance Act, which was passed on 23 November 1988 (see https://www.fema.gov/media-library-data/ 1519395888776-af5f95a1a9237302af7e3fd5b0d07d71/StaffordAct. pdf). This important law describes federal responsibility to prepare the nation for disasters as well as various programs to help state and local governments react when they occur. The Stafford Act recommends that plans be developed and reviewed annually. It also discusses federal financial and technological assistance that may be given to state and local governments. Although the Stafford Act has been amended periodically, it serves as the cornerstone of emergency management in the United States.

After the numerous failures witnessed in response to Hurricane Katrina, senators and representatives proposed ways to strengthen the ability of the United States to deal with all types of disasters. Known as the **Post-Katrina Emergency Management Reform Act**, this law (signed in October 2006) specifies ways to avert the slow and disjointed federal response to the catastrophe in New Orleans, Louisiana. For instance, after being severed when the DHS was created, the close organizational ties that once existed between the Director of FEMA and the President were reinstated. Some of the national preparedness programs were returned to the FEMA after being integrated elsewhere into DHS and the FBI. FEMA's budget was also enhanced substantially since much of its funding was diverted for DHS start-up costs. The Reform Act also points out ways

Post-Katrina Emergency Management Reform Act:
A law which specifies ways to avert the slow and disjointed federal response to the catastrophe in New Orleans, Louisiana.

IN THE REAL WORLD

Important Legislation and Resources

There are a number of important documents of which you should be aware if you work in homeland security. Some of these may include Homeland Security Policy Directives and Presidential Policy Directives (e.g. HSPD 5 and PPD 8). You should also be aware of National Strategy Documents, the National Mitigation Framework (NMF), the National Response Framework (NRF), and the National Disaster Recovery Framework (NDFR). There are other laws that are also very important:

Federal Employees' Compensation Act (FECA). Provides workers compensation to federal employees and volunteers of federal agencies who are killed or injured during the course of their duties.

Federal Tort Claims Act (FTCA). Immunizes federal government employees from liability in most instances.

National Emergencies Act (NEA). Allows the President to declare a national emergency.

Pandemic and All Hazards Preparedness Act (PAHPA). Addresses organization of public health preparedness and response activities including medical surge capacity and countermeasures for biological threats.

Public Health Service Act (PHSA). Authorizes the Secretary of Health and Human Services to declare a public health emergency.

Public Readiness and Emergency Preparedness Act (PREPA). Protects health workers from liability when responding to public health emergencies.

Volunteer Protection Act (VPA). Ensures immunity from ordinary negligence to volunteers of nonprofit organizations.

to enhance the nation's ability to cope with chemical and radiological incidents. It is significant and will likely have a positive impact on preparedness for terrorism and all types of disasters. This is particularly important since terrorists may attack during or after natural and other types of disasters.

National laws do not always solve every problem facing those involved in emergency management. In fact, some people suggest that it is the federal laws themselves that are actually the problem! Regardless of the validity of this point, organizational and operational changes are also required for success. One of the strategies developed after 9/11 was the **National Incident Management System (NIMS)**. NIMS is defined as a comprehensive national approach for incident management (see https://www.fema.gov/nims-doctrine-supporting-guides-tools). It was initiated after it was illustrated that police and fire units could not or would not operate jointly in New York City when the World Trade Center was attacked. NIMS

National Incident Management System (NIMS):
A comprehensive national approach for incident management in the United States.

consequently specified the procedures and structures to improve interoperable communications and collaboration among responding organizations. It also gives guidelines for resource management and promotes compatible technologies. NIMS helps to standardize expectations in disasters, and it will likely improve communication ability in disasters. Nevertheless, NIMS might focus excessively on technological solutions to coordination problems, and it may prove too rigid in the dynamic conditions of disasters. Furthermore, it may not always be applicable because of the politics of response operations, and it may have trouble relating to mitigation and recovery activities (Buck et al. 2006).

IN THE REAL WORLD

Target Capabilities List (TCL)

In light of the threat of terrorism and other catastrophes, the President and Congress recently advocated the creation of an improved national preparedness system. The vision proposed by the National Preparedness Guidelines is "A nation prepared with coordinated capabilities to prevent, protect against, respond to, and recover from all hazards in a way that balances risk with resources and need." This objective will require a consensus approach among all of the relevant homeland security stakeholders in order to build capabilities. These capabilities include common capabilities such as planning and communications; prevention capabilities such as intelligence gathering, counterterrorism, and law enforcement; protection capabilities such as food and agricultural safety and epidemiological surveillance; response capabilities such as incident and EOC management, search and rescue, and warning and evacuation; and recovery capabilities such as damage assessment and lifeline (utility) restoration. Everyone involved in homeland security and emergency management is encouraged to work toward the building of capabilities in these and other areas. This is particularly important for the Homeland Security Exercise and Evaluation Program (HSEEP).

National Response Plan (NRP):
A document that describes the procedures for responding to all-types of hazards with a multi-disciplinary perspective.

Similar charges have been made against the DHS's National Response Plan. In December 2004, DHS created this planning document for the United States. The **National Response Plan (NRP)** described national procedures for responding to all types of hazards with a multidisciplinary perspective (see https://www.dhs.gov/xlibrary/assets/NRP_Brochure.pdf). It listed 15 vital post-disaster functions such as transportation, mass care, and search and rescue and divides those responsibilities among primary and support agencies. The goal of the NRP was to define what federal agencies and all other actors are to do when terrorism or disasters occur. While the intentions were laudable, critics argue that the plan focused too heavily on terrorism and that it was far too complicated (Tierney 2006). The fact that the Federal Response Plan (the existing plan at the time) was not simply revised led to controversy. And the inability of FEMA to significantly influence the content of the NRP proved problematic. Many of the individuals and agencies that reviewed the initial drafts of the NRP found it unwieldy. This is because the relationship between the NRP and NIMS was unclear. The complexity of the NRP was also faulted, in part, for the poor response to Hurricane Katrina. Moreover, those involved in emergency management did not understand the plan and did not receive adequate training on it. As a result, the NRP was rescinded a short time later. Its successor is the National Response Framework.

National Response Framework (NRF):
The successor to the National Response Plan; a document that describes the principles, roles and structures of response and recovery operations.

The **National Response Framework (NRF)** is a document that describes the principles, roles, and structures of response and recovery operations. It is written for all elected and appointed leaders at the federal, state, and local levels of government. The NRF is based on five key principles:

- **Engaged partnerships.** Leaders at all levels must communicate and support one another in times of crisis.

- **Tiered response.** Incidents are managed at the lowest level of government and supported by others when needed.

- **Flexible operational capabilities.** Management activities will change to meet the size, scope, and complexity of events.

- **Unified command.** Clear understanding of the roles of others is required as is collaboration.

- **Readiness to act.** Individuals, families, community organizations, and all levels of government must prepare to deal with incidents of national significance.

Unlike the NRP, the NRF did a better job of clarifying roles and responsibilities, describing what must be done to improve response and recovery operations, and explaining how concepts and structures are applied to incident management objectives. Regional Advisory Boards provided feedback on the NRF and other preparedness initiatives. Since the NRF included comments from the emergency management and homeland security communities, it is an important plan at the national level.

In addition to the federal government, states are also heavily involved in preparedness activities. State homeland security departments are being established around the nation. Focus groups in these political jurisdictions are meeting to consider important policy decisions. Laws are being passed to better protect infrastructure and key assets. Tax revenues are being used to improve security, law enforcement, and emergency management functions. States are also working together to improve post-disaster operations. In 1996, Congress approved the multistate initiative titled the

Emergency Management Assistance Compact (EMAC):
An agreement among states to render assistance to one another in time disaster.

Emergency Management Assistance Compact (EMAC). The EMAC is an agreement among states to render assistance to one another in time of need. The goal is to establish guidelines for the sharing of material resources and to resolve in advance legal questions about personnel (e.g. who will pay overtime or death benefits). EMAC has been activated

Figure 11-2

The National Response Framework is a plan that describes the principles, roles and structures of response and operations.
Source: © FEMA.

National Emergency Management Association:
A professional association of state emergency management agencies.

Emergency Management Accreditation Program:
A standard-based assessment and certification initiative for local and state emergency management agencies.

in several disasters and is administered by the National Emergency Management Association. The **National Emergency Management Association** is a professional association that is composed mainly of officials from state emergency management agencies. It was initiated in 1974 when the state directors of emergency management desired to discuss common concerns around the nation. It has been a key organization for the development of the EMAC (an interstate mutual aid agreement) and the **Emergency Management Accreditation Program** (a standard-based assessment and certification initiative for local and state emergency management agencies).

As has been noted, it is vital that the federal government be fully involved in emergency management activities throughout the nation. The federal government provides policy direction and financial resources that can have a significant impact upon national preparedness. However, it is imperative that state governments are prepared to respond as well since they are likely to be on their own for at least 72 hours after a disaster. When Hurricane Katrina struck Louisiana, it took nearly a week before sufficient help arrived. The same principle applies to local governments. Cities and counties should take increased responsibility to be ready for any type of event, including terrorist attacks. Local governments will be impacted most by terrorism and may be on their own for several days before outside assistance arrives. For this reason, it is imperative that you promote local government preparedness.

IN THE REAL WORLD

The Emergency Management Accreditation Program

After a conference presentation on the importance of standards in emergency management in 1997, the National Emergency Management Association began to discuss the need to establish recommendations for emergency management programs around the nation. In time, the Emergency Management Accreditation Program (EMAP) was developed and implemented. EMAP is a voluntary accreditation initiative that attempts to improve emergency management capabilities around the nation. It is based on the National Fire Protection Association's Standard on Disaster/Emergency Management and Business Continuity Programs that encourages norms regarding laws and authorities, program management, mutual aid, training, and many other preparedness activities. Emergency management officials who desire accreditation must write a self-assessment document and invite a team of independent assessors to review his or her program. Based on the findings of the review committee, the EMAP commission may accredit state and local programs. Accreditation implies that the jurisdiction is in compliance with widely accepted preparedness guidelines. An added benefit is that external reviews will point out weaknesses that can be corrected in the future.

SELF-CHECK

1. Preparedness deals more with improving response and recovery capabilities rather than avoidance and deterrence. True or False?

2. There is complete consensus on the benefits of federal policies and legislation, such as the National Incident Management System. True or False?

3. The successor of the National Response Plan is the:
    (a) Emergency Management Assistance Compact
    (b) Comprehensive Homeland Security Act of 2003
    (c) National Response Framework
    (d) Post-Katrina Emergency Management Reform Act

4. Why is it essential that local governments take responsibility to prepare for acts of terrorism?

11.2 FOUNDATIONS OF PREPAREDNESS

In order to foster preparedness for terrorist attacks, it will be imperative that you work closely with key stakeholders, establish legal guidelines, and obtain financial resources. You will therefore need to organize a preparedness committee, draft ordinances, and seek funding through budget or grants. When this has been accomplished, you should also consider if your community needs an EOC.

11.2.1 Preparedness Councils

Preparedness council:
A group of individuals that provide recommendations for policy and assist with program administration.

Because homeland security is both complex and interdisciplinary, it will be necessary for you to create a preparedness council. A **preparedness council** is a group of individuals in a local or tribal government that provide recommendations for policy and assist with program administration. Such councils may be composed of representatives from law enforcement, public health, public works, hospitals, key businesses, the American Red Cross, and volunteer groups, among others. The goal is to ensure that many diverse viewpoints and areas of expertise are incorporated into the activities of the preparedness council. It is also wise to make sure that there are sufficient members to get the work done, but avoid excessive numbers because that may prove overwhelming and unmanageable.

Local Emergency Planning Committees (LEPCs):
Preparedness councils promoted in the 1980s to help communities prepare for hazardous materials releases.

Local Emergency Planning Committees (LEPCs) are one type of preparedness council. LEPCs were promoted in the 1980s to help communities prepare for hazardous materials releases (Lindell 1994). During this decade, there was a desire on the part of government leaders to avoid some of the mistakes being made in disasters associated with industrial accidents. For instance, doctors had major problems responding to the toxic gas release in Bhopal, India, in 1984. The failure to identify the released chemical and appropriately treat victims resulted in nearly 3000 deaths. LEPCs were accordingly seen as a way to identify hazardous materials concerns and help the jurisdiction anticipate how best to deal with fires and deadly toxins.

Emergency manager:
A local government official in charge of disaster mitigation, preparedness, response and recovery.

It should be noted that there will likely be multiple committees to assist with preparedness at the federal, state, and local levels. One might focus on weapons of mass destruction, while another is geared toward natural disasters. Some committees are in charge of public health emergencies, and others deal with security and preparedness at community sporting events. Thus, in reality, there will likely to be multiple preparedness committees or subcommittees instead of a single preparedness council. It is also probable that the emergency manager will be the leader of these preparedness networks. An **emergency manager** is a local government official in charge of disaster mitigation, preparedness, response, and recovery. Emergency managers have

IN THE REAL WORLD

Local Emergency Planning Committees

Well-known disaster scholar Michael Lindell has conducted several important studies on Local Emergency Planning Committees (LEPCs). His research illustrates that LEPCs are composed of representatives from fire departments, environmental protection agencies, hospitals, and corporations from the petrochemical industry (Lindell 1994). Lindell notes that LEPCs are beneficial in that they promote collaboration among organizations involved in preparedness. LEPCs are also advantageous in that they help to acquire additional funding, foster risk assessment, and rely on the expertise of highly committed members. Each jurisdiction should ensure that they have developed an advisory committee that focuses on terrorism and other types of disasters.

been leading preparedness councils for decades and should be recognized by homeland security officials as experts in the disaster profession.

11.2.2 Ordinances

Ordinance:
An authoritative order or law issued by a government.

Passing local laws pertaining to the preparedness aspect of homeland security and emergency management will also be necessary. An **ordinance** is an authoritative order issued by a government. In terms of homeland security or emergency management, an ordinance will justify the need for community preparedness for terrorism and other types of disasters. It will specify the creation of an office or department to deal with these threats and permit the appointment of an official to help the community build capabilities for such events. Duties of this employee will be outlined in the ordinance along with powers that may be granted to him or her in time of a crisis. In some cases, mutual aid will be addressed in ordinances. **Mutual aid** is a collaborative agreement between jurisdictions when external help is warranted. Such promises are made to assist one another when internal resources prove insufficient. Other issues, including penalties for failure to comply with local laws, may be discussed in ordinances.

Mutual aid:
A collaborative agreement between jurisdictions when external help is warranted.

Sample ordinances can be obtained from other jurisdictions, and states may have recommended templates for those working in homeland security and emergency management. The input of political leaders (e.g. the mayor, city manager, and city council) and members of the preparedness council will be helpful in the creation of ordinances. Drafts must be approved by the city attorney since these are legal documents. The important point to remember is that ordinances dictate what should be done (and not undertaken) when preparing for terrorism and other types of disasters.

11.2.3 Budgets and Grants

Besides ordinances, every organization will need resources if it is to survive and accomplish its mission. This is also the case with homeland security and emergency management offices. Without people and monetary support, it will be impossible to prepare a city for terrorist attacks. Resources can be acquired from local budgets as well as state and federal grants.

Each year, you will be asked to submit a proposed budget to the mayor and city council. This budget may include money needed to fund your position and that of your coworkers and staff. Estimated costs for office supplies, computers, phone lines, and other expected expenses will need to be outlined in your recommendation. The city manager and budget office can help you understand the rules that must be followed in your jurisdiction.

Once your budget draft is completed, you will probably need to present your proposal to city leaders. Concise communication, with supporting evidence and documentation, will help you to get as much money for your preparedness program as is possible. Because you will be competing for funds with many other departments, you will probably not get everything you desire. However, persuasive argument, accountability for existing funds, and visible activity in your program will enable you to increase your budget over time.

Grants:
Funds given to local governments to support or enhance homeland security and emergency management programs.

Since local monetary resources are limited, it may be advisable for you to seek grants from federal or state governments. **Grants** are funds given to local governments to support or enhance homeland security and emergency management programs. They may provide monies for personnel costs and material resources. There are numerous grants that can be obtained by local jurisdictions, for instance:

- Emergency Management Performance Grants help fund emergency manager's positions and their general office expenses.
- Assistance to Firefighters Grants provide money to purchase equipment to fight fires.
- Public Safety Interoperable Communications Grants are awarded to acquire and utilize improved communication equipment.
- The Homeland Security Grant Program gives financial assistance to help local jurisdictions prepare to deal with terrorism involving weapons of mass destruction.
- The Infrastructure Protection Program shares money to improve security at seaports, rail stations, bus terminals, and other transportation hubs and networks.
- The Citizen Corps Support Program provides money to help train civilians teams to prepare for terrorist attacks and other disasters.
- The Law Enforcement Terrorism Prevention Program gives resources to police departments to gather intelligence and share information about possible terrorists and criminals.
- The Metropolitan Medical Response System Program funds public health organizations to response effectively to bioterrorism attacks and cope with mass fatality incidents.

There are also grants for hospital and school planning, urban search and rescue teams, and chemical stockpile emergency preparedness, among others.

IN THE REAL WORLD

Urban Area Security Initiative (UASI)

The most recognized government grant program in homeland security is the Urban Area Security Initiative (UASI). The purpose of UASI is to help local governments build capabilities to deal with terrorist attacks and catastrophic disasters. Funds are directed toward large and dense metropolitan areas that are considered to be vulnerable targets of future terrorist attacks. Those applying for the grants must take a regional approach toward planning. In other words, cities will only be eligible for funds if they collaborate with nearby jurisdictions. UASI grants can be used to purchase equipment, train responders, and conduct exercises. Monies are also given to help prevent and protect against the use of weapons of mass destruction. The UASI program is multidisciplinary and supports numerous organizations working in preparedness, warnings, public health, search and rescue, triage, mass care, firefighting, fatality management, etc. UASI is funded by the federal government and managed by the state.

These and other grants are awarded on a competitive basis. That is to say, there are a fixed number of grants, and they will only be given to a limited number of jurisdictions that put together the best applications. As a result, it is imperative that you carefully read the grant instructions and ensure that you have met all requirements in the application documents. Clear writing is key, and it is wise to have the budget or grant office help you prepare your application.

Another important consideration is to illustrate your ability to manage the grant. In some cases, your city will need to fund a portion of the program you are proposing and match federal government monies. If you receive the grant, you will also need to work closely with your grant team to accomplish all of the goals that were identified in the proposal. Documentation of expenses must also be meticulous and reported on a periodic basis (depending on the type of grant). Failure to follow up on required paperwork and use funds as outlined could result in termination of the grant or even imprisonment of those failing to meet expectations or misusing government funds.

11.2.4 Emergency Operations Centers

Emergency operations center (EOC):
A location from which disaster response and recovery activities can be overseen and managed.

Another fundamental step for preparedness is to establish an **emergency operations center (EOC)**. An EOC is a location from which disaster response and recovery activities can be overseen and managed. While not every city has a designated EOC, they are becoming the norm for medium- and large-sized jurisdictions around the nation. In these EOCs, government and other community leaders will meet to coordinate all of the functions that have to be performed after terrorist attacks or other disasters. This may include members of the preparedness council and others who have specialized knowledge and skills required in case of an emergency.

EOCs may include a large office space with tables, phones, computers, whiteboards, and TV monitors. At times, EOCs may be a designated area adjoined to other rooms (for top officials, media briefings, a break area, rest rooms, etc.). In other cases, an EOC will be set up quickly when an incident occurs. Thus, there is no standard layout for EOCs. It could be set up by department, function, or any other organizational arrangement. The important point to remember is that you will need desks for many organizations as well as common office supplies (e.g. pencils, paper, copiers, computers, etc.). You will also need to develop procedures for activating the EOC. For instance, you will want to determine when you will open the EOC and how you will contact participants who should report to that location (e.g. a phone call, text, or e-mail). You will want to create an EOC that works for the agencies in your jurisdictions.

While temporary EOCs can be established in training rooms, most communities now prefer to build permanent facilities. Designated EOCs have the advantage of being ready at a moment's notice, whereas temporary EOCs take time to be established and activated. Controlling access to EOCS and having a backup facility is a good idea. On 9/11, New York City's EOC was disabled and later destroyed due to the terrorist attacks and resulting collapse of the World Trade Center. As a result, the city had to quickly set up a temporary EOC at a pier on the Hudson River. It is also possible that EOCs could be intentionally selected as targets by terrorist organizations in

Figure 11-3

EOCs are equipped locations to help you manage response and recovery operations. Source: © FEMA.

order to add to the chaos and disruption associated with attacks. They should be carefully guarded as a key asset.

SELF-CHECK

1. Local Emergency Planning Committees are a type of a preparedness council. True or False?

2. Ordinances justify the need for community preparedness for terrorism, but not other types of disasters. True or False?

3. Who in the community is responsible for most daily disaster mitigation, preparedness, response, and recovery activities?

   (a) Mayor

   (b) Emergency manager

   (c) City manager

   (d) Preparedness council

4. What is needed to have a well-equipped emergency operations center?

11.3 PLANNING

Emergency operations plan (EOP): A document that describes what may be anticipated in terms of homeland security and emergency management and how to best to react.

One of the central priorities of preparedness is writing an emergency operations plan. An **emergency operations plan (EOP)** is a document that describes what may be anticipated in terms of terrorism and how best to react. The plan may note what types of terrorist attacks or disasters may occur in a community. It also provides an educated guess on the types of issues that will arise and how they will be met. The EOP outlines who will be in charge of specific post-event functions (outlined in Chapters 12 and 13).

For this reason, plans help to foster coordination and speed up response and recovery operations.

Writing an EOP can be a lengthy and technical task. Fortunately, guidance for writing plans can be obtained from homeland security and emergency management personnel in neighboring jurisdictions or from the state. FEMA has also provided details about planning in SLG 101 (see https://www.fema.gov/pdf/plan/slg101.pdf). This document describes the importance of plans and value to the community. It also discusses the format and content of plans so you will be able to help your community prepare for terrorism and other disasters.

EOPs should be based on a thorough assessment known as **Threat and Hazard Identification and Risk Assessment (THIRA)**. As mentioned in Chapter 10, this is a comprehensive study that outlines what could happen along with possible consequences. The THIRA should serve as the foundation of EOPs and all other actions relating to prevention, mitigation, preparedness, response, and recovery.

EOPs are commonly divided into three sections. The **basic plan** is an overview of the entire document. It describes the general strategy for dealing with response and recovery operations. The **annexes** discuss specific hazards or functions that will need to be addressed if an event takes place. The basic plan and annexes often contain at least six sections:

- **Authority.** The first section of the plan often mentions the federal, state, and local laws pertaining to homeland security and emergency management. The goals of the document are taken from the Stafford Act, the NRP, state mandates, and local ordinances.
- **Purpose.** This portion of the plan covers the objectives of the plan. It may mention, among other things, the need to protect life, reduce property loss, minimize societal disruption, and promote coordination among participating organizations.
- **Situation and assumptions.** The third part of the plan examines the context of terrorism and other hazards in the community. The potential for attacks and disasters is mentioned along with expected impacts. This portion of the plan is vital for the understanding of what response and recovery functions will have to be performed.
- **Concept of operations.** The fourth component of plans typically identifies, in brief fashion, what organizations are in charge of specific functions. It often notes that departments will respond based on daily activities and areas of expertise.
- **Organization and assignment of responsibilities.** The segment of the plan describes in detail the roles of each responding organization. It is far more explicit than the concept of operations section.
- **Direction and control.** The final section of the plan is concerned with the management of the entire post-event operation. It gives highest attention to top officials in the EOC and their decision making and oversight duties.

Finally, the **appendices** contain additional information to support the plan including resource and contact lists, maps, standard operating procedures, and checklists.

Threat and Hazard Identification and Risk Assessment (THIRA): A comprehensive study that outlines what could happen along with possible consequences.

Basic plan: An overview of the entire emergency operations plan.

Annexes: A portion of the emergency operations plan that discusses specific hazards or functions that will need to be addressed if an event takes place.

Appendices: Additional information at the end of the emergency operations plan which includes resource and contact lists, maps, standard operating procedures and checklists.

When putting together an EOP, several principles should be kept in mind. First, it is vital that you do not plan alone! Be sure to work with others to develop the plan as it will help you generate a better game plan for anticipated response and recovery operations. Your preparedness council, city manager, and legal offices can help you develop a useful and logical document. There are also useful guidelines from the FEMA (see Comprehensive Preparedness Guide (CPG) 101) (Department of Homeland Security 2010). Second, your plan should be as comprehensive as possible. It should include all types of events (e.g. terrorism and other disasters) and all actors involved in homeland security and emergency management (e.g. those from the public, private, and nonprofit sectors). Third, your plan should be reviewed and updated annually. Failing to do so may result in the plan being outdated, incomplete, or obsolete. Fourth, your plan must ensure that the government is, itself, preparing for disaster. Such continuity of operations plans specifies how to keep the government functioning in time of crisis as well as a line of succession. Finally, you must remember that writing the plan is only one aspect of preparedness. Far too many jurisdictions write a plan and assume they are ready to react in an effective manner. Known as the **paper plan syndrome**, this attitude implies that having a plan assumes you are adequately prepared (Auf der Heide 1989). Nothing could be further from the truth. Don't be fooled into thinking that your compliance with state and federal planning mandates is sufficient. Dwight D. Eisenhower once stated: "in preparing for battle, I have always found that plans are useless. But planning is indispensable!" Planning is vital, but should not overshadow other preparedness activities to build community capacity.

Paper plan syndrome: An attitude that assumes that having a plan ensures you are prepared to deal with terrorism and other types of disasters.

FOR EXAMPLE

The Paper Plan Syndrome

Public officials sometimes comment that they are prepared for any terrorist attack because "we have a plan." Writing an emergency operations plan is necessary since it describes what could happen and how response and recovery functions are to be performed. Planning also helps to clarify roles and therefore increases effectiveness and efficiency of service delivery. While planning is important, it should not be regarded as a panacea. Planning is a process, not a checklist that is completed once and never revisited. Concentrating on plans ignores the greatest challenge in emergency management – developing capabilities to enhance your ability to react successfully in a crisis situation. Preparedness cannot be pursued without planning, but writing an emergency operations plan does not ensure you are ready for a terrorist attack. It is imperative that those working in homeland security and emergency management do not fall into the paper plan syndrome.

SELF-CHECK

1. Writing an emergency operations plan ensures that a local government is ready for a terrorist attack. True or False?

2. The appendices in an EOP discuss specific hazards or functions that will need to be addressed if an event takes place. True or False?

3. Which of the following is not one of the principles for putting together an EOP?

    (a) The plan should be as comprehensive as possible.
    (b) The plan should be created by one person.
    (c) The plan should be reviewed and updated annually.
    (d) The plan must be considered as only one aspect of preparedness.

4. What are the usual sections contained within the basic plan and annexes of an EOP?

11.4 OTHER MEASURES

Preparedness entails much more than those activities described above (McEntire and Myers 2004). Training, exercises, and community education are vital if a jurisdiction is to be ready to deal with terrorism. Training helps police, fire, emergency medical personnel, and others to respond in a safe and effective manner. Exercises identify weaknesses in the plan and illustrate room for improvement. Community education enlists the support of citizens since response and recovery require a joint effort with the populous.

11.4.1 Training

Training:
Information sharing in classroom or field settings to help familiarize people with protocol.

First responders:
The first official government responders in the field including police, fire fighters and emergency medical technicians.

According to the well-known disaster sociologist E.L. Quarantelli, training is a vital component of community preparedness (Quarantelli 1984, p. 29). **Training** includes information sharing in classroom or field settings to help familiarize people with protocol. Training helps all of those involved in response and recovery to anticipate what could happen and how best to react. It may be focused on **first responders**, such as police, firefighters, and emergency medical technicians, who know how to save lives and communicate one with another. Training can help the directors of public works and the water department know their roles when terrorist attacks occur. Mayors and city managers can also be taught how to seek state and federal assistance. Everyone – regardless of position or department – should have some training about terrorism and how to deal with it.

Training courses are provided by FEMA as well as the FBI, the Department of Defense, the Environmental Protection Agency, the Department of Transportation, and other federal agencies. State agencies including public health, public safety, and emergency management departments often provide training on a variety of subjects pertaining to

IN THE REAL WORLD

The Coming Storm

In October of 2015, the Federal Bureau of Investigation (FBI) released a 40-minute video entitled *The Coming Storm*. Part of the movie is a 13-minute documentary called *Managing the Storm*. This short training film portrays a mass shooting at a college campus and details lessons and important information pertinent to those types of events. It features interviews with both victims and first responders from previous shootings and explains what steps need to be taken immediately following these tragedies. Additionally, this training tool illustrates what FBI resources are available to assist local law enforcement and contains extensive research on the most effective aftermath strategies. The film was distributed nationwide to police departments and other first responders. The hope is that this video spurs future discussions on preparedness and response capabilities in active shootings.

terrorism and on a rotating basis. Emergency management associations and regional council of government organizations will also be aware of training opportunities for you and your jurisdiction.

SWAT:
Special Weapons and Tactics relating to well-trained police forces.

One of the most important types of training for terrorism preparedness relates to SWAT teams. **SWAT** stands for Special Weapons and Tactics and has the purpose of developing well-trained police forces. SWAT teams were initially created in the 1960s to handle riots. However, during the 1980s and 1990s, they were used in the war on drugs and in terrorism. In 2005, SWAT teams were deployed more than 50 000 times in the United States. The fact that terrorist attacks are increasing underscores the importance of SWAT teams. For this reason, these teams must be trained in the use of assault rifles, riot control agents, and stun grenades. They must also be well equipped with body armor, ballistic shields, armored vehicles, and night vision devices. Their deployment in many terrorist attacks and civil disturbances illustrates why they are vital for society.

Another important type of training relates to emergency medical care and responses to weapons of mass destruction. Emergency medical technicians and paramedics are vital in responses to terrorist attacks. They must be trained not only in medical care but ways to protect themselves during violent activities like mass shootings. In addition, other medical personnel – such as doctors and nurses – must be educated on how to deal with victims who have been affected by terrorist attacks (Goralnick et al. 2017). The Ebola outbreak in Dallas, Texas, illustrated that more needs to be done to decontaminate victims, treat symptoms, and dispose of hazardous materials. There are also major medical concerns about explosives, chemical weapons, and biological agents (as will be noted in Chapter 14).

If you are responsible for training, make sure you recognize that it must be continual. New employees will be hired. People will take on new positions in city government. Everyone can forget what they have learned in the

Figure 11-4

Training is a great way to educate your public servants or first responders about terrorist attacks. Source: © FEMA.

past. New policies and procedures will be instituted by federal and state officials. A training program will be incomplete and limited in impact if it is not repeated and updated over time.

11.4.2 Exercises

Exercises:
Drills and mock events that test the knowledge and skills of those in charge of reacting to attacks.

Tabletop exercises:
Informal discussions about hypothetical scenarios that occur in an office setting.

Functional exercises:
Practice scenarios that explore one or a few of the annexes in the plan.

Full-scale exercises:
Major scenarios that test many functions or the entire response system.

Because disasters and terrorist attacks are infrequent, experience in dealing with them is generally limited. For this reason, homeland security and emergency management officials should be proactive and take initiative in their efforts to develop and participate in exercises. **Exercises** are drills and mock events that test the knowledge and skills of those in charge of reacting to attacks. They are the semirealistic methods to evaluate and test the validity of the EOP (Daines 1991). Exercises indicate where planning and training fall short so they can be remedied in the future.

There are three types of exercises. **Tabletop exercises** are informal discussions about hypothetical scenarios. They occur in an office setting and often involved the key leaders of each department. Tabletop exercises are useful to help decision makers reflect upon how they would respond should a terrorist attack occur. **Functional exercises** are drills that explore one or a few of the annexes in the plan. Such exercises may include a field component as well as equipment and a mild degree of stress. **Full-scale exercises** are major scenarios that test many functions or the entire response system. They often have an EOC and field component and explore the interaction of the broad array of responding agencies. They may include realistic props, "moulaged" victims, and most department leaders from the community.

The City of Denton, Texas, has participated in each of these types of exercises. The emergency manager frequently invites his/her preparedness council to review how they would respond to different scenarios. These tabletop exercises are a great way to contemplate what you might do in a difficult situation. At other times, the city has tested its ability to decontaminate victims in a mock exercise of a school bus crashing into a tanker truck carrying hazardous materials. Functional exercises such as this can test any operation that might be needed after a terrorist attack. In a final exercise, city departments responded to a mock bombing at a utility company headquarters. This full-scale exercise involved communications, emergency medical care, law enforcement, and the EOC.

IN THE REAL WORLD

TOPOFF Exercises

In order to prepare for anticipated terrorist attacks, the federal government has instituted an exercise program known as TOPOFF. TOPOFF stands for "top officials" and therefore has the purpose of assessing how key government leaders and others respond to fictitious terrorist attacks. One TOPOFF exercise, which took place on 15–19 October 2007, focused on intelligence gathering and analysis, victim decontamination, coordination with the military, and the implementation of large-scale recovery activities. Thousands of federal, state, and local participants played roles in this exercise. The lessons learned from such events are vital in that they can facilitate national preparedness for future terrorist attacks. For more information, see https://www.cnn.com/2013/10/30/us/operation-topoff-national-level-exercise-fast-facts/index.html.

In order to develop a solid exercise program, it is first necessary to identify the potential weaknesses in the plan or emergency management system. Once you have determined what areas need improvement, an exercise scenario can then be developed with the assistance of an exercise design team (probably to include the members of your preparedness council). The scenario may include some contextual information about the event as well as specific injects from participants who act out certain roles (e.g. a victim calling 911, a firefighter in the field, or an emergency manager from a neighboring jurisdiction). As the scenario is being developed, you should also schedule the date and location of the exercise and notify all of the participants. Be sure to assign evaluators to determine the success or shortcomings in responding to the mock event.

During the exercise, a controller will make sure the scenario is unfolding at a logical pace. Those responding to the event will then react according to the plan, their training, and the specific nature of the scenario. While there are many "right" ways to react to terrorist events, it is important that evaluators look for major errors so they can be corrected in the future. Mistakes may include safety violations, failure to communicate and coordinate with others, and general ineffectiveness in dealing with the problems presented to them.

When the exercise is over, evaluators should write up findings so they can be addressed. Many emergency management organizations fail to follow up on lessons learned, which can make the exercise a useless waste of time, energy, and taxpayer dollars. Sometimes local politicians do not want to hear recommendations for improvement because they fear political support. Regardless, you will also need to submit paperwork to state and federal officials to explain exercise findings and mention your actions to address weaknesses. Failure to do so may result in you losing grants or your good standing among your peers. It would also be wise to fully understand the **Homeland Security Exercise and Evaluation Program (HSEEP)**. This federal program provides guiding principles for exercises and will help to improve planning before drills and follow up on lessons learned after they are undertaken.

Homeland Security Exercise and Evaluation Program: is a federal program that provides guiding principles for exercises.

11.4.3 Community Education

Because the government is not the only one involved in response and recovery activities, it is vital that you educate businesses, churches, volunteer groups, and citizens about terrorism. These nonofficial partners can be of great assistance to you if you harness their potential and channel their efforts in constructive ways. Alternatively, if you ignore or neglect these

Figure 11-5

The Red Cross can help you educate your community about terrorist attacks and other disasters. Source: © FEMA.

groups and individuals, your response and recovery operations can be more problematic. For instance, people may visit the scene of attacks out of curiosity and put themselves at risk. They may also donate goods and supplies that really are not needed after most terrorist attacks and disasters. Educating others about terrorism, homeland security, and emergency management is a great way to foster compliance and effectiveness.

There are many ways to share information with the public. Community education may include speeches at schools, booths at fairs and other community gatherings, and the distribution of pamphlets and related information about homeland security and emergency management. Developing a useful website can also help people acquire information about what they should do to be prepared for the threat of terrorism. For instance, the DHS has a website (www.ready.gov) that helps individuals and families develop their own plans, anticipate supplies that will be needed, and become more self-sufficient until further help arrives. Since most people rely on the computer to acquire information today, it is imperative that your website be as user friendly as possible.

IN THE REAL WORLD

Citizen Corps

Citizen Corps is a network of a variety of volunteer associations. Its mission is to "harness the power of every individual through education, training, and volunteer service to make communities safer, stronger, and better prepared to respond to the threats of terrorism, crime, public health issues and disasters of all kinds." Besides CERT, Citizen Corps includes Neighborhood Watch, Volunteers in Police Service, Medical Reserve Corps, and the Fire Corps. According to the Citizen Corps website (https://www.ready.gov/citizen-corps), Local Citizen Corps Councils will:

- Promote and strengthen the Citizen Corps programs at the community level, such as Volunteers in Police Service programs, CERTs, Medical Reserve Corps units, and Neighborhood Watch groups.
- Provide opportunities for special skills and interests.
- Develop targeted outreach for the community, including special needs groups.
- Provide opportunities of training in first aid and emergency preparedness.
- Organize special projects and community events.
- Encourage cooperation and collaboration among community leaders.
- Capture smart practices and report accomplishments.
- Create opportunities for all residents to participate.

Unfortunately, many government programs like Citizen Corps could be dismantled in the future because of funding issues.

Community Emergency Response Team (CERT):
A group of citizens who receive basic training response operations.

Another excellent way to educate your citizens is to develop a **Community Emergency Response Team (CERT)**. A CERT is a group of citizens who receive basic training on response operations. They are taught general information about terrorism and disasters and learn how to perform small-scale fire-fighting, search and rescue, and medical functions. CERT members also gain knowledge about shutting off gas valves and helping victims with emotional distress. Having multiple CERTs in your jurisdiction will augment preparedness beyond normal levels. Establishing CERTs is one of many important ways to promote preparedness in your community.

While there is no single or correct way to educate your community, there are probably some mistakes to avert. For instance, assuming someone else will share vital information about terrorism with the public is incorrect and problematic. Also, failing to coordinate your public education campaign with others will result in the provision of conflicting and contradictory information. Finally, educating the public on a one-time basis will ensure that citizens forget what is relayed, which will limit ongoing preparedness activity. Avoiding these mistakes will go a long way to ensure your community is ready to deal with terrorist attacks.

IN THE REAL WORLD

KnoWhat2Do

In 2007, the North Central Texas Council of Governments produced a public education campaign to reach out to millions of people in the 16-county region surrounding Dallas–Fort Worth. Funded by a grant from the Department of Homeland Security, the KnoWhat2Do initiative included the distribution of calendars, playing cards, DVDs, and brochures to help citizens understand what to do in case of a terrorist attack or other types of disaster. A website, accessed at www.KnoWhat2Do.com, has also been created to help people anticipate possible hazards/threats and take measures to protect themselves from harm. KnoWhat2Do is a creative example of reaching out to the community for the purpose of preparedness.

SELF-CHECK

1. A training program does not need to be repeated in order to ensure success. True or False?

2. The first step in developing an exercise program is to identify weaknesses in the plan or emergency management system. True or False?

3. Which of the following is the best example of a first responder?
   (a) Mayor
   (b) City manager
   (c) Police officer
   (d) Governor

4. How do Community Emergency Response Teams help increase preparedness beyond normal levels?

SUMMARY

Preparing for terrorism is one of your central responsibilities in homeland security. In order to help your community get ready for possible terrorist attacks, you will need to comprehend the executive orders and legislation issued by the President and Congress. You should also set the foundation for preparedness by creating an advisory council, passing ordinances, acquiring monetary resources, and establishing an EOC. Writing plans and promoting training, exercises, and education are other ways to improve the degree of preparedness in your jurisdiction. Setting up a CERT is also helpful to increase post-attack capabilities. Preparedness is vital if you are to effectively respond to and recover from the effects of terrorism.

ASSESS YOUR UNDERSTANDING

UNDERSTAND: WHAT HAVE YOU LEARNED?

 Go to **www.wiley.com/go/mcentire/homelandsecurity2e** to assess your knowledge of preparedness.

SUMMARY QUESTIONS

1. National preparedness is solely the responsibility of the Department of Homeland Security and the Federal Emergency Management Agency. True or False?

2. The National Emergency Management Association is mainly composed of emergency management offices from city governments. True or False?

3. Grants always cover the full financial need of a proposed program. True or False?

4. An important consideration for preparedness councils is the interdisciplinary nature of homeland security. True or False?

5. Assistance with writing an emergency operation plan can be sought from homeland security and emergency management personnel in neighboring jurisdictions or from the state. True or False?

6. A paper plan syndrome occurs when a plan provides a false assurance of effective preparation. True or False?

7. Training is meant only for first responders. True or False?

8. It is important to educate the public only once to ensure they get the same message. True or False?

9. The process by which government functions are maintained after terrorism is best known as:

   (a) Preparedness

   (b) Continuity of operation

   (c) Prevention

   (d) Mitigation

10. Which law serves as the cornerstone of emergency management in the United States?

    (a) The Robert T. Stafford Disaster Relief and Emergency Assistance Act

    (b) The National Defense Authorization Law

    (c) The Comprehensive Homeland Security Act of 2003

    (d) The Anti-terrorism and Effective Death Penalty Act of 1996

11. A collaborative agreement between jurisdictions that ensures external help is coordinated is best known as:

 (a) An ordinance

 (b) Mutual aid

 (c) Annexes

 (d) An emergency operations plan

12. Which of the following is not one of the three sections of an emergency operations plan?

 (a) Annexes

 (b) Basic plan

 (c) Appendices

 (d) The National Response Plan

13. Training and education about terrorism and how to deal with it should be provided to:

 (a) City managers and mayors

 (b) Emergency managers

 (c) First responders

 (d) Everyone

14. Functional exercises are best described as:

 (a) Scenarios that explore one or a few annexes in a plan

 (b) Informal discussions about hypothetical situations

 (c) Major scenarios that test the entire response system practice

 (d) Scenarios that are studied in an office setting

APPLYING THIS CHAPTER

1. As an emergency manager, it is important that you organize a preparedness council. Who could you get to participate on the council?

2. As financial officer of your emergency management program, you need to submit a proposed budget to the mayor and city council. What can you do to get as much money as possible for your preparedness program and, over time, increase your budget?

3. Due to your role in homeland security, you have been asked to talk with local governments about the importance of community education. What reasons would you give in support of a strong community education program?

4. You have just completed a full-scale exercise as the new fire chief in your jurisdiction. What steps could you take to properly follow up on the exercise?

BE A HOMELAND SECURITY PROFESSIONAL

Presentation to the City Council

You are the emergency manager for a local government that is not well prepared for a possible terrorist attack. In order to accomplish your office's mission of increasing the city's level of preparedness, you need more people and monetary support. The city council is considering an increase in your budget, but first you must persuade them that such a step is an important and effective use of the taxpayers' money. When you are asked by the council about why preparedness is important, how could you respond?

Assignment: Federal and State Governments

Write a one-page paper comparing and contrasting the roles of federal and state governments in preparedness. Be as thorough as possible.

Creating Ordinances

You were just hired as the emergency manager for a local government. You are aware that ordinances are a necessary component in justifying and executing measures aimed at increasing preparedness. Such regulations indicate what should and should not be done in preparing for terrorism. What methods could you utilize to facilitate the development of ordinances that take into account these issues?

KEY TERMS

Annexes	A portion of the emergency operations plan that discusses specific hazards or functions that will need to be addressed if an event takes place
Appendices	Additional information at the end of the emergency operations plan that includes resource and contact lists, maps, standard operating procedures, and checklists
Basic plan	An overview of the entire emergency operations plan
Community Emergency Response Team (CERT)	A group of citizens who receive basic training response operations
Continuity of operation	The maintenance of government functions after terrorist attacks through the identification of leader succession, alternate work sites, and resumption of operational practices

Emergency Management Accreditation Program	A standard-based assessment and certification initiative for local and state emergency management agencies
Emergency Management Assistance Compact (EMAC)	An agreement among states to render assistance to one another in time of disaster.
Emergency manager	A local government official in charge of disaster mitigation, preparedness, response, and recovery
Emergency operations center (EOC)	A location from which disaster response and recovery activities can be overseen and managed
Emergency operations plan (EOP)	A document that describes what may be anticipated in terms of homeland security and emergency management and how best to react
Exercises	Drills and mock events that test the knowledge and skills of those in charge of reacting to attacks
First responders	The first official government responders in the field including police, firefighters, and emergency medical technicians
Full-scale exercises	Major scenarios that test many functions or the entire response system
Functional exercises	Practice scenarios that explore one or a few of the annexes in the plan
Grants	Funds given to local governments to support or enhance homeland security and emergency management programs
Homeland Security Exercise and Evaluation Program	A federal program that provides guiding principles for exercises
Local Emergency Planning Committees	Preparedness councils promoted in the 1980s to help communities prepare for hazardous materials releases
Mutual aid	A collaborative agreement between jurisdictions when external help is warranted
National Emergency Management Association	A professional association of state emergency management agencies

National Incident Management System (NIMS)	A comprehensive national approach for incident management in the United States
National Response Framework (NRF)	The successor to the National Response Plan; a document that describes the principles, roles, and structures of response and recovery operations
National Response Plan (NRP)	A document that describes the procedures for responding to all types of hazards with a multidisciplinary perspective
Ordinance	An authoritative order or law issued by a government
Paper plan syndrome	An attitude that assumes that having a plan ensures you are prepared to deal with terrorism and other types of disasters
Post-Katrina Emergency Management Reform Act	A law that specifies ways to avert the slow and disjointed federal response to the catastrophe in New Orleans, Louisiana
Preparedness	Concerted efforts to improve response and recovery capabilities
Preparedness council	A group of individuals that provide recommendations for policy and assist with program administration
SWAT	Special Weapons and Tactics relating to well-trained police forces
Tabletop exercises	Informal discussions about hypothetical scenarios that occur in an office setting
Threat and Hazard Identification and Risk Assessment (THIRA)	A comprehensive study that outlines what could happen along with possible consequences
Training	Information sharing in classroom or field settings to help familiarize people with protocol

REFERENCES

Auf der Heide, E. (1989). *Disaster Response: Principles for Preparation and Coordination*. St. Louis, MO: C.V. Mosby.

Buck, D.A., Trainor, J.E., and Aguirre, B.E. (2006). A critical evaluation of the incident command system and NIMS. *Journal of Homeland Security and Emergency Management* 3 (1): 1–27.

Daines, G.E. (1991). Planning, training, and exercising. In: *Emergency Management: Principles and Practices for Local Government* (ed. T.E. Drabek and G.G. Hoetmer), 161–200. Washington, DC: International City/County Management Association.

Department of Homeland Security. (2004). National Incident Management System. www.dhs.gov (accessed 10 November 2006).

Department of Homeland Security. (2010). Developing and Maintaining Emergency Operations Plans: Comprehensive Preparedness Guide (CPG) 101. https://www.fema.gov/media-library-data/20130726-1828-25045-0014/cpg_101_comprehensive_preparedness_guide_developing_and_maintaining_emergency_operations_plans_2010.pdf (accessed August 2017).

Donahue, T.A. (2014). *National Security and Preparedness: Issues, Development and Analyses*. New York: Nova Science Publishers, Inc.

Gillsepie, D.F. and Streeter, C.L. (1987). Conceptualizing and measuring disaster preparedness. *International Journal of Mass Emergencies and Disasters* 5 (2): 155–176.

Godschalk, D.R. (1991). Disaster mitigation and hazard management. In: *Emergency Management: Principles and Practices for Local Government* (ed. T.E. Drabek and G.G. Hoetmer), 131–160. Washington, DC: International City/County Management Association.

Goralnick, E., Van Trimpont, F., and Cali, P. (2017). Preparing for the next terrorism attack: lessons from Paris, Brussels, and Boston. *JAMA Surgery* 152 (5): 419–420.

Kirschenbaum, A. (2002). Disaster preparedness: a conceptual and empirical reevaluation. *International Journal of Mass Emergencies and Disasters* 20 (1): 5–28.

Lindell, M.K. (1994). Are local emergency planning committees effective in developing community disaster preparedness? *International Journal of Mass Emergencies and Disasters* 5 (2): 137–153.

McEntire, D.A. and Myers, A. (2004). Preparing communities for disasters: issues and processes for government readiness. *Disaster Prevention and Management* 13 (2): 140–152.

Quarantelli, E.L. (1984). *Organizational Behavior in Disasters and Implications for Disaster Planning*. Washington, DC: Federal Emergency Management Agency.

Richardson, L. (2007). *What Terrorists Want: Understanding the Enemy, Containing the Threat*. New York: Random House.

Tierney, K.J. (2006). Recent developments in U.S. homeland security policies and their implications for the management of extreme events. In: *Handbook of Disaster Research* (ed. H. Rodrigues, E.L. Quarantelli and R.R. Dynes), 405–412. New York: Springer.

12

RESPONDING TO ATTACKS
Important Functions and Coordination Mechanisms

What You Will Find Out	What You Will Be Able To Do
12.1 How human behavior relates to safety, search and rescue, emergency medical care, decontamination, and investigation	• Predict what types of activities will take place after terrorist attacks and evaluate the effectiveness of investigative practices
12.2 The importance of warnings, evacuations, and sheltering	• Perform necessary functions relating to life safety
12.3 Ways to coordinate responses to terrorist attacks	• Set up incident command and EOC coordination mechanisms

Introduction to Homeland Security: Understanding Terrorism Prevention and Emergency Management,
Second Edition. David A. McEntire.
© 2019 John Wiley & Sons, Inc. Published 2019 by John Wiley & Sons, Inc.
Companion website: www.wiley.com/go/mcentire/homelandsecurity2e

INTRODUCTION

When terrorist attacks occur, it is vital that you know how to respond successfully. This entails understanding that resources will arrive on the scene of an attack along with altruistic citizens. You will also need to fulfill many priorities including investigation, apprehension, site security, search and rescue, emergency medical care, decontamination, and investigation. Where possible or when required, you may also need to warn citizens of impending attacks or evacuate them away from harm. Because so many organizations are involved in these functions, you may need to rely on various coordination mechanisms. The incident command system and emergency operations centers (EOCs) are two tools that can help deal with negative terrorism effects in an effective manner.

12.1 BEHAVIOR AND MAJOR PRIORITIES

When a terrorist attack occurs, both first responders and citizens will assist with post-incident operations. In the vast majority of cases, official governmental first responders will arrive after they are notified by citizens who call emergency numbers (e.g. 911). In this sense, the title of first responder is somewhat of a misnomer. It is actually ordinary people who will typically be present on the scene before police, fire, and emergency medical personnel arrive. Citizens are almost always first to react because they are located everywhere – at home, in their cars, at work, in the shopping mall, at the movie theater, in the sports stadium, running errands in government offices, etc. Every day people will generally see or hear of the event first and then do what they can to help victims. Their behavior has been described by sociologists as "convergence" and "emergence."

Convergence:
The flow of people and resources to the scene of an emergency or disaster.

Convergence is the flow of people and resources to the scene of an emergency or disaster (Kendra and Wachtendorf 2003). When victims have been impacted by a major incident, bystanders will stop what they are doing and go to the location of the attack. In some cases, they will bring needed supplies with them (e.g. a fire extinguisher, a first aid kit, or any other resource that might be useful). Their goal is to come to the focal point of the incident to provide assistance to those in need. In turn, first responders and government officials will be notified and also arrive on the scene. Until this happens, citizens will engage in new types of behaviors, which is called emergence. **Emergence** is the appearance of altruistic behavior that is unfamiliar to the participants (Drabek and McEntire 2002). In emergency or disaster situations, people will take on new roles and interact cooperatively with strangers (e.g. providing basic first aid). They will also develop new relationships that often end when emergency needs have been addressed (e.g. groups that form initially to address victim donation needs).

Emergence:
The appearance of altruistic behavior that is unfamiliar to the participants.

The terrorist attacks on 9/11 provide vivid examples of convergence and emergence. For instance, people from around the nation and world sent supplies for first responders and monetary support for the victims' families. Also, occupants from different floors in the World Trade Center worked together to evacuate the disabled or injured. Carrying someone down stairs is something people don't normally do. But, in a disaster like 9/11, citizens will take on new responsibilities to care for others.

To be sure, the activities of every day citizens and official responders will vary significantly, depending on the type of attack that occurs. For instance, people will run, hide, or even fight with a mass shooter. A mass shooting will also necessitate heavy police involvement and tactical EMS.

Tactical emergency medical services:
The name given to a team of paramedics that are armed and trained in weapons use.

Tactical emergency medical services (TEMS) is the name given to a team of paramedics that are armed and trained in weapons use. Tactical emergency services teams have been given greater attention since the mass shootings at Columbine High School, Virginia Tech, the Pulse nightclub, and San Bernardino. In other cases, an arson event may require firefighters and investigators from multiple stations. A bombing, in contrast, will cause the ATF to become involved to determine what type of explosive was used. A biological attack will necessitate the involvement of public health officials. Since the type of terrorist event can vary dramatically, it is also imperative that you understand how to respond to any incident effectively.

12.1.1 Initial Investigation and Apprehension

One of the first priorities of response is to thwart the attack before it begins or as soon as possible after it unfolds. This proactive measure requires lots of information from intelligence sources as noted in Chapter 8. However, while preventing an attack internationally requires the Central Intelligence Agency (CIA) and military involvement, it is the Federal Bureau of Investigation (FBI) and local law enforcement officials who play the crucial role in domestic investigation and apprehension. If there is any tip or any evidence that an attack is unfolding, federal officials and local police will investigate

Figure 12-1

The FBI is one of many agencies that attempt to find terrorists, prevent attacks, or bring perpetrators to justice. Source: © FEMA.

further and attempt to apprehend or neutralize potential or active terrorists. This is clearly seen in the response to the Boston Marathon bombing.

After the Boston Marathon bombing, the FBI took the lead on the attack with the support of the CIA and the National Counterterrorism Center (NCTC), among others. The dissemination of information online by law enforcement played a significant role in keeping the public correctly informed about the bombing and in eventually solving the case itself. The Boston Police Department and FBI also collected video surveillance and photographs of the suspects from nearby cameras and accepted uploads from the public via social media sites like Facebook and Twitter. On 18 April, the FBI released this information through multiple sources online and were able to identify the Tsarnaev brothers as the perpetrators that day. However, these siblings took more innocent lives before law enforcement personnel were successful in capturing them. They fatally shot a police officer at the Massachusetts Institute of Technology (MIT) and then carjacked a civilian vehicle, taking a hostage inside. Tamerlan confessed to the hostage that they were responsible for the marathon bombing and the death of the policeman. Shortly after being forced to withdraw money from an ATM, the hostage escaped and called 911.

Law enforcement was able to locate the brothers who were driving in separate vehicles in Watertown, and a shootout ensued shortly after midnight. In the fight, two police officers were wounded, and one ended up passing away from his injuries almost a year later. Tamerlan was shot multiple times and was subsequently run over and killed by his brother who was driving the car. Dzhokhar soon abandoned the vehicle and escaped on foot. While law enforcement pursued Dzhokhar, additional information was released to the public through the media and online. Watertown residents were told to shelter in place and avoid leaving their homes. Everyone in the search area was put on lockdown as the manhunt continued for several hours.

Dzhokhar was discovered on the evening of 19 April when a Watertown citizen saw a man covered in blood lying inside his boat that was parked in his backyard. The citizen notified police, and Dzhokhar was finally taken into custody. Interrogation later revealed that the brothers were about to bomb Times Square in New York City after their attack in Boston. Dzhokhar was eventually sentenced to death by lethal injection. The brothers were self-radicalized, but influenced by propaganda from an Al-Qaeda affiliate. Their motive for this attack was to avenge Muslims who were affected by the US wars in Afghanistan and Iraq.

IN THE REAL WORLD

San Bernardino Shooting

On 2 December 2015, Syed Farook and his wife Tashfeen Malik entered the Inland Regional Center and shot several people with AR-15 rifles during a holiday party. Farook was present in the meeting but left at about 10:36 a.m. A short time later, Farook and his wife entered the facility wearing dark clothing. They shot between 100 and 225 rounds into the room. The result was 14 people killed and another 22 injured. 911

was contacted immediately, and police responded within four minutes after being notified. The first officer on scene had no tactical gear nor did the first team, which was assembled a short time later. Law enforcement officials encountered a chaotic scene with a blaring fire alarm, heavy gunpowder smell, malfunctioning lights, and water coming out of the fire sprinklers. Police also found numerous victims and hiding survivors. They began to stabilize the scene and evacuate victims.

Paramedics stationed themselves at a golf course across the street and began providing emergency medical care to those in need. Four hospitals received victims as they were transported from the scene of that attack. The San Bernardino SWAT team arrived within 11 minutes of the call, as they were training only a few miles away at the time of the incident. Roads were shut down to clear the area, and buses were used to pick up witnesses and take them to the Rock Church for interviews to begin the investigation.

During the investigation, one of the employees noted that he saw Farook leave the party and believed it was he that returned. This tip led police to the couple's home. Other departments rushed to assist, including the FBI and the Department of Homeland Security, which provided aircraft surveillance in the area in search of the rented black SUV the suspects used to flee the scene. When police arrived at the couple's home in Redlands, the SUV was seen leaving an alleyway. The police followed the vehicle, and the Malik shot at the officers through the back window. Syed exited the vehicle and began shooting at the police as well. Armored police vehicles surrounded the perpetrator's SUV, and the shootout continued. The exchange of over 500 rounds lasted 6½ minutes and involved 23 officers. Both Farook and Malik were killed by police, about four hours after the terrorist attack began.

Back at the scene and at Farook's house, several bombs were found. Robots were used to dispose of the three explosive devices found. Farook's friend and former neighbor, Enrique Marquez, Jr., also called 911 to turn in Farook. On 17 December 2015, Marquez was arrested in connection with terrorism. He purchased the two rifles that Farook and Malik used in the shooting, as well as materials used in the pipe bombs. Marquez claimed he did not know their plans to attack the building in San Bernardino. But, in the past, he conspired with Farook to execute other terrorist attacks that were never carried out. Subsequent investigation revealed that Malik posted allegiance to al-Baghdadi, a terrorist leader, on social media. Although the shooting was a terrible tragedy, this incident is a prime example of how preparedness and speed of response limited further impact. Lessons learned revealed that there is a need for cross-training among police and fire departments. The importance of tactical EMS, automatic weapons, and body armor with plate carrier systems was also noted in after-action discussions.

12.1.2 Safety and Security

As can be seen in the cases above, terrorist attacks will produce property destruction, injury, and death. For these reasons, there will be a strong

Figure 12-2

Numerous law enforcement officials will confront terrorists and initiate investigation into the event. Source: © FBI.

Size-up:
The process of evaluating the nature of the attack site.

Secondary devices:
The detonation of other bombs to add to the disruption and fear of the initial attack.

Dirty bombs:
Explosive devices laden with dangerous chemicals or radioactive material.

Situational awareness:
Continual monitoring of safety concerns at the scene of a terrorist attack.

inclination for people to rush into the area to help victims. It is important, however, that everyone resist this temptation – at least initially. The first priority, if possible, is to assess the situation from afar to determine what has occurred and how to respond safely. The process of evaluating the nature of the attack site is known as a **size-up**. This quick assessment is imperative because the location of terrorist attacks is inherently dangerous. Citizens and first responders can be injured by glass, twisted metal, falling debris, unstable buildings, broken gas lines that catch on fire, and many other hazards. Knowing what conditions you will be dealing with is central to your safety and that of others (Levy 2014).

There are other potential dangers that you must be concerned about as well. It is possible that terrorists may detonate additional bombs (i.e. **secondary devices**) to add to the disruption and fear. By setting off further explosions, terrorists attempt to kill those who are trying to aid initial victims. This only adds to the casualty count and creates compounded problems for those trying to react to the mayhem. As an example, Eric Rudolph, a terrorist who opposed abortion, used secondary devices when he attacked an abortion clinic in 1998. **Dirty bombs**, or explosives combined with hazardous materials (e.g. chlorine or nuclear material), have been used in Iraq and could also be utilized in the United States in the future. While the blast area is generally limited to a certain geographic area, chemical fumes can be transported by wind far from the scene of an attack. Someone should therefore be given the task of monitoring safety concerns and other issues such as air quality. Known as **situational awareness**, this is vital under dangerous working conditions. You should expect that terrorists will do all they can to hinder response operations.

Figure 12-3

The scene of a terrorist attack can be extremely dangerous.
Source: © FEMA.

There are at least three principles to remember to keep first responders out of harm's way at the scene of a terrorist attack (FEMA 1999). First, those responding to a terrorist event should not stay at the location for any extended length of time. There may be hazardous agents that can do physical harm to people. Besides dangerous materials, fatigue resulting from extensive work periods at the location can lead to many accidents and injuries. Second, keeping a distance between you and the site of the attack or harmful chemicals will enhance your safety. While this is not always feasible for those involved in response operations, the goal should be promoted where possible. Finally, if you must enter a dangerous area, be sure you have the proper personal protective equipment. Fire gear and hazardous materials suits may be needed to ensure your survivability in hostile conditions. Therefore, time, distance, and shielding are central ways to keep you safe when responding to terrorist attacks.

In addition to these recommendations, there is also the need for site security. As soon as is feasible, first responders should gain control over the scene. This may include the use of squad cars to block off roads as well as barricades, fences, and police or National Guard units on foot patrol. Trained individuals should sweep the area for other devices. The main priority is to prevent further attacks so that additional lives can be spared and a comprehensive response can take place without further constraints. While site security is essential, the scene must not be impermeable. Other responders, public works employees, and contractors may need to enter the area to accomplish vital post-disaster missions. For this reason, a check-in system can be established by locating tables, chairs, and personnel at the site entrance. The intentions, legitimacy, and qualifications of those wishing to enter the scene can then be determined by checking ID cards, reviewing licenses, or making phone calls. Any donations coming into the area should also be carefully checked to ensure they do not include bombs or WMD. This can limit the probability of secondary attacks and protect your safety.

12.1.3 Search and Rescue

Search and rescue (SAR):
Response activities undertaken to find disaster victims and remove them from danger or confinement.

While safety and site security issues are major priorities, they are only means to an end. Safety and security will enhance your ability to care for the victims, which ranks among your ultimate goals after a terrorist attack. One of the first steps you will need to take is to participate in SAR operations. **Search and rescue (SAR)** is defined as "response activities undertaken to find disaster victims and remove them from danger or confinement" (McEntire 2007, p. 142). There are many different types of SAR ranging from swift water to wildland contexts. In relation to terrorism, SAR includes finding the victims under rubble and extracting them to a safe location.

SAR will be undertaken initially by emergent groups. Later on, firefighters, who have specialized knowledge for this important function, will take over. Firefighters have personal protective equipment and tools such as helmets, goggles, dust masks, and other gear (e.g. saws and jacks) to reach and retrieve victims. Local fire departments may be insufficient however. In major events, national Urban Search and Rescue (USAR) teams may be required. FEMA has nearly 30 such teams made up of firefighters, engineers, doctors, and paramedics. They can be activated by within hours and transported by C-130 aircraft and/or bus to the scene of an attack. USAR teams are especially valuable when destroyed areas are extensive or when SAR operations will last long periods. Such teams can be rotated periodically to keep them fresh, alert, and productive. USAR teams were used extensively after the Oklahoma City bombing and after the 9/11 attacks on the World Trade Center.

12.1.4 Medical Care and Triage

As victims are extracted from or around damaged buildings, it will be necessary to provide them necessary medical care. Much of the medical attention will be provided by citizens (similar to those engaged in SAR operations). When firefighters and paramedics arrive, they will take over. They have expertise and supplies that citizens will not possess. Treatment will vary depending on the nature and extent of injuries.

Triage:
The assessment, sorting, and treatment of the injured in such a way as to maximize limited resources.

Some individuals may suffer from minor cuts and bruises to smoke inhalation. Others will have broken bones or life-threatening injuries (e.g. damaged internal organs). If the number and extent of injuries are limited, first responders will be able to handle the load easily. They will stop the bleeding, provide oxygen, or immobilize fractures. If there are many casualties and serious injuries, the emergency medical system can be severely taxed. In this case, triage may need to be implemented.

Triage is the assessment, sorting, treatment, and transportation of the injured in such a way as to maximize limited medical resources (Mayer

Figure 12-4

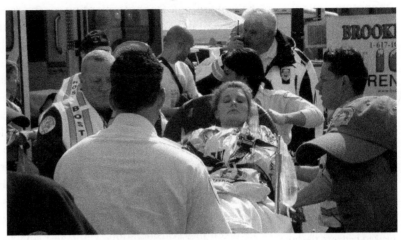

An important priority after a terrorist attack is emergency medical care. Source: © FEMA.

1997). At the scene of a terrorist attack, there may be large numbers of victims. Because of quantity of casualties in comparison to available paramedics, choices will have to be made about who will receive care. For instance, those with minor injuries and those with fatal injuries will be treated last or not at all. Attention will be given to those who require immediate help and have a strong chance of survival. This will help determine who should be sent to hospitals. The practice of triage sounds cruel or inhumane, but the reality of terrorist attacks often dictates the extent to which medical personnel can assist everyone. Difficult choices have to be made to do the most good for the most number of people.

Another major advantage of triage is that it limits the number of people who go to the hospital for further treatment. In most disasters (terrorist attacks included) people will often be taken to the hospital by friends, coworkers, and neighbors. That is to say, they are **self-referred**, walking wounded or ambulatory, meaning they arrive at the hospital whether they require immediate care or not. This often clogs the hospital with patients who may not always have critical injuries. Therefore, hospitals also have to practice triage, thereby limiting the chance that nurses and doctors will be overwhelmed with patients that do not require immediate or lifesaving help. Interestingly, this is a continuation of a practice that occurs every day in the hospital. Nurses and doctors in the ER always determine who should be admitted immediately or who can wait for treatment.

Self-referred:
Patients who arrive at the hospital whether they require immediate care or not.

12.1.5 Decontamination

Regardless of how patients arrive at the hospital, it may be necessary to clean them before they receive additional treatment. Patients may be covered in hazardous materials that could result in harm to themselves, firefighters, paramedics, and medical staff in hospitals. If a hospital receives

Decontamination:
The removal of hazardous materials from victims through clothing removal and the washing of bodies.

Hot zone:
The area contaminated by the terrorist attack.

Warm zone:
The location where victims are washed. It is located between the hot and cold zones.

Cold zone:
The uncontaminated area where responders and victims may enter and leave.

contaminated patients or even contaminated gurneys, its operations could be jeopardized. **Decontamination,** or the removal of hazardous materials from victims through clothing removal and the washing of bodies, must therefore be performed at the scene, at a field hospital, or before entering a permanent medical facility. If victims are not decontaminated, the chemicals on them may adversely impact physicians and nurses as was the case after the Tokyo sarin gas attacks in 1995.

The process of decontamination is technical and must be followed meticulously. When responding to a terrorist incident involving hazardous materials, three zones should be identified near the attack site. A **hot zone** is the area that has been contaminated by the terrorist attack. A **warm zone** is the location where victims are washed. A **cold zone** is the uncontaminated area. It is where responders and victims may enter and leave the area. When setting up and cordoning off these zones, it is important that wind direction be taken into consideration. The zones should be set up in such a way that wind blows toward the hot zone. This will ensure that hazardous materials are not sent in the direction of responders and decontaminated individuals.

Decontamination in the warm zone must take into account several important factors. Those involved in decontamination must have the proper protective gear and training. Inadequate hazardous materials suits, incorrect breathing apparatus, and mistakes in operations can lead to the loss of further lives. Another important priority is to protect the privacy of those being decontaminated. Decontamination tents or colored plastic sheeting can be hung to shield undressing, washing, and dressing areas. In order to properly clean victims, clothing should be removed. Known as "dry decon," this process may remove up to 85 or 95% of contaminants. If needed, water, a mild soap, brushes, and/or sponges can also be used. Contaminated runoff can be captured in children's plastic swim pools or other devices made especially for this purpose. Affected clothing or gurneys with hazardous residues should also be properly disposed. Dirty liquids can then be treated in an environmentally sensitive way. Responders should also be decontaminated in the same manner before they leave the scene. This will ensure their safety as well. When finished with the decontamination process, new clothing or medical gowns can be given to victims. At this point, victims can be transported, receive further medical treatment, or admitted into hospitals.

Once again, the hospital will also ensure decontamination occurs when a patient is admitted. In fact, the Joint Commission requires hospitals to have a process to decontaminate victims. This includes a location to wash off patients as well as personal protective equipment and training of staff. Remediation teams and the Environmental Protection Agency may need to be involved after attacks to determine the impact on the environment and what can be done to clean up hazardous chemicals.

12.1.6 Closing the Investigation

Another major priority after a terrorist attack is to finalize the investigation (McEntire et al. 2001). After life safety issues have been addressed,

Figure 12-5

Decontamination is vital to prevent the transmission of
dangerous chemicals or hazardous materials. Source: © FEMA.

additional attention can be shifted toward law enforcement activities
(i.e. investigation). In order to apprehend or prosecute terrorists, evidence must be collected. It is vital that you remember that anything at
the scene of a terrorist attack – debris, a body, or anything else – may
provide evidence. For this reason, responders should be aware that the
scene of an attack should be protected to the fullest extent possible.
Unauthorized people should not be allowed to enter the area, or they
should operate with minimal disruption in mind. Evidence should be
meticulously recorded and stored for future court proceedings. Photos
can also be taken of the scene, and maps can be drawn to assist with the
investigation. Other measures, including information gathering from
witnesses, or laser maps can help you piece together critical facts and
data that will be needed in court.

All of these measures could help you identify who committed the
attacks, prevent further terrorist acts, and facilitate successful prosecution. Cases have been solved because of seemingly insignificant clues.
For instance, the serial numbers of blown-up vehicles have helped law
enforcement officials track down the terrorists who rented or owned
them. A 2007 terrorist plot in London was thwarted because a terrorist
parked a car illegally. When police went to move the vehicle, they detected explosives and were able to track down the people involved in
the diabolical plan. Alternatively, legal battles may be lost on a technicality because evidence has not been carefully collected and recorded
with a clear chain of custody. Investigation conducted by the police is
one of the things that separate terrorism from other types of disaster
operations.

IN THE REAL WORLD

Responding to 9/11

The attacks on the World Trade Center in New York illustrate the variety of functions that have to be performed when terrorism occurs. Ground Zero and the area surrounding it was a dangerous area due to fires, unstable debris piles, broken glass, and twisted metal. This situation required additional equipment and instructions be given to first responders. Because a secondary attack by terrorists could not be ruled out, anyone wishing to enter the area had to be carefully screened. Only those with legitimate reasons for entering Ground Zero were permitted to do so once they were approved and given proper identification documents. Urban Search and Rescue teams arrived from around the nation to find the injured and deceased. 9/11 also produced the largest crime scene in America. Evidence from more than a 16-block area had to be collected by numerous agencies. One of the major concerns was the presence of hazardous materials (e.g. dust, soot, dangerous chemicals). First responders were adversely affected by breathing the contaminated air around Ground Zero. Many required long-term medical care to treat their symptoms. The major lesson from 9/11 is that those working in homeland security and emergency management will be preoccupied with many responsibilities after terrorist attacks occur.

SELF-CHECK

1. Usually, the very first people to help out with a post-disaster operation are not first responders, but ordinary citizens. True or False?
2. Emergence is the flow of people and resources to the scene of an emergency or disaster. True or False?
3. The process of assessing and evaluating the situation at an attack site is best known as:
   (a) Triage
   (b) Search and rescue
   (c) Situational awareness
   (d) A size-up
4. Why should responders be aware that the attack scene should be protected to the fullest extent possible?

12.2 OTHER CRUCIAL FUNCTIONS

There are many other important functions that will need to be addressed when terrorist attacks occur. If possible, warnings should be issued and information must be shared with the public. People must be evacuated out of dangerous areas and sheltered if required. These measures can keep citizens safe and minimize the impact of terrorism.

12.2.1 Warning, Intelligence, and Public Information

Warnings:
Notifications sent out to the public so they can take protective measures.

Warnings are notifications sent out to the public so they can take protective measures. Warnings have been issued several times since 9/11. Warnings were given due to possible attacks against the financial district in New York as well as when terrorists attempted to smuggle explosives on airliners crossing the Atlantic Ocean from England to the United States. Unfortunately, most terrorist attacks will not allow advanced warning. Terrorists often make threats against their enemies, but they rarely explain exact details about what they intend to do. The element of surprise is one of their greatest strengths. It is true that intelligence officers may at times intercept communications and obtain terrorist plans. However, this information may be sketchy or incomplete and require corroboration. In addition, there is always the difficulty of knowing what and how much to share with the public.

On the one hand, the intelligence community may wish to avoid sharing sensitive information in a warning because it may compromise the safety of their agents or make terrorists aware of their tracking methods. This, in turn, will harm future intelligence efforts. On the other hand, sharing information with the public could help avert attacks or capture terrorists. For instance, if terrorists threaten to attack airports, relaying this information to the public could help them be more aware of the activities taking place around them. While this dilemma may never be completely resolved, authorities should use their best judgment about what to do. The particulars of the situation will probably dictate which course of action to follow.

Regardless of whether or not a warning is possible or desirable, it is imperative that officials in emergency management and homeland security communicate often to the public after a terrorist attack. Citizens will want to know:

- What happened?
- Who was responsible for the attack?
- What are the impacts?
- Are they in danger?
- What steps should they take to protect themselves?
- What is the government doing?
- What should they do if they need assistance?

Weather radios:
Electronic devices that receive information from the National Weather Service to warn people of approaching severe weather.

To notify people of impending attacks or to answer their questions, emergency management and homeland security officials should rely heavily on existing warning systems (McEntire 2007). **Weather radios** are electronic devices that receive information from the National Weather Service to warn people of approaching severe weather. If needed, they could be used to

Emergency alert system:
An announcement that interrupts TV and radio programs and relays information about what is taking place and what people should do for protection.

Reverse 911 systems:
Computerized messages sent over phone lines rapidly to anyone in a designated area.

Public information officer:
The person who gathers information for the incident commander(s) and shares information with the media, or a city employee who specializes in working with the media.

relay information about terrorist attacks. Alternatively, the **emergency alert system** can be activated. This warning system interrupts TV and radio programs and provides an announcement about what is taking place and what people should do for protection. The drawback of these systems is that not everyone has a weather radio or is watching TV or listening to the radio.

Some cities have **reverse 911 systems**, which are essentially computerized phone messages sent rapidly to large numbers of people in a designated area. Reverse 911 is useful because it can relay detailed information to thousands of citizens and businesses within a specific area code or zip code. It allows you to target a specific group of people with a detailed message. The drawback of reverse 911 systems is that they are expensive, require constant updating and data entry, and have not always been applicable to cell phones.

The most common method of communicating with the public is the media. Before and after terrorist attacks, emergency management and homeland security officials should interact frequently with reporters representing the television, radio, the Internet, and print media. Press conferences can be held periodically to make sure information is getting to the public. Because the media wants lots of information, it is vital that you meet their requests to the best of your ability. Failing to do so will likely result in them seeking knowledge elsewhere or reporting inaccurate information. Anytime you hear anything that is incorrect, it should be brought to the attention of reporters and clarified. The rule is to provide clear, consistent, and repeated information by a credible authority (Quarantelli 1990). Anytime this rule is not followed, public information will be ineffective and even counterproductive. A **public information officer**, a city employee who specializes in working with the media, can help you share information successfully to the media and the citizens you are trying to inform.

Figure 12-6

Sharing information to the public via the media can help your community respond successfully to a terrorist attack.
Source: © FEMA.

12.2.2 Evacuation and Sheltering

Depending on the consequences of the attack, you may need to evacuate your citizens and shelter them in safer locations. Terrorist attacks will result in burnt-down buildings or unstable structures. A bomb may release toxic chemicals into the atmosphere for a short period of time. A dirty bomb, an explosive device laden with radiation, could contaminate the environment for an extended period of time. The detonation of the nuclear device would level a large city and leave it uninhabitable for decades. Those victims that survive would need to leave or risk radiation contamination. While not terrorist attacks, events like Chernobyl illustrate this point clearly. The location of this radiation leak from the reactor has generally been unpopulated since the release occurred. For these reasons, you may need to evacuate the citizens in your community.

Evacuation:
The movement of people away from hazardous areas or situations.

Evacuation is the movement of people away from hazardous areas or situations. When attacks threaten the lives or well-being of individuals, an evacuation request should be made. This decision should not be taken lightly since "unnecessary evacuations are expensive, disruptive, and un-popular" (Baker 1990, p. 3). However, evacuation for short or long periods may be required before or after terrorist attacks. It is therefore important that you notify people of the need to evacuate and provide clear instructions about when and how they will leave. In addition, after a major attack, you may need to make transportation arrangements for those without vehicles. Buses, trains, and planes can help you evacuate large numbers of people. As neighborhoods or communities are evacuated, you will want to have sufficient law enforcement personnel to help monitor and direct traffic. Contraflow plans – reversing the flow of transportation arteries as is done before hurricane landfall – can help to speed up the evacuation process. This will enable a quicker and safer exit from the location of the terrorist attack. However, it is important to recognize that some people may not evacuate even when warned or advised to do so. This experience has been seen in many disasters, including Hurricane Katrina. In some cases, people simply ignore requests to leave. In other cases, individuals and families may not have the means to travel to a safer area.

If people are leaving their homes and neighborhoods, they will logically require a place to go. Some individuals and families will stay in hotels, while others will locate with friends and families in other areas. Some people will not have financial resources or supportive networks. In other cases, the number of evacuees is so large that this puts an extreme burden on receiving communities. In these cases, sheltering will be required elsewhere.

Sheltering:
The location of individuals in places of safety and refuge.

Sheltering is the location of individuals in places of safety and refuge (Mileti et al. 1992). It includes not only a roof overhead but also other life-sustaining activities. There are a number of factors that need to be considered when opening shelters:

- The number of evacuees versus the number of shelters needed to house them
- Occupancy rates in relation to the size of the buildings or rooms
- Electrical supply
- Sleeping arrangements (e.g. beds, cots, sleeping bags, pillows, blankets).
- Food and water (i.e. mass care arrangements)

- Bathroom and shower facilities
- Medical care
- Law enforcement presence
- Records of who was staying in the shelter

Churches and organizations like the American Red Cross and Salvation Army are frequently involved in sheltering operations. Faith-based agencies and volunteer groups can help you understand what else needs to be taken into account when establishing and running shelters.

When possible, you will want to encourage those in the shelter to find temporary or permanent housing (e.g. apartments or homes). The time frame of this may depend largely on whether or not evacuees can return home or start a new life elsewhere. Because some individuals and families will lack resources, the transition from an evacuee status to a returned or permanent resident can be long and challenging. You may need to provide government assistance or financial support from nonprofit organizations.

IN THE REAL WORLD

Sheltering First Responders

When sheltering is discussed by the public, the impression is given that it is directed toward the victims of terrorist attacks and disasters. While this is undoubtedly true, it ignores the fact that those responding to the event may also need to place to stay. After the terrorist attacks on 9/11, hundreds of emergency workers had to be sheltered in the Jacob Javits Convention Center in New York City. Cots and bedding were acquired for this purpose. Shower facilities and food were also required to care for those responding to the terrorist attack. The sheltering operations at the Javits Center went on for an extended period of time and were vital to the success of the recovery activities at Ground Zero.

SELF-CHECK

1. Most terrorist attacks will not allow advanced warning. True or False?
2. The most common method of communicating with the public is through the emergency alert system. True or False?
3. The movement of people away from hazardous areas or situations is best known as:
   (a) A warning
   (b) Sheltering
   (c) An evacuation
   (d) The emergency alert system
4. Why is there a dilemma in the intelligence community about whether or not to share sensitive information?

12.3 COORDINATION MECHANISMS

As can be seen, there are numerous activities that have to be performed after terrorist attacks. They range from site security and medical care to SAR and sheltering. Because of this wide array of responsibilities, there are countless organizations involved in incident response. Besides first responders, public works will be involved in damage assessment and debris removal. Public information officers will work closely with the media to provide information to citizens. Public health may assist with medical needs along with hospitals. State and federal government officials will arrive to provide security and investigate. Businesses can provide resources and nonprofit organizations will assist with sheltering. As can be seen, there are countless people involved after terrorist attacks.

Coordination:
Cooperative efforts to pursue common goals in the wake of terrorist attacks.

Due to this disparate set of activities and actors, coordination becomes imperative. **Coordination** is defined as cooperative efforts to pursue common goals in the wake of terrorist attacks. Such goals may include protecting life, assisting victims, investigating leads, and minimizing social disruption. Coordination helps to identify who will be in charge of vital functions, what collective problems exist, and how they will be overcome. These joint endeavors help to limit gaps in service and promote efficiency and effectiveness in response operations. Conversely, the lack of coordination may result in "an inability to determine priorities, misunderstanding among organizations, failure to fully utilize equipment and personnel, overly-taxed organizations, delays in service, omission of essential tasks, duplication of effort, safety problems, and counterproductive activity among other things" (McEntire 2007, p. 293).

12.3.1 The Incident Command System

Incident Command System (ICS):
A set of personnel and procedures that helps facilitate coordination among first responders.

One of the best ways to promote coordination among field-level personnel is to employ the **Incident Command System (ICS)**. The ICS is "a set of personnel, policies, [and] procedures ... integrated into a common organizational structure designed to improve emergency response operations of all types and complexities" (Irwin 1989, p. 134). It was developed in California after responses to forest fires witnessed several problems including poor communications, lack of joint planning, and inadequate resource management. ICS helps to overcome these challenges and manage organizations involved in response operations.

ICS is typically a field organization mechanism and is based on an incident commander and various supporting officers. It also includes four organizational sections and a number of widely accepted principles. While ICS can help promote coordination, first responders must be aware of its potential weaknesses if response operations are to be successful.

Incident command:
The on-scene leader or leaders in the incident command post.

Under the strategy of ICS, the position of incident command will be established. **Incident command** is the on-scene leader or leaders for field operations. When a terrorist attack occurs, incident command will be established by the first person on the scene and later taken over by those with more expertise or higher authority. Incident command may also include more than one commander. In other words, a variety of individuals may meet to make decisions about response priorities and methods.

Figure 12-7

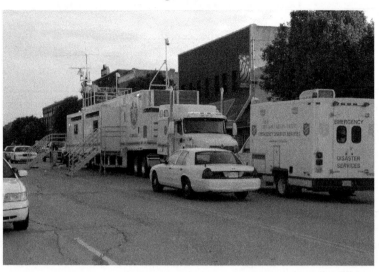

Incident Command Vehicles like this one may facilitate coordination at the scene. Source: © FEMA.

IN THE REAL WORLD

GEDAPER

When you or the incident commander(s) arrives on scene, you should take several steps to accurately assess the situation. The National Fire Academy recommends the acronym GEDAPER (FEMA 1999, p. 43). GEDAPER includes:

- Gathering information about the event
- Estimating potential impact of the attack
- Determining response goals
- Assessing tactical options and resources at hand
- Planning and implementing response actions
- Evaluating progress
- Reviewing results

By following these recommendations, you will be more likely to protect yourself and successfully respond.

Safety officer:
The person who evaluates the dangers at the scene and makes sure everyone is operating according to safety policies.

Liaison officer:
The person who serves as the link between the incident commander(s) and other organizations.

The incident commander/commanders work(s) closely with three officers. These officers are attached laterally to incident command and include the public information officer, the safety officer, and the liaison officer. The **public information officer** gathers information for the incident commander/commanders and shares information with the media. The **safety officer** evaluates the dangers at the scene and makes sure everyone is operating according to safety policies. The **liaison officer** serves as the link between the incident commander/commanders and other organizations. Together, the incident commander/commanders and officers oversee the entire field response operation.

The incident commander/commanders and officers do not have to do everything however. They have four organizational sections below them to assist them in responding to terrorist attacks. These sections include planning, operations, logistics, and finance/administration. Each section may include one person or scores of people to fulfill important preplanning and post-event functions.

Planning:
The section under ICS in charge of collecting information about the terrorist attack, including operational priorities.

Operations:
The name given to the section under ICS that is in charge of implementing the strategy created by those in planning.

Logistics:
A section that supports operations. It acquires people, equipment, and other resources needed by those responding to the attack.

Finance/administration:
The final section under ICS. This section tracks the expenses associated with response operations and logistics.

- **Planning** is the section in charge of collecting information about the terrorist attack, including operational priorities given to them by the incident commander. It determines what has happened and what may occur and identifies a strategy to accomplish response goals.
- **Operations** is the name given to the section that is in charge of implementing the strategy and tactics to satisfy the objectives of the incident commander and the planning section. It includes a number of activities ranging from fire suppression and triage to SAR and decontamination.
- **Logistics** is the section that supports operations. It acquires people, equipment, and other resources needed by those responding to the attack.
- **Finance/administration** is the final section under ICS. This section tracks the expenses associated with response operations and logistics.

As can be seen, ICS helps to organize key functions in response operations. It also promotes coordination and effectiveness because it is based on commonly accepted principles. ICS encourages people to use common terminology when communicating with others; jargon and "ten" codes (e.g. 10-4) are avoided. ICS likewise allows for expansion of the organizational structure based on the nature and scope of the incident; it may be very simple or include additional layers (e.g. divisions, branches, and strike teams). ICS tries to integrate communications; frequencies are assigned and clearly identified. Unity of command is promoted under ICS; this implies that each person reports to one supervisor only. Unified command is also an important priority in ICS; all major organizations may be involved in joint decision making. Another principle is consolidated incident action plans; written documents help guide operations on a 12-hour period. Three other principles are a manageable span of control, designated incident facilities, and comprehensive resource management. Span of control implies that each supervisor should have between 3 and 7 people to manage and oversee. Designated incident facilities refer to desire to make everyone aware of the incident command post, staging areas, camps, helibases, etc. Comprehensive resource management suggests that all resources, whether human or material, must be checked in and carefully tracked during response operations. Such principles are believed to help promote coordination among field personnel.

12.3.2 Strengths and Weakness of ICS

The ICS has both advantages and disadvantages (McEntire 2007, p. 329). On the one hand, ICS may help promote collaboration among key leaders, increase safety among responders, and enhance communication among many organizations. Realistic management processes and improved use of resources are other benefits of ICS. On the other hand, ICS may not resolve all of the challenges inherent in response operations, and it can even exacerbate some (Dynes 1994; Neal and Phillips 1995). Critics argue that incident command may be too rigid for the dynamic nature of post-disaster operations and fail to appreciate the need for collaboration instead of control. Some feel that first response organizations do not work well with other organizations and that ICS becomes less important in larger terrorist attacks. Regardless of this controversy, ICS remains the principal system for field response operations. Those working under ICS will be more successful if they are aware of the potential pitfalls (e.g. the dangers of focusing too much on technological solutions instead of addressing organizational communication problems or the problems of stressing who should be in charge vs. how can organizations work together harmoniously).

12.3.3 Utilization of Emergency Operations Centers

Area command:
An ICS organization that supervises several incident command posts.

Multiagency coordination centers (MACCs):
An ICS organization level that supervises incident command across several jurisdictions.

Joint field office (JFO):
An incident command organization with federal personnel (and state and local officials on certain occasions).

Because terrorist incidents will most likely include more than a field response, other organizational layers will be required. This is especially true when terrorist attacks are large and have significant consequences. ICS is helpful for dealing with field operations at a specific location (e.g. SAR, medical care, and decontamination). Incident command activities will also be needed to oversee the larger picture of terrorist attacks. This may result in the establishment of **area command** (which supervises several incident command posts) and **multiagency coordination centers** (**MACCs**) (which supervises incident command across several jurisdictions). If national assets are required, a **joint field office (JFO)** will be established. The JFO is an incident command organization with federal personnel (and state and local officials on certain occasions). Their purpose is to provide resource support to incident command teams at lower levels. Area command, MACCs, and JFO are known in emergency management as EOCs.

In contrast to incident command posts, EOCs are more concerned with the broader issues pertaining to incident response and disaster recovery. As noted in Chapter 11, EOCs are the locations where information is gathered, processed, and acted upon by key decision makers. EOCs will be activated in the jurisdiction, in neighboring communities, in regional organizations, at the state level, and even among numerous federal government agencies. Multiple EOCs can therefore be running and even interacting at the same time.

When working in an EOC, you must ensure that numerous organizations are represented. This may include police, fire, and emergency medical departments. However, EOCs will also incorporate all major city departments and even major businesses and nonprofit organizations. These participants will assist all community-wide response operations such as public information, evacuation, and sheltering. In terrorist attacks, public health and intelligence officials should logically be given presence in EOCs. This will aid with bioterrorism attacks and investigation processes.

EOCs can and have been organized under the principles of incident command. However, in other cases, EOCs are laid out based on organizational units or according to functions (e.g. Emergency Support Functions such as warning, evacuation, public information, debris management, resource management, etc.). The main point to remember is that EOCs can be organized in dramatically different ways and based on the needs and interests of those involved. Nevertheless, all EOCs should endeavor to facilitate response coordination.

IN THE REAL WORLD

Responsibilities of Local Departments and Organizations

When responding to a terrorist attack, it is imperative that you are aware of the other important participants. In cities and counties, this may include several organizations as noted in the following chart:

Dept./organization	Roles and responsibilities
Fire	• Isolate impact area and set up perimeter • Position equipment and responders upwind, uphill, and upstream from the incident site • Assess downwind hazards and implement evacuation or shelter in place decisions • Identify agenda and adjust scene layout if required • Respond to victim needs with appropriate PPE • Decontaminate all victims, responders, and equipment as needed
EMS	• Implement mass casualty triage procedures • Provide medical treatment as dictated by the incident • Transport victims to definitive care facilities • Determine mental health impact and treat accordingly
Police	• Share preliminary intelligence data with incident command and the EOC • Notify and interact with the FBI • Deploy law enforcement personnel, including bomb squads and tactical operations teams • Assure incident security for first responders • Collect and control evidence • Apprehend and assume custody of suspects at the scene

(Continued)

(Continued)

Dept./organization	Roles and responsibilities
Hospitals	• Implement lock-down of facility to ensure security • Decontaminate and triage all arriving patients • Track patients, including their symptoms, and communicate with public health officials • Decide where to treat patients (internally or externally) • Treat as dictated by nature of injuries
Public health	• Conduct surveillance for evidence of epidemics • Identify and control agent • Determine and implement protective measures for the population, including immunizations or prophylactic medicines • Work with police to implement quarantines if needed
Coroners	• Receive human remains • Safeguard personal property • Identify the deceased and notify next of kin • Prepare and complete file for each decedent • Photograph, fingerprint, and collect DNA specimens as appropriate • Provide death certificates • Coordinate and release remains for final disposition

Source: Adapted from Perry (2003)

12.3.4 EOC Management

One of your major priorities in the EOC is to acquire and manage resources. For instance, if the incident commander and logistics section requests additional body bags, the EOC may be tasked with the responsibility of obtaining and shipping them to the right location. E.L. Quarantelli (1979) notes that EOCs also help determine response policies, host visitors, and keep records.

Because EOCs are in charge of so many functions, they can be very noisy and stressful. The nature of response operations is also dynamic, and the impacts of terrorism can unfold quickly. For this reason, it may be necessary to have everyone stop what they are doing every few hours and report on the key issues they are dealing with. This is similar to the planning function of ICS. In both cases, such briefings will ensure that everyone is up to speed on what is taking place and what yet needs to be done.

Those working in EOCs may be required to work long hours under emotionally draining circumstances. Breaks should be taken periodically, and healthy food should be supplied to keep energy levels up. Shifts should be designated so that employee burnout does not occur. When shift transitions take place, transfer of command briefings should be given to the fresh crew. These same principles must also be applied to those working in field response.

SELF-CHECK

1. Under the Incident Command System (ICS), incident command is always given to a single on-scene leader. True or False?
2. There is only one EOC operating during a terrorist attack. True or False?
3. Under the strategy of ICS, who serves as a link between incident command and other organizations?
   (a) The information officer
   (b) The safety officer
   (c) The liaison officer
   (d) The emergency manager
4. Why is coordination an important aspect in responding to attacks?

SUMMARY

This chapter illustrated that successful response operations after a terrorist attack do not occur by chance. They require you to be familiar with convergent and emergent behavior. In addition, effective reactions to terrorist attacks include giving priority to investigations, safety, and interdictions to neutralize the threat. Many functions are involved in responses such as the protection of police officers and firefighters as well as the decontamination of the victims of terrorist attacks. At times, you may also need to warn citizens before an attack or evacuate them to safer areas after terrorism occurs. To help you with your responsibilities, ICS and EOCs can be utilized. By anticipating your responsibility after a terrorist attack, you will be better able to protect life, prosecute terrorists, and collaborate effectively with others.

ASSESS YOUR UNDERSTANDING

UNDERSTAND: WHAT HAVE YOU LEARNED?

 Go to **www.wiley.com/go/mcentire/homelandsecurity2e** to assess your knowledge of response operations.

SUMMARY QUESTIONS

1. In emergency or disaster situations, people will take on new roles and interact cooperatively with strangers. True or False?

2. When providing medical care at an attack site, those with minor or fatal injuries are treated last or not at all. True or False?

3. Triage is the process by which harmful chemicals are removed from victims' clothes and bodies. True or False?

4. Sheltering is the location of people to places of safety and refuge. True or False?

5. Weather radios are never used to relay information on terrorist attacks. True or False?

6. ICS is the principal system to coordinate field response operations. True or False?

7. EOCs have a narrower scope in disaster response than ICS. True or False?

8. Logistics is the ICS section that supports operations by acquiring and distributing people, equipment, and other needed resources. True or False?

9. Initial search and rescues are often undertaken by:
   (a) Firefighters
   (b) Urban Search and Rescue teams
   (c) Emergent groups
   (d) Police officers

10. An important way to prevent overloading of hospitals after a terrorist attack is best known as:
    (a) Triage
    (b) Situational awareness
    (c) A size-up
    (d) Decontamination

11. All of the following are drawbacks of reverse 911 systems, except that such systems:
    (a) Are able to reach large numbers of people in an expedited manner
    (b) Call only homes and not businesses
    (c) Require constant updating of data
    (d) Are expensive

12. To better share information with the media after an attack, it could be most helpful to obtain communication assistance from:

    (a) An emergency manager

    (b) A public information officer

    (c) A homeland security official

    (d) A preparedness committee

13. Under the strategy of ICS, who evaluates the dangers at an attack scene?

    (a) The information officer

    (b) The liaison officer

    (c) The safety officer

    (d) The emergency manager

14. The cooperative effort to identify common goals in the wake of a terrorist attack is best known as:

    (a) ICS

    (b) Logistics

    (c) Planning

    (d) Coordination

APPLYING THIS CHAPTER

1. As a homeland security expert, you have been asked to speak at an emergency management seminar on the importance of safety in responding at a terrorist attack site. What could you say about the importance of a size-up?

2. You are in charge of medical operations and have been asked to speak at a press conference about the response to the attack. One reporter asks you about the process and importance of decontamination. How could you respond?

3. As an emergency manager, you are concerned about how best to communicate with the public. How could you effectively utilize the media for this goal?

4. Your duty with the Red Cross is to deal with sheltering in the case of an evacuation. What are some factors that you would need to be considered if sheltering was required?

BE A HOMELAND SECURITY PROFESSIONAL

Advising a Local Government

You are a consultant on emergency management. A local government has asked you for suggestions on how to keep their first responders safe in the event of a terrorist attack. What recommendations could you provide?

Assignment: Convergence and Emergence

Write a one-page paper describing the concepts of convergence and emergence and how these processes factor into the response to terrorist attacks. Be as thorough as possible.

Managing an EOC

You are an emergency manager. Your office has recently created an emergency operations center. When an EOC opens up to respond to a disaster, the work environment is often noisy, fast-paced, and exhausting. What management strategies could you use to maintain high levels of communication and staff energy in the event your EOC responds to an attack?

KEY TERMS

Area command	An ICS organization that supervises several incident command posts
Cold zone	The uncontaminated area where responders and victims may enter and leave
Convergence	The flow of people and resources to the scene of an emergency or disaster
Coordination	Cooperative efforts to pursue common goals in the wake of terrorist attacks
Decontamination	The removal of hazardous materials from victims through clothing removal and the washing of bodies
Dirty bombs	Explosive devices laden with dangerous chemicals or radioactive material
Emergence	The appearance of altruistic behavior that is unfamiliar to the participants
Emergency alert system	An announcement that interrupts TV and radio programs and relays information about what is taking place and what people should do for protection
Evacuation	The movement of people away from hazardous areas or situations
Finance/ administration	The final section under ICS. This section tracks the expenses associated with response operations and logistics.
Hot zone	The area contaminated by the terrorist attack
Incident command	The on-scene leader or leaders in the incident command post
Incident Command System (ICS)	A set of personnel and procedures that helps facilitate coordination among first responders
Joint field office (JFO)	An incident command organization with federal personnel (and state and local officials on certain occasions)

Liaison officer	The person who serves as the link between the incident commander(s) and other organizations
Logistics	A section that supports operations. It acquires people, equipment, and other resources needed by those responding to the attack.
Multiagency coordination centers (MACCs)	An ICS organization level that supervises incident command across several jurisdictions
Operations	The name given to the section under ICS that is in charge of implementing the strategy created by those in planning
Planning	The section under ICS in charge of collecting information about the terrorist attack, including operational priorities
Public information officer	The person who gathers information for the incident commander(s) and shares information with the media, or a city employee who specializes in working with the media
Reverse 911 systems	Computerized messages sent over phone lines rapidly to anyone in a designated area
Safety officer	The person who evaluates the dangers at the scene and makes sure everyone is operating according to safety policies
Search and rescue	Response activities undertaken to find disaster victims and remove them from danger or confinement
Secondary devices	The detonation of other bombs to add to the disruption and fear of the initial attack
Self-referred	Patients who arrive at the hospital whether they require immediate care or not
Sheltering	The location of individuals in places of safety and refuge
Situational awareness	Continual monitoring of safety concerns at the scene of a terrorist attack
Size-up	The process of evaluating the nature of the attack site
Tactical emergency medical services	The name given to a team of paramedics that are armed and trained in weapons use
Triage	The assessment, sorting, and treatment of the injured in such a way as to maximize limited resources
Warm zone	The location where victims are washed. It is located between the hot and cold zones
Warnings	Notifications sent out to the public so they can take protective measures
Weather radios	Electronic devices that receive information from the National Weather Service to warn people of approaching severe weather

REFERENCES

Baker, E.J. (1990). Evacuation Decision making and Public Response in Hurricane Hugo in South Carolina. *Quick Response Research Report no.39*. Boulder, CO: Natural Hazards Research and Applications Information Center, University of Colorado.

Drabek, T.E. and McEntire, D.A. (2002). Emergent phenomena and the sociology of disaster: lessons, trends and opportunities from the research literature. *Disaster Prevention and Management* 12 (2): 97–112.

Dynes, R.R. (1994). Community emergency planning: false assumptions and inappropriate analogies. *International Journal of Mass Emergencies and Disasters* 12 (2): 141–158.

FEMA (1999). *Emergency Response to Terrorism*. Independent Study Course. Washington, DC: FEMA.

Irwin, R.L. (1989). The incident command system. In: *Disaster Response: Principles of Preparedness and Coordination* (ed. E. Auf der Heide), 133–161. St. Louis, MO: C.V. Mosby Company.

Kendra, J.M. and Wachtendorf, T. (2003). Reconsidering convergence and converger legitimacy in response to the world trade center disaster. In: *Terrorism and Disaster: New Threats, New Ideas*, Research in Social Problems, vol. 11 (ed. L. Clarke), 97–122. New York: Elsevier.

Levy, J. (2014). *The First Responder's Guide to Hazmat & Terrorism Emergency Response*. Firebelle Productions.

Mayer, T.A. (1997). Triage: history and horizons. *Topics in Emergency Medicine* 19 (2): 1–11.

McEntire, D.A. (2007). *Disaster Response and Recovery: Strategies and Tactics for Resilience*. New York: Wiley.

McEntire, D.A., Robinson, R.J., and Weber, R.T. (2001). Managing the Threat of Terrorism. *IQ Rep. 33(12)*. Washington, DC: International City/County Management Association.

Mileti, D.S., Sorensen, J.H., and O'Brien, P.W. (1992). Toward an explanation of mass care shelter use in evacuations. *International Journal of Mass Emergencies and Disasters* 10 (1): 25–42.

Neal, D.M. and Phillips, B.D. (1995). Effective emergency management: reconsidering the bureaucratic approach. *Disasters* 19 (4): 327–337.

Perry, R.W. (2003). Municipal terrorism management in the United States. *Disaster Prevention and Management* 12 (3): 190–202.

Quarantelli, E.L. (1979). *Studies in Disaster Response and Planning*. Newark, DE: Disaster Research Center, University of Delaware.

Quarantelli, E.L. (1990). The Warning Process and Evacuation Behavior: The Research Evidence. *Preliminary Paper no. 148*. Newark, DE: Disaster Research Center, University of Delaware.

CHAPTER 13

RECOVERING FROM IMPACTS
Short- and Long-term Measures

Do You Already Know?

- How to assess damages resulting from terrorism
- Ways to deal with debris and mass fatalities
- What makes a relief operation effective

 For additional questions to assess your current knowledge of recovery activities, go to **www.wiley.com/go/mcentire/homelandsecurity2e**

What You Will Find Out	What You Will Be Able To Do
13.1 The importance of disaster declarations	• Assess the impact and consequences of terrorist attacks
13.2 The key functions of disaster recovery, including mass fatality management and debris management	• Justify the need for outside disaster assistance and support the emotionally traumatized
13.3 Types of assistance available after terrorist attacks	• Assemble an effective relief operation

Introduction to Homeland Security: Understanding Terrorism Prevention and Emergency Management,
Second Edition. David A. McEntire.
© 2019 John Wiley & Sons, Inc. Published 2019 by John Wiley & Sons, Inc.
Companion website: www.wiley.com/go/mcentire/homelandsecurity2e

INTRODUCTION

Reacting to terrorist attacks includes much more than initial lifesaving measures. If you are employed in homeland security or emergency management, you should also be aware of the steps that must be taken for recovery. For instance, you should understand the importance of assessing damages and the steps required to declare a disaster. You must be able to deal with mass fatalities, debris, and psychological issues resulting from terrorist attacks. You should likewise be aware of the different types of assistance that can be provided to both governments and citizens. Applying the novel approaches to recovery as noted in this chapter can also help your community rebound quickly from the consequences of terrorist attacks.

13.1 INITIAL RECOVERY STEPS

If you are to promote recovery after a terrorist attack, you will need to understand the impact of the event. You may also need to seek help from the state or federal government by acknowledging the limited capabilities you may have to react to the attack. Assessing damages and declaring a disaster are the initial steps to start your recovery after terrorism occurs.

13.1.1 Damage Assessment

One of the first things you will need to do to facilitate recovery is to assess the effects of an attack. As the emergency period begins to wane and after you have addressed urgent response operations, you must now begin to think about short- and long-term recovery issues. In order to comprehend what needs to be done, you must carry out an evaluation of damages. **Damage assessment** is a survey of physical destruction and economic losses. It may include an evaluation of the number of deaths and degree of social disruption caused by terrorists. In most cases, damage assessment should identify major needs. For instance, a bombing could result in the requirement to address debris removal, housing shortages, crisis counseling, etc. Therefore, the assessment of impacts is really your first priority for fostering recovery (Oaks 1990, p. 6). Without an assessment, the community or nation will not be able to effectively and efficiently overcome the negative consequences of terrorist attacks.

There are typically three types of damage assessments as well as different ways of completing them (McEntire 2002). A **rapid assessment** is a quick survey of impacts. It is designed to gain comprehension of the scope of the attack so immediate needs can be met and additional help can be summoned. This type of assessment is undertaken by local government officials. A **preliminary damage assessment (PDA)** is a more detailed evaluation of impacts that typically takes place within days or weeks of the event. The goal of this assessment is to determine if and to what degree state and federal help is warranted and in what ways. A PDA is performed by the affected community as well as state and federal officials. This type of assistance is labeled as "preliminary" because it occurs before the federal government verifies needs and provides relief.

Damage assessment: A survey of physical destruction, economic losses, deaths, social disruption, and recovery needs.

Rapid assessment: A quick survey of impacts designed to gain an appreciation of the scope of the attack.

Preliminary damage assessment (PDA): A more detailed assessment of impacts that typically takes place within days or weeks of the event; it determines possibility and extent of outside assistance.

Technical assessment:
A survey of damages that points out methods and costs for rebuilding.

A **technical assessment** points out alternative methods and anticipated costs for rebuilding. It identifies what materials and labor will be required for demolition and/or reconstruction. This assessment is completed by engineers, insurance agents, contractors, and Federal Emergency Management Agency (FEMA) employees. It is a more thorough type of assessment than the PDA.

The three types of damage assessments are not accomplished in the same fashion. The rapid assessment may be completed by driving near the attack site to view damages or flying overhead to gain an aerial perspective. In other cases, a rapid assessment may require that the damaged area be toured by foot. Such walkthroughs are most likely to be used for preliminary and technical damage assessments. At times, PDAs and technical assessment may require those involved to talk to victims, impacted businesses, and community leaders to tally deaths, estimate economic losses, and determine societal disturbance. The important point to remember is that the goals of the assessment will determine how it is conducted. Safety should also be a top priority.

13.1.2 Damage Assessment Concerns and Procedures

When completing damage assessments, it will be imperative that you recognize the extreme danger of the attack site. Sharp glass and twisted metal may be present from bombings. Fires and unstable structures are also associated with explosions. Hazardous materials could be located in and around the area of the terrorist attack. There are many other variables that could cause injury or death to those who are involved in damage assessment. For these reasons, access to the area should be carefully controlled. You should also do all you can to ensure that the damage assessment is accurate and complete. Recovery will be slowed down if your evaluation is incorrect or performed in a superficial manner.

In order to ensure that your damage assessments are successful, it is a good idea to hold a meeting to discuss who will evaluate the site of the attack and how it will be accomplished. Participants can be trained in safety precautions and given assignments based on geographic location or type of damage to look for. For instance, those doing the assessment can be told to search a particular floor in a building or visit a block in a particular neighborhood. Assessment teams can also be advised if the building lacks structural integrity or if there is the possibility of gas leaks. Protective equipment and communication devices can also be distributed at this meeting. This will facilitate communication in case people have questions or if someone gets hurt. Cameras and forms should likewise be given to those assessing damages along with guidelines on when reports are to be turned in.

At the scene of the attack, you will need to determine if buildings are safe, sanitary, and secure. In other words, you will need to determine if the building poses a danger, if it can be inhabited, and if its windows and doors allow for it to be locked. Depending on the degree of damage, you may need to categorize structures in one of three ways. Buildings designated as "green" are habitable and occupants are allowed to return. "Yellow" structures have known or unknown safety concerns and should only be entered by well-trained and properly equipped individuals. Buildings labeled as "red" are unsafe and should be condemned and destroyed. Once the assessments are completed, they should be reviewed for accuracy, compiled with other assessments, and then given to state and federal authorities. Organizations like FEMA will subsequently help you to determine your top priorities for recovery.

13.1.3 Declaring a Disaster and Seeking Help

Disaster declaration:
An acknowledgement of the severity of the event and that outside response and recovery assistance is required.

Depending on the findings of your damage assessment, you might need to issue a statement acknowledging that you have experienced an emergency or even a major disaster. If the attack is limited in scope and you are able to address relief needs without significant federal assistance, it will be declared as an emergency. If the needs are greater than your resources, you should declare a state of disaster. A **disaster declaration** is an acknowledgement of the severity of the event and that outside response and recovery assistance is required. It is one of the many requirements for obtaining state or federal funds for rebuilding. Without this acknowledgement and justification, you may not get help from other levels of government.

The FBI will automatically become involved in investigation activities as long as they are informed about attacks. That is to say that this agency will arrive on scene and support local and state efforts to determine who was responsible and to investigate for apprehension and prosecution. Also, the damage and impact of a terrorist attack may be so obvious that the President of the United States will publicly acknowledge the event and take additional measures to deal with the situation at the federal level (e.g. by deploying personnel to the area and sending needed material resources). After a terrorist attack, a national emergency may be declared by the President. This measure goes beyond a disaster declaration and often has more of an overtone of war or concerns about ongoing security. However, not all situations may require this top-down initiation. For this reason, you should know the process of declaring a disaster at the local level.

Figure 13-1

Political leaders are often present when a disaster is declared
or to remember the victims of attacks. Source: © National Guard.

After an attack occurs, it will be important for you to initiate your response and recovery operations. You will determine the negative consequences of the event through your damage assessment process along with your ability to handle such challenges. If the municipal and county governments determine that the event will overstretch their abilities, a disaster is declared. This usually includes a formal statement recognizing the death and damages, societal impact, economic losses, and the need for outside assistance. Disaster declarations may also discuss if the damage is covered by insurance, if the attack has traumatized the community, and if the consequences result in unemployment or evacuation and sheltering. At this point, the state will contact you to discuss the situation and may send representatives to verify impact. If the state feels it may also be unable to deal with the consequences effectively, it will also declare a disaster and relay this information to the FEMA regional office responsible for their area. If the officials in 1 of the 10 regional offices around the nation concur with the state's assessment, the declaration will be forwarded to the FEMA Administrator and to the President. A large or significant event will result in a presidential disaster declaration. This action will free up funds and mobilize the federal government to the aid of the affected community. However, if the event is less serious, the process of declaration could theoretically be stopped at any point. Because of the political nature of terrorism and homeland security, it is likely that the federal government will be involved in some fashion in any and all attacks against our nation. This should not discount the fact that there will be many functions that will require the attention of local governments.

IN THE REAL WORLD

Declaring a Disaster

When Timothy McVeigh blew up the Murrah Federal Building in Oklahoma City, first responders initially thought the explosion was a result of a broken gas line. A short time later, it became apparent that the devastation was the outcome of an intentional attack. After consulting with local officials, the governor of Oklahoma called the Regional Director of FEMA Region VI in Denton, Texas. The Regional Director then notified James Lee Witt, the director of FEMA in Washington, D.C. By that afternoon, President Clinton was made aware of the terrorist attack in Oklahoma. He addressed the nation publicly and declared a state of emergency. This freed up funds, personnel, and federal resources so the government could support the response operations at and around the Murrah Federal Building. Declaring a disaster is often the first step toward getting the help you need.

SELF-CHECK

1. A survey of physical destruction and economic losses is known as a damage assessment. True or False?

2. A rapid assessment is generally undertaken by federal officials. True or False?

3. In assessing damage, the color "red" indicates:
   (a) The building is safe.
   (b) The building is sanitary and secure.
   (c) The building is completely destroyed, unsafe or beyond repair.
   (d) The building should be entered with caution.

4. An acknowledgement of the severity of an event that requires outside response and recovery assistance is best known as:
   (a) A rapid assessment
   (b) A preliminary damage assessment
   (c) Emergence
   (d) A disaster declaration
   (e) A windshield assessment

13.2 KEY RECOVERY FUNCTIONS

Besides assessing damages and declaring a disaster, there are many other activities that must be undertaken if you are to promote recovery for your community. You may have to deal with mass fatalities, clean up debris, and address emotional issues. These are some of the major priorities during recovery operations.

13.2.1 Mass Fatality Management

Terrorism may produce a large quantity of deaths. Small attacks around the world may result in numerous fatalities. Israel has been experiencing this situation for decades, and Iraq and Syria are now plagued with similar situations. Larger attacks, such as Al-Qaeda's bombings in Africa on 7 August 1998, claim even more lives. In Nairobi (Kenya) and Dar es Salaam (Tanzania), 212 people died when US embassies were blown up with explosives in cars parked near the buildings. In addition, on 12 October 2002, over 200 people died when Jemaah Islamiyah initiated three bombings in the tourist area of Bali, Indonesia. On 19 April 1995, 168 people died when Timothy McVeigh parked a Ryder truck laden with explosives near the Murrah Federal Building. And, on 11 September 2001, an appalling 2974 people died when 19 terrorists hijacked planes and flew them into the World Trade Center (WTC), the Pentagon, and a field in Pennsylvania. These numbers are significant, but experts anticipate greater losses in the future if terrorists use nuclear or biological weapons. It is no exaggeration to suggest that terrorist attacks could result in thousands, hundreds of thousands, and even millions of fatalities.

Mass fatality incident:
An attack that creates so many deaths that the processing of remains is beyond the ability of local government.

Because of the significant numbers of victims and the possibility of even more consequential attacks down the road, it will be imperative for you to understand the challenges of and recommendations for dealing with a mass fatality incident. A **mass fatality incident** is an attack that creates so many deaths that the processing of remains stretches government agencies or is beyond the ability of local government. In other words, the large number of deceased is greater in comparison to the personnel that are able to collect, identify, and bury them. Besides the large quantity of dead, there are other challenges associated with mass fatality incidents. While dead bodies do not normally pose a threat to public health, a terrorist attack involving weapons of mass destruction can complicate mass fatality management. Some of the bodies may be contaminated and that can adversely affect those trying to process remains and bury them. In addition, well-intentioned citizens may move bodies in an attempt to help public officials (Scanlon 1998). This may complicate investigation and record keeping (because they are no longer located at the scene of the attack). A third problem deals with the heavy emotions of survivors. Family members may be distraught over their losses, and those working in mass fatality management should be sensitive to the situation. In fact, this situation could be so disturbing that it may also impact responders emotionally. Finally, it is also possible that remains may not be identified. Some bodies can be obliterated in attacks and be beyond recognition. After 9/11, searchers found 19 893 separate body parts. However, the remains of 1268 individuals were never found (Hampson and Moore 2003). DNA can help determine who people are, but it is not 100% successful as we discovered after the WTC attacks.

In order to process large numbers of bodies for burial or cremation, several steps must be taken (Hooft et al. 1989):

1. If possible, the location of bodies should be recorded. This will help with investigation. ID tags on the deceased and maps of their location can assist with this objective.

2. Remains should be stored for processing. This may occur at hospitals or county morgues. Innovative ideas can help you when bodies outstrip storage facilities. Bodies have been stored in unmarked refrigerated trucks or even at ice skating rinks.

3. Clothing, jewelry, and other items (e.g. wallets or berets) should be removed and saved for family members. The height, weight, gender, and other identifying features (e.g. tattoos, mustaches, dentures, and cavities) must be recorded. Fingerprints and pictures of the body should also be taken to facilitate identification.

4. After bodies have been identified, they can be returned to families for burial. If remains are not claimed, they can be buried in recorded graves.

5. Respect for the wishes of the surviving family members (e.g. cultural burial practices) should be ensured.

Disaster Mortuary Operations Response Team (DMORT):
A group of private citizens from around that nation who may be activated by the federal government to assist with mass fatality incidents.

Should mass fatality incidents warrant substantial outside involvement, a **Disaster Mortuary Operations Response Team (DMORT)** can be requested. A DMORT is a group of private citizens from around the nation who may be activated by the federal government to assist with mass fatality incidents. They include funeral directors, medical examiners, coroners, pathologists, and medical record technicians. Their purpose is to recover bodies and issue death certificates. These teams can be sent to any location and can assist communities with their portable morgue units. DMORTs can augment the capabilities of any community impacted by a terrorist attack. They will be a vital asset if fatalities outstretch local resources.

13.2.2 Debris Management

Because of the nature of most terrorist attacks (i.e. bombings), there could be a great deal of rubble that will need to be cleaned up. This will include concrete, glass, metal, wood, wiring, and other construction materials. The quantity of debris can be overwhelming. For instance, when the Murrah Federal Building was demolished after the Oklahoma City bombing, an average of 800 tons of debris was removed on a daily basis. The amount of debris at the WTC is even more noteworthy. As many as 10 major buildings were destroyed, which left behind 1.2 million tons of debris (McEntire et al. 2003, p. 451). It took several months working around the clock to remove this large quantity of debris. This brings up the important concept of debris management. **Debris management** is the removal, storage, disposal, or recycling of rubble produced from terrorist attacks. It is an extremely important function to facilitate recovery.

Debris management: The removal, storage, disposal, or recycling of rubble produced from terrorist attacks.

Debris management after a terrorist attack sounds simple in theory, but it is actually a very complex and complicated issue. There are a variety of factors that must be considered when dealing with rubble. First, trained personnel with adequate gear and heavy equipment will be needed to remove debris. People may not be able help if they do not have gloves, hard hats, steel-toed boots, shovels, backhoes, or dump trucks. Debris can also pose a danger to those trying to remove it. After the Oklahoma City bombing, a large piece of concrete broke loose from an upper floor and fell on a nurse who was helping with search and rescue operations. She was killed instantly. There are numerous cases where debris has created injuries among those trying to clean it up. Cuts, bruises, and crushing from debris are all possible at the site of a terrorist attack. Safety should be a top priority when removing debris.

Debris management operations are also problematic in that debris may contain evidence as well as human remains. Sorting of debris must be painstakingly careful. Law enforcement and coroners/medical examiners may need to be involved in the debris removal process in order to find corpses or body parts. Another challenge relates to where to take the debris. Because of the large quantity, debris may need to be stored somewhere temporarily until the waste can be recycled or buried. This will require a large holding area. Eventually debris will need to be sent to a designated landfill, burned, or disposed of in other ways. The location and disposal of debris brings up another difficulty. The expense associated with moving and burying debris can be enormous. Local governments may need to seek federal assistance for debris management. Community officials will also need

Figure 13-2

Debris from 9/11: Debris is an important, but often neglected, function that must be addressed after a terrorist attack.
Source: © FEMA.

to monitor contractors to make sure they are being honest. Some companies involved in debris management have defrauded the government for their services. Continual oversight will be needed. As you deal with debris after a terrorist attack, organizations like the FEMA and the Environmental Protection Agency can assist you.

IN THE REAL WORLD

Debris from the WTC

The terrorist attacks on 9/11 resulted in the collapse of the World Trade Center towers. When these buildings came down, at least eight other buildings were completely destroyed or substantially damaged. The pile of rubble that was produced was equivalent to 1.2 million tons of debris. In order to deal with this large amount of debris, the government divided the 16-acre World Trade Center site into quadrants. It then assigned a number of contractors to remove, ship, and dispose of debris. Cranes, trucks, and even barges were used in the process. A special challenge was the sorting of debris in order to search for and collect bodies, body parts, evidence, and personal belongings. In spite of the monumental undertaking, debris was removed much quicker than initially anticipated. In May 2002, Ground Zero was emptied of steel beams, broken concrete, and other demolished building materials.

13.2.3 Emotional Issues

Terrorism may create a great deal of emotional distress. The victims of terrorism and even witnesses recognize the toll of attacks in terms of injuries, fatalities, and economic disruption. The death of a loved one, resulting disabilities, and monetary losses could be unbearable to certain individuals in some cases. But many people are most troubled by the fact that terrorism is an intentional act undertaken to instill fear. It is violence that is often directed against the most vulnerable: ordinary citizens. A common response is "why was this done and how could someone do this?" These issues and questions bring up a major function that you should address during recovery.

Crisis counseling:
The treatment of psychological problems that may arise from the stress produced by terrorism.

Crisis counseling is the treatment of psychological problems that may arise from the stress produced by terrorism. It includes active listening, sympathetic understanding, and emotional support (both direct and indirect) for the victims of terrorism. These victims may include first responders who experience critical incident stress. **Critical incident stress (CIS)** is defined as the inability of emergency service personnel to cope with the trauma that is experienced while on the job. For instance, a firefighter may do all he/she can to save a child after a terrorist attack, but ultimately be unsuccessful. This experience, along with the sights, smells, and sounds at the attack site, may be emotionally burdensome over time.

Critical incident stress (CIS):
The inability of emergency service personnel to cope with the trauma that is experienced while on the job.

Post-traumatic stress disorder (PTSD):
The clinical diagnosis for individuals who become depressed due to a traumatic event in their lives.

Alternatively, citizens may suffer from symptoms of **post-traumatic stress disorder (PTSD)**. PTSD is the clinical diagnosis for individuals who become depressed due to a traumatic event that they personally witness or experience indirectly in their lives. As seen after 9/11, terrorism certainly constitutes such an experience. Many people were psychologically disturbed by the terrorist attacks on this day.

Victims experiencing CIS or PTSD may exhibit a number of symptoms. Besides depression, they may gain or lose weight, become angry, abuse alcohol and drugs, have headaches, and experience mood swings. Facial twitches, social withdrawal, sleeplessness, and flashbacks are also common signs indicating that someone has been affected psychologically. If a person has difficulty coping with everyday stress and does not have a strong support network, they are considered to be vulnerable to CIS or PTSD.

Defusing:
A short, unstructured meeting to allow a person to discuss an experience as soon as it takes place.

Debriefing:
A recurring and more in-depth discussion designed to redirect harmful thinking and develop improved coping mechanisms.

After a terrorist attack occurs, homeland security and emergency management personnel may set up a clinic to help those who suffer psychologically. There are two strategies for dealing with the emotional problems created by terrorism. A **defusing** is a short, unstructured meeting to allow a person to discuss an experience as soon as it takes place. It is commonly provided to first responders as they wrap up at the scene so they can vent and unload frustration among colleagues and peers. A defusing is one way to relieve pent-up stress and reduce their compounding effects over time. A **debriefing** is a recurring and more in-depth discussion designed to redirect harmful thinking and develop improved coping mechanisms. Therapists reiterate the fact that humans have normal reactions to disappointing events and offer practical suggestions for stress management. The goal is to allow people to talk after the attack, provide victims support, and help them find ways to deal with or overcome negative psychological impacts.

The success rate of defusings and debriefings is debated among scholars (Barnett-Queen and Bergmann 1989; Mitchell 1988). Some research seems to indicate that crisis counseling helps people recover more quickly, but other evidence suggests that repeated exposure to a traumatic event through discussion could be counterproductive. While this issue remains to be resolved, you can seek the most appropriate help for your first responders and citizens. Police departments, fire departments, and the American Red Cross are organizations that have experience in dealing with CIS and PTSD. They can provide advice in order to help your community recover emotionally from terrorist attacks.

IN THE REAL WORLD

Memorials

After terrorist attacks, communities frequently honor the victims of the incident. For instance, a memorial was created in Oklahoma City after the bombing of Murrah Federal Building. It includes a reflection pool and an empty chair for each of the victims. The Flight 93 memorial in Pennsylvania incorporates a visitor's center and plaques to remember the victims of this hijacking. The largest and most visible memorial is in New York City. The 9/11 museum is building on the footings of the twin towers at the World Trade Center. It includes artifacts from the site of the attack, video and audio recordings of the response, pictures of the victims, and other notable information about the event. The goal of these memorials is to remember those who perished and educate people about the nefarious impacts of terrorism. Such steps also help the community to recover from the impacts of the attacks.

SELF-CHECK

1. Experts anticipate that there will be less loss of life from terrorist attacks in the future. True or False?
2. Defusing is a recurring and in-depth discussion to improve coping mechanisms for those suffering from emotional problems after an attack. True or False?
3. The removal, storage, and disposal of rubble produced by a terrorist attack is best known as:
   (a) Defusing
   (b) Debriefing
   (c) Rapid assessment
   (d) Debris management
4. What challenges are associated with mass fatality incidents?

13.3 THE IMPORTANCE OF DISASTER ASSISTANCE

As individual victims and the community as a whole begin the process of recovery after a terrorist attack, aid will arrive from unofficial and official sources. Unofficial sources include volunteers and donations from concerned citizens. Official sources of assistance will come from organizations like the FEMA. In either case, it will be your responsibility to harness these resources and implement innovative strategies to promote recovery.

13.3.1 Volunteer and Donation Management

After a terrorist attack, citizens will experience a deep and sincere interest in helping victims and the impacted jurisdiction. A study of volunteer behavior after 9/11 reveals that people sympathize with those affected and desire to find ways to assist them in coping with the aftermath. For instance, a woman who wanted to donate blood after the WTC towers came down stated, "there needs to be some positive that comes out of it, and the only way it's positive is if I and other people make it positive" (Lowe and Fothergill 2003, p. 299). This strong feeling will motivate people to volunteer their time, talent, and energy for altruistic causes.

On 9/11, spontaneous volunteers arrived at the WTC to participate in search and rescue operations, provide basic first aid, cheer on first responders, serve food to those removing debris, and give massages to tired workers. Others offered translation services or were willing to perform any other duty that might be required after such a devastating event (e.g. clerical duties, crisis counseling, transportation, etc.). In events such as 9/11, it is not uncommon for there to be hundreds or even thousands of volunteers. While not everyone was able to assist because of the dangerous conditions, the arrival of so many volunteers can be truly impressive – and perhaps overwhelming.

The influx of significant quantities of volunteers is only matched by the number of donated items that pour into a community after a terrorist attack. The recovery efforts after the Oklahoma City bombing provide a good case in point (ODCEM 1996). Southwestern Bell donated cell phones and a cell tower to help those responding to the event. Fast-food companies brought in meals to feed emergency workers. Clothing, pharmaceuticals, water, and other supplies and equipment arrived from around the state, region, nation, and world. Besides these **in-kind donations**, money was also sent to Oklahoma City. Hundreds of thousands of dollars were sent to care for the victims and their families. Donations of money and supplies will occur after almost every significant terrorist attack. Experience suggests that large quantities of donations will poor into affected communities.

This mass assault of volunteers and donations, as it has been described by Thompson and Hawkes (1962), can create several problems for those working in emergency management and homeland security. For example, there can be too many volunteers in comparison with the number of individuals needed to manage them effectively. Some may be untrained or lack

In-kind donations: Physical donations including food, water, clothing, supplies, and equipment.

the skills you require after a terrorist attack. Another difficulty is keeping them safe in spite of the dangerous conditions of the attack site. Others may become frustrated if you do not put them to work immediately or if they are given tasks that they feel are not "making a difference."

In order to overcome the challenges associated with those who want to help out, you should implement a coherent strategy for volunteer management. **Volunteer management** is the harnessing of volunteers to take advantage of their potential contributions while averting potential negative consequences. Successful volunteer management often requires a volunteer management center. A **volunteer registration center** is a location where citizens fill out forms noting their skills and share other information that can help you when making assignments. When giving responsibilities to volunteers, it is wise to review some basic safety rules and briefly train them on what they will be doing. You will then need to evaluate their progress and care for them as needed (e.g. provide food, water, or safety equipment). Without ensuring the safety and well-being of volunteers, injury and death can result. In addition, liability will be increased if volunteers are not carefully supervised. No community wants to be sued if not enough was done to protect volunteers. Although too many uncoordinated volunteers can be a headache, their strength in numbers and desire to serve can have a dramatic and positive impact upon recovery operations.

Volunteer management:
The harnessing of volunteers to take advantage of their potential contributions while averting potential negative consequences.

Volunteer registration center:
The location where citizens fill out forms noting their skills and other information that can help you when making assignments.

Figure 13-3

People will donate goods and supplies to the Red Cross for distribution to victims. Source: © FEMA.

Donations management:
The collection, sorting, and distribution of goods and money for the benefit of victims of terrorist attacks.

Unmet needs committee:
A group of concerned citizens and community leaders who work together to collect donations and address long-term needs of victims.

Individual assistance:
Relief programs for citizens and businesses impacted by terrorist attacks.

Public assistance:
Relief programs that make aid available to government entities that have been affected by terrorism.

The problems resulting from excessive and unrequested donations may also be addressed through effective donations management (Neal 1994). **Donation management** is the collection, sorting, and distribution of goods and money for the benefit of victims of terrorist attacks. It entails recognizing your needs after an attack and relaying your specific requests to the public through the media. Once received at designated areas (e.g. a warehouse), you will need to have a team in place to help sort and disperse needed items. Faith-based groups and nonprofit organizations can be very helpful in this respect. Tracking donations with the use of computers can also help you determine what you are lacking, what is coming in, and where it should be sent.

An even better way to avoid the hassle of donations is to request monetary contributions. Cash funds prevent unwanted items from arriving, eliminate some of the labor needed to deal with them, speed up assistance, and help the local economy (if goods and services are purchased in the affected or nearby areas). If in-kind and monetary donations are not getting to the appropriate individuals, an unmet needs committee may be established. An **unmet needs committee** is a group of concerned citizens and community leaders who work together to collect donations and address long-term needs of victims (Wedel and Baker 1998). They play a positive role in recovery operations.

13.3.2 Individual and Public Assistance

If a terrorist attack results in a presidential declaration, citizens and communities alike may receive federal disaster assistance. Thus, there are two types of disaster assistance. **Individual assistance** provides relief to citizens and businesses impacted by terrorist attacks. **Public assistance** makes aid available to government entities that have been affected by terrorism. Both types of assistance have special programs and requirements.

Individual assistance includes loans at low interest rates as well as grants that do not have to be repaid. Some of the loans are directed toward homeowners and renters who have lost personal property. In this case up to $200 000 can be provided for primary residences and $40 000 to replace personal property. Other loans are for businesses. Loans up to $1 500 000 can be obtained to repair or replace structures and machinery. If the business has suffered economic hardship because of the attack, another $1 500 000 can be acquired. Small grants up to $27 000 can also be obtained by individuals and families who do not qualify for loans. This money can be used to provide temporary housing in mobile homes, help with hotel/motel stays, or repair or replace destroyed property.

Individuals and families may also obtain needed services after a terrorist attack. Federal and state assistance can help victims understand the types of programs that are available, file and settle insurance claims, protect against price gouging and fraud, and obtain counseling from attorneys regarding legal issues and contracts. Food stamps, unemployment assistance, and social security and veterans' benefits can all be given to victims of terrorist attacks.

National Processing Service Center:
A FEMA office set up to help victims apply for federal assistance programs.

Disaster Recovery Center (DRC):
A temporary facility near the attack location where victims can seek information about federal assistance programs.

Emergency assistance:
Financial help given to local governments to take care of immediate needs such as debris removal or safety precautions.

Permanent assistance:
Financial aid for the repairing of publicly owned critical infrastructure and key assets.

In order to obtain individual assistance, victims of terrorism should call the National Processing Service Center at 1 (800) 621-FEMA. The **National Processing Service Center** is a FEMA office set up to help victims apply for federal assistance programs. Call takers will input information about the victim's needs into a computer. Alternatively, the victim may go to a Disaster Recovery Center for help. A **Disaster Recovery Center (DRC)** is a temporary facility near the attack location where victims can seek information about federal assistance programs. It includes phone and Internet access to federal disaster programs. The selection of the location of the DRC is a local and state responsibility. However, the DRC is usually set up in a building that can accommodate tables, chairs, phones, copiers, and parking. Federal officials will help to publicize and run the DRC. Regardless of how citizens apply for assistance, the information they provide will be reviewed and verified by FEMA employees and contractors. Eventually, decisions will be made about loans, grants, services, and benefits. When warranted, funds will be distributed to individuals, families, and businesses.

If a local or state government, Indian tribe, or private nonprofit organization is adversely impacted by a terrorist attack, it may also qualify for public assistance. Public assistance is divided into two types: emergency assistance and permanent assistance. **Emergency assistance** is financial help given to local governments to take care of immediate needs. It may include monetary and technical support for debris removal and safety precautions. **Permanent assistance** is financial aid for the repairing of publicly owned critical infrastructure and key assets. It may include the help to

Figure 13-4

Victims of large terrorist attacks may be able to seek assistance at a FEMA Disaster Recovery Center. Source: © FEMA.

reconstruct roads, bridges, and lights; dikes, levees, and dams; public buildings and equipment; water, gas, and sewage systems; or parks, airports, and recreational facilities.

If individual or public assistance is required, community leaders will need to declare a disaster and share damage assessment findings with federal officials. If assistance is deemed as justified, a kickoff meeting will be held. A **kickoff meeting** is a gathering of local, state, and federal officials for the purpose of explaining public assistance programs in detail (e.g. application materials and deadlines). This meeting will help answer questions about public assistance and begin the process of obtaining outside aid to promote recovery.

The oversight of federal public assistance programs will take place in a **Joint Field Office (JFO)**. The JFO is an established but temporary office that includes local, state, and federal representatives who will manage the paperwork regarding public assistance. Those working in the JFO will ensure that recovery projects are being completed, check for fraudulent activities, and consider the special circumstances surrounding historic buildings, environmental concerns, and rebuilding with mitigation in mind. However, this does not mean that the process will be smooth or easy. Some jurisdictions and states are highly critical of FEMA and the federal government after disasters and terrorist attacks. They assert that the process is bureaucratic, inflexible, and even wasteful. Some people have even called for the dissolution of FEMA or a distribution of recovery funds directly to local and state governments (thereby bypassing FEMA). Recovery can therefore be a contentious process as people seek resources or attempt to control the outcome of disaster assistance and rebuilding efforts.

Kickoff meeting:
A gathering of local, state, and federal officials for the purpose of explaining public assistance programs in detail.

Joint Field Office (JFO):
An established but temporary office that includes local, state, and federal representatives who will manage the paperwork regarding public assistance.

13.3.3 Novel Approaches

As can be seen there are many aspects associated with recovery operations. But performing the functions listed above will not necessarily ensure that long-term issues will be successfully addressed. Innovative ideas are needed to help the community rebound quickly from terrorist attacks. One exemplary case is from Manchester, England (Bathos et al. 1999).

On 15 June 1996, the Irish Republican Army called officials in this city and advised them of a bombing that would be detonated shortly. A warning was issued, and efforts were made to evacuate the area of approximately 80 000 people. About 40 minutes later, a 3000-lb. fertilizer bomb in an illegally parked Ford van exploded. Fortunately, no one was killed in the bombing. Nevertheless, over 200 people were injured. At least 12 buildings were damaged, and many of these had such severe structural problems that they had to be demolished. As a result, 672 businesses were displaced, and nearly 50 000 m² of office space was lost. Residents in the area were forced to leave their homes due to fears about the effects of infrastructure damage. The event provided both a test for responders and an opportunity for those involved in recovery.

When the emergency period involving fire suppression and lifesaving activities ended, attention soon focused on long-term concerns. In accordance with the community disaster plan, the area was cordoned off. This "protected people from physical danger, helped preserve criminal evidence at the disaster scene, and [was central to] the city-council's re-occupancy strategy" (Bathos et al. 1999, p. 222). On the next day, a task force if made up of the local leaders, police officials, and representatives from the private sector. They toured the area and devised a methodical strategy to help the community recover.

The city's architectural department was put in charge of assessing damages and determining what could be done to make the area safe enough for further recovery activities (e.g. demolition of buildings). As structures were deemed or made safe, business owners and citizens were allowed back into the structures to retrieve belongings and resume normal activities. Over the next several days, police presence diminished and companies hired their own security staff to monitor the destroyed buildings. The cordoned-off area was reduced to five buildings.

During the first week, a major challenge for city officials was the large number of people (between 5000 and 10 000) who arrived at city hall wanting information or assistance after the bombing. At first, there was no system in place to address citizen concerns. In time, however, various meetings were held for owners and occupants in different geographic areas. This helped to provide details about getting back into damaged buildings, making them safe, and the process of recovery.

The city council also helped large businesses relocate to available retail property so the private sector could resume normal operations. A massive media campaign was initiated to help citizens understand what was taking place and how they could assist in the recovery efforts. By the end of the first month, the city created a committee to oversee the rehabilitation of the area. Three priorities became evident.

First, the Mayor created a fund and asked people to donate to it to help those experiencing hardship from the attack. Over £2.5 million was raised for victims over an 18-month period. Second, the Deputy Prime Minister announced an international urban planning competition in July to generate a vision and plan for recovery. The decision on the winning design was made public 16 weeks later. Finally, an organization called the Manchester Millennium Task Force was created to oversee rebuilding of the area. It was put in charge of recovery activities until they were completed in spring 2000.

A review of the reaction to this bombing reveals a number of positive features. Prior planning and training helped to ensure a quick response to the event. The oversight of post-attack functions was also successful due to the use of a designated emergency operations center. Police were effective in evacuating most people out of the area and maintaining security presence after the attack occurred. Although determining who should have access to the area was problematic, the City Architect Department was soon made responsible for issuing passes to the area. The leadership and innovation of city officials helped to channel resources and ideas to facilitate recovery. While the rehabilitation of the area was not problem-free, the aftermath of the Manchester bombing illustrates the benefit of organizations working together to overcome post-attack problems. Partnerships and cooperation among various parties were cited as reasons for a speedy recovery.

FOR EXAMPLE

Unmet Needs After the Oklahoma City Bombing

Because Timothy McVeigh's terrorist attack on the Murrah Federal Building produced so many deaths and injuries, there was an almost overwhelming sense of responsibility for the victims and their families. Within a short time, the community shifted from short-term emergency needs to long-term concerns. A committee was formed with the participation of city, business, and nonprofit organizations (Wedel and Baker 1998). Its goal was to collect monetary and in-kind donations and ensure that the donations were directed to those in need. Cars, tuition scholarships, and many other resources were given to those in need. The unmet needs committee also tracked relief assistance to make sure that it was not duplicated by other organizations or abused by disaster victims. The superb handling of donations and the treatment of victims were labeled the "Oklahoma Standard." However, in time, the distribution of resources has taken a long time, and a minority of victims are claiming the resources are not being used as intended.

SELF-CHECK

1. A gathering of local, state, and federal officials for the purpose of explaining public assistance programs in best known as a kickoff meeting. True or False?

2. Contributions of money to help out victims of a terrorist attack are also known as in-kind donations. True or False?

3. Financial aid for repairing publicly owned critical infrastructure and key assets is best known as:
   (a) Permanent assistance
   (b) Emergency assistance
   (c) Individual assistance
   (d) In-kind donations

4. What problems can volunteers create in the recovery process?

SUMMARY

If a terrorist attack occurs in your jurisdiction, you will need to perform a variety of recovery measures. After assessing damages, you will need to ensure that a disaster or state of emergency is declared. It will also be imperative that other functions are addressed – mass fatality management, the disposal of debris, and provision of emotional support for those who have been emotionally impacted by the event. As you begin to address long-term issues, you will want to ensure that your community applies for public and individual assistance. If you successfully address the impacts of terrorist attacks through donations and volunteer management, you will speed up the time it takes for recovery and help your community rebound from disturbing events.

ASSESS YOUR UNDERSTANDING

UNDERSTAND: WHAT HAVE YOU LEARNED?

 Go to **www.wiley.com/go/mcentire/homelandsecurity2e** to assess your knowledge of recovery activities.

SUMMARY QUESTIONS

1. A preliminary damage assessment is a quick survey of attack-related impacts undertaken by local government officials. True or False?

2. A technical assessment identifies what materials and labor will be required for demolition and/or construction. True or False?

3. If a local government declares a disaster, the federal government must provide aid. True or False?

4. If an attack causes so many deaths that a local government is unable to collect, identify, and bury all of the deceased, it is called a mass fatality incident. True or False?

5. DNA is generally, but not always, 100% successful in helping to identify remains after an attack. True or False?

6. The Environmental Protection Agency is one of the organizations that can assist local governments in debris management. True or False?

7. After a terrorist attack, people are afraid and will not want to volunteer or help out. True or False?

8. Only local or state governments can qualify for public assistance after a terrorist attack. True or False?

9. If a mass fatality incident warrants substantial outside help in dealing with remains, then a request can be made for:

   (a) A Disaster Mortuary Operations Response Team
   (b) Tactical emergency medical services
   (c) Crisis counseling
   (d) Defusing

10. Critical incident stress is best described as:

    (a) The process of determining which buildings are safe after an attack
    (b) A clinical diagnosis for individuals suffering from depression or trauma
    (c) The inability of first responders to cope with trauma from work
    (d) A treatment for psychological problems associated with attacks

11. A short, unstructured meeting to allow a first responder to discuss job-related experiences and reduce emotional stress is best known as:

    (a) A damage assessment
    (b) Defusing
    (c) Debriefing
    (d) Decontamination

12. The oversight of federal public assistance programs after a terrorist attack takes place in a:

(a) National Processing Service Center
(b) Joint Field Office
(c) Disaster Recovery Center
(d) Volunteer Registration Center

13. Financial help given to local governments for immediate needs, such as debris removal, is best known as:

(a) Permanent assistance
(b) In-kind donations
(c) Individual assistance
(d) Emergency assistance

14. Relief provided to citizens and businesses affected by terrorist attacks is best known as:

(a) Permanent assistance
(b) Emergency assistance
(c) Individual assistance
(d) Public assistance

APPLYING THIS CHAPTER

1. As a homeland security expert, you are asked by a local government official about the process by which a municipality can obtain federal assistance after a terrorist attack. How could you respond?

2. When having lunch with friends, you mention that you are studying emotional issues related to terrorist attacks in your homeland security class. Your friends are curious about how authorities deal with the stress faced by first responders. How could you answer their question?

3. As a homeland security expert, a local government has asked you about the potential resources that may become available for their community in the event of a terrorist attack. They are curious about the different types of disaster assistance. How could you respond?

4. As an emergency manager, you have been asked by your organization to come up with some strategies for volunteer management in case of a terrorist attack. What are some recommendations that you could provide?

BE A HOMELAND SECURITY PROFESSIONAL

Planning for Debris Management

You are an emergency manager with a local government. In the event of a terrorist attack, there could be a large quantity of debris that needs to be removed, stored, disposed, or recycled. You have been asked to prepare a report on this aspect of recovery in case of an attack. What concerns would you address in your report on debris management?

Assignment: Damage Assessments

Write a 2-page paper discussing the concerns you might want to address if you were to complete a damage assessment. Be as thorough as possible.

Addressing Donations Management

You are an employee in an emergency management office. In order to be prepared for recovery in case of a terrorist attack, your personnel should be ready to handle the large influx of donations that usually accompanies such an event. Without proper management, donations can become excessive or irrelevant. What recommendations could you provide on how to effectively manage donations?

KEY TERMS

Crisis counseling	The treatment of psychological problems that may arise from the stress produced by terrorism
Critical incident stress (CIS)	The inability of emergency service personnel to cope with the trauma that is experienced while on the job
Damage assessment	A survey of physical destruction, economic losses, deaths, social disruption, and recovery needs
Debriefing	A recurring and more in-depth discussion designed to redirect harmful thinking and develop improved coping mechanisms
Debris management	The removal, storage, disposal, or recycling of rubble produced from terrorist attacks
Defusing	A short, unstructured meeting to allow a person to discuss an experience as soon as it takes place

Disaster declaration	An acknowledgement of the severity of the event and that outside response and recovery assistance is required
Disaster Mortuary Operations Response Team (DMORT)	A group of private citizens from around that nation who may be activated by the federal government to assist with mass fatality incidents
Disaster Recovery Center (DRC)	A temporary facility near the attack location where victims can seek information about federal assistance programs
Donations management	The collection, sorting, and distribution of goods and money for the benefit of victims of terrorist attacks
Emergency assistance	Financial help given to local governments to take care of immediate needs such as debris removal or safety precautions
Individual assistance	Relief programs for citizens and businesses impacted by terrorist attacks
In-kind donations	Physical donations including food, water, clothing, supplies, and equipment
Joint Field Office (JFO)	An established but temporary office that includes local, state, and federal representatives who will manage the paperwork regarding public assistance
Kickoff meeting	A gathering of local, state, and federal officials for the purpose of explaining public assistance programs in detail
Mass fatality incident	An attack that creates so many deaths that the processing of remains is beyond the ability of local government
National Processing Service Center	A FEMA office set up to help victims apply for federal assistance programs
Permanent assistance	Financial aid for the repairing of publicly owned critical infrastructure and key assets
Post-traumatic stress disorder (PTSD)	The clinical diagnosis for individuals who become depressed due to a traumatic event in their lives
Preliminary damage assessment (PDA)	A more detailed assessment of impacts that typically takes place within days or weeks of the event; it determines possibility and extent of outside assistance
Public assistance	Relief programs that make aid available to government entities that have been affected by terrorism
Rapid assessment	A quick survey of impacts designed to gain an appreciation of the scope of the attack

Technical assessment	A survey of damages that points out methods and costs for rebuilding
Unmet needs committee	A group of concerned citizens and community leaders who work together to collect donations and address long-term needs of victims
Volunteer management	The harnessing of volunteers to take advantage of their potential contributions while averting potential negative consequences
Volunteer registration center	The location where citizens fill out forms noting their skills and other information that can help you when making assignments

REFERENCES

Barnett-Queen, T. and Bergmann, L.H. (1989). Counseling and critical incident stress. *The Voice* (August/September), pp. 15–18.

Bathos, S., Williams, G., and Russell, L. (1999). Crisis management to controlled recovery: the emergency planning response to the bombing of the Manchester city centre. *Disasters* 23 (3): 217–233.

Hampson, R. and Moore, M.T. (2003). Two years after Sept. 11, NYC couple to Bury Son. *USA Today* (Thursday, 4 September), pp. 1A–2A.

Hooft, P.J., Noji, E.K., and Van De Voorde, H.P. (1989). Fatality management in mass casualty incidents. *Forensic Science International* 40: 3–14.

Lowe, S. and Fothergill, A. (2003). A need to help: emergent volunteer behavior after September 11th. In: *Beyond September 11th: An Account of Post-Disaster Research* (ed. L. Jacquelyn), 293–314. Boulder, CO: Natural Hazards Research and Applications Information Center, University of Colorado.

McEntire, D.A. (2002). Understanding and improving damage assessment. *IAEM Bulletin* (May), pp. 9, 12.

McEntire, D.A., Robinson, R.J., and Weber, R.T. (2003). Business responses to the world trade center disaster: a study of corporate roles, functions and interaction with the public sector. In: *Beyond September 11th: An Account of Post-Disaster Research* (ed. L. Jacquelyn), 431–457. Boulder, CO: Natural Hazards Research and Applications Information Center, University of Colorado.

Mitchell, J.K. (1988). Stress: the history, status and future of critical incident stress debriefings. *JEMS* 13 (11): 47–52.

Neal, D.M. (1994). The consequences of unrequested donations: the case of hurricane Andrew. *Disaster Management* 6 (1): 23–28.

Oaks, S.D. (1990). The damage assessment process: an overview. In: *The Loma Prieta Earthquake: Studies of Short-Term Impacts. Program on Environment and Behavior Monograph #50* (ed. R. Bolin), 6–16. Boulder, CO: Institute of Behavioral Science, University of Colorado.

Oklahoma Department of Civil Emergency Management (1996). Donations Management Case Study of the Alfred P. Murrah Federal Building Bombing, 19 April 1995 in Oklahoma City, OK: Summary and Lessons Learned. Oklahoma City, OK.

Scanlon, J. (1998). Dealing with mass death after a community catastrophe: handling bodies after the 1917 Halifax explosion. *Disaster Prevention and Management* 7 (4): 288–304.

Thompson, J. and Hawkes, R. (1962). Disaster community organization and administrative process. In: *Man and Society in Disaster* (ed. G. Baker and D. Chapman), 268–300. New York: Basic Books.

Wedel, K.R. and Baker, D.R. (1998). After the Oklahoma City bombing: a case study of the resource coordination committee. *International Journal of Mass Emergencies and Disasters* 16 (3): 333–362.

ASSESSING SIGNIFICANT THREATS
WMD and Cyberterrorism

Do You Already Know?

- Future threats that will confront homeland security
- The dangers of radiological weapons
- How to minimize the spread of nuclear weapons
- Ways to respond to biological weapons
- Steps to prevent the use of chemical weapons
- How to define cyberterrorism

 For additional questions to assess your current knowledge of the future of homeland security, go to **www.wiley.com/go/mcentire/ homelandsecurity2e**

What You Will Find Out	What You Will Be Able To Do
14.1 Anticipated risks facing homeland security	• Predict new threats confronting the United States
14.2 The threat of radiological weapons	• Estimate the outcome of dirty bombs
14.3 The potential impact of nuclear weapons	• Evaluate the consequences of nuclear terrorism
14.4 What to do about biological weapons	• Select ways to respond to biological attacks
14.5 The types of chemical weapons	• Plan how to respond to chemical weapons
14.6 The vulnerabilities associated with cyberterrorism	• Implement measures to prevent cyberterrorism attacks

Introduction to Homeland Security: Understanding Terrorism Prevention and Emergency Management,
Second Edition. David A. McEntire.
© 2019 John Wiley & Sons, Inc. Published 2019 by John Wiley & Sons, Inc.
Companion website: www.wiley.com/go/mcentire/homelandsecurity2e

INTRODUCTION

If you are to prevent terrorist attacks and minimize their consequences, you must anticipate future threats. In the following chapter, you will learn about the probability of terrorist attacks involving radiological, nuclear, biological, and chemical weapons. You will gain knowledge about the threat these weapons pose, the ability of terrorists to acquire such capabilities, and the effects of their use. You will also learn what steps can be taken to minimize these types of attacks or respond effectively should they occur. In addition, the nature of cyberterrorism will be explored along with a number of measures to prevent these types of attacks against the nation. Knowing this information will be imperative as terrorist attacks will likely be more significant in the future.

14.1 THE FUTURE OF TERRORISM AND WMD

In order to succeed in homeland security, it is vital that you are aware of the innumerable concerns about future threats. There are new terrorist groups appearing each day, and their motivations for attacks are becoming more intense and entrenched. For instance, right-wing domestic terrorist groups remain a constant threat, in spite of the fact that they are not as active as they have been in the past. Left-wing groups have become more vocal in recent years, and even people like school teachers and Madonna have asserted that they would like to shoot President Trump and blow up the White House. Regardless of the actual intent of these statements, the actions of many on the left have included riots and other violent protests in recent years.

In addition, terrorism may also take on new forms in the future. For instance, there is a strong chance of increased suicide bombings in crowded public areas. Terrorists employ this tactic around the world, and it is likely this type of terrorism will soon come to the United States. Also, the success of shootings in Florida, California and Nevada will likely lead to more mass slayings. Terrorists can take out large numbers of people with automatic weapons. All of these threats have implications for homeland security policy and programs.

Of course, the main area of focus right now is on radical Islamic terrorists. They are constantly fighting American troops in Afghanistan, Iraq, and Syria, among other locations. Attacks from groups like ISIS are becoming more brutal, and the impacts may have broader and more negative consequences. These individuals and groups have also vowed to bring the fight to the United States. Radical Islamic terrorists' desire is to affect the West directly by launching attacks on our own soil.

Countries, including Iran and Syria, are also increasing their support of terrorism (financially and in other ways). For instance, Iran trains terrorists within its borders, funds operations in Lebanon and Israel, and sends soldiers and weapons into Iraq to be employed against American soldiers. More worrisome yet is the fact that Iran is developing nuclear technology. While the leaders of this country maintain they are taking this course of action to meet future energy needs, it is also possible that highly enriched uranium could be used for belligerent purposes. If this occurs, Israel or the United States could be targeted or blackmailed by Iran. It is also possible that Iran could share nuclear materials or weapons with terrorist organizations. Such an action would theoretically make it more difficult to prevent attacks or place blame. In any case, Iran is regarded by many to be a major threat in the Middle East and toward the United States. Its leaders have clearly stated their desire to attack Israel, and this country is no fan of the United States. In response to this situation, President Obama focused on a diplomatic solution. But many feel his approach is paving the way for Iran to obtain nuclear weapons. It appears that diplomacy has not really worked as intended, and the Trump Administration is implementing new sanctions. Continued conflict and even all-out war are not out of the question. If things turn more violent, the use of nuclear weapons cannot be ruled out.

IN THE REAL WORLD

Al-Qaeda, ISIS, and WMD

Research illustrates that terrorist groups like Al-Qaeda and ISIS are taking numerous measures to acquire and use weapons of mass destruction (WMDs). Dunn's study (2008) revealed that Al-Qaeda has been working diligently to obtain WMDs. For instance, it is believed the Al-Qaeda operatives attempted to purchase radiological material in Russia and elsewhere. Concrete evidence suggests that Al-Qaeda contacted scientists in Pakistan to learn more about nuclear weapons. Training manuals seized in Afghanistan reveal that labs were beginning to develop ricin and botulinum toxin. Al-Qaeda ran experiments to test the impact of cyanide on dogs in 2001. ISIS is another group that covets WMD, and it appears that they have used them against US troops in Syria. In recent years, ISIS established a unit to seek and develop chemical weapons. The *Washington Times* reported that ISIS fired a shell with mustard agent in Iraq where US troops were operating. The shell landed within the security perimeter, and tests confirmed mustard gas. It is also believed that ISIS may have acquired iridium-192 from a storage facility in southern Iraq. This radioactive isotope is highly dangerous and could injure or kill those who come in contact with it. Belgian police also disrupted an ISIS plot to obtain radioactive materials in that country. It appears that terrorists are intent on obtaining and using WMDs.

Weapons of mass destruction (WMD): Weaponry that will create major injuries, carnage, destruction, and disruption when utilized.

The possibility of Iran developing nuclear weapons brings up the most pressing concern for the future homeland security: weapons of mass destruction. As noted in earlier chapters, **weapons of mass destruction (WMDs)** are weaponry that will create major carnage, destruction, and disruption when utilized. WMD is not only possible but also probable in the future. Many scholars and policy experts agree that forthcoming attacks

Figure 14-1

The Ayatollah Khamenei is an example of an Iranian leader who has espoused revolution and violence. Source: © Shutterstock. Reproduced with permission of Shutterstock.

will rely on WMDs in the future (Gurr and Cole 2000; Kelley 2014; Mahan and Griset 2013).

There are numerous reasons why this is the case. *America's Achilles' Heel*, a study by three terrorism experts, Falkenrath et al. (1998, pp. 5–6), reveals that terrorists may seek and use WMDs for the following reasons:

- **Massive casualties**. WMDs may result in an overwhelming number of injuries and casualties. Hundreds, thousands, and even millions of people could be adversely impacted by WMDs. While the number of fatalities was limited, over 5000 people sought medical care after the 1995 sarin gas attack on a Tokyo subway in Japan. The potential for mass death is certainly a concern going forward.

- **Degraded response capabilities**. Terrorism involving WMDs will have at least three consequences for first responders. First, police, fire, and EMS personnel will be overwhelmed by the demands placed upon them by the initial wave of victims. Second, countless first responders could be numbered among the victims of these types of attacks because of secondary devices or unanticipated exposure and contamination. Third, responding to WMD attacks will require a great deal of knowledge and skill. Unfortunately, this expertise is not as widespread as it needs to be due to the technical nature of WMD and insufficient training programs or funding sources.

- **Contamination**. The use of WMD has a significant negative consequence on the environment. Because of the dangers associated with WMDs, the impacted area may require remediation. In certain cases, the location of the attack may be uninhabitable for days, weeks, months, and even years. For instance, the accidental release of radiation from a nuclear power plant in Chernobyl in 1986 illustrates this potential in vivid manner. Decades after the incident, the area is still considered hazardous and is therefore officially declared uninhabitable. Some studies suggest the area won't be completely safe for 20 000 years.

- **Economic damage.** An attack involving WMDs will have extensive financial consequences. Direct financial expenses will include the loss of buildings, property, and the infrastructure as well as the costs associated with response and recovery. Indirect economic losses are inevitable and could result from disruptions in business transactions, astronomical insurance payouts or unsettled claims, and resulting unemployment. The terrorist attacks on 9/11 cost at least $40 billion; future costs could be unimaginable.

- **Psychological impact.** Because the outcome of any WMD attack is likely to be significant in so many ways, victims and others witnessing this type of terrorism may feel intense fear. Anxiety, sleeplessness, stress, and other emotional tolls are probable. While most people are resilient after major events, terrorism adds psychological distress because it is intentionally caused.

- **Political change.** The use of WMD could result in significant governmental transformation. The freedoms we enjoy could be seriously curtailed in an attempt to respond effectively after an attack occurs. Isolationism or vengeance in foreign policy is another possibility if terrorists use WMD. The organizational and policy changes after 9/11 are indicative of how societies can change after major terrorist attacks. New laws were passed, and the creation of the Department of Homeland Security resulted in the most sweeping transformation of government in a half a century.

IN THE REAL WORLD

WMD Identifiers

When responding to terrorist attacks, you should pay special attention to WMD identifiers. FEMA has identified several of them (1999, pp. 25–26):

Biological
- Unusual numbers of sick or dying people or animals
- Dissemination of unscheduled and unusual sprays, especially outdoors and/or at night
- Abandoned spray devices with no distinct odors

(Continued)

(Continued)

Nuclear

- Presence of Department of Transportation placards and labels
- Monitoring devices

Incendiary

- Multiple fires
- Remains of incendiary devices
- Odors of accelerants
- Heavy burning
- Fire volume

Chemical

- Massive onset of similar symptoms in a large group of people
- Mass fatalities
- Hazardous materials or lab equipment that are not relevant to the location
- Exposed individuals reporting unusual odors and tastes
- Explosions dispersing liquids, mists, or gases
- Detonations that destroy a package or the bomb device alone
- Unscheduled dissemination of an unusual spray
- Abandoned spray devices
- Numerous dead animals, fish, and birds
- Absence of insect life in a warm climate
- Mass casualties without obvious trauma
- Distinct pattern of casualties and common symptoms
- Civilian panic in potential target areas, e.g. government buildings, public assemblies, subway systems, etc.

Explosive

- Large-scale building damage
- Blown-out windows
- Scattered debris
- Victims with shrapnel-induced trauma
- Appearance of shock-like symptoms
- Damage to eardrums

Of course, not all types of WMD will have each of these impacts or to the same degree. This is because WMDs may range from crude bombs made out of common household cleaning products as well as more elaborate and large-scale explosives composed of fuel and fertilizers acquired from commercial outlets. However, the most feared WMDs include radiological, nuclear, biological, and chemical weapons. For this reason, each of these will be discussed in turn.

SELF-CHECK

1. Scholars and practitioners are increasingly fearful of the use of WMD in the future. True or False?

2. WMD produces injuries and deaths, but not social disruption. True or False?

3. Responding to WMD attacks is difficult because:
   (a) Responders are likely to be victims.
   (b) There will be a large number of victims.
   (c) Responses to WMD require technical expertise.
   (d) All of the above.

4. Discuss three reasons why terrorists may use WMD in future attacks.

14.2 RADIOLOGICAL WEAPONS

Radiological weapons:
Weapons that spread dangerous radiological material but do not result in a nuclear explosion. Radiological weapons are also known as radiological dispersion devices (RDDs) or dirty bombs.

Radiological weapons spread dangerous radiological material, but do not result in a nuclear explosion. Instead, **radiological dispersion devices (RDDs)** as they are known are made out of a combination of conventional explosives and nuclear materials. RDDs are commonly known as **dirty bombs**. Terrorism involving radiological material can also occur by simply exposing it to people and the environment. In other words, terrorists could place a container with radiological material in a subway and then remove the lid. This would potentially affect all those in the immediate vicinity. As will be seen, the alpha, beta, and gamma radiation in these bombs generate additional complications beyond more routine terrorist activities.

Radioactive substances are not readily available to the average person. However, they can be obtained from hospitals, industrial facilities, and elsewhere (e.g. the black market or smugglers). Philip Purpura, a well-known security expert, asserts that radiological materials are used for various commercial purposes, including food sterilization and the treatment of cancer (2007, p. 74). Unfortunately, the sources for dirty bombs or RDDs are not always secure. "Since 1999 … federal investigators have documented 1300 cases of lost, stolen, or abandoned radiological material" in the United States (Purpura 2007, p. 74). There are also over 100 countries that have not adequately controlled radiological substances. The ease of access (in comparison with other types of WMD) as well as their potential negative impacts makes radiological weapons inviting to terrorists.

It is true that radiological weapons are not commonplace – at least when compared with conventional bombings. Nevertheless, there have been confirmed attempts or actual uses of radiological weapons in the United States. José Padilla, a US citizen trained by Al-Qaeda in Afghanistan, was arrested when he plotted to use an RDD in Chicago. Although the attack was thwarted, it did generate a significant degree of media interest. Since instilling fear in others is a major motivator for terrorists, the recognition gained by RDDs makes them attractive weapons. For these reasons, it is highly likely that radiological weapons will be used in the future.

IN THE REAL WORLD

Radiological Terrorism

Terrorism involving radiological material is not a theoretical proposition, but an empirical reality. Gavin Cameron, an expert at the Centre for Military and Strategic Studies, observes that radiological terrorism is more common than one might think. In 1974, a man called police and noted that he had placed a nonlethal amount of iodine-131 on a train bound to Rome. The material was stolen as it was being shipped to a hospital. The man took this measure due to his grievance about the treatment of mentally ill patients in Austria. In 1985, a man sent a letter to the Mayor of New York demanding the release of a prisoner. If the city failed to respond adequately, plutonium trichloride would be placed in reservoirs serving New York. Although there was no proof that the threat was acted upon, the US Department of Energy did find elevated levels of plutonium in the water. In 1993, a Moscow businessman was killed when the Russian mafia placed gamma-ray-emitting pellets in his office. In 1996, three men attempted to kill officials of the Republican Party by placing radium in the victims' cars, food, and toothpaste. One culprit was found unfit to stand trial (on grounds of insanity), and the other two were sentenced for their participation in the attack. In 1995, the Chechen guerrilla leader, Shamil Basayev, placed radioactive material in Izmailovo Park. Russian authorities were able to find the cesium-137 wrapped in a yellow plastic bag within a case. In 2001, Ivan Ivanov, a Bulgarian businessman, told British officials that he was asked by bin Laden's associates to obtain radiological material. He was also offered $200 000 to acquire fuel rods from the Kozlodui nuclear power plant in Bulgaria. After the 2015 terrorist attacks in Paris, authorities uncovered video surveillance of a scientist employed at the Belgian Nuclear Research Center. It was feared he was working on radiological weapons. Radiological weapons have been used in the past, and the efforts of terrorists indicate that they are attempting to employ them in the future.

If deployed, radiological weapons could pose health hazards to humans. The length of exposure will determine the extent of injuries and deaths. Those who are exposed for a brief time may not suffer any notable consequences. However, a strong dose or prolonged exposure could lead to immediate fatalities or cancer that develops over time. In addition, radiological weapons could contaminate geographic locations for an extended period of time. Even if the amount of radiological material dispersed is insignificant, the presence of such substances could create social disruption and psychological concern. People will not want to live or work in an area that has been exposed. This could lead to major evacuations, housing shortages, and economic decline around the nation.

The theft of radioactive material from a medical clinic in Brazil illustrates the potential negative outcome of dirty bombs. In 1987, scavengers entered an abandoned medical facility and came across a container with radiological material. They broke the source open, thereby releasing the radioactive material into the environment. As a result, "four people died, more than 100,000 others had to be monitored for contamination, and cleanup costs amounted to tens of millions of dollars" (Ferguson and Lubenau 2008, p. 139).

In order to prevent the use of radiological weapons, it will be imperative to secure the sources of this material. For instance, each year, 50 radioactive gauges are stolen from the oil industry in Nigeria (Ferguson and Lubenau 2008, p. 141). If such thefts are to be prevented, the material will have to be held under lock and key or protected by armed guards. In addition, the issuing of licenses (allowing the legal use of radiological materials) should also be carefully controlled. As an example, Stuart Lee Adelman posed as a professor in 1996 and illegally obtained radiological material. He pled guilty to this fraud and was sentenced to five years in prison (Ferguson and Lubenau 2008, p. 143). It is believed he may have been trying to obtain money from terrorists. Regardless of Adelman's motive, terrorists themselves may also seek radiological materials through similar deception. Records should therefore be carefully kept, and shipments should also be meticulously monitored. Homeland security personnel should ensure that steps are taken to prevent terrorists from acquiring radiological material.

If radiological weapons are used by terrorists, it will be imperative to rely on the expertise of highly trained individuals. Normally, this will require military personnel or others who have knowledge and understanding of how to isolate and clean up radiological material. The Department of Defense has 58 **Civil Support Teams** around the nation, with more on the way. These teams can be quickly activated and mobilized to respond to this type of event anywhere in the country. They assist local and state governments in identifying hazardous agents (including RDDs), determining consequences and appropriate response techniques, and requesting additional support if required. Other military personnel, from US Northern Command (NORTHCOM), may also be activated to assist when circumstances warrant their assistance. If an attack occurs, medical personnel and coroners will also be needed to treat the injured and dead. A major priority is to wash those affected by the radiation and "purge inhaled or ingested materials" (Purpura 2007, p. 305). The disposal of deceased must be completed in the proper manner (assuring that others are not contaminated in the process).

In order to be prepared for terrorism involving radiological materials, monitoring devices should be placed strategically around cities to detect the presence of the weapon. This is especially important in that RDDs may or may not have an obvious and associated explosion. The lack of forewarning or the desire to avert drawing attention to this type of attack means that these weapons can be employed covertly. In addition, radiological materials cannot be detected by human senses because they are colorless and odorless. The only way to know that they have been used is through symptoms of victims or constant monitoring of the environment. Having adequate equipment will also be necessary for those responding to RDDs. This may

Civil Support Teams: Specialized military units that assist local and state governments that have been affected by weapons of mass destruction.

Figure 14-2

Civil Support Teams can help local jurisdictions deal with attacks involving weapons of mass destruction.
Source: © US Department of Homeland Security.

include Geiger counters, personal protective clothing covering the entire body, and breathing apparatus. Keeping a safe distance from the radiological materials or limiting time of exposure is another recommendation when responding to this type of terrorist attacks.

IN THE REAL WORLD

Treating Radiation Poisoning

Three medical experts in the Dallas–Fort Worth area (Elvin Adams, Ira Nemeth, and John White) assert that radiological poisoning can be minimized in some cases. If a person has been exposed to radioactive U-235, an antidote of baking soda and water can be administered to eliminate the radioactive isotope from the body. If cesium has been used in an attack, the pigment Prussian blue can bind the cesium and carry it out in the stool. If iodine-131 is present in the environment, the administration of potassium iodide will help. Large doses are required to saturate the thyroid in order to block exposure to radioactive I-131. If given to the victim quickly, some forms of cancer can be prevented. The most critical treatment to prevent dangerous internal exposure is to prevent ingestion of a radiological agent. Use of an N-95 mask will prevent inhaling of the agent. When drinking is required, using a straw to minimize ingestion of materials on the lips will reduce significantly the number of radioisotopes taken into the body.

SELF-CHECK

1. Examples of radiological weapons include dirty bombs and radiological dispersion devices. True or False?

2. There have been no cases of radiological weapons used in the past. True or False?

3. Which country illustrates the potential deaths and economic impact of radiological terrorism?

   (a) Nigeria
   (b) Brazil
   (c) Colombia
   (d) Iran

4. What experts will be needed to react effectively to radiological terrorism?

14.3 NUCLEAR WEAPONS

Nuclear weapons:
Weapons that produce massive explosions due to the release of vast amounts of energy through fission or fusion.

Suitcase bomb:
Portable nuclear weapons that can be carried or rolled to the target location.

Nuclear weapons also contain radiological material as dirty bombs or RDDs do. However, **nuclear weapons** produce massive explosions due to the release of vast amounts of energy through the process of nuclear fission or fusion. Most nuclear weapons are placed in the tip of rockets and cruise missiles. However, portable nuclear weapons are also possible. In fact, many experts in homeland security fear the use of a **suitcase bomb**. A suitcase bomb is a portable weapon that could be carried or rolled to the target location.

Nuclear weapons are possessed by major powers including China, France, Great Britain, Russia, and the United States. India, Israel, North Korea, and Pakistan also have nuclear weapons, and it is believed that Iran is actively seeking to develop them. While it would be difficult for a terrorist organization to acquire highly enriched material for nuclear bombs, it is not impossible to rule out their success in obtaining them. Theft, blackmail, and bribery are all potential ways of acquiring plutonium or other nuclear material. Once attained, organizations with sufficient knowledge and technological sophistication may theoretically build nuclear weapons. Information on their construction is accessible in scientific journals, in academic books, or even on the Internet. It is also true that states possessing nuclear weapons may also simply give them to known terrorists. This is why the United States and others are currently concerned about Iran and their nuclear energy program.

Should nuclear weapons be acquired and used in a terrorist attack, the impacts are almost unimaginable. The devastation produced by the nuclear weapons at the end of World War II was imposing. America's use of the A-bomb killed approximately 130 000 people in Hiroshima and 65 000 more in Nagasaki. But today's technology is far superior. The destruction and death of a modern nuclear weapon would certainly be more notable.

The explosion of a nuclear weapon produces a mushroom cloud that can be seen from miles and miles away. In the blink of an eye, people and property in the immediate area (perhaps a 15-mile radius or greater) would simply be vaporized. Those on the outskirts would be killed by the intense heat or injured by flying debris and blinded by the extreme light produced in the explosion. Sickness and death from radiological poisoning would also occur, requiring a major medical and mass fatality response. The infrastructure would be severely damaged, and the environment would be contaminated for decades. Living near the blast or fallout zone would be impossible due to the health consequences of radiation. Because of the loss of business and impact on the stock market, serious economic repercussions would be inevitable. Government agencies would cease to exist or function in the immediate area, and nearby jurisdictions would be severely hampered. The results truly bring up images of Armageddon.

In order to prevent the use of nuclear weapons by terrorists, those involved in homeland security must work closely with intelligence officials,

Figure 14-3

The atomic bomb in Japan was devastating. Today's nuclear weapons are far superior and will inflict even more death and destruction if utilized. Source: © Getty Images/Alamy Stock Photo. Reproduced with permission of Getty Images.

Proliferation:
The acquisition, sharing, and spread of nuclear weapons and materials to those who do not currently possess them.

Non-Proliferation Treaty (NPT):
An international regime designed to prevent nuclear states from giving nuclear weapons or materials to those who do not possess them.

International Atomic Energy Agency (IAEA):
The international organization responsible for the enforcement of the Non-Proliferation Treaty.

foreign governments, military agencies, and multilateral institutions to avert proliferation. **Proliferation** is the acquisition, sharing, and spread of nuclear weapons and materials to those who do not currently possess them. The **Non-Proliferation Treaty (NPT)** is an international regime designed to prevent nuclear states from giving nuclear weapons or materials to those who do not possess them. It was initiated in 1968 due to the Cold War and has been signed by over 180 governments around the world. It is administered by the **International Atomic Energy Agency (IAEA)**.

Unfortunately, not everyone has signed the NPT, and others may not adhere to IAEA requirements. As an example, Iran has disregarded the wishes of the NPT repeatedly and hindered the activities of the IAEA and others. Furthermore, terrorist organizations are not signatories of the treaty because they are not nation-states. They may seek to develop nuclear weapons outside of international law. Therefore, the loopholes in the NPT and desire of others to acquire nuclear materials and technology limit 100% compliance. In addition, one radical Saudi cleric states that it would be morally permissible to use a nuclear bomb against the United States as a way to stop American actions against Muslims (Bunn and Wier 2008, p. 125).

Bunn and Wier's chapter in *Weapons of Mass Destruction and Terrorism* dispels seven myths pertaining to nuclear terrorism (2008):

- Some terrorists do want to use nuclear weapons against the United States and others. Osama bin Laden declared this to be a major priority before he was killed.

- Acquiring nuclear material is not impossible. Bribery and theft are only two of the many ways terrorists may acquire highly enriched uranium or plutonium.

- Building a nuclear weapon is not improbable. The US Office of Technology Assessment asserts that a small group of individuals could build such a device if they were sufficiently committed.

- Setting off a nuclear weapon is not as unlikely as is commonly believed. Some of the older weapons in the possession of Russia do not have permissive action links (electronic locks requiring coded access).

- State sponsorship in obtaining nuclear weapons is not a requirement. As long as nuclear materials can be acquired, individuals and groups will be able to manufacture nuclear weapons alone.

- Smuggling a nuclear device into the United States is likely to be achieved. It would be very difficult for border officials to guarantee that a nuclear weapon or its component parts could be complete because of the vast quantity of goods that enter our nation each day through legal and illegal means.

- A strong military offensive cannot always stop terrorists from using nuclear weapons. Counterterrorism operations have not prevented terrorist attacks in the past, and there is no reason to believe they will be 100% successful in the future.

For these and other reasons, it is wise to prepare for a terrorist attack involving a nuclear weapon. Getting ready for this scenario is likely to be undertaken especially by the military and medical communities. Personnel in the armed forces have special training on nuclear weapons in addition to personnel protective gear and radiological monitoring devices. Doctors, nurses, and paramedics will also be needed to care for the injured. Those exposed to radiation will lose hair and experience the destruction of the cells that are vital for the brain, heart, and other internal organs. There is no way to reverse the effects of this type of radiation exposure, although symptoms can be relieved through various medical treatments.

Because of the dangers of radiation, government leaders will also need to plan on ways to evacuate hundreds of thousands of people from the impacted area. Such an evacuation could take place if a credible threat is issued or after a nuclear detonation has occurred. Doing so would require detailed and comprehensive evacuation plans that take into account all exit routes and all methods of transportation. Contraflow strategies with the use of countless law enforcement personnel would be needed along with others to monitor vehicle breakdowns and fuel shortages. However, many vehicles will be rendered useless due to the electromagnetic pulse associated with nuclear weapons.

Any mass evacuation will also necessitate large quantities of sheltering and housing. Hurricane Katrina resulted in one of largest evacuation in US history. The destruction of New Orleans and surrounding cities caused over one million people to migrate to other locations. Every state received evacuees. This led to the need for short-term shelters operated by organizations like the American Red Cross. The integration of evacuees into long-term residential housing will also be required after terrorist attacks, which will lead to severe shortages in the housing market and place significant burdens on the construction industry. This is to say nothing about the need to help evacuees find schools, obtain jobs, and gain a sense of belonging in their new community. Evacuation is a short-term action, but it has long-term consequences for those involved.

FOR EXAMPLE

Future Possibilities of Nuclear Terrorism

Research reveals differing opinions about the future possibility of nuclear terrorism (Maerli et al. 1998). Some assume that terrorists will attack a US city as soon as they are able to acquire nuclear weapons. Others assert that other types of WMD are more likely to be employed due to the technical requirements associated with developing nuclear weapons. While the risks of nuclear terrorism may be low, the consequences should warn us about complacency or a false sense of security. If terrorists cannot obtain nuclear weapons from supporting governments, they may be able to make crude weapons such as those that destroyed Hiroshima and Nagasaki during World War II. In addition, one nuclear physicist warns if terrorists are able to obtain nuclear material, "even a high school kid could make a bomb in short order" (Alvarez in Maerli et al. 1998, p. 115).

SELF-CHECK

1. The only threat of nuclear terrorism comes from missiles and rockets. True or False?

2. Pakistan currently possesses a nuclear weapon. True or False?

3. Which of the following is not associated with nuclear weapons?

    (a) Radiation sickness

    (b) Vaporization of people in the immediate detonation area

    (c) Immunity through vaccination programs

    (d) Injuries due to fires and flying debris

4. What is the Non-Proliferation Treaty?

14.4 BIOLOGICAL WEAPONS

Biological weapons:
Living organisms or agents produced by living organisms that may be used in terrorist attacks.

Bacteria:
A single-cell organism that causes disease in plants, animals, and humans.

Virus:
A microscopic genetic particle that infects the cells of living organisms but cannot multiply outside a host cell.

Toxin:
A poison that is produced by plants or animals.

Another major concern among those in homeland security is biological weapons (Guillemin 2005). **Biological weapons** are living organisms – or agents produced by living organisms – that may be used in terrorist attacks. There are three types of biological agents that can be converted into weapons of mass destruction:

- **Bacteria** are single-cell organisms that cause disease in plants, animals, and humans. Anthrax is an example of such pathogens that can be reproduced on their own.

- A **virus** is a microscopic genetic particle that infects the cells of living organisms. It lives inside a host cell and cannot multiply outside of this location. Ebola, smallpox, and AIDS are well-known viruses.

- A **toxin** is a poison that is produced by plants or animals. They vary in strength but can destroy blood cells, tissues, and the central nervous system. Ricin is frequently mentioned as toxin.

Developing and using biological weapons in attacks is ironically straightforward and difficult at the same time (Falkenrath et al. 1998). On the one hand, converting biological agents into weapons is relatively simple. A seed stock of the agent can be acquired and then it must be produced in bulk. Information to accomplish this objective is widely available in the scientific literature and medical community. Equipment to reach this goal is also present in many locations because of numerous research or commercial enterprises engaged in bioengineering. On the other hand, it is admittedly more challenging to store, transport, and employ biological weapons. For instance, there are significant technical hurdles inhibiting the development of aerosol dissemination, unless the perpetrator is willing to utilize less effective methods for spreading the biological agent.

IN THE REAL WORLD

The 2001 Anthrax Crisis

Shortly after the 9/11 attacks, Bruce Edwards Ivins sent four envelopes containing powdered anthrax spores from Trenton, New Jersey (Thomas 2003). The first victim was a photo editor who worked with the National Enquirer. Over the next several weeks, 21 others became ill. Four of these individuals succumbed to the effects of inhalation anthrax and died. Because antibiotics can stop infection and treat anthrax disease, the government implemented an aggressive prophylactic treatment. 32 000 people were given antibiotics for 10 days. Of these, 10 000 were also given a 60-day treatment. Although it was impossible to tell who was infected, public health officials and the CDC believed that this measure saved countless lives. As the emergency period ended, focus shifted to other issues. The post office and other buildings had to be cleaned of any remaining anthrax. These facilities had to be shut down for an extended period of time until they were believed to be free of any remaining biological agent. The FBI initiated a massive manhunt to determine who was involved in the attacks. Clues eventually lead the FBI to Ivins. The anthrax crisis in 2001 illustrates the deadly and disruptive potential of bioterrorism along with the difficulty of prosecution.

Category A agents: Biological weapons that pose a serious risk to people because they are easily transmitted to others and they result in high mortality rates.

Category B agents: Biological weapons that have a moderate chance of contagion and generally result in lower morbidity rates than category A agents.

Category C agents: Biological weapons that could be used for mass dissemination and high morbidity if engineered for that purpose.

Bioterrorism: Terrorism that employs biological weapons.

The impacts of biological weapons will vary dramatically, depending on the type of agent used and the method of distribution. **Category A agents** pose a serious risk to people because they are easily transmitted to others and they result in high mortality rates. Smallpox is an example of these types of biological weapons. **Category B agents** have a moderate chance of contagion and generally result in lower morbidity rates than category A agents. Typhus fever is an example of category B agents. **Category C agents** could theoretically be used for mass dissemination and high morbidity if engineered for that purpose. An example of this type of agent is hantavirus.

	Category A agents	Category B agents	Category C agents
Example	Plague	Viral encephalitis	West Nile virus
Transmissibility	High	Moderate	Low
Mortality rates	High	Moderate	Low

The effects of **bioterrorism** – terrorism that employs biological weapons – will also be dependent on whether it is absorbed through cracks in the skin, ingestion, or inhalation. Depending on the agent used, extent of exposure, and health of the victim, symptoms may appear quickly or over time. Signs of infection may include fever, respiratory distress, vomiting and diarrhea, painful lesions, blackened fingers and toes, shock, paralysis, and death in certain cases. Ricin is one example of a biological agent. It is a toxin that is produced by castor bean plants and can be very deadly. While ricin may kill only those who have been directly exposed to it, other types of biological weapons could kill countless people. Respiration (e.g. coughing) and physical contact (e.g. touching pustules) are factors in contagion. The ease of travel today may also spread diseases around the nation and world within days. In 2007, an infected passenger traveled from Europe to the United States even though he was known to have been diagnosed with tuberculosis. In another case, severe acute respiratory syndrome (SARS) spread rapidly in Canada and Hong Kong as people traveled within cities or to distant locations.

It is vital to recognize that humans may not be the only target of biological attacks however. David Franz, the director of the National Agricultural Biosecurity Center, notes that hoof-and-mouth disease could easily be used in a terrorist attack (1998, p. 190). It is readily available in the natural environment, it does not pose a risk to humans, and it would easily spread through the livestock population. This brings up the concept of agroterrorism. **Agroterrorism**, or terrorism against farming industries and products, must therefore be taken into consideration as well. Agroterrorism could limit or severely disrupt the supply of food. Death and disease could result if terrorists employed this type of tactic.

Agroterrorism:
Terrorism against farming industries and products.

Biological Weapons Convention (BWC):
An international treaty designed to prevent the proliferation of biological agents around the world.

Preventing bioterrorism or agroterrorism is similar to efforts to inhibit terrorism involving radiological or nuclear weapons. That is to say, the proliferation of biological agents among states and nonstate actors should be strongly opposed by the international community. The **Biological Weapons Convention (BWC)** has this purpose, but it also suffers from the

Figure 14-4

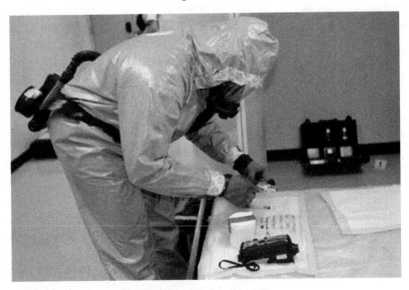

Deadly diseases can be acquired by terrorists from bio-medical labs. Source: © National Guard.

weaknesses of the NPT. As an example, Iraq successfully hid its anthrax program from the United Nations until after the first Gulf War. For this reason, George W. Bush's administration observed that the BWC was "inherently unverifiable" in 2001.

Minimizing the threat of bioterrorism will likewise require the close monitoring of biological agents in other ways. Efforts, including security of facilities and verification of legitimate use, should be taken to limit access to qualified medical personnel and researchers only. Protecting air intakes of buildings and using high efficiency particulate air (HEPA) filters in large occupancy buildings are other methods to minimize the possible use or impact of bioterrorism. Recurring evaluation of herbs and crops should also be a top priority of those trying to prevent agroterrorism. Inspection personnel in the agricultural and ranching sectors must maintain situational awareness at all times. If cattle and agricultural produce appear to have been tainted in any way, they should be reported to the proper authorities immediately. This may include the US Department of Agriculture, the Federal Bureau of Investigation (FBI), or the Department of Homeland Security.

Effective responses to a bioterrorism attack will require a great deal of collaboration among doctors, nurses, public health officials, emergency managers, the National Disaster Medical System (NDMS), and the Center for Disease Control (CDC). It will also necessitate quick distribution of medicines through the strategic national stockpile to state and local governments. The **strategic national stockpile (SNS)** is a cache of medicines in secret locations that can be quickly sent to affected locations around the country. This includes 14 push-pack components such as antibiotics that can easily fill a 747 aircraft. Medicines can also be obtained from the vendor-managed inventory (VMI), which includes drugs manufactured and distributed by large pharmaceutical companies. The goal is to break these pallets of supplies down and send them to the **points of distribution (PODs)** as soon as possible. PODs are locations where medicines may be given to victims. PODs may be set up at government buildings, schools, churches, or any location that can handle large numbers of people. Depending on the type of agent, victims may need to be given appropriate shots or pills within as little as 48 hours.

Strategic National Stockpile (SNS):
A cache of medicines in secret locations that can be quickly sent to affected locations around the nation.

Points of distribution (PODs):
Locations where medicines may be given to victims.

In some cases, vaccines can be administered to prevent the agent from negatively affecting victims. For instance, smallpox vaccinations have been given to soldiers, medical personnel, and first responders around the nation. If a biological attack does take place, the general population may also be given necessary antibiotics, respiratory treatments, or other forms of prophylaxis. This obviously assumes that the biological agent is identified early enough and that medicines are readily available to be dispersed. Unfortunately, it may take days or weeks to ascertain a bioterrorist attack, and some medicines can only be created once the proper strain of the pathogen has been identified.

Planning activities must likewise take into consideration the important process of resource distribution. Preparedness measures must also involve the public. For example, the washing of hands is the single most effective way of reducing the spread of disease. Steps must be taken to isolate infected people and animals from others. Home nursing care, work-at-home programs, and even quarantines may need to be implemented after a biological terrorist attack. Unfortunately, we lack sufficient information on the best methods and effectiveness of quarantines. The last time they were used extensively was during the Spanish flu outbreak in the early 1900s. More studies of how to deal with bioterrorism will be required in the future.

IN THE REAL WORLD

Terrorist Attacks Versus Other Types of Disasters

Responding to a terrorist attack involving WMD is similar, in some ways, to other types of disasters. All events may require emergency medical care, media relations, and donations management. However, there are also some significant differences between WMD events and natural disasters. For instance, there may be no warning for a terrorist attack, whereas some events like hurricanes provide advanced notification. Debris removal should be handled with care after a terrorist attack since destroyed buildings may contain evidence and deadly contaminants. There may be greater demand for crisis counseling after a terrorist attack because it has been caused by humans. It is also possible that terrorist attacks involving biological weapons could kill millions of people. People may also overrun hospitals because they do not know if they have been affected or not. It is important to be able to compare and contrast the impact of terrorist attacks and other types of disasters so your actions will be appropriate for the situation at hand.

SELF-CHECK

1. Health impacts of biological weapons may include fever, vomiting, paralysis, and death. True or False?

2. A category B agent is more deadly than a category A agent. True or False?

3. Which type of biological weapon is a poison produced by plants or animals?

   (a) Bacteria
   (b) Toxin
   (c) Virus
   (d) Category C agents

4. What is the Strategic National Stockpile?

14.5 CHEMICAL WEAPONS

Chemical weapons:
Lethal man-made poisons that can be disseminated as gases, liquids, or aerosols.

Nerve agents:
Chemical weapons that prevent the transmission of electrical signals in the nervous system.

Vesicants:
Blister agents that produce chemical burns.

Blood agents:
Chemical weapons that prevent the flow of oxygen in the blood.

Choking agents:
Chemical weapons that cause respiratory distress.

Irritants:
Agents that lead to allergic reactions.

Terrorists may also attempt to access and use chemical weapons in the future. Lethal man-made poisons that can be disseminated as gases, liquids, or aerosols are known as **chemical weapons** (Falkenrath et al. 1998, p. 17). Chemical weapons are divided into five categories:

- **Nerve agents** prevent the transmission of electrical signals in the nervous system. An example of nerve agent is soman.
- **Vesicants** are blister agents that produce chemical burns on the body. Lewisite is a type of vesicant.
- **Blood agents** prevent the flow of oxygen in the blood. Cyanide is an example of blood agents.
- **Choking agents** inhibit the pulmonary system. Phosgene falls into the category of choking agents.
- **Irritants** are agents that lead to allergic reactions (e.g. tearing, runny nose, or respiratory distress). Mace is a common example of an irritant.

	Example	Impacts
Nerve agents	Sarin	Convulsion of muscles
Vesicants	Mustard gas	Burns/blisters on the skin
Blood agents	Cyanide	Depletion of oxygenated blood
Choking agents	Chlorine	Suffocation
Irritants	Pepper spray	Allergic reactions

Many countries used chemical weapons during World War I, and the consequences were devastating to soldiers on the battlefield. Today, many countries have eliminated their stockpiles to avoid aggravating an arms race in this area. However, these same nations could produce chemical weapons on a moment's notice. Others, including Iran and Syria, are believed to be current possessors of chemical weapons. Thus, it is possible that terrorists could obtain chemical weapons from governments around the world. Theft and bribery are, again, possible ways for terrorists to obtain chemical weapons.

Virtually any individual or organization could produce chemical weapons since their precursor materials are available from legitimate commercial suppliers (Falkenrath et al. 1998, p. 103). It is estimated that the United States produces 300 000 metric tons of cyanide to be used in electroplating, dyeing, printing, and the production of plastics (Tucker 2008, p. 217). Ordinary household chemicals or supplies from mail-order companies could also be used to acquire chemical weapons.

For instance, terrorist organizations like Aum Shinrikyo have developed chemical weapons in the past. Aum Shinrikyo was a quasi-Buddhist sect composed of disillusioned intellectuals from Japan and Russia during the late 1980s (Tucker 2008, p. 214). Led by Shoko Asahara, this terrorist organization was able to acquire a net worth of $1 billion through legitimate and illegitimate practices. With this money, it desired to instigate a major

Figure 14-5

The Tokyo Subway is one of the world's busiest commuter transport systems, and the Sarin gas attack was the deadliest attack against it to occur in Japan since the end of World War II. Source: © Getty Images/iStockphoto.

war between the United States and Japan by using chemical weapons. Scientists were subsequently hired to develop this type of weaponry within the organization's "Ministry of Science and Technology." In time, these technicians were successful in producing sarin, which was later tested on sheep on a remote ranch in Australia. In the mid-1990s, Aum Shinrikyo then used sarin to kill three judges in Matsumoto. Seven others were later killed with the use of aerosolized sarin during an attack on a subway in Tokyo. Fortunately, the sarin gas in this latter attack was diluted and not as potent as it could have been. That attack brought more attention to the use of chemical weapons by terrorist organizations.

Chemical weapons may be composed of conventional explosives that disperse hazardous materials into the atmosphere (e.g. a bomb that disperses chlorine). Alternatively, chemical weapons may be employed by simply releasing chemicals that are normally stored in protective containers (e.g. opening up a valve on a chlorine tanker). Opening a lid and using a spray device to impact others are various means to distribute chemical agents. For instance, chemical weapons could be introduced into a heating, ventilation, and air conditioning (HVAC) system inside a building. Product tampering, injection with a syringe, and the sending of letters or packages with powdery substances are other ways to deliver chemical weapons. Jonathan Tucker, a senior fellow at the Center for Nonproliferation Studies, provides a list of three more types of chemical weaponry:

- Distribution of military-grade chemical warfare agent into the air.
- Use of toxic agents to contaminate water or food supplies.
- Assassination of a specific individual or group with chemical agents (2008, p. 213).

In conjunction with the type of attack, the impact of chemical agents could vary significantly. Some chemicals are persistent (meaning that they evaporate slowly), while others dissipate quickly. Certain chemical agents may lead to minor medical problems, while others lead to immediate death. Depending on the type of chemical agent used and environmental conditions (i.e. temperature, humidity, and wind speed), physical results could include physical annoyance, long-term respiratory or central nervous system damage, and widespread mortality. Environmental problems are also likely consequences of chemical weapons. Water and soil can remain contaminated long after a chemical agent has been used in a particular geographic area.

Much like radiological, nuclear, or biological weapons, the development of chemical weapons can be minimized by carefully controlling the manufacturing, use, transportation, and storage of hazardous materials. Suppliers can also ensure that those requesting chemicals have legitimate and peaceful purposes. Nevertheless, it could be impossible to prevent the acquisition of chemical weapons. Materials and knowledge to make them are everywhere. Known state possessors could also give them to terrorist organizations. Even industry and transportation methods can be used against us. A bomb could release dangerous chemicals at a manufacturing plant. A tanker truck or railcar could also be penetrated, thereby releasing toxic materials in the air near a school, business district, or residential area.

The possibility of chemical weapons suggests that much more attention should be given to detection, decontamination, emergency medical response, and environmental reclamation. Planning with the Metropolitan Medical Response System, the Department of Health and Human Services, and the NDMS needs to be improved. More paramedics, doctors, and nurses will be required to treat the victims of chemical weapons. Training of these individuals should focus on ways to identify chemical weapons and respond effectively. For instance, those involved in homeland security should be aware that the FBI has labs to help you to identify what agent is being used. In addition, atropine may need to be administered quickly to victims if their lives are to be spared. Along these lines, military personnel and some paramedics may have Mark I autoinjector kits for this purpose. Mark I is a spring-loaded injector that has been developed by the military. It contains atropine and an oxime, which can help treat patients affected by nerve agents. Mark I kits and other drugs may only help to save those with moderate exposure however. Also, such medicines will certainly be lacking in a major attack. For instance, only 29% of hospitals that responded to a survey had sufficient medicines to care for 50 victims (Tucker 2008, p. 222). Some larger jurisdictions do have CHEMPACK antidotes strategically placed across the city, but it is unclear if funding is adequate to replace them when the drugs reach their expiration date. Organizational resources, including the Disaster Medical Assistance Teams and environmental restoration companies, will need to be deployed quickly after a chemical attack takes place. Chemical weapons, along with other types of WMDs, are all likely to be used by terrorists in the future. It will be crucial that homeland security personnel take measures now to prevent their use or be ready to respond if that cannot be averted.

FOR EXAMPLE

Chemical Terrorism

Between 1960 and 2001, there were 125 incidents of terrorists using chemical weapons (Tucker 2008). Most of these were small in scope and were committed by a wide range of terrorists (e.g. nationalists, religious extremists, antiabortion or environmental groups, left-wing and right-wing organizations). However, it is anticipated that the number of chemical weapons attacks will rise in the future. One case in Russia illustrates how easy it is for scientists to develop chemical weapons. A man named Valery Borzov was fired from the Moscow Scientific Research Institute of Reagents in 1997. In order to maintain an income, the 40-year-old chemist started to develop blister agents in his own clandestine laboratory. His desire was to sell vials of the poisonous substance for $1500 each to the Russian mafia or other criminal organizations. When arrested, investigators found recipe books, equipment, and 50l of dangerous products in his home. Borzov was found incompetent to stand trial, and he was committed to a mental institution. Police were fortunate to interdict his efforts to make money at the expense of others' lives.

SELF-CHECK

1. Chemical weapons are disseminated as liquids only. True or False?
2. Responding to chemical weapons may involve decontamination, emergency medical response, and environmental reclamation. True or False?
3. Which type of agent prevents the transfer of electrical signals in the body?
   (a) Blood agents
   (b) Vesicants
   (c) Irritants
   (d) Nerve agents
4. Why are attacks involving chemical weapons increasingly likely in the future?

14.6 CYBERTERRORISM

The WMDs mentioned above get a lot of attention from those working in homeland security and for good reason. However, another threat – which is often underestimated – is cyberterrorism (CEDAT 2008). Cyberterrorism, which is also known as electronic terrorism, is not the same thing as cybercrime or hacking. Cybercrime has the goal of economic gain, while hacking

Cyberterrorism:
A terrorist activity that utilizes or attacks computer networks to instill fear and force some type of change.

could be equated to electronic vandalism. In contrast to cybercrime or hacking, **cyberterrorism** is defined as terrorist activity that utilizes or attacks computer networks to instill fear and force some type of change. An example of cyberterrorism is the use of computer viruses, worms, malware, coded programs, and technology in such a way as to impact people, the infrastructure, and the economy. Cyberterrorism targets cyberspace systems that are composed of computers, networks, servers, routers, fiber optic, etc.

Barry Collin, who coined the term cyberterrorism in the 1980s, stated that cyberterrorism occurs at the intersection of the physical and virtual worlds. Along these lines, Pluschinsky suggests that "a cyber-attack involves digitally targeting a computer information system so as to destroy, damage, or steal data and thereby disrupt or disable telecommunications, health, transportation, finances, utilities, food distribution, and other critical infrastructure systems. The primary target of a cyber-attack is information, but such attacks can ultimately cause casualties, depending on the system targeted" (2006, p. 367).

Almost everyone – reporters, researchers, practitioners, and politicians – fears the threat of cyberterrorism. The concern is that terrorists could gain access to computers via networks and disrupt vital services including dams, power generating stations, air traffic control systems, emergency services, and even the self-driving cars of the future. Thomas Friedman painted such a picture. He said "If someone is able to knock out a handful of key Internet switching and addressing centers in the US, ... here's what happens: many trains will stop running, much air traffic will grind to a halt, power supplies will not be able to shifted from one region to another, there will be no e-mail, your doctor's CAT scanner ... won't work" (Nacos 2006, p. 238). Such access and impacts are not farfetched. Students, hackers, and amateur computer programmers have entered secure sites relating to banking, the military, and NASA. Disruption of our critical systems is a very real possibility. Even death could be the consequence of cyberterrorism if

Figure 14-6

A computer may look like an innocent piece of technology, but it can be a very disruptive tool in the hands of a terrorist. Source: © FBI.

critical infrastructure is impacted. Perhaps for this reason, Michael Chertoff noted: "Of the many challenges facing ... the twenty-first century, one of the most complex and potentially consequential is the threat of large-scale cyber attack against shared information technology and cyber infrastructure, including the Internet" (2009, p. 95).

Examples of cyberterrorism, although not numerous or well known, are notable. For instance, during the 1990s, Iraq set up over 100 websites around the world. Their goal was to launch denial-of-service attacks against companies from the United States. In Japan, Aum Shinrikyo was able to access the computers of the Metropolitan Police Department, and they developed capability to track 150 police vehicles. After 9/11, the armed services obtained Al-Qaeda laptops in Afghanistan that revealed significant research on computer systems relating to water systems, nuclear power plants, and sports stadiums. More recently, France was hit by more than 19 000 cyber-attacks after Islamic terrorists attacked the Charlie Hebdo news organization that killed 12 and injured 11 others. ISIS has similarly attempted to launch cyber-attacks on computers that control US electric power grid.

The appeal of cyberterrorism is owing to several factors. According to Gabriel Weimann (2004), the author of "Cyberterrorism: How Real is the Threat?" cyberterrorism is cheaper than other methods of terrorism because all that is required is a computer and an Internet connection. Cyberterrorism occurs from a distance and also allows anonymity, which could limit apprehension and prosecution. Finally, cyberterrorism expands available targets and has the potential to affect millions of people.

Because of the horrifying potential of cyberterrorism, the US government is taking this threat seriously. New laws are being created as necessary including the Computer Fraud and Abuse Act. In addition, October has been designated each year as Cyber Security Awareness Month. Federal agencies are likewise spending $5 billion spent annually on cyber-defense. The US government has created a National Cybersecurity and Communications Integration Center (NCCIC). This is a 24 × 7 center composed of officials from the federal government, the intelligence communities, and law enforcement officials to monitor the Internet, respond to threats, and manage incidents. In addition, the government has proposed a **National Strategy to Secure Cyberspace**. This program is under the Information Analysis and Infrastructure Protection Unit and takes into account home users/small business, larger enterprises, critical infrastructure, and national and international Internets. The strategy includes the following priorities:

National Strategy to Secure Cyberspace: A component under the Information Analysis and Infrastructure Protection Unit and takes into account home users/small business, larger enterprises, critical infrastructure, and national and international Internets.

1. **A National Cyberspace Security Response System**. Efforts need to be taken to assess attacks and work with private sector to share information. Continuity plans must also be created and exercised.

2. **A National Cyberspace Threat and Vulnerability Reduction Program**. The goal is to enhance law enforcement capabilities to prevent attacks and prosecute terrorists. In addition, there is a need to prioritize research and development to secure emerging systems.

3. **A National Cyberspace Security Awareness and Training Program**. This promotes a national awareness program and fosters training.

4. **Securing Governments' Cyberspace**. The federal government must maintain access for authorized users only and secure federal wireless networks.

5. **National Security and International Cyberspace Security Cooperation**. This objective relates to strengthening cyber-counterterrorism intelligence. It also entails interaction with international organizations to promote global cybersecurity.

Virus:
It reproduces itself and overloads a single computer.

Worm:
It is similar to a virus, but it is capable of reproducing itself over many computer systems.

Trojan horses:
They contain malicious codes that destroy files.

Denial of service:
This means that computers cannot operate as intended.

While the National Strategy to Secure Cyberspace is a government-initiated program, this should not imply that the average person has no role in cyberterrorism prevention. Robert Jorgensen, the director of Cybersecurity at Utah Valley University, asserts that cybersecurity requires a "cyber citizen." In other words, people must recognize that their actions at home or work have a big impact on national vulnerability. Simple efforts to protect passwords and avoid phishing scams are basic steps to limit cyberterrorism the future.

In addition, the private sector can be a valuable asset in efforts to reduce cyberterrorism. For instance, the National Cyber Security Alliance is a partnership that was created after 9/11. Its goal is to spread information about what people, businesses, and the government can do to limit cyberterrorism. Everyone needs to know how to protect themselves online. Personal responsibility is imperative in the view of this organization. Their motto for the country is "Stop. Think. Connect."

IN THE REAL WORLD

Example of Cyberterrorism

If a terrorist can gain access to computers and computer networks, they may be able to wreak havoc. Some terrorists may infect computers with a **virus**, which reproduces itself and overloads a single computer. A **worm** is similar to a virus, but it is capable of reproducing itself over many computer systems. Some attacks are **Trojan horses**, which contain malicious codes that destroy files. These types of activities may produce what is known as **denial of service**. This means that computers cannot operate as intended. There are numerous examples of these activities. In 1996, a Swedish hacker tied up phone lines in 11 counties, and this stopped 911 systems for a time. In 1998, two high school students hacked into Pentagon, NASA, and nuclear sites. These students routed the attack through the United Arab Emirates. If students can create such consequences, it will only be a matter of time before terrorists engage in these types of activities.

SELF-CHECK

1. Cyberterrorism is expected to decline in frequency in the future. True or False?

2. A denial-of-service attack overloads computers and slows down computer processing. True or False?

3. What is another name for cyberterrorism?
   (a) Electronic terrorism
   (b) Network terrorism
   (c) Phishing terrorism
   (d) Fiber-optic terrorism

4. Explain the National Strategy to Secure Cyberspace.

SUMMARY

As a participant in homeland security, it is imperative that you prepare for the future. It will be necessary for you to comprehend the impacts of dirty bombs and RDDs. You must recognize the possible devastation that may result if nuclear weapons are acquired by terrorists. Preparing for biological or chemical weapons should be one of your top responsibilities. It will also be vital that you consider the possibility of cyberterrorism in the future and prepare accordingly. Working with key partners in each of these areas will be essential. Without anticipating future attacks like these and taking preventive and preparatory measures, you will not be successful in your efforts to promote homeland security.

ASSESS YOUR UNDERSTANDING

UNDERSTAND: WHAT HAVE YOU LEARNED?

 Go to **www.wiley.com/go/mcentire/homelandsecurity2e** to assess your knowledge of the future of homeland security.

SUMMARY QUESTIONS

1. Terrorists do not intend to use WMD. True or False?

2. Theft of radiological material has been a problem in recent years. True or False?

3. The International Atomic Energy Agency is not responsible for the Non-Proliferation Treaty. True or False?

4. The nature and extent of impact from biological weapons is dependent on the type of agent used as well as health of the victim and extent of exposure. True or False?

5. Irritants are the most deadly type of chemical agent. True or False?

6. The creation of new response plans should take into account complicated responses to terrorist attacks and other disasters in the nation. True or False?

7. Agroterrorism has no relation to biological agents. True or False?

8. The IAEA is in charge of preventing the spread of chemical weapons. True or False?

9. Radiological agents:
   (a) Can be obtained from hospitals, industrial facilities, and the black market
   (b) Are not used in dirty bombs
   (c) Never pose health threats to humans
   (d) Do not necessitate the involvement of the military or expert medical physicians

10. Which of the following causes the least concern among terrorism experts?
    (a) A suitcase bomb involving conventional explosives
    (b) A declared nuclear possessor giving nuclear weapons or material to a terrorist organization
    (c) Iran developing nuclear weapons
    (d) The United States losing one of its nuclear weapons

11. Which type of biological agent is composed of single-cell organism that causes diseases in plants, animals, and humans?
    (a) Bacteria
    (b) Virus
    (c) Toxin
    (d) Category A agents

12. Which of the following helps to prevent the spread of biological weapons?
    (a) IAEA
    (b) NPT
    (c) BWC
    (d) NTW

13. Which type of chemical weapon damages the pulmonary system?
    (a) Nerve agents
    (b) Vesicants
    (c) Blood agents
    (d) Choking agents

APPLYING THIS CHAPTER

1. While serving as an intelligence analyst for the CIA, you have been asked to testify in a closed session with congressional representatives. A Senator from California wonders why the United States government should be concerned about weapons of mass destruction today (when the Cold War ended a long time ago). What would you say?

2. During dinner, you tell your family what you have learned about radiological weapons. They ask you what radiological weapons are. What would you tell them?

3. An official from the State Department expresses concern about the potential for nuclear attack from a terrorist organization. During the press briefing, a reporter wonders how serious the threat really is. What should the State Department official say?

4. In your role as an analyst for the Department of Defense, your supervisor has requested a report about the types of chemical weapons. What would you include in your report?

BE A HOMELAND SECURITY PROFESSIONAL

Nuclear Proliferation

Write a paper on the proliferation of nuclear weapons and how it relates to terrorism. Be sure to explain who is responsible for halting the spread of nuclear weapons around the world.

Bioterrorism

As a seasoned analyst in the Center for Disease Control, you have been asked to identify the risk of bioterrorism. Be sure to explain why bioterrorism is both likely and unlikely.

Cyberterrorism

Imagine that you have been asked to write a report on cyberterrorism. Can you explain what it is? Why is cyberterrorism a concern today? What can be done to prevent this type of attack?

KEY TERMS

Agroterrorism	Terrorism against farming industries and products
Bacteria	A single-cell organism that causes disease in plants, animals, and humans
Biological weapons	Living organisms or agents produced by living organisms that may be used in terrorist attacks
Biological Weapons Convention (BWC)	An international treaty designed to prevent the proliferation of biological agents around the world
Bioterrorism	Terrorism that employs biological weapons
Blood agents	Chemical weapons that prevent the flow of oxygen in the blood
Category A agents	Biological weapons that pose a serious risk to people because they are easily transmitted to others and they result in high mortality rates
Category B agents	Biological weapons that have a moderate chance of contagion and generally result in lower morbidity rates than category A agents
Category C agents	Biological weapons that could be used for mass dissemination and high morbidity if engineered for that purpose
Chemical weapons	Lethal man-made poisons that can be disseminated as gases, liquids, or aerosols
Choking agents	Chemical weapons that cause respiratory distress
Civil Support Teams	Specialized military units that assist local and state governments that have been affected by weapons of mass destruction
International Atomic Energy Agency (IAEA)	The international organization responsible for the enforcement of the Non-Proliferation Treaty
Irritants	Agents that lead to allergic reactions
National Strategy to Secure Cyberspace	A component under the Information Analysis and Infrastructure Protection Unit and takes into account home users/small business, larger enterprises, critical infrastructure, and national and international Internets.
Nerve agents	Chemical weapons that prevent the transmission of electrical signals in the nervous system
Non-Proliferation Treaty (NPT)	An international regime designed to prevent nuclear states from giving nuclear weapons or materials to those who do not possess them

Nuclear weapons	Weapons that produce massive explosions due to the release of vast amounts of energy through fission or fusion
Proliferation	The acquisition, sharing, and spread of nuclear weapons and materials to those who do not currently possess them
Radiological dispersion devices (RDDs)	See radiological weapons
Radiological weapons	Weapons that spread dangerous radiological material but do not result in a nuclear explosion. Radiological weapons are also known as radiological dispersion devices (RDDs) or dirty bombs
Strategic national stockpile (SNS)	A cache of medicines in secret locations that can be quickly sent to affected locations around the nation
Suitcase bomb	Portable nuclear weapons
Toxin	A poison that is produced by plants or animals
Vesicants	Blister agents that produce chemical burns
Virus	A microscopic genetic particle that infects the cells of living organisms but cannot multiply outside a host cell
Weapons of mass destruction (WMD)	Weaponry that will create major injuries, carnage, destruction, and disruption when utilized

REFERENCES

Bunn, M. and Wier, A. (2008). The seven myths of nuclear terrorism. In: *Weapons of Mass Destruction and Terrorism* (ed. R.D. Howard and J.J.F. Forest), 125–137. New York: McGraw-Hill.

Center of Excellence Defense Against Terrorism (CEDAT) (2008). *Responses to Cyber Terrorism*. NATO Security Through Science Series. Amsterdam: IOS Press.

Chertoff, M. (2009). *Homeland Security*. Philadelphia, PA: University of Pennsylvania Press.

Dunn, L.A. (2008). Can Al Qaeda be deterred from using nuclear weapons? In: *Weapons of Mass Destruction and Terrorism* (ed. R.D. Howard and J.J.F. Forest), 295–316. New York: McGraw-Hill.

Falkenrath, R.A., Newman, R.D., and Thayer, B.A. (1998). *America's Achilles' Heel: Nuclear, Biological and Chemical Terrorism and Covert Attack*. Cambridge, MA: MIT Press.

FEMA (1999). *Emergency Response to Terrorism*. Washington, DC: Independent Study Course.

Ferguson, C.D. and Lubenau, J.O. (2008). Securing US radiological sources. In: *Weapons of Mass Destruction and Terrorism* (ed. R.D. Howard and J.J.F. Forest), 139–166. New York: McGraw-Hill.

Franz, D. (1998). International Biological Warfare Threat in CONUS. Posture Statement for the Joint Committee on Judiciary and Intelligence. United States Senate, Second Session, 105th Congress, International Biological Warfare Threats in CONUS (4 March). https://fas.org/irp/congress/1998_hr/s980304-franz.htm

Guillemin, J. (2005). *Biological Weapons: From the Invention of State-Sponsored Programs to Contemporary Bioterrorism*. New York: Columbia University Press.

Gurr, N. and Cole, B. (2000). *The New Face of Terrorism: Threats from Weapons of Mass Destruction*. New York: I.B. Tauris.

Kelley, M. (2014). *Terrorism and the Growing Threat of Weapons of Mass Destruction*. Anchor: Hamburg.

Maerli, M.B., Schaper, A., and Barnaby, F. (1998). The characteristics of nuclear terrorist weapons. In: *Weapons of Mass Destruction and Terrorism* (ed. R.D. Howard and J.J.F. Forest), 100–124. New York: McGraw-Hill.

Mahan, S. and Griset, P.L. (2013). *Terrorism in Perspective*. Thousand Oaks, CA: Sage.

Nacos, B.L. (2006). *Terrorism and Counterterrorism: Understanding Threats and Responses in the Post-9/11 World*. New York: Penguin Academics.

Purpura, P.P. (2007). *Terrorism and Homeland Security: An Introduction with Applications*. Burlington, MA: Butterworth-Heinemann.

Thomas, P. (2003). *The Anthrax Attacks. The Century Foundation's Homeland Security Project Working Group on the Public's Need to Know*. New York: The Century Foundation.

Tucker, J.B. (2008). Chemical terrorism: assessing threats and responses. In: *Weapons of Mass Destruction and Terrorism* (ed. R.D. Howard and J.J.F. Forest), 213–226. New York: McGraw-Hill.

Weimann, Gabriel. 2004. Cyberterrorism: How Real is the Threat? Special report, May 13. United States Institute of Peace.

15

LOOKING TOWARD THE FUTURE
Challenges and Opportunities

Do You Already Know?

- The major lessons to be drawn from this book
- The need for accountability in homeland security
- What concepts can guide homeland security policy
- Where research in homeland security is incomplete

For additional questions to assess your current knowledge of the future of homeland security, go to **www.wiley.com/go/mcentire/ homelandsecurity2e**

What You Will Find Out	What You Will Be Able To Do
15.1 The importance of reviewing the material presented in this book	• Recall the major recommendations for homeland security
15.2 Why accountability is imperative for homeland security	• Promote responsible stewardship for government resources
15.3 Homeland security policy lacks a simple but comprehensive conceptual guide	• Assess how liability reduction and capacity building can improve homeland security
15.4 What research will improve homeland security	• Implement practical recommendations for homeland security

INTRODUCTION

As has been illustrated throughout this book, your role as a participant in homeland security is vital for the national interests of the United States and countries everywhere. Advancing the homeland security profession will occur when you and others remember and apply the major lessons in this book. Another important obligation you have is to promote accountability and develop coherent policies in homeland security to ensure that resources are spent carefully and that strategic priorities are clearly identified. It is also imperative that you understand what research is required to improve homeland security and how principles can be applied to reduce the threat and consequences of terrorism. The central theme of this chapter is that success can only be achieved when those working in homeland security are knowledgeable, when they use resources wisely, when they recognize where scholarship is incomplete, and when they work diligently to accomplish strategic goals.

15.1 THE LESSONS OF THIS BOOK

If you work now in homeland security or will be employed in this profession in the future, chances are that you have or will have a very specialized function. That is to say, you probably will work in one agency and within a limited scope of responsibility. Nevertheless, it is vital that you gain a broad understanding of terrorism and what to do about it. The threat of terrorism is extremely complex, and countless measures must be taken to prevent attacks or successfully respond if they occur. Many of these activities overlap with others. For this reason, it is wise to review the major lessons of this book in this concluding chapter.

Chapter 1 introduced you to the threat of terrorism along with the impact of 9/11 and the nature of homeland security and emergency management. You learned that terrorism is a serious problem and that it should not be discounted going forward. Events like 9/11 illustrate the significant impact of terrorism on society. Accordingly, the emerging profession of homeland security will be vital to reduce the loss of life and disruption terrorist attacks produce. It, along with the discipline of emergency management, will help to reduce the probability and consequences of terrorism.

Chapter 2 defined terrorism as a violent behavior (or the threat of violence) that instills fear in others and aims to force people to acquiesce to the demands of ideological extremists. Terrorism is characterized by public attacks that coerce others to support the goals of the perpetrators. It may take on various forms including mass terror, assassination, random terror, or terror against the government. Although terrorism may be regarded as one of many different types of threats or hazards, it has elements of both conflict and consensus disasters. That is to say, discord leads to terrorism, but terrorist attacks are often followed by increased altruistic behavior as people work together to solve mutual problems.

Chapter 3 explored the factors that lead people to engage in terrorism. It was revealed that some individuals and groups are violent due to their frustrations with prior social interactions, while others focus on problematic foreign policy or their impoverished condition. Terrorism may also result from disagreements about politics or ineffective political systems. Culture and religion are major explanations of terrorism today. However, it is clear that all terrorists share strong ideological stances that lead them to act violently. These attitudes (e.g. being unwilling to compromise on beliefs) seem to be more engrained than before.

Chapter 4 concentrated on understanding who terrorists are and how they operate. It was illustrated that many individuals, groups, and even nation-states participate in terrorism. These terrorists are categorized as being criminals, crusaders, or crazies. However, contrary to popular belief, there is no typical stereotype of a terrorist. Nevertheless, the people who advocate terrorism see the world through a unique lens and assume that they are justified in attacking others in order to correct the wrongs they perceive and address the issues that are important to them. Terrorists are also very calculating in their planning operations, and their attacks may be manifested through assassination, mass shootings, arson, bombings, etc. No one should discount the threats and actions of terrorists.

Chapter 5 outlined the evolution of terrorism over time. Violent behavior with the goal of creating fear in others has always existed, and terrorist attacks can specifically be traced back to the Roman and Greek republics. Nonetheless, the concept of terrorism did not appear until the period of the Enlightenment. Europe's bout with terrorism is long, but the United States has also experienced terrorism (as a victim and some would even argue as a participant). Terrorism has changed dramatically over time and is far different today than in the past. For instance, terrorists are less hierarchical, more independent, increasingly creative, and more intent on violence than their peers in prior decades.

Chapter 6 exposed the unique relation between terrorism and the media. The ability to share stories around the world in minutes and seconds is one of the reasons why terrorists want to portray their attacks through the media. Indeed, terrorists thrive on the publicity given to them through the media. Television, radio, and news organizations also benefit from the increased attention terrorist attacks bring even though they may be the target of attacks themselves. For their part, the government utilizes the media to discredit those who engage in terrorism and works with reporters to find and apprehend the perpetrators of attacks. The fact that terrorists rely so heavily on the media is one of the reasons why self-censorship may be required at times. Without responsible reporting, additional attacks may occur, and the rights of victims may be disregarded. Of course, social media is changing the relationship between terrorists and the media, and it will be interesting to see how this alters terrorist activity in the future.

Chapter 7 identified the major dilemma facing those who create and implement homeland security policy. This section of the book reveals that terrorists do not operate according to Geneva Convention rules of warfare. Instead, those engaging in terrorism attack innocent civilians and do so in a brutal manner. Some people therefore advocate the goal of security – even if it may jeopardize rights and freedoms. Others reject this viewpoint and alternatively argue the virtues of maintaining liberty in spite of the threat of terrorism. Various cases indicate the challenges of balancing each of these priorities. For this reason, those working in homeland security should be ever vigilant of ways to prevent attacks while also protecting rights and liberties.

Chapter 8 discussed the causes of terrorism with the hopes of finding ways to reduce such violent behavior. It first expressed the need to address "root causes" relating to poverty, political oppression, and the socialization of violence. Without addressing these fundamental problems, terrorism will remain a never-ending problem. In addition, this chapter explained that laws are required to prohibit terrorism and prosecute those who support or engage in such dastardly deeds. Organizations like the CIA and FBI play an important role in gathering and distributing information about terrorists through the intelligence cycle. If it is determined that attacks have been planned, relying on the special forces or terrorism task forces may be needed. Counterterrorism operations will be required in cases where terrorists are intent upon inflicting death, damage, and disruption upon others.

Chapter 9 considered measures to secure the nation as well as our vital businesses and societal interests. While controversial in the minds of certain people, the policies and actions that enhance border control may be needed to keep terrorists out of the United States. In addition, steps will be required to defend various segments of the economy. Terrorists have targeted and will continue to attack railways, air transportation, and seaports. Chemical facilities are also vulnerable to terrorist attacks because of the hazardous materials they contain. For these reasons, efforts must be taken to increase transportation security and regulate requirements for those handling dangerous chemicals.

Chapter 10 reviewed ways to protect people and property from terrorist attacks. It suggested that threat assessments are important to understand the true risk facing critical infrastructure, key assets, and soft targets. It was argued that more should be done to defend power and water systems, government institutions, sporting venues, and other locations where people are congregated. Buildings must also be constructed in such a way as to reduce the likelihood or impact of attacks. Besides this type of structural mitigation technique, it will be vital that nonstructural mitigation actions like proper zoning be implemented as well. What is more, the use of landscaping, access control, lighting, cameras, security guards, and other measures may deter terrorist attacks in the future. The goal is to reduce the desirability of certain locations as possible targets to be attacked.

Chapter 11 concentrated on various emergency management functions relating to preparedness. The concept of preparedness was defined as activities that increase readiness for possible terrorist attacks. It was conveyed that the federal government has created a National Response Framework and a National Disaster Recovery Framework to facilitate planning relating to the threat of terrorism. State governments have also instituted the Emergency Management Accreditation Program and the

Emergency Management Assistance Compact to increase capabilities when attacks do occur. At the local level, the establishment of broadly represented advisory councils, the passing of well-designed ordinances, and the acquisition of grants will increase preparedness as will thorough planning, training, exercises, and community education. The goal is to augment capacity to deal with terrorism beyond the simple development of an emergency operations plan.

Chapter 12 reflected on the importance of response operations when terrorist attacks occur. The chapter exposed common behavioral patterns exhibited during extreme events (e.g. convergence and emergence). It was also illustrated that the first priority is to deploy SWAT teams to thwart attacks and/or apprehend would-be terrorists. If this is not possible, it was noted that the primary responsibility of any official or unofficial first responder is to ensure the safety of personnel so further deaths and injuries can be avoided. Searching for victims, providing medical care, triaging and decontaminating victims, and investigating the attack to find the perpetrators are all necessary aspects of terrorism response. The incident command system and emergency operations centers may help you to complete and coordinate the myriad of functions that have to be performed immediately after terrorist organizations strike.

Chapter 13 discussed the short- and long-term recovery phases. In order to increase the resiliency to a terrorist attack, the community must adequately assess damages, human losses, unmet needs, and other impacts. Once the nature of the situation is understood, an emergency or disaster can be declared by the mayor, county officials, the governor, and the President. At this point, it will be easier for the impacted jurisdiction to focus on mass fatality operations, debris removal, psychological counseling, and volunteer and donations management. Federal programs, including individual assistance and public assistance, can also bring much needed resources to victims, their families, businesses, and local and state governments. However, affected jurisdictions must be aware of potential pitfalls and do all they can to rebound in an expedited manner.

Chapter 14 assessed the probability that terrorists will launch more unique and devastating attacks in the future. The concept of weapons of mass destruction was defined. And the threat of radiological, nuclear, biological, and chemical weapons was discussed along with numerous recommended actions to counter such assaults. In these situations, it was noted that homeland security officials should call upon the assistance of specialized military and public health officials since sophisticated technical knowledge and capabilities will be required. Cyberterrorism was also described, and the measures being taken by the government and even citizens were praised.

While these and other actions are necessary to improve the homeland security profession, they are insufficient in and of themselves. You will therefore also need to increase accountability in homeland security, improve policy guidance, foster research, and implement well-established principles to deal with terrorism. Each of these will be discussed in turn.

IN THE REAL WORLD

Academic and Professional Journals

Learning about terrorism and homeland security should be a lifelong process. With this in mind, you may want to be aware of and read the following academic and professional journals:

Disasters

Disaster Prevention and Management

Government Security

Homeland Defense Journal

Homeland Security Affairs

Homeland Security Professional

Homeland Security Today

Journal of Homeland Security

Journal of Homeland Security and Emergency Management

Journal of Emergency Management

Natural Hazards Review

Studies in Conflict and Terrorism

SELF-CHECK

1. Homeland security is a relatively simple profession. True or False?
2. Homeland security includes a broad range of activities to prevent attacks or improve post-event responses. True or False?
3. What functions are included in homeland security and when dealing with attacks?
   (a) Intelligence gathering
   (b) Border control
   (c) Community education and preparedness
   (d) Emergency medical care
   (e) All of the above
4. Can homeland security be accomplished easily? Why or why not?

15.2 ACCOUNTABILITY IN HOMELAND SECURITY

Those working to counter terrorist activities and minimize their impacts may have some – but not complete – control over the actions of terrorists. However, homeland security officials certainly have power over the administration of prevention, protection, and preparedness initiatives. National leaders can also shape the direction of policy in the areas of response and recovery in the future.

Unfortunately, it appears that limited vision and poor management have at times been weaknesses among those responsible for or involved in this national priority (Perrow 2006; Wise 2006). At its inception, homeland security suffered significant problems. Leaders and employees of homeland security have at times created and/or ignored innumerable challenges:

- The burial of FEMA within a massive department that focuses almost exclusively on security or law enforcement concerns jeopardized natural hazard mitigation, terrorism preparedness, and response coordination (Perrow 2006). The overarching focus on terrorism in this organization and the movement of different programs away from FEMA hurt the nation's ability to deal with all types of crisis events.

- The structural changes resulting from the creation of DHS also resulted in the loss of ties between the FEMA Director and the President. The lack of communication between Michael Brown and President Bush was readily apparent after Hurricane Katrina struck the United States in 2005. This weakness resulted in additional layers of bureaucracy that were added to emergency management in recent years.

- The rejection of emergency operations plans that proved to be effective in prior disasters and terrorist attacks resulted in unclear expectations for subsequent response activities. For instance, the new strategies of the National Response Plan were too complex, convoluted, and unclear. Time will tell if the National Response Framework will correct these mistakes, but the initial indications are positive.

- The introduction of the Homeland Security Advisory System (HSAS) has lessened the credibility of the government to issue warnings (Aguirre 2004). The HSAS was not based on the scientific literature on how to most effectively notify people of impending harm or suggest what should be done as a result.

- The distribution of $4.3 billion for communication equipment has not led to any real improvement in interoperability (Laskow 2010). Jurisdictions now have more communication equipment, but the lack of concrete national standards may continue to hamper the ability to coordinate with each other.

- A portion of the billions of dollars dedicated to homeland security appears to have been squandered on questionable projects or spent in unscrupulous ways. Homeland security funds have been spent on baseball caps and leather bomber jackets instead of on major prevention, protection, or preparedness initiatives as intended.

- The failure to protect US borders against outside infiltration has been one of the most glaring weaknesses of homeland security (Flynn 2002; GAO 2011). In spite of the growing threat of terrorism around the world, it seems as if little has been done to prevent people from simply walking across national boundaries into the United States.

- Presidential and political decisions have substantial consequences. Some people felt that President Bush was too aggressive in the war on terrorism and assert that he aggravated the conflict. In contrast, President Obama often denied or downplayed the fact that terrorists want to kill Americans. Early indications suggest that President Trump will be less agreeable to tolerate terrorism than his predecessor. This pendulum has a significant impact on coherent and consistent policies to build homeland security.

It appears, therefore, that many of the troubles we are currently facing are a result of incorrect planning assumptions as well as ineffective government oversight and follow-through. This is not to deny the significant threat of terrorism or the major trials of undertaking the most sweeping reform of government policies and organization in history. Problems are to be expected when cunning enemies are present and anytime a reorganization of this magnitude takes place. The criticisms against homeland security are not meant to diminish the important roles of the military, intelligence, and law enforcement communities either. Fighting against terrorism would be impossible without these important actors. It is also necessary to note that many of the aforementioned problems were corrected under the Post-Katrina Emergency Management Reform Act. For example, the President now has closer ties to the FEMA Administrator, and some of the prepared-ness programs have been put back into this important disaster organization. Problems – particularly in relation to mitigation and recovery – remain in emergency management.

Accountability:
The expectation of being responsible for decisions and activities.

Nevertheless, accountability was lacking at least initially when home-land security emerged. **Accountability** is the expectation of being respon-sible for decisions and activities that impact citizens in democratic nations. It includes being answerable for failed policies, misused resources, and

IN THE REAL WORLD

Accountability in Practice

On 16 February 2017, the Oversight and Management Efficiency Sub-committee held a hearing to explore ways to better manage the Depart-ment of Homeland Security (DHS) to prevent fraud, waste, abuse, and dysfunction. Representative Scott Perry (R-PA) gave an opening state-ment about the problems in DHS. He noted that this department should do a better job of getting its employees the resources they need and do so in a more streamlined process. However, Perry also complained that DHS has wasted millions of dollars on the Human Information Tech-nology Program as well as the Federal Protective Vehicle Program (in which it purchased more vehicles than drivers). Representative Perry also mentioned the failure to follow up on misconduct by members of the Secret Service. He argued that each of these types of mismanage-ment put the nation at risk. Consequently, Americans are demanding more of their government. He recommended that DHS do more to follow up on high-risk report the Government Accountability Office produces each year to identify areas of improvement. He also suggested that DHS adhere to the recommendations of the Office of the Inspector General.

incomplete goal attainment (Peters 2014). In other words, accountability includes constant review of goals and programs in order to overcome mistakes and capitalize on successes. Accountability in homeland security should be a major priority for the future. But accountability will not resolve all of the problems of evidence in the past. Success will also depend upon solid policies.

SELF-CHECK

1. Poor management has been one of the glaring weaknesses in homeland security. True or False?

2. Some of the money devoted to homeland security has been misdirected or used in fraudulent purposes. True or False?

3. Correcting problems and ensuring policies are effective may be labeled as:
   (a) Accountability
   (b) Adaptability
   (c) Flexibility
   (d) Command and control

4. Why is accountability important for homeland security?

15.3 CLARIFICATION OF HOMELAND SECURITY POLICY

Perhaps one of the reasons why homeland security programs have failed at times is because our nation does not have a fully developed and comprehensive policy for homeland security (May et al. 2011). Without a definitive statement on the goals of homeland security and methods of attaining them, our efforts to deal with terrorism could flounder aimlessly. For this reason, it is vitally important that you also consider policy issues in homeland security.

As this book reveals, the objectives of homeland security are surprisingly straightforward. The goals of those working in this field are twofold: (i) reduce the probability of terrorism and (ii) minimize the consequences of attacks that do occur. Put differently, homeland security attempts to limit both the possibility and impact of terrorist attacks. Such intentions will require not only prevention and protection measures, but preparedness, response, and recovery activities as well. Emergency management must therefore be viewed as an equal partner in the homeland security process.

Although clarifying the purpose of homeland security is imperative, this does not necessarily outline the means for implementing the desired priorities. For this reason, you might want to consider two proposed concepts to help guide your work in homeland security. These principles are liability reduction and capacity building (McEntire 2005).

Liability reduction:
A strategy that attempts to address the factors that result in or permit terrorist attacks.

The means for reducing the *probability* of terrorism are policies and actions that focus on liability reduction. **Liability reduction** is the name given to the strategy that attempts to address the factors that result in or permit terrorist attacks. This includes both proactive actions and defensive measures. Examples include:

- Understanding what motivates terrorists and working to alleviate root causes.
- Enhancing national security while protecting personal liberty.
- Reducing the permeable nature of the borders.
- Guarding vulnerable infrastructure and key assets.
- Stopping the proliferation of weapons of mass destruction.

Capacity building:
A strategy that attempts to enhance the ability of the nation, states, and communities to effectively deal with terrorist attacks.

The way to effectively deal with the *consequences* of terrorism is to enhance response and recovery capabilities. This is known as capacity building. **Capacity building** is a strategy that attempts to enhance the ability of the nation, states, and communities to effectively deal with terrorist attacks. This includes:

- Establishing laws and ordinances in homeland security and emergency management.
- Meeting with an advisory council to plan how to best react to terrorist attacks.
- Training responders on important functions including warning, evacuation, sheltering, decontamination, search and rescue, and emergency medical care.
- Conducting exercises and educating the community about how to prepare for terrorist attacks and other disasters.
- Helping leaders to understand their roles in disaster declarations, EOC activities, debris management, and individual and public assistance programs.

While liability reduction and capacity building have thus far been treated as isolated strategies, the reality is that these processes are inherently intertwined. Minimizing liabilities necessitates the development of additional capacities. For instance, surprise attacks can only be averted by augmenting human intelligence. Strengthening capabilities can likewise limit liabilities. As an example, the provision of additional training for first responders could promote increased safety at the scene of an attack.

Other complicated relationships among liability reduction and capacity building are also possible. Counterterrorism activities could aggravate additional terrorist attacks if they result in the death of innocent people, while well-justified counterterrorism operations could increase our ability to protect life and freedoms. In another example, media reports may intensify terrorist behavior unless reporters are aware of the potential negative impact their portrayals may have on such conduct. Failing to understand how terrorists operate will subsequently lead to future attacks, although improved recognition of the dynamic nature of terrorism can augment readiness for unprecedented violence. Liability reduction and capacity building could thus be seen as mutually reinforcing policies, leading to an effective homeland security apparatus.

IN THE REAL WORLD

DHS Performance

On 6 September 2007, Paul A. Schneider, the Under Secretary for Management in the Department of Homeland Security (DHS), testified before the US Senate Committee on Homeland Security and Governmental Affairs. After reviewing 24 performance expectations dealing with emergency preparedness and response, he revealed that DHS has produced mixed results since it was established. The department succeeded in five areas including grant funding, exercise programs, and the development of a national incident management system. However, DHS was unsuccessful in 18 other areas. Risk assessments, planning, training programs, and interoperable communications were regarded to be unsatisfactory. Other problems included the lack of an inventory of federal capabilities, unclear national goals, and a failure to provide assistance to individuals and communities during emergency events. The Government Accountability Office and other government oversight organizations have also been highly critical of the activities of the DHS. Fortunately, recommendations are being made to correct prior problems. They include improved strategic planning, sharing information with key stakeholders, partnering with other agencies, and integrating DHS's management functions. It is anticipated that progress will be made in these areas.

SELF-CHECK

1. Homeland security does not lack a coherent policy guide. True or False?
2. An example of liability reduction is efforts to minimize the root causes of terrorism. True or False?
3. Funding the Department of Homeland Security, hiring and training employees, and writing response and recovery plans are examples of:
   (a) Risk reduction
   (b) Capacity building
   (c) The paper plan syndrome
   (d) The National Response Framework
4. Explain how the concepts of liability reduction and capacity building could improve homeland security in the future.

15.4 RESEARCH NEEDS AND RECOMMENDATIONS FOR THE FUTURE

If homeland security is to be successful, your focus on liability reduction and capacity building must rely on the unique insights of scholars and implement the recommendations of dedicated practitioners. For their part, researchers must increase knowledge about terrorism and share it with government officials, business leaders, and everyday citizens. On the other hand, professionals must concentrate efforts on ways to improve the performance of critical responsibilities in homeland security (Wise 2006). While countless suggestions for the future could be mentioned, this book will conclude with five recommendations for both scholars and professionals.

15.4.1 Direction for Researchers

In order to improve homeland security, scholars must advance knowledge about terrorism and homeland security in several areas, for instance:

1. Homeland security will never maximize success unless we fully understand the causes of terrorism. It will be imperative that knowledge is generated about why people are willing to kill themselves and others for ideological goals (Pedahzur 2005). Without understanding this fundamental explanation and how to counter it, terrorist attacks will continue to grow in frequency and intensity.

2. Security and liberty are important values for societies, but insufficient information exists about how to protect each of these vital goals. Scholars should explore if it is possible to protect each objective simultaneously and promote ways to ensure neither perspective supersedes the other.

3. A major threat today relates to the possible use of radiological, nuclear, chemical, and biological weapons. Numerous research grants were given to scholars from the 1950s to the 1980s to understand human behavior in natural and technological disasters. Less is known about human behavior in response to weapons of mass destruction, and this shortfall needs to be corrected.

4. Terrorism has changed dramatically over time, but there are limited studies about modern-day threats. In particular, there is a dearth of awareness about cyberterrorism. Research must uncover both the threat of cyberterrorism and provide solutions that pertain to government, the private sector, and everyday citizens.

5. The massive reorganization of government after 9/11 revealed several shortcomings relating to public administration. Additional scholarship must determine how best to improve government operations in relation to complex problems such as terrorism and homeland security.

IN THE REAL WORLD

Working Across the Academic/Practitioner Divide

The Training and Education Synergy Focus Group was established with the support of the FEMA Higher Education Program. It provides a great example of how scholars and practitioners may work together. Although this group focused on emergency management, the model is one that could be applied to homeland security. The group asserts that it is the responsibility of everyone in both higher education and practice to contribute to emergency management training and education synergy. Individuals do not have to do the same thing. The key is that everyone does at least one thing and sustains it over time.

Ideas for Training Partners and Practitioners

- Meet and develop a relationship with people in emergency management higher education programs.
- Offer to host student interns to support their professional development and enhance their classroom education.
- Mentor college students that are interested in your emergency management career path.
- Invite students to attend emergency management training.
- Encourage student professional development by introducing students to your emergency management professional network.
- Promote the value of an emergency management education as a complement to relevant training and experience.
- Invite students and faculty to participate in exercises; planning efforts; hazard, risk, and vulnerability assessments; and after-action reviews.
- Invite higher education partners to present at practitioner conferences.
- Invite emergency management scholars to design and deliver training.
- Allow emergency management researchers to conduct research on your jurisdiction's emergency management activities.
- Subscribe to EM academic journals for the benefit of all staff.
- As personal and professional circumstances permit, emergency managers should consider taking an emergency management higher education course.

Ideas for Education Partners and Scholars

- Meet emergency managers from various sectors in your local area, state, and region.
- Form an advisory board composed of practitioners from different emergency management practice settings and specialties.
- Promote internships that allow students to develop skills and additional knowledge related to the sector in which they desire a career.
- Join local, state, and/or regional emergency management associations and volunteer for committees.
- Attend practitioner conferences and pursue offers to present at those conferences.

- Collaborate with practitioners to identify research projects that would be useful to them.
- Share research findings in practitioner-valued outlets.
- Offer continuing education opportunities that would help practitioners earn and maintain emergency management certifications.
- Make students aware of various career paths in emergency management and professional development needs related to those paths.
- Invite practitioners to be guest speakers in academic courses.
- Invite practitioners to present at conferences or other academic meetings or, better yet, co-present with them.
- Identify service learning opportunities that benefit both students and practice.
- Make internships in emergency management a degree requirement.

Figure 15-1

Professors and practitioners must work with students to help advance knowledge about terrorism and homeland security.
Source: © FEMA.

15.4.2 Guidance for Practitioners

Professionals in homeland security may also wish to focus on several measures to improve their efforts to prevent or react to terrorist attacks, for instance:

1. Terrorism is ultimately a reflection of a breakdown of respect and an unwillingness to permit alternative lines of thinking. Therefore, ways must be found to promote mutual understanding and stop radicalization. The socialization of young children into a life of terrorism is one of the greatest challenges to be overcome by current and future generations (Lombardi 2015).

2. Acts of violent extremism can only be halted if there is sufficient information about diabolical plans in advance of their implementation.

Figure 15-2

We must reverse the socialization of children into violence. Source: ©
ZouZou/Shutterstock. Reprinted with permission of Shutterstock.

For this reason, intelligence gathering and information sharing must
remain a top priority for organizations like the FBI and CIA.

3. The threat of terrorism is now self-evident and cannot be downplayed or
ignored. It will be imperative that we build a modern police and military
force to counter violent individuals and groups. Law enforcement agencies and the armed services must have the necessary equipment and training to react quickly and decisively to the danger posed at home or abroad.
However, "the trick, if one has the political acumen to learn it, is to avoid
fueling it while claiming to fight it" (Chaliland and Blin 2007, p. 11).

4. Terrorists have repeatedly expressed their intentions to attack the US
homeland. Accordingly, the porous border must be strengthened, and
infrastructure must be protected through more stringent antiterrorism
measures. The consequences of failing to meet these obligations are
dangerous and unacceptable.

5. It will unfortunately be impossible to prevent terrorism if people are
committed to undertaking such atrocities. As a consequence, there will
be a need to improve emergency preparedness at federal, state, and
local levels. Emergency managers should therefore be included as crucial partners in the development of homeland security policies and procedures. In addition, more attention should be given to education and
training. Fortunately, FEMA recently established the National Training
and Education System. The goal is to improve knowledge and capabilities, build and sustain a community of practice, and establish a defined
career path for those working in homeland security.

As can be seen, future success in homeland security will largely be dependent upon the ability of scholars and professionals to formulate a logical
mission for homeland security, identify major priorities to reduce terrorism,
and craft and implement appropriate policies to deal with ideologically

Figure 15-3

Professionals are needed in homeland security to advance
efforts to prevent attacks or respond effectively when they occur.
Source: © FEMA.

motivated acts of violence. Ongoing support and monitoring of necessary programs as well as the intentional adaptation of strategy will be required if we are to thwart terrorism and cope with its adverse effects. In short, the threat of future attacks is real and menacing. It is up to you and others involved in homeland security to meet this challenge and do so in an efficacious manner. In the words of a former director of the Defense Intelligence Agency, "The question is not whether such an attack will occur ..., but when and where. It is up to you ... to be prepared" (Chaliand and Blin 2007, p. 2).

 SELF-CHECK

1. Scholars play no role in homeland security policy or its practical application. True or False?

2. Stopping the socialization of children into terrorist behavior is one of the most important solutions in homeland security. True or False?

3. There is currently insufficient information about how to deal with which type of terrorism?

   (a) Conventional terrorism
   (b) Terrorism involving explosives
   (c) Cyberterrorism
   (d) Shootings
   (e) Hijackings

4. Describe why it is important for scholars and practitioners to work together to resolve the challenges facing homeland security.

SUMMARY

This book has illustrated countless issues that must be considered and addressed if efforts to prevent or deal with terrorism are to be effective. Therefore, you should review the major lessons of homeland security often so you do not forget all of the things that need to be accomplished to minimize the probability and impact of terrorism. In addition, it is advisable that you promote continued accountability in homeland security and the development of clear policies so that resources can be maximized and strategy can be simplified. The goals of preventing attacks, limiting their negative consequences, and reacting to them effectively can only be achieved if you work astutely and diligently to counter the deadly intents of terrorists. For this reason, the concepts of liability reduction and capacity building may help to direct your actions in this important field and profession. Furthermore, cutting-edge research will help you to know what else needs to be done to counter the threat of terrorism. However, the application of existing principles will also determine if you will be successful in protecting the homeland against terrorist attacks. Consequently, your work in homeland security will be both challenging and rewarding. It is up to you to prevent terrorist attacks, prepare for adverse consequences, and react effectively.

ASSESS YOUR UNDERSTANDING

UNDERSTAND: WHAT HAVE YOU LEARNED?

 Go to **www.wiley.com/go/mcentire/homelandsecurity2e** to assess your knowledge of the future of homeland security.

SUMMARY QUESTIONS

1. Terrorist attacks have occurred more frequently in recent years and pose a serious risk to people. True or False?

2. Homeland security includes only a few functions that have to be performed. True or False?

3. The Department of Homeland Security has created and experienced a few problems since its inception as a government entity. True or False?

4. Accountability is the expectation of being responsible for decisions and activities that impact citizens in democratic nations. True or False?

5. The United States has a comprehensive and fully developed policy to guide homeland security. True or False?

6. Liability reduction implies a strategy to minimize the probability of terrorist attacks. True or False?

7. Liability reduction and capacity building are mutual exclusive activities. True or False?

8. What systems can help to increase coordination after terrorist attacks?
   (a) Incident command
   (b) Emergency operations centers
   (c) The homeland security consortium
   (d) Answers a and b

9. Many of the shortcomings in homeland security result from a failure of:
   (a) Terrorists to advocate nonviolent solutions
   (b) Inaction
   (c) Accountability
   (d) Effort

10. Examples of historic failures in homeland security include:
    (a) The introduction of the Homeland Security Advisory System
    (b) The distribution of millions of dollars for interoperable communications
    (c) An inability to control the borders of the United States
    (d) All of the above

11. The central goals of homeland security include:
    (a) Reducing probability of attacks and minimizing consequences
    (b) Providing intelligence and responding to attacks

    (c) Engaging in counterterrorism and stopping cyber-attacks

    (d) Strengthening SWAT teams and facilitating recovery

12. Which of the following is representative of capacity building?

    (a) Launching a preemptive strike against known terrorists

    (b) Sealing off the borders so terrorists cannot enter the United States

    (c) Planning, training, and exercises

    (d) Promoting tolerance among different religions

13. There is currently insufficient knowledge about which threat(s)?

    (a) Cyberterrorism

    (b) Bombings

    (c) Arson

    (d) None of the above

APPLYING THIS CHAPTER

1. What are the major lessons of this book?

2. Why is accountability important in homeland security?

3. What can be done to reduce fraud, waste, abuse, and mismanagement?

4. What is liability reduction and capacity building, and how are they related?

5. What are some recommendations for future research and practical application?

BE A HOMELAND SECURITY PROFESSIONAL

Learn About Homeland Security Resources

Go to the library or look online to become familiar with homeland security and emergency management journals. What ones exist? How are they similar or different than others?

Accountability in Homeland Security

Review some of the government reports on the status of homeland security in the United States. Explain whether or not you think the Department of Homeland Security has been effective or ineffective in its responsibilities.

Future Research Needs

You have been asked to recommend future studies to assist the Department of Homeland Security. What types of research projects would you recommend?

KEY TERMS

Accountability — The expectation of being responsible for decisions and activities

Capacity building — A strategy that attempts to enhance the ability of the nation, states, and communities to effectively deal with terrorist attacks

Liability reduction — A strategy that attempts to address the factors that result in or permit terrorist attacks

REFERENCES

Aguirre, B.E. (2004). Homeland security warnings: lessons learned and unlearned. *International Journal of Mass Emergencies and Disasters* 22 (2): 103–115.

Chalian, G. and Blin, A. (2007). Introduction. In: *The History of Terrorism: From Antiquity to Al Qaeda* (ed. G. Chalian and A. Blin), 1–11. Berkeley, CA: University of California Press.

Flynn, S.E. (2002). America the vulnerable. *Foreign Affairs* 81 (1): 60–74.

Governmental Accountability Office (2011). *Border Security: Additional Steps Needed to Ensure that Officers Are Fully Trained.* Washington, DC: USGAO.

Laskow, S. (2010). Homeland security's billion-dollar bet on better communications. *The Center for Public Integrity* (17 February). www.publicintegrity.org (accessed 20 February 2017).

Lombardi, M. (2015). *Countering Radicalization and Violent Extremism Among Youth to Prevent Terrorism.* Amsterdam: IOS Press.

May, P.J., Jochim, A.E., and Sapotichne, J. (2011). Constructing homeland security: an anemic policy regime. *Policy Studies Journal* 39 (2): 285–307.

McEntire, D.A. (2005). Why vulnerability matters: exploring the merit of an inclusive disaster reduction concept. *Disaster Prevention and Management* 14 (2): 206–222.

Pedahzur, A. (2005). *Suicide Terrorism.* Malden, MA: Polity Press.

Perrow, C. (2006). The disaster after 9/11: the department of homeland security and the intelligence reorganization. *Homeland Security Affairs* 1 (11).

Peters, B.G. (2014). Accountability in public administration. In: *The Oxford Handbook of Public Accountability* (ed. M. Bovens, R.E. Goodin and T. Schillemans). Oxford: Oxford University Press.

Wise, C.R. (2006). Organizing for homeland security after Katrina: is adaptive management what's missing? *Public Administration Review* May/June: 302–318.

GLOSSARY

9/11   the most consequential terrorist attack involving hijacked planes against the United States.

Absolute poverty   a situation where people lack so many resources that they cannot even meet basic necessities such as food, clothing, and shelter.

Abu Musab al-Zarqawi   a Sunni terrorist who was responsible for many atrocities in Iraq, including the beheading of an American businessman named Nicolas Berg.

Abu Sayyaf   a jihadist separatist group in the Philippines that desires an independent Islamic state in Mindanao.

Accountability   the expectation of being responsible for decisions and activities that impact citizens in democratic nations.

Affect dimension   feeling or emotions that are generated in conjunction with beliefs.

Agro-terrorism   terrorism against farming industries and products.

Al Jazeera   the most widely viewed TV station based in Qatar that often serves as the vehicle to disseminate terrorist information.

Al-Qaeda   an extreme Islamic fundamentalist organization affiliated with Osama bin Laden.

Anarchists   those opposing specific governments or all governments.

Anders Behring Breivik   a terrorist who espoused far-right ideology and conducted one the worst attacks in Norway.

Annexes   a portion of the emergency operations plan that discusses specific hazards or functions that will need to be addressed if an event takes place.

Appendices   additional information at the end of the emergency operations plan that includes resource and contact lists, maps, standard operating procedures, and checklists.

Arab Spring   a series of uprising and armed rebellions that spread across the Middle East in 2010 and 2011.

Area command   an ICS organization that supervises several incident command posts.

Armed Forces of National Liberation   a Puerto Rican terrorist organization seeking liberation of Puerto Rico from the United States.

Asymmetrical warfare	terrorist attacks on the part of the militarily weak against those who are powerful.
Bacteria	a single-cell organism that causes disease in plants, animals, and humans.
Basic plan	an overview of the entire emergency operations plan.
Biological Weapons Convention (BWC)	an international treaty designed to prevent the proliferation of biological agents around the world.
Bioterrorism	terrorism that employs biological weapons.
Black Panthers	an organization composed of African Americans to revenge the actions of the KKK and other white supremacists.
Black September	an operational unit of the Al-Fatah terrorism organization that launched a terrorist attack against Israeli athletes during the Munich Olympics.
Blood agents	chemical weapons that prevent the flow of oxygen in the blood.
Bojinka plot	a planned attack on airliners over the Pacific Ocean.
Bollards	metal or concrete posts installed into the ground or cement, used to keep vehicles from entering restricted areas.
Border	the territorial boundary of any nation along with its various points of entry.
Capacity building	a strategy that attempts to enhance the ability of the nation, states, and communities to effectively deal with terrorist attacks.
Category A agents	biological weapons that pose a serious risk to people because they are easily transmitted to others and result in high mortality rates.
Category B agents	biological weapons that have a moderate change of contagion and generally result in lower mortality rates than category A agents.
Category C agents	biological weapons that could be used for mass dissemination and high morbidity if engineered for that purpose.
CBRNE	chemical, biological, radiological, nuclear, or explosive devices.
Cells	branches and members of terrorism around the world.
Censorship	the withholding, banning, or altering of information the media shares with the public.
Central Intelligence Agency (CIA)	the federal government agency that is responsible for intelligence collection outside of the United States.
Chemical Facility Anti-Terrorism Standards (CFATS)	a program that identifies risk at chemical facilities (as well as at power plants, refineries, and universities) and regulates stands to ensure sufficient security measures are in place.
Choking agents	chemical weapons that cause respiratory distress.

Civil defense
a government initiative to prepare communities and citizens to react effectively to nuclear war against the Soviet Union.

Civil Support Teams
specialized military units that assist local and state governments that have been affected by weapons of mass destruction.

Classified intelligence
information given only to a very specific and limited number of people to protect sources of acquisition and deny adversaries information that would lead them to alter their communications or operations.

Cognitive dimension
the knowledge and beliefs of the ideology.

Cold zone
the uncontaminated area where responders and victims may enter and leave.

Communism
an ideology that sympathizes with the poor and downtrodden and attempts to do away with private property and capitalism.

Community Emergency Response Team (CERT)
a group of citizens who receive basic training on response operations.

Comprehensive Homeland Security Act
a law passed in 2003 containing new regulations for critical infrastructure security, railroad security, and more stringent measures related to border control and weapons of mass destruction.

Computer Assisted Passenger Prescreening System II (CAPPS II)
a database that ensured that passengers are screened by every airliner and airport that operates within the United States.

Conflict disaster
an event that involves a riot, violence, or some type of warfare.

Consensus disaster
an event like an earthquake or tornado that brings the community together.

Consequence management
preparedness, response, and recovery operations.

Container Security Initiative (CSI)
one of the first measures taken by the government to protect maritime trade and ports against terrorism.

Continuity of operations
the maintenance of government functions after terrorist attacks through the identification of leader succession, alternate work sites, and resumption of operational practices.

Convergence
the flow of people and resources to the scene of an emergency or disaster.

Coordination
cooperative efforts to pursue common goals in the wake of terrorist attacks.

Corporatist model
a model that stresses the integration of various components of society into the government (e.g. close ties to business, churches, clubs, etc.).

Counterterrorism
the active pursuit of known terrorists that includes preemptive military strikes or the involvement of law enforcement officials.

Crazy	a psychologically disturbed individual.
Criminal	a person who seeks personal gain by breaking the law.
Crisis counseling	the treatment of psychological problems that may arise from the stress produced by terrorism.
Crisis management	prevention, protection, and prosecution activities.
Critical incident stress (CIS)	the inability of emergency service personnel to cope with the trauma that is experienced while on the job.
Critical infrastructure	interdependent networks composed of industrial, utility, transportation, and other distribution systems.
Crusader	a terrorist that promotes high moral goals.
Crusades	wards endorsed by the Pope to recapture the Holy Land of Jerusalem from Muslims.
Culture	the lifestyle of groups based on their shared history, language, religion, and moral system.
Customs-Trade Partnership Against Terrorism (C-TPAT)	an agreement between the public and private sectors to protect international commerce from terrorist attacks.
Cyberterrorism	terrorist activity that utilizes or attacks computer networks to instill fear and force some type of change.
Damage assessment	a survey of physical destruction, economic losses, deaths, social disruption, and recovery needs.
Daniel Pearl	a reporter with the *Wall Street Journal* who as was captured and killed by the National Movement for the Restoration of Pakistani Sovereignty.
Debriefing	a recurring and more in-depth discussion designed to redirect harmful thinking and develop improved coping mechanisms.
Debris management	the removal, storage, disposal, or recycling of rubble produced from terrorist attacks.
Decontamination	the removal of hazardous materials from victims through clothing removal and the washing of bodies.
Defusing	a short, unstructured meeting to allow a person to discuss an experience as soon as it takes place.
Denial of service	computer attacks that result in blocked operations.
Department of Defense	the public entity responsible for the military.
Department of Homeland Security	a government organization created to prevent terrorist attacks and react to those that may occur.
Department of State	the federal agency in charge of diplomatic relationships among nations.

Dirty bombs	explosive laden with dangerous chemicals or radioactive material.
Disaster declaration	an acknowledgment of the severity of the event and that response and recovery assistance is required.
Disaster Mortuary Operational Response Team (DMORT)	a group of private citizens from around the nation who may be activated by the federal government to assist with mass fatality incidents.
Disaster Recovery Center (DRC)	a temporary facility near the attack location where victims can seek information about federal assistance programs.
Domestic terrorism	terrorism that occurs within a single country.
Donations management	the collection, sorting, and distribution of goods and money for the benefit of victims of terrorist attacks.
Dynastic assassination	the murder of the head official in government.
Economic class model	a model that suggests a division of society based on the amount of wealth one possesses.
Emergence	the appearance of altruistic behavior that is unfamiliar to the participants.
Emergency alert system	an announcement that interrupts TV and radio programs and relays information about what is taking place and what people should do for protection.
Emergency assistance	financial help given to local governments to take care of immediate needs such as debris removal or safety precautions.
Emergency Management Accreditation Program	a standard-based assessment and certification initiative for local and state emergency management agencies.
Emergency Management Assistance Compact (EMAC)	an agreement among states to render assistance to one another in time of disaster.
Emergency management	a profession that specifies how to prevent or react successfully to various types of disasters.
Emergency manager	a local government official in charge of disaster mitigation, preparedness, response, and recovery.
Emergency operations center (EOC)	a location from which disaster response and recovery activities can be overseen and managed.
Emergency operations plan (EOP)	a document that describes what may be anticipated in terms of homeland security and emergency management and how best to react.
Enlightenment	a period in history when a new way of looking at the world emerged.
Evacuation	the movement of people away from hazardous areas or situations.
Exercises	drills and mock events that test the knowledge and skills of those in charge of reacting to attacks.

Fascism	an ideology that promotes the uniting of citizens in support of the state.
Fatwa	a religious edict.
Federal Air Marshal Service	an organization of a few thousand marshals who act under the Transportation Security Administration to prevent hijacking of aircraft.
Federal Bureau of Investigation	a government organization that concentrates on the enforcement of US law.
Federal Emergency Management Agency	the national entity in charge of disaster management.
First responders	the first official governmental responders in the field including police, firefighters, and emergency medical technicians.
Focused terror	terrorism directed toward a specific group of people deemed as the enemy.
Freedom of religion	people cannot be denied their right to worship according to the dictates of their own conscience.
Freedom of speech	people are allowed to express their opinions, even when they criticize the government.
Full-scale exercises	major scenarios that test many functions or the entire response system.
Functional exercises	practice scenarios that explore one or a few of the annexes in the plan.
Geneva Conventions	a set of internationally accepted laws pertaining to the conduct of war.
Grants	funds given to local governments to support or enhance homeland security and emergency management programs.
Group competition model	a model that asserts that interest groups interact with or counteract one another in their attempt to sway government policy.
GSG9	a German counterterrorism organization, whose name means "Border Guards, Group 9."
Guerilla	a Spanish term for little war, which is an armed protest of occupying forces.
Gunpowder plot	a disagreement between King Henry VIII and Pope Clement VII that led to a terrorist attack in England in 1605.
Hazard	refers to physical or other agents that may trigger or initiate disaster events and processes.
Holocaust	the extermination of approximately eight million Jews by the Nazi regime.

Homeland security	a concerted national effort to prevent terrorist attacks within the United States, reduce America's vulnerability to terrorism, and recovery from and minimize the damage of attacks that do occur.
Homeland Security Act	a law passed in 2002 that mandated the creation of the Department of Homeland Security.
Homeland Security Advisory System	the nation's method for warning the population of potential and actual terrorist attacks after 9/11.
Homeland Security Exercise and Evaluation Program	a federal program that provides guiding principles for exercises.
Hot zone	the area contaminated by the terrorist attack.
HUMINT	intelligence collected by people from people (and can be done overtly or covertly).
Ideology	a set of beliefs related to values, attitudes, ways of thinking, and goals.
IED	improvised explosive devices.
IMINT	geospatial imagery collected by satellites and aircraft.
Immigration and Customs Enforcement (ICE)	the largest investigative organization within the Department of Homeland Security that attempts to deter illegal immigration and the smuggling of money and materials that support terrorism.
Incident command	the on-scene leader or leaders in the incident command post.
Incident Command System (ICS)	a set of personnel and procedures that helps facilitate coordination among first responders.
Individual assistance	relief programs for citizens and businesses impacted by terrorist attacks.
In-kind donations	physical donations including food, water, clothing, supplies, and equipment.
Intelligence	the function of collecting, assessing, and distributing information about an enemy, criminal, or terrorist.
Intelligence adjustment	adaptation of the intelligence cycle that is required when collection is incomplete, analysis seeks to "connect the dots," production generates new questions, and dissemination results in the anticipation of future concerns.
Intelligence analysis	efforts to make sense of the voluminous data that is gathered from the field.
Intelligence collection	activities to gather information about terrorist organizations and their operations and potential attacks.
Intelligence cycle	a four-step process of gathering, understanding, and synthesizing data and then sharing it with those who will use it.

Intelligence dissemination	sharing information with end users (e.g. policy makers, FBI Special Agents, homeland security personnel, etc.).
Intelligence production	the creation of written reports, briefings, images, or maps to influence operational decisions.
International Atomic Energy Agency (IAEA)	the international organization responsible for the enforcement of the nonproliferation treaty.
International terrorism	terrorism that spans two or more nations.
INTERPOL	an international police organization that is involved in intelligence.
Iran	a state in the Middle East that has a long-standing history of participation in terrorism.
Irritants	agents that led to allergic reactions.
Islamic fundamentalists	individuals or groups of Muslims that violently oppose Israel and the United States.
Islamic State of Iraq and Syria	a group that seeks to establish an Islamic government in the Middle East.
Japanese Red Army	a terrorist organization that protested the presence of the United States in Japan after World War II, disapproved of the Vietnam War, and rejected capitalism.
Jihad	an internal struggle to pursue righteousness or a war of self-defense.
Joint field office (JFO)	an incident command organization with federal personnel (and state and local officials on certain occasions).
Key assets	a variety of unique facilities, sites, and structure that require protection.
Kickoff meeting	a gathering of local, state, and federal officials for the purpose of explaining public assistance programs.
Ku Klux Klan	a white supremacist group that has been involved in terrorism in the United States since the Civil War.
Liability reduction	a strategy that attempts to address the factors that result in or permit terrorist attacks.
Liaison officer	the person who serves as the link between the incident commander(s) and other organizations.
Local Emergency Planning Committees (LEPCs)	preparedness councils promoted in the 1980s to help communities prepare for hazardous materials releases.
Lone-wolf terrorists	individuals who act alone.
Libya	a country in Africa that has been sympathetic to the Palestinian cause in Israel.

Madrasahs	schools that offer basic education in the Middle East and are exploited by terrorists.
MASINT	measurement and signature intelligence that looks for the characteristics of certain types of actions (e.g. the presence of nuclear material when one is trying to develop a nuclear weapon).
Mass fatality incident	an attack that creates so many deaths that the processing of remains is beyond the capability of local government.
Mass terror	terrorism by the government in power against its own citizens.
Metadata	information gathered from communication through electronic devices.
Minuteman Project	activities to promote border security carried out by a group of volunteers that found the Minuteman Civil Defense Corps in Arizona.
Mitigation	activity that attempts to avoid disasters or minimize negative consequences.
Molly Maguires	a group of Irish citizens that joined together to dispute the treatment of coal mine workers in the United States.
Money laundering	the process of hiding where money is coming from and what it is being used for.
Multi-agency coordination centers (MACCs)	an ICS organization level that supervises command across several jurisdictions.
Muslims	those following the prophet Muhammad and adhering to the religion of Islam.
Mutual aid	a collaborative agreement between jurisdictions when external help is warranted.
National Cybersecurity and Communications Integration Center (NCCIC)	a 24×7 center composed of officials from the federal government, the intelligence communities, and law enforcement officials to monitor the Internet, respond to threats, and manage incidents.
National Emergency Management Association	a professional association of state emergency management agencies.
National Incident Management System	a comprehensive national approach for incident management in the United States.
National Processing Service Center	a FEMA office set up to help victims apply for federal assistance programs.
National Response Framework (NRF)	the successor to the National Response Plan that describes the principles, roles, and structures of response operations.
National Response Plan (NRP)	a document that describes the procedures for responding to all types of hazards with a multidisciplinary perspective.

National Strategy to Secure Cyberspace	a national strategy to reduce cyberterrorism and cyber-crime in the United States.
Nationalist movements	efforts on the part of group or nation to obtain political independence and autonomy.
NBC	nuclear, biological, and chemical weapons.
Nerve agents	chemical weapons that prevent the transmission of electrical signals in the nervous system.
Non-Proliferation Treaty (NPT)	an international regime designed to prevent nuclear states from giving nuclear weapons or materials to those who do not possess them.
Nonstructural mitigation	methods beyond construction that may limit the possibility or consequences of terrorist attacks.
Operation Mongoose	an attempt by the United States to kill Cuban leader Fidel Castro with a poison cigar.
Operations	the name given to the section under ICS that is in charge of implementing the strategy created by those in planning.
OPINT	open-source intelligence acquired through publicly available materials including academic research, newspaper articles, library books, etc.
Ordinance	an authoritative order or law issued by a government.
Paper plan syndrome	an attitude that assumes that having a plan ensures you are prepared to deal with terrorism and other types of disasters.
Permanent assistance	financial aid for the repairing of publicly owned critical infrastructure and key assets.
Point of distribution	locations where medicines may be given to victims.
Political elite model	a model that describes a situation where the leaders are ruling over the masses.
Political system	a governing body that operates in a self-contained environment.
Politics	the authoritative allocation of values and resources in society.
Post-Katrina Emergency Management Reform Act	a law that specifies ways to avert the slow and disjointed federal response to the catastrophe in New Orleans, Louisiana.
Post-traumatic stress disorder (PTSD)	the clinical diagnosis for individuals who become depressed due to a traumatic event in their lives.
Preliminary damage assessment (PDA)	a more detailed assessment of impacts that typically takes place within days or weeks of the event; it determines the possibility and extent of outside federal assistance.
Preparedness	readiness measures in anticipation of a disaster.
Preparedness council	a group of individuals that provide recommendations for policy and assist with program administration.

Profiling	the practice of law enforcement officials (including security personnel) using race, ethnicity, religion, or national origin as the decisive factors in targeting an individual for suspicion of a wrongdoing.
Programs dimension	plans and actions to support ideological goals.
Proliferation	the acquisition, sharing, and spread of nuclear weapons and materials to those who do not currently possess them.
Protection	an attempt to deny attacks and defend oneself from terrorism.
Public assistance	relief programs that make aid available to government entities that have been affected by terrorism.
Public information officer	the person who gathers information for the incident commander(s) and shares information with the media or a city employee who specializes in working with the media.
Random terror	an attack on larger numbers of people wherever they gather.
Rapid assessment	a quick survey of impacts designed to gain an appreciation of the scope of the attack.
Recovery	long-term activities to rebound after disasters or terrorist attacks.
Reign of terror	a period during the French Revolution where an estimated 20 000 persons were killed by France's Committee of Public Safety.
Relative poverty	some people are less wealthy than their fellow citizens or peers in other countries.
Religion	the beliefs and practices espoused by those sharing a common spiritual faith.
Response	the immediate reaction to an emergency situation like a terrorist attack.
Reverse 911 systems	computerized messages sent over phone lines rapidly to anyone in a designated area.
Right to assemble	people are permitted to join in politically motivated gatherings.
Right to bear arms	guns can be purchased and owned without government interference.
Risk	a measure of probability and consequences.
Safety officer	the person who evaluates the dangers at the scene and makes sure everyone is operating according to safety policies.
Sayeret Matkal	a strike team devoted to finding terrorists before they attack Israeli interests.
Search and rescue	response activities undertaken to find disaster victims and remove them from danger or confinement.
Secondary devices	the detonation of other bombs to add to the disruption and fear of the initial attack.

Secure flight	an advanced passenger screening program that is administered by the Transportation Security Administration.
Self-referred	patients who arrive at the hospital whether they require immediate care or not.
Set-back requirements	laws that describe the proximity of buildings to roads and parking lots.
Sheltering	the location of individuals in places of safety or refuge.
SIGINT	interception and interpretation of electronic communications such as phone conversations and e-mails.
Situational awareness	continual monitoring of safety concerns at the scene of an attack.
Size-up	the process of evaluating the nature of the attack site.
Social base dimension	the individuals and groups that espouse an ideology.
Soft targets	potential sites of terrorist attacks because they are open and accessible to the public.
Special Air Service (SAS)	a British counterterrorism organization.
Strategic national stockpile (SNS)	a cache of medicines in secret locations that can be quickly sent to affected locations around that nation.
Strategic Rail Corridor Network	a network of railroads that transport Department of Defense munitions and other materials, including hazardous items.
Structural mitigation	special construction practices and materials to limit the impact of terrorist attacks.
Structure	the organizational relationships within the political system.
Suitcase bomb	portable nuclear weapons that can be carried or rolled to the target location.
Surface Transportation and Public Transportation Information Sharing and Analysis Center (ST-PT ISAC)	a system that interfaces with government leaders, intelligence agencies, law enforcement personnel, and computer emergency response teams to spread top-secret information among railroad operators.
SWAT	Special Weapons and Tactics used to train police forces.
Tabletop exercises	informal discussions about hypothetical scenarios that occur in an office setting.
Tactical emergency medical services	the name given to a team of paramedics that are armed and trained in weapons use.
Tactical terror	the use of attacks against the government for revolutionary or other purposes.
Taliban	the name of the government that provided safe haven for Al-Qaeda.
Technical assessment	a survey of damages that points out methods and costs for rebuilding.

Terrorism	the use or threat of violence to support ideological purposes.
Theocracy	a government run by clerics in the name of God.
Theodore "Ted" Kaczynski	the "Unabomber" who opposed technology and wrote a manifesto that decried advances in this area.
Threat assessment	a careful study of the targets that might be appealing to terrorists.
Trojan horses	computer attacks that contain malicious codes to destroy files.
Toxin	a poison that is produced by plants or animals.
Training	information sharing in classroom or field settings to help familiarize people with protocol.
Transportation Security Act	a law designed to protect transportation systems in the United States.
Transportation Security Administration	a federal agency under the Department of Homeland Security created to protect our transportation systems from terrorist attacks.
Triage	the assessment, sorting, and treatment of injured in such a way as to maximize limited resources.
United Nations	an international organization that establishes security rules regarding access and security at ports.
United States Coast Guard (USCG)	a military branch within the Department of Homeland Security that is in charge of maritime law, environmental protection of waterways, search and rescue operations at sea, and interdiction of illegal aliens and contraband.
United States Visitor and Immigrant Status Indicator Technology (US-VISIT)	a computer database used to screen passengers who wish to travel to the United States.
Unmet Needs Committee	a group of concerned citizens and community leaders who work together to collect donations and address long-term needs of victims.
USA PATRIOT Act	a homeland security law that stands for "Uniting and Strengthening America by Providing Appropriate Tools Required to Intercept and Obstruct Terrorism" meant to prevent terrorist attacks and enhance law enforcement's ability to investigate and punish offenders.
Vesicants	blister agents that produce chemical burns.
Virus	a microscopic genetic particle that infects the cells of living organisms but cannot multiply outside a host cell.
Volunteer management	the harnessing of volunteers to take advantage of their potential contributions while averting potential negative consequences.
Volunteer registration center	the location where citizens fill out forms noting their skills and other information that can help you when making assignments.
Vulnerability	a high degree of disaster proneness and/or limited disaster management capabilities.

Wahhabism a very stringent and legalistic religious movement that attempts to ensure the purity of the Muslim faith with no deviations whatsoever.

Warm zone the location where victims are washed for decontamination.

Warnings notifications sent out to the public so they can take protective measures.

Weather radios electronic devices that receive information from the National Weather Service to warn people of severe weather.

WMD weapons of mass destruction.

Writ of habeas corpus a law protecting citizens from unlawful imprisonment.

Zoning regulations that delineate where buildings can be located.

INDEX

Introduction to Homeland Security: Understanding Terrorism Prevention and Emergency Management,
Second Edition. David A. McEntire.
© 2019 John Wiley & Sons, Inc. Published 2019 by John Wiley & Sons, Inc.
Companion website: www.wiley.com/go/mcentire/homelandsecurity2e